INDIVIDUAL AND ORGANIZATIONAL PERSPECTIVES ON EMOTION MANAGEMENT AND DISPLAY

RESEARCH ON EMOTION IN ORGANIZATIONS

Series Editors: Neal M. Ashkanasy, Wilfred J. Zerbe
and Charmine E. J. Härtel

Volume 1:   The Effect of Affect in Organizational Settings,
Edited by Neal M. Ashkanasy, Wilfred J. Zerbe
and Charmine E. J. Härtel

RESEARCH ON EMOTION IN ORGANIZATIONS   VOLUME 2

INDIVIDUAL AND ORGANIZATIONAL PERSPECTIVES ON EMOTION MANAGEMENT AND DISPLAY

EDITED BY

WILFRED J. ZERBE

University of Calgary, Alberta, Canada

NEAL M. ASHKANASY

University of Queensland, Brisbane, Australia

CHARMINE E. J. HÄRTEL

Monash University, Victoria, Australia

ELSEVIER
JAI

Amsterdam – Boston – Heidelberg – London – New York – Oxford
Paris – San Diego – San Francisco – Singapore – Sydney – Tokyo

JAI Press is an imprint of Elsevier

JAI Press is an imprint of Elsevier
The Boulevard, Langford Lane, Kidlington, Oxford OX5 1GB, UK
Radarweg 29, PO Box 211, 1000 AE Amsterdam, The Netherlands
525 B Street, Suite 1900, San Diego, CA 92101-4495, USA

First edition 2006

British Library Cataloguing in Publication Data
A catalogue record for this book is available from the British Library

ISBN-13: 978-0-7623-1310-5
ISBN-10: 0-7623-1310-2
ISSN: 1746-9791 (Series)

For information on all JAI Press publications
visit our website at books.elsevier.com

Printed and bound in The Netherlands

06 07 08 09 10 10 9 8 7 6 5 4 3 2 1

Working together to grow
libraries in developing countries

www.elsevier.com | www.bookaid.org | www.sabre.org

ELSEVIER   BOOK AID   Sabre Foundation
            International

CONTENTS

ABOUT THE EDITORS

Neal Ashkanasy is professor of Management in the UQ Business School at the University of Queensland, and research director for the Faculty of Business, Economics, and Law. He has a PhD (1989) in Social and Organizational Psychology from the University of Queensland. His research in recent years has focused on emotions in organizational life. He has published in journals such as the *Academy of Management Review*, the *Academy of Management Executive*, and the *Journal of Management*. He is associate editor of *Academy of Management Learning and Education*, and the incoming editor-in-chief of the *Journal of Organizational Behavior*.

Charmine Härtel is professor of Organizational Behavior in the Department of Management at Monash University in Melbourne, Australia. She is co-editor of four books on research and theory relating to emotional experience, expression, and management in the workplace. Her research has been published in *AMR*, *JOM*, *JAP*, *Leadership Quarterly*, *Industrial Marketing Management* and *Applied Psychology: An International Review*. Charmine has been recognised with a number of awards including the Richard M. Suinn Commendation Award for Excellence in Research and the Advancement of Psychology, the Martin E. P. Seligman Applied Research Award, the Jacob E. Hautaluoma Distinguished Alumni Award, the Janet Chusmir Service Award, and the Vice Chancellors Award for Postgraduate Supervision. Her current research and consulting activities focus on employee and customer emotions and patterns of relating; management practices and organizational characteristics which promote inclusion, ethical behavior and well-being; poverty alleviation and the improvement of the status of women in developing countries.

Wilfred J. Zerbe is professor of Human Resources and Organizational Dynamics in the Haskayne School of Business at the University of Calgary, and adjunct professor, Theseus International Management Institute, Nice, France. His research interests focus on emotions in organizations, organizational research methods, service sector management, business ethics, and leadership. His publications have appeared in books and journals including *The Academy of Management Review, Industrial and Labour Relations Review, Canadian Journal of Administrative Sciences, Journal of Business Research, Journal of Psychology, Journal of Services Marketing,* and *Journal of Research in Higher Education.* He is also an active consultant and executive educator.

LIST OF CONTRIBUTORS

Céleste M. Brotheridge	Départment d'organisation et ressources humaines École des sciences de la gestion, Université du Québec à Montréal, Montréal, QC, Canada
Stéphane Côté	Joseph L. Rotman School of Management, University of Toronto, Toronto, ON, Canada
Lorna M. Doucet	Department of Business Administration, University of Illinois at Urbana-Champaign, IL, USA
Vanessa Urch Druskat	Department of Management, Whittemore School of Business and Economics, University of New Hampshire, NH, USA
Dorthe Eide	Bodø Graduate School of Business, Norway
Andrea Fischbach	Department I – Psychology, University of Trier, Germany
Markus Groth	Australian Graduate School of Management, University of New South Australia
Thorsten Hennig-Thurau	Department of Marketing and Media Research, Bauhaus-University of Weimar, Germany
Annabelle Mark	Middlesex University Business School, The Burroughs, Hendon, London, UK
Janet R. McColl Kennedy	UQ Business School, The University of Queensland, Brisbane, Australia

Katrin Meyer-Gomes   Psychiatry Department, University of
                              California, San Diego, CA, USA

Christopher T.H. Miners   Joseph L. Rotman School of
                              Management, University of Toronto,
                              Toronto, ON, Canada

Nanette Monin   Department of Management and
                              International Business, Massey
                              University, New Zealand

Sue Moon   Joseph L. Rotman School of
                              Management, University of Toronto,
                              Toronto, ON, Canada

Anthony T. Pescosolido   Department of Management, Whittemore
                              School of Business and Economics,
                              University of New Hampshire, NH, USA

Fleur Piper   School of Communication Studies,
                              Auckland University of Technology,
                              Faculty of Design and Creative
                              Technologies, New Zealand

Johannes Rank   University of South Florida/University of
                              Giessen, Germany

Arja Ropo   Department of Management Studies,
                              School of Economics and Business
                              Administration, University of Tampere,
                              Finland

Erika Sauer   Department of Management Studies,
                              School of Economics and Business
                              Administration, University of Tampere,
                              Finland

Amy K. Smith   School of Business, The George
                              Washington University, Washington, DC,
                              USA

Matthias Spörrle   Department Psychology, Ludwig-
                              Maximilians-Universität, Munich,
                              Germany

Ian Taylor	P. O. Box 28444 Dubai, UAE
Gianfranco Walsh	Strathclyde Business School, Glasgow, UK
Isabell M. Welpe	Institute for Information, Organisation and Management, Ludwig-Maximilians-Universität, Munich, Germany
Kay Yoon	Department of Communication, DePaul University, Chicago, IL, USA
Dieter Zapf	Work and Organizational Psychology, Department of Psychology, Johann Wolfgang Goethe-University, Germany

OVERVIEW: INDIVIDUAL AND ORGANIZATIONAL PERSPECTIVES ON EMOTION MANAGEMENT AND DISPLAY

Scholarly writing on emotions in organizations has passed an important marker of progress, albeit an informal one. Specifically, up until recently it seemed almost required of theoretical or empirical papers that they begin with a lament that emotions in organizations represented an area that was understudied, misunderstood, neglected, discriminated against, and so on. This is no longer the case. It can safely be reported that, alongside the continuing strength of cognitive approaches to understanding organizational behavior, the study of affect and emotion has achieved legitimacy, and the role of affect and emotion as important factors in understanding behavior in organizations is well established. The markers of this legitimacy are many and varied, including numerous conferences devoted to emotion, emotions tracks within broader conferences, books in the popular business press, the increasing number of articles appearing in scholarly journals with emotions as a central focus or as an important explanatory construct, and special journal issues devoted to emotions. Notable among these markers is the presence of this series, which provides an annual forum for current research on emotions in organizational behavior.

THE 2004 EMONET CONFERENCE

As reported in Volume 1 of *Research on Emotions in Organizations* (Ashkanasy, Zerbe, & Härtel, 2005), the chapters in this volume are drawn from the best contributions to the 2004 *International Conference on Emotion and Organizational Life* held at Birkbeck College, London, complemented by additional, invited chapters. (This biannual conference has come to be known as the "Emonet" conference, after the listserv of members.) Previous edited volumes (Ashkanasy, Härtel, & Zerbe, 2000; Ashkanasy, Zerbe, & Härtel, 2002; Härtel, Zerbe, & Ashkanasy, 2004) were published every two years following the Emonet conference. With the birth of this annual Elsevier series came the opportunity for greater focus in the theme of each volume, and for greater scope for invited contributions. This volume contains eight chapters selected from conference contributions for their quality, interest, and appropriateness to the theme of this volume, as well as four invited chapters. We again acknowledge in particular the assistance of the conference paper reviewers (see the appendix). In the year of publication of this volume the 2006 Emonet conference will be held in Atlanta, USA and will be followed by Volumes 3 and 4 of *Research on Emotions in Organizations*. Readers interested in learning more about the conferences or the Emonet list should check the Emonet website http://www.uq.edu.au/emonet/.

THE THEME OF THIS VOLUME

The theme of this volume, *Individual and Organizational Perspectives on Emotion Management and Display*, reflects the central premise underlying the resurgence of interest in emotions in organizations, namely that organizations do manage the emotions of employees and this management has effects on individuals. The seminal work of Hochschild (1983) and Rafaeli and Sutton (1987, 1989) are fundamental examples. From this starting point the field has grown to include study of the antecedents of emotions and the individual and organizational moderators of their effects, group emotional processes such as emotional contagion and organizational affective climate, the role of culture, and so on.

THE CHAPTERS

Studies of the effects of emotional display for employees and organizations, such as the later chapters in this volume, generally point to the importance of emotion management and regulation. As Stephane Côté, Christopher Miners, and Sue Moon point out in Chapter 1, this begs the question of what constitutes "good" or "wise" regulation of emotions. The authors develop a process model of emotion regulation that outlines the effective regulation of emotion through (1) the setting of goals with respect to which emotion is appropriate for display and at what intensity, (2) the selection of an effective strategy for attainment of these goals, (3) implementation of this strategy, and (4) the adaptation of emotional regulation choices in response to events in the environment. For each of these stages, Côté et al. outline the nature of the choices facing individuals and the factors affecting their choices. In the second half of their chapter, Côté et al., consider how and why individuals who are higher in ability-based emotional intelligence are likely to be more effective in their emotion regulation at each of the four phases of their model. In contrast to previous studies of emotional labor, in which employees are viewed as displaying emotions to meet organizational demands, or as being deviant by resisting such demands, Côté et al. consider how employees can use the display of emotion to meet their own objectives within a work setting.

In Chapter 2, Vanessa Druskat and Anthony Pescosolido continue the topic of the intelligent use of emotions in an empirical study of the effect of leader behavior in self-managed work teams. Specifically, Druskat and Pescosolido test propositions following from the socio-emotional theory of group effectiveness (Druskat & Wolff, 2001; Wolff & Druskat, 2003) that leader behaviors which contribute to the development of emotionally competent team norms would result in higher levels of trust, greater openness of team communication, engagement with team tasks, and higher team performance and viability. Further they investigated the mediating role of social capital and task processes. In a methodologically impressive study of ongoing, intact self-managed teams in a manufacturing setting, Druskat and Pescosolido showed that emergent leaders who build the emotional competence of their teams are much more effective than those who use directive leadership styles.

Erika Sauer and Arja Ropo take a very different approach to the study of team leadership in Chapter 3. Using a social constructivist analysis of narrative they describe the use of shame by a leader to drive the performance of a theatre ensemble. Rather than opposing directive and supportive leadership styles, as in the previous chapter, Sauer and Ropo consider leadership as a social process that is inherently paradoxical, in which leaders create emotional tensions – such as the simultaneous experience of shame and joy. Interviews and participant observation are used to gather information that is then presented in the form of a fictional narrative, a story of the experience of a leader and the lead that engages the reader in the turbulence and contradictions of leadership in practice.

In Chapter 4, Fleur Piper and Nanette Monin examine similarly emotionally charged incidents involving workers and their supervisors. Using a grounded-theory approach, Piper and Monin found that the emotions experienced by workers (whether expressed, repressed, or edited), following an altercation were overwhelmingly negative with the most commonly cited emotions being feelings of powerlessness and frustration. Furthermore, their research revealed that a key cause for dissonance was the substantial gap between the supervisor's respect and value for them as workers and the personal and the professional values and expectations of the workers, leading a number of them to reveal that they had lost respect for their supervisor and felt disillusioned about the morality and ethicality of the workplace environment itself. Their findings show the importance of a psychologically safe organizational climate in which discontent is acknowledged and discussed and the goal of interpersonal health held in high regard.

The effective management of emotion is particularly relevant to organizational outcomes in service organizations. In Chapters 5 and 6, Dorthe Eide and Annabelle Mark look at emotion work performed by employees in the hospitality industry and healthcare organizations where emotional labor is not explicitly considered to be a part of organizational activities, while in Chapters 7 and 8, Celeste Brotheridge and Ian Taylor, and Andrea Fischbach and colleagues consider the role that culture plays in the perceptions of service workers regarding the emotion work that they undertake.

Dorthe Eide presents an interesting conceptualization of the role of emotion in service work looking at the phenomenon of care in organizations. Eide presents a framework for the ideal types of practice in frontline work and suggests that emotions are a vital component of the care work undertaken by frontline workers.

In the following chapter, conceptualizing patients in lifecycle terms and emphasizing the need to consider the role of emotion at different stages in this journey, Annabelle Mark considers the role of emotion in the context of healthcare, in particular the National Health Service in the UK. Mark discusses the importance of understanding the role that emotions play in healthcare at both the macro and the micro levels and suggests that "an approach to healthcare based on rational systems approach alone, although necessary, is not sufficient to the task ahead". The importance of emotion in healthcare is highlight by Mark's claim that the "distances being created between doctors and their patients, through a lack of attention to emotion, are dysfunctional in enabling recovery". Overall, this chapter shows how accepting emotion as a driving force in healthcare organizations can increase motivation, enrich job performance, reduce stress and enhance relationships as well as present ethical and legal benefits. Ignoring it, in contrast, reduces the quality and quantity of acceptable patient outcomes.

In Chapter 7, Celeste Brotheridge and Ian Taylor explore an issue of considerable international relevance in their examination of cross-cultural differences in emotional labor performed by flight attendants working in a multicultural setting. Using four different perspectives, they examine differences in how workers perform emotional labor. Findings from their research indicate that there appears to be cultural variations in how workers perform emotional labor, "notably deep acting and the hiding feelings dimension of surface acting, but not the faking emotions dimension of surface acting".

The findings of Fischbach and colleagues, which compares emotion work carried out by travel agents in Germany and the United States, also indicates differences in the way that people from different cultures perform emotion work. The frequency of both neutrality requirements and emotional dissonance were found to be lower in the US than in Germany. However, while sensitivity requirements were expected to be higher in the US sample than the German sample the reverse was found to be true. Furthermore, the data did not support their predictions regarding the frequency of either positive or negative emotion display requirements or sympathy display requirements. Results also indicated that at least in the case of the travel agent role, job requirements for emotion work appear to exert a greater influence on emotion regulation than did cultural difference. The superiority of some emotion work strategies in terms of consequences for workers well-being are also noted and suggested as a model for sales occupations across cultures.

In Chapter 9, Markus Groth, Thorsten Hennig-Thurau, and Gianfranco Walsh deal with the other side of the service encounter – customer emotions. They present a model, which includes 13 propositions relating to the antecedents and mechanisms of customer satisfaction and retention. In their model, service provider job satisfaction and organizational citizenship behavior, together with the strength of the service relationships and service scripts affect emotional labor strategies (deep versus surface acting). These strategies, in turn, influence customer attitudes including the customer's perceptions of the service provider's service orientation, of benefit relationships, and of trust. In the final step of this model, these attitudes together determine customer satisfaction and, ultimately, customer behavior in terms of retention.

In Chapter 10, Janet McColl-Kennedy and Amy Smith address an area that, surprisingly, has attracted little research attention to date: customer emotions following a "service failure". In this model, a customer experiencing an unsatisfactory service encounter experiences a range of negative emotions, culminating in emotions of anger, and even rage. McColl-Kennedy and Smith discuss the nature of customer emotion, including measurement issues, and develop a model based on principles of cognition–emotion, attribution theory, and emotional contagion. Finally, they suggest that customer characteristics such as gender and national culture play a role.

While Chapters 9 and 10 present theoretical models of customer emotion, Kay Yoon and Lorna Doucet in Chapter 11 provide data from 1,000 telephone service interactions involving 125 service providers in a retail bank. The focus of this research is on the negative emotions of the service provider associated with "problematic service interactions". Results of this research show that the service providers' negative emotional displays are determined by their prior history of negative emotional displays, especially when they perceive that the customer, rather than the bank, is to blame for the service failure in the first instance.

Finally, in Chapter 12, Matthias Spörrle and Isabell Welpe provide an innovative perspective on emotional intelligence. Based on the theoretical framework of Ellis's (1973) Rational Emotive behavior Therapy (REBT), they hypothesized, among other things, that people who engage in rational thinking will experience more "adaptive emotions" (fear, annoyance, sadness, regret) in response to stressors in the workplace, while those who engage in irrational thinking will experience "maladaptive emotions" (anxiety, rage, depression, guilt, pride) in the same situation. Moreover, rational thinking (as opposed to irrationality) will tend to be experienced by people with high emotional intelligence. They tested this theory in two studies, and found general support for their hypotheses. In addition, they found that irrationality was associated with lower levels of life and job satisfaction.

CONCLUSIONS

The chapters in this volume constitute a tour of the emotion management and display landscape. We begin with consideration of what effective management of emotion is and how it can and should be undertaken, we examine emotional incidents in the workplace, the role of culture, and management of both employee and customer emotions in service contexts, and conclude, having returned to our staring point, with an examination of emotionally intelligent, constructive responses to workplace stressors. One sign of a maturing area of study is how each of the papers in this volume speaks to the others; how they form a complementary body of work. This is not to say that there are not many fruitful avenues yet to be explored, or that diversity of topical, theoretical, or methodological approach should be at all discouraged, but rather to say that the study of emotions is coming to enjoy coherence that again reflects its importance in understanding organizational behavior. In particular, we encourage scholars to continue to push methodological and theoretical boundaries, going beyond the "low hanging fruit" that this young field still enjoys. For example, scholars in mainstream psychology and sociology have a long history of research and theory about emotion. Have organizational scholars effectively leveraged that work to enhance our own understanding? And conversely, how can we make a theoretical contribution to essential understanding of emotions through what we study in organizational settings? One answer to this latter question, we suggest, is to take advantage of the interdisciplinarity and multiplicity of methods that organizational studies are open to. This would mean, for example, undertaking studies at organizational levels of analysis or that cross-levels of analysis. The title of this volume is *Individual and Organizational Perspectives on Emotional Management and Display*, yet because emotions reside in individuals we tend toward the "individual" at the cost of the "organizational". It would also mean encouraging study that takes an anthropological, or historical, or dramaturgical point of view, as chapters in this series have. The future is bright, we have a strong foundation from which to go forward, and we look forward to the efforts of our colleagues in this community.

APPENDIX. CONFERENCE REVIEWERS

Alia Al-Serkal
Hillary Anger Elfenbein
Claire Ashton-James
Yvonne Athanasaw
Remi Ayoko
Julie Baker
Lisa Beesley
Rebekah Bennett
Geetu Bharwaney
Joyce Bono
Maree Boyle
Celeste Brotheridge
Ethel Brundin
John C. Byrne
Yochi Cohen-Charash
Shane Connelly
Marie Dasborough
Catherine Daus
Norma Davies
James Diefendorff
Lorna Doucet
Vanessa Druskat
Dorthe Eide

Gerard Finnemore
Yuka Fujimoto
Deanna Geddes
Don Gibson
Markus Groth
Sally Hall-Thompson
Anne Herman
Olivier Herrbach
Elaine Hollensbe
Alice Hsu
Ron Humphrey
Eisenberg Jacob
Bob Jones
Peter Jordan
Tammy Kostecki-Dillon
Janet Kellett
Gail Kinman
Susan Kruml
John Lamuch
Yongmei Liu
Annabelle Mark
Marty Mattare
Stefan Meisiek

Stéphane Moriou
Jane Murray
Apolonia Niemirowski
Ben Palmer
Ann Parkinson
Ken Parry
Neeta Patil-Adhau
Anthony Pescosolido
Fleur Piper
Michelle Pizer
Mauricio Puerta
Roni Reiter-Palmon
Erin Remi
Erin Richard
Anna L. Rosche
Arie Shirom
Micheal Stratton
Peter Totterdell
Sue Vickers-Thompson
Terry Waters-Marsh
Xin Yao
Vanda Zammuner

REFERENCES

Ashkanasy, N. M., Härtel, C. E. J., & Zerbe, W. J. (Eds) (2000). *Emotions in the work place: Theory, research, and practice.* Westport, CT: Quorum Books.

Ashkanasy, N. M., Zerbe, W. J., & Härtel, C. E. J. (Eds) (2002). *Managing emotions in the work place.* Armonk, NY: ME Sharpe.

Ashkanasy, N. M., Zerbe, W. J., & Hartel, C. E. J. (Eds) (2005). *Research on emotions in organizations, Volume 1: The effect of affect in organizational settings.* Oxford, UK: Elsevier JAI.

Druskat, V. U., & Wolff, S. B. (2001). Building the emotional intelligence of groups. *Harvard Business Review, 79*, 81–90.

Ellis, A. (1973). *Humanistic psychotherapy: The rational-emotive approach.* New York: McGraw-Hill.

Härtel, C. E. J., Zerbe, W. J., & Ashkanasy, N. M. (Eds) (2004). *Emotions in organizational behavior*. Mahwah, NJ: Erlbaum.

Hochschild, A. (1983). *The managed heart: Commercialization of human feeling*. Berkeley: University of California Press.

Rafaeli, A., & Sutton, R. I. (1987). Expressions of emotion as part of the work role. *Academy of Management Review, 12*, 23–37.

Rafaeli, A., & Sutton, R. I. (1989). The expression of emotion in organizational life. In: L.L. Cummings & B.M. Staw (Eds), *Research in organizational behavior* (Vol. 11, pp.1–42). Greenwich, CT: JAI Press.

Wolff, S. B., & Druskat, V. U. (2003). A socio-emotional theory of workgroup effectiveness. Paper presented at the annual meeting of the American Psychological Association, Toronto.

Wilfred J. Zerbe, Neal M. Ashkanasy and Charmine E. J. Härtel

CHAPTER 1

EMOTIONAL INTELLIGENCE AND WISE EMOTION REGULATION IN THE WORKPLACE

Stéphane Côté, Christopher T. H. Miners and Sue Moon

ABSTRACT

In organizations, it is common to talk about how wisely people manage their emotions. Even so, it is often not obvious whether a particular act of emotion regulation is wise or unwise and, to date, research has provided little guidance to judge the wisdom of emotion regulation efforts. We develop a model that construes wise emotion regulation as a process that involves: (a) setting an effective emotion regulation goal, (b) choosing an appropriate strategy to achieve that goal, (c) implementing that strategy effectively, and (d) adapting emotion regulation over time. We also develop propositions linking emotional intelligence to wise emotion regulation. Finally, we discuss the implications of our model and propositions for research and practice.

INTRODUCTION

Early in his tenure as the CEO of Microsoft, Steven Ballmer made a particularly memorable address to his company's employees. He ran onto the stage and jumped up and down wildly while screaming "Whoa! Whoa!

Individual and Organizational Perspectives on Emotion Management and Display
Research on Emotion in Organizations, Volume 2, 1–24
Copyright © 2006 by Elsevier Ltd.
All rights of reproduction in any form reserved
ISSN: 1746-9791/doi:10.1016/S1746-9791(06)02001-3

Whoa! Come on! Get up! Get up! Come on! Come on! Come on! Who said sit down? I've got four words for you: I love this company!" During his opening remarks, the audience applauded loudly, but it is not clear whether they were genuinely enthusiastic or mortified and deferential to a senior executive. Thus, it is unknown whether his efforts to project enthusiasm had a positive, a negative, or no effect on his employees.

As this example illustrates, determining whether a specific act of emotion regulation is wise or unwise is challenging. Some behaviors that seem wise at first glance may in fact be unwise, and vice versa. Research has so far provided little guidance to evaluate the wisdom of specific acts of emotion regulation. The slow progress in this area of research is unfortunate because it is common to talk about people who manage their emotions wisely or unwisely. For example, "Today" show host Matt Lauer received praise for how he handled an interview with actor Tom Cruise. In particular, after Cruise called Lauer ill-informed and "glib," Lauer maintained his composure and responded with reason. Howard Dean, an American candidate for the 2002 Democratic presidential nomination, emitted an unusual scream to rally his supporters during a speech following a disappointing third place finish in the Iowa caucus. The speech was dubbed the "I have a scream" speech and it lost Dean a number of key supporters.

The practical importance of the concept of wise emotion regulation renders the development of theories of wise emotion regulation important. The first goal of this chapter is to develop a model of wise emotion regulation that we label the Process of Wise Emotion Regulation (PoWER) model. To the extent that specific emotion regulation behaviors can be identified as wise or unwise, a related question concerns whether such behaviors can be predicted. We believe that they can be predicted from emotional intelligence, a set of abilities pertaining to emotions (Mayer & Salovey, 1997). For example, it is conceivable that Lauer maintained his composure during his interview with Cruise because he is emotionally intelligent and that Dean's lack of emotional intelligence contributed to the poor emotion regulation that impacted his political success. The second goal of this chapter is to delineate mechanisms and offer propositions linking emotional intelligence to the wisdom of organization members' emotion regulation.

WHAT IS WISE EMOTION REGULATION?

Emotion regulation is defined as the efforts that people exert to increase, maintain, or decrease one or more aspects of an emotion (Gross, 1999).

Building on this definition, the term *wise emotion regulation* implies that some efforts to increase, maintain, or decrease aspects of emotion can be considered wiser than others. As a starting point to developing a model of wise emotion regulation, we reviewed the literature to find out how wise emotion regulation has been conceptualized in the past. We identified four conceptualizations in the literature. Although these conceptualizations are not entirely independent of one another, we believe that they are sufficiently distinct to discuss them separately.

The first conceptualization of wise emotion regulation involves identifying a set of emotion regulation behaviors, studying the consequences of these behaviors, and judging the wisdom of these behaviors based on their consequences. Salovey, Bedell, Detweiler, and Mayer (1999), for instance, identified three types of emotion regulation behaviors: rumination, social support seeking, and disclosure of emotional experiences. Based on empirical evidence, they concluded that rumination (i.e., mulling over symptoms or circumstances surrounding distress) is an unwise way to manage emotion. Conversely, they considered tapping into social resources and disclosing emotional experiences to be wise ways to manage emotion.

This conceptualization of wise emotion regulation implicitly assumes that the consequences of emotion regulation behaviors are similar across situations. Evidence that emotion regulation behaviors are not equally effective in all situations casts doubt on its viability. For example, despite evidence that expressing emotional experiences improves people's psychological and physical health (Pennebaker, 1997), Clark and Finkel (2004) argued that the effectiveness of this strategy depends on the social context. On the basis of a series of empirical studies, they argued that expressing emotions is beneficial in communal relationships because expressions of emotion tend to elicit social support. In contrast, they argued that expressing emotions is unwise in non-communal relationships because expressions of emotion within the context of these relationships tend to elicit rejection and dislike.

The second conceptualization of wise emotion regulation concerns the flexible application of emotion regulation strategies (Bonanno, Papa, Lalande, Westphal, & Coifman, 2004; Diamond & Aspinwall, 2003; Gross & John, 2002). According to this conceptualization, individuals possess an array of emotion regulation strategies and make decisions about which strategy to use depending on the features of the context. The features of the context may include the nature of the task and the people with whom one interacts. According to this conceptualization, it is wise to use a strategy that fits a certain context and it is unwise to use a strategy that does not fit the context. This conceptualization differs from the first because emotion egulation strategies are not assumed to have the same effects across situations. In support of this conceptualization, Bonanno et al. (2004) showed that the ability to flexibly enhance or suppress emotion in response to situational demands contributed to relatively low levels of distress among students following the September 11 terrorist attacks.

The third conceptualization of wise emotion regulation concerns the successful implementation of the strategy that one has selected (Gross & John, 2002). To our minds, this conceptualization has not been fully delineated. We believe that successful implementation consists of several elements. One element may be the degree to which the target emotion actually changes as a result of emotion regulation efforts. For example, two salespeople may employ the same strategy to enhance their displays of enthusiasm. The first salesperson may exhibit an appropriate amount of enthusiasm and the other may fail to generate enough enthusiasm to have an effect on customers. Another element of the successful implementation of an emotion regulation strategy may be the automaticity of the implementation. Wise emotion regulation may possibly be characterized as being automatic and consuming minimal mental resources.

The final conceptualization of emotion regulation concerns adaptation to varying circumstances over time (Gross & John, 2002). Sutton (1991) found that bill collectors' success at garnering payment from debtors entails tailoring their emotional expressions to debtors' responses. For instance, bill collectors learn to respond with calmness to angry debtors and irritation to sad debtors. Adaptation to different debtors' responses is important to success and therefore, it may be wise for bill collectors to change their emotion regulation strategies over time. This implies that the dimension of time is important, such that changing strategies when necessary is a critical component of wise emotion regulation.

The different conceptualizations of emotion regulation suggest that wise emotion regulation may be construed as a process as opposed to a discrete event. To our knowledge, these conceptualizations of emotion regulation have never been integrated in a comprehensive model. Such integration would provide a parsimonious theoretical framework to guide future research. Thus, we integrate the conceptualizations in a model of wise emotion regulation. We also introduce a new conceptualization that we believe is necessary to fully describe the PoWER model. We combine these conceptualizations to create the PoWER model.

PROCESS OF WISE EMOTION REGULATION MODEL

We propose a four-step model of wise emotion regulation. The steps constitute a process that unfolds over time. In Step 1, the organization members set an emotion regulation goal. In Step 2, they choose the best strategy available to achieve that goal given the context. In Step 3, they implement that strategy effectively. Finally, in Step 4, they modify their emotion regulation goals and strategies when necessary. The PoWER model is displayed in Fig. 1. The first three steps are arranged in a circle, while the circle itself illustrates the fourth step and the idea that the PoWER model is a cycle that unfolds over time.

Our model focuses on the regulation of one's own emotions and excludes the regulation of other people's emotions. Regulating other people's emotions may be an important part of at least some jobs. For example, leaders may enhance the positive emotions of subordinates to increase teamwork (Sy, Côté, & Saavedra, 2005). For the sake of parsimony, however, our model focuses on the regulation of one's own emotions. Future research is needed to develop models of the wise regulation of other people's emotions. Similarly, for the sake of simplicity, we focus on the regulation of one emotion at a time. People may experience two or more emotions simultaneously and we believe that our propositions can be extended to apply to these experiences.

We also note at the outset that the emotion regulation behaviors we describe within our model fall along a continuum from controlled to automatic (Lord & Harvey, 2002; Pugh, 2002). Controlled emotion regulation can be characterized as conscious and effortful, such as when a person makes a conscious effort to disclose feelings of sadness to a close friend. Automatic emotion regulation can be characterized as unconscious and effortless, such as when a customer service agent with considerable work experience smiles automatically at customers. Through practice, controlled emotion regulation may become automatic. Each step in our model can be more or less conscious and effortful and, as such, our model accommodates emotion regulation behaviors that range from controlled to automatic.

Step 1. Set an Effective Emotion Regulation Goal

In the first step, wise emotion regulation entails setting an effective emotion regulation goal. We define an emotion regulation goal as a target for which emotion to regulate and at what intensity that emotion is to be felt and

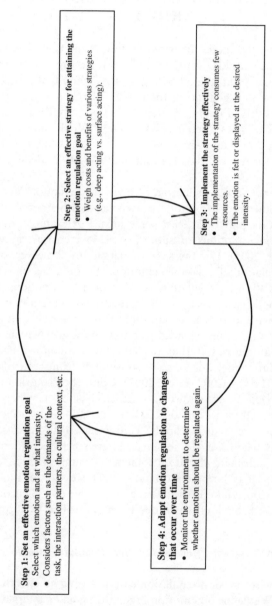

Fig. 1. Process of Wise Emotion Regulation Model.

displayed. For example, a salesperson may set the goal of experiencing and displaying a moderate level of enthusiasm.

We contend that emotion regulation goals vary in their effectiveness. Emotion regulation goals are effective to the extent that the appropriate emotion and level of intensity are chosen for a given situation. For example, it is often wise for a salesperson to aim for a moderate level of enthusiasm. Conversely, emotion regulation goals are ineffective to the extent that an inappropriate emotion or level of intensity is chosen for a given situation. For example, it is usually unwise for a salesperson to aim for an intense level of fear. It is also unwise to fail to set a goal, a circumstance that may occur when individuals get engulfed by their emotions or passively accept them. Goals have directive functions (Locke & Latham, 2002) and therefore, in the absence of a set goal, workers' emotion regulation behaviors will lack direction. Workers will regulate a variety of emotions in a variety of directions, as opposed to a specific emotion in a specific direction.

There are a number of characteristics of the situation that may be considered when determining what is the right emotion and intensity and, hence, what is an effective emotion regulation goal. We focus on three characteristics: the demands of the task, the characteristics of one's immediate interaction partners, and the cultural context.

The Demands of the Task

Research on the effects of emotions on information processing and decision-making specifies to some degree which emotion may be best to feel for a given task. Given a certain task that calls for a specific emotion, individuals may exhibit wise emotion regulation to the extent that they choose to regulate that specific emotion. For example, research suggests that a moderate level of happiness often helps people to think in creative ways, for example, by naming unusual associations to neutral words (Isen, Johnson, Mertz, & Robinson, 1985), using inclusive categories to group stimuli (Isen & Daubman, 1984), and processing material in an integrative and flexible fashion (Isen, 1987; Isen & Daubman, 1984). This research suggests that experiencing a moderate level of happiness is wise if the task demands broad and creative thinking. While happiness can be beneficial in certain contexts, research reveals that anger also has its place. For instance, displaying anger in negotiations often leads others to concede (van Kleef, De Dreu, & Manstead, 2004) and therefore, setting the goal of expressing a moderate level of anger may also sometimes be wise.

It is important to note that the associations between emotions and task performance are not yet understood well enough to always confidently determine which emotion is best to experience during tasks with particular demands. For example, George and Zhou (2002) identified circumstances in which negative moods are positively related to creativity. The available research makes us confident about some emotions and some tasks, but more research is needed. We return to this issue below when discussing future research on the PoWER model.

The Characteristics of Interaction Partners

Certain characteristics of interaction partners may determine the correct emotion and intensity to experience that emotion and, therefore, what is an effective emotion regulation goal. These characteristics include relative status, gender, the closeness of the relationship, and the personality traits of interaction partners. For example, Clark and Finkel (2004) argued that expressions of sadness are interpreted as calls for help in communal relationships, but not in other types of relationships. This indicates that experiencing and expressing a moderate level of sadness in communal relationships may be considered wise (Clark & Finkel, 2004). Expressing the same sadness in other types of relationships, however, may be considered unwise.

The Cultural Context

Culture reflects a way of living shared by most members of a social group (Adler, 1997). As such, culture structures people's perceptions of the world and shapes their behavior. One important way in which cultures differ is the extent to which they are individualistic versus collectivistic (Triandis, 1983). While individualistic cultures reinforce looking after oneself and one's immediate family, collectivistic cultures reinforce groups, such as extended families and organizations where everyone takes responsibility for others. This cultural difference has consequences for emotion regulation behavior. For example, the Netherlands and the Philippines represent near opposite ends of the individualism–collectivism continuum. This, in turn, leads to a significant difference in how workers from the two cultures manage shame (Bagozzi, Verbeke, & Gavino, 2003). In the Netherlands, an individualistic culture, workers manage shame via withdrawal behavior as they devote mental resources inward. In the Philippines, a collectivist culture, workers manage shame via enhanced customer service and organizational citizenship behavior as they seek to repair relationships. The influence of culture on behavior operates at such a deep level that most people are unaware of it (Triandis, 1983). Culture may nonetheless have powerful effects on what emotions and levels of intensity are appropriate and, hence, what emotion regulation goals are effective.

Step 2. Select an Effective Strategy for Attaining One's Emotion Regulation Goal

In the second step of the PoWER model, workers regulate their emotions wisely if they choose an effective strategy to attain the emotion regulation goal that they set in the first step. Choosing an effective strategy is important because multiple strategies are available to organization members.

Theorists have distinguished between strategies broadly by identifying whether a strategy occurs relatively early or relatively late during the unfolding of an emotion. Strategies that occur early during the unfolding of an emotion have been grouped under the rubric of deep acting, or antecedent-focused emotion regulation (Grandey, 2000; Gross, 1998; Hochschild, 1983). Deep acting concerns the manipulation of components of an emotion before the emotion is fully under way. For example, individuals can appraise a threat as harmless to avoid both the internal experience and the public display of fear. Gross (1998) distinguished among four specific deep acting strategies. Situation selection consists of approaching or avoiding certain people or situations on the basis of their likely emotional impact. Situation modification involves modifying the environment to alter its emotional impact. Attention deployment refers to efforts to turn attention toward or away from something in the environment. Finally, cognitive change concerns re-evaluating either the immediate situation or one's capacity to manage the situation.

Strategies that occur late during the unfolding of an emotion have been grouped under the rubric of surface acting, or response-focused emotion regulation (Grandey, 2000; Gross, 1998; Hochschild, 1983). Surface acting concerns the manipulation of components of an emotion once the emotion is fully under way. For example, angry employees can reduce their public display of anger while leaving their internal experience of anger intact. In his program of research, Gross (1998) focused on one type of surface acting, response modulation, which involves the manipulation of aspects of emotions such as physiology and facial display.

In addition to choosing between deep and surface acting, people have the choice of amplifying or suppressing emotion, or maintaining emotion at the current level (Hochschild, 1983; Levenson, 1994). Emotion amplification consists of initiating or enhancing public displays of emotion. For example, sales clerks may exert efforts to enhance their public displays of enthusiasm. Emotion suppression consists of reducing or eliminating public displays of emotion. For instance, negotiators may exert efforts to reduce their public displays of happiness (Thompson, Nadler, & Kim, 1999). Maintaining an emotion consists of preserving the level at which an emotion is publicly displayed. For example, students who show sadness following a poor performance in an examination may wish to maintain their display of sadness to elicit sympathy from friends.

The availability of different emotion regulation strategies underscores the choice of a strategy as a core component of wise emotion regulation. There are several elements involved in determining which strategy to use. First, given the context, one must accurately assess the benefits and the costs of various strategies. For example, employees who are angry about their pay may choose to modify the situation by voicing complaints. Employees may benefit from this strategy if their supervisors increase their pay, but this strategy may also incur costs such as damaged relationships with supervisors. An analysis of the costs and benefits of different emotion regulation strategies is central to choosing the best strategy from the available options.

In addition, one must accurately assess the likelihood of successfully implementing various strategies. For instance, an employee may implement the strategy of voicing a complaint effectively if the complaint is communicated clearly. A person with poor communication skills may not implement this strategy effectively. Such considerations need to be taken into account when making the decision about which strategy to employ.

Emotion regulation becomes less wise as the selected strategy becomes less likely to achieve the goal set in Step 1. An employee with poor communication skills who chooses the strategy of voicing a complaint may not exhibit wise emotion regulation because the strategy is unlikely to be implemented effectively. Emotion regulation is also unwise when an organization member fails to choose any strategy once a goal has been set. When such inertia exists, the probability that the goal set in Step 1 will be achieved is reduced considerably.

Step 3. Implement the Selected Strategy Effectively

In the third step of our model, workers effectively implement the strategy that they have selected. Merely choosing an effective strategy is insufficient because a well-chosen strategy can be poorly implemented. For example, imagine that a worker has correctly selected the amplification of happiness via surface acting as the best strategy in a given context. This strategy involves "putting on a show" to display happiness. Selecting that strategy does not necessarily mean that it will be implemented effectively, as the worker may fail to display any happiness.

As we argued above, successful implementation may be conceptualized in at least two ways. First, implementation becomes more successful to the extent that the target emotion actually changes. For example, two leaders may employ the same strategy to increase their cheerfulness prior to delivering an important speech. The first leader may exhibit an appropriate amount of cheerfulness during the speech, while the other leader may only generate a small amount of cheerfulness. The difference would be that the first leader has implemented the strategy more effectively than the second leader.

Second, successful implementation may be automatic and consume few resources. Two doctors may employ the same strategy to decrease their sadness prior to informing a patient about a poor prognosis. The first doctor may have worked for many years longer than the second doctor and have far more experience in reporting unfortunate circumstances to patients. The implementation of the strategy to decrease sadness may be automatic for the first doctor, but it may require deliberate effort on the part of the second doctor. The mental resources of the first doctor will be largely, if not entirely, preserved during the implementation of the emotion regulation strategy. This may enable the first doctor to use resources to respond more readily to the peculiarities of the situation such as the presence or absence of the patient's spouse and children and the nuances of the patient's response. Accordingly, it can be argued that the most successful implementation is automatic, leaving more resources available.

Step 4. Adapt Emotion Regulation to Changes that Occur over Time

In the fourth and final step, workers repeat the earlier steps and modify their emotion regulation as events in the environment change. The events that workers encounter in the work environment are dynamic. For example, new interaction partners and changes in the demands of a task are encountered. This suggests that wise emotion regulation is also dynamic in that workers should adapt their emotion regulation behaviors to constantly changing circumstances. More precisely, when events change, it is possible that a new emotion regulation goal must be set, a new strategy must be chosen to achieve that goal, and that strategy must be implemented effectively. This involves a constant monitoring of events and reading of the situation to decide whether a new goal must be set. We contend that remaining flexible in the face of changing events in the environment is a core component of wise emotion regulation. For example, when a product is being designed, pleasant moods may be desirable because they foster creativity, but the same moods may be undesirable when the design has been agreed upon and more systematic thinking is required to evaluate the practical issues that surround its manufacture (Schwarz & Clore, 1996). Emotion regulation becomes wiser as the person becomes more attuned with the varying demands of the task and sets different goals and selects and implements different strategies as the demands of the task change.

In contrast, we believe that it is unwise to remain rigid in the face of changing events. It is unwise to be unaware of changing circumstances. It is also unwise to know that circumstances have changed and fail to set a new emotion regulation goal and employ a new strategy to achieve that goal.

EMOTIONAL INTELLIGENCE AND WISE EMOTION REGULATION

Having described our model of wise emotion regulation, we explore the possibility that emotional intelligence is associated with wise emotion regulation, such that emotionally intelligent employees regulate their emotions more wisely than their counterparts. Prior to discussing associations between the two concepts, we define emotional intelligence.

Emotional Intelligence

Emotional intelligence is a set of abilities that pertain to emotions. Emotional intelligence includes the abilities to perceive emotion in the self and in others, use emotion to facilitate performance, understand emotion, and regulate emotion in the self and in others (Mayer & Salovey, 1997; Salovey & Mayer, 1990). A central issue in the debate about the scientific status of emotional intelligence concerns its definition (cf. Jordan, Ashkanasy, & Härtel, 2003; Landy, 2005; Zeidner, Matthews, & Roberts, 2004). To our minds, progress can be made on this issue by paying careful attention to the definition of ability. The definition of ability is rarely presented in the emotional intelligence literature, and we believe that this severely hinders progress.

A precise definition of ability was offered in Carroll's (1993) analyses of the structure of human abilities. Abilities are "the possible variations over individuals in the liminal levels of task difficulty (or in derived measurements based on such liminal levels) at which, on any given occasion in which all conditions appear to be favorable, individuals perform successfully on a defined class of tasks" (Carroll, 1993, p. 8). As such, abilities represent what a person *can do* in situations that are favorable. For example, the emotion recognition ability represents whether a person can perceive the emotions that an interaction partner expresses in situations that are favorable (Elfenbein & Ambady, 2002). Carroll's (1993) definition implies that abilities are not necessarily reflected in behavior. Indeed, it is possible for a person to have a specific ability and never use it. The ability would exhibit no relation with what the person does across situations and over time. For example, a computer programmer who infrequently interacts with others would rarely use the ability to recognize emotions in others and, therefore, this ability would infrequently be reflected in this person's behavior. The colloquial term "squandered ability" illustrates the possible gap between abilities and behavior.

Because Carroll's (1993) definition of ability is central to our conceptualization of emotional intelligence, we do not subscribe to mixed models of emotional intelligence and, by extension, we believe that research that employs mixed models has serious limitations. Some researchers have proposed models of emotional intelligence that subsume both abilities and additional constructs that evade the definition of abilities, such as personality traits. For example, Bar-On's (2001) mixed model includes, among other characteristics, social responsibility and optimism – characteristics that are not typically thought of as abilities. Consequently, Bar-On's measure of emotional intelligence (Emotional Quotient Inventory (EQ-i); Bar-On, 1997) suffers from substantial overlap with the Big Five (Daus & Ashkanasy, 2005). This has contributed to the consistent criticism that emotional intelligence is little more than "old wine in a new bottle." In effect, by including concepts that evade the definition of abilities, mixed models fail to represent emotional intelligence.

Development of Emotional Intelligence

Based on previous theorizing, we propose that emotional intelligence reflects a specialization of general intelligence that results from experience and learning in the domain of emotions (Côté & Miners, in press). Indeed, empirical evidence reveals that emotional intelligence, defined as a set of abilities pertaining to emotions, may be developed through experience and learning. First, Saarni (1999) showed that children's development of emotional abilities is influenced by their family environment, so that two children with the same genetic influences could develop different levels of emotional intelligence. Second, Mayer, Caruso, and Salovey (2000) provided evidence that adults have significantly higher emotional intelligence than adolescents, suggesting that it develops with age. Third, Elfenbein (in press) found that the ability to recognize emotions in photographs can be improved in a laboratory training session, at least in the short term. Finally, through a field study, Totterdell and Parkinson (1999) demonstrated that trainee teachers instructed to attribute positive meaning to events experienced more positive emotions than trainee teachers instructed to distract themselves, suggesting that interventions can help people better manage their emotions. These studies accord an important role to experience and learning in the development of emotional intelligence.

Distinction between Emotional Intelligence and Emotion Regulation

Emotional intelligence and emotion regulation are distinct theoretical concepts because the former encompasses abilities while the latter encompasses behaviors. Emotion regulation has been defined as efforts to increase, maintain, or decrease one or more components of an emotion (Gross, 1999). The term *effort* implies behavior, so that a person behaves in a way that is more or less effortful. Emotion regulation differs from emotional intelligence because emotional intelligence represents the potential for behavior and not actual behavior. The link between emotional intelligence and wise emotion regulation pertains to whether emotional abilities predict the emotion regulation behaviors described in the PoWER model.

RESEARCH PROPOSITIONS ON EMOTIONAL INTELLIGENCE AND WISE EMOTION REGULATION

For the most part, research on emotional intelligence and emotion regulation has proceeded independently. We believe that this may be the case because, as noted, it is not clear what types of emotion regulation may correspond to high and low emotional intelligence. The PoWER model identifies emotion regulation behaviors that may be related to emotional intelligence. We propose that emotional intelligence leads to more effective behavior along each of the four steps of the PoWER model.

First, we propose that individuals with high emotional intelligence *set more effective emotion regulation goals* than individuals with low emotional intelligence. The first reason is that emotionally intelligent individuals can identify their own and others' emotions more accurately than their counterparts. This is critical because, to set an effective emotion regulation goal, people must identify their emotions accurately. If people fail to accurately identify the emotion that they are experiencing, the goal that is then set might involve the amplification, suppression, or maintenance of an inappropriate emotion. It is also important to identify other people's emotions. For example, emotionally intelligent teachers may have the ability to detect test-taking anxiety among their students and understand the impact that anxiety has on their students' test performance. These teachers may set the goal of increasing their own displays of calmness to reduce students' anxiety because they know that this will help them perform better.

The second reason that emotionally intelligent individuals may set more effective emotion regulation goals than their counterparts is that they understand the nature of emotions more readily. For example, in response to an argument with co-workers, individuals with high emotional intelligence may be more likely to anticipate the emotions that they and other people are likely to experience, and understand how one emotion can fold into another emotion.

The third reason that emotionally intelligent individuals may set more effective emotion regulation goals than their counterparts is that they are more likely to be aware of the consequences of experiencing and displaying a particular emotion such as the cognitions and the behaviors that the emotion will likely encourage.

The preceding discussion suggests that people with high emotional intelligence are more likely than their counterparts to target the correct emotion and set a goal involving the emotion that is well-suited to the particular characteristics of a situation.

Proposition 1. Emotional intelligence is positively associated with the effectiveness of emotion regulation goals.

We also propose that individuals with high emotional intelligence generally *choose better strategies* to regulate their emotions than their counterparts. First, individuals with high emotional intelligence may possess a wider array of strategies from which to choose. Emotional intelligence, in part, reflects experience and learning that is unique to each individual. Thus, individuals high in emotional intelligence are more likely to have had greater exposure to situations in which emotions play an important part and to have accumulated a large number of emotion regulation strategies. Accordingly, compared to their counterparts, people with high emotional intelligence may be less likely to be in a situation that calls for a strategy that they do not possess.

The second reason why individuals with high emotional intelligence may choose a better emotion regulation strategy than their counterparts is that, in theory, they understand the consequences of the different emotion regulation strategies better than their counterparts. For example, people with high emotional intelligence may be likely to know that surface acting may have more pernicious consequences in most situations than deep acting because displays emanating from surface acting tend to be less authentic than displays emanating from deep acting (Côté, 2005). As a result, people with high emotional intelligence may be more likely to choose deep acting than their counterparts in the many situations where it is likely to be a better choice than surface acting. Furthermore, people with high emotional intelligence may be more sensitive to the characteristics of a situation that may influence the consequences associated with choosing one emotion regulation strategy over another, including the demands of the task and the characteristics of interaction partners.

The third reason that individuals with high emotional intelligence may choose better strategies to regulate their emotions than their counterparts is that they may be more aware of their own ability with respect to implementing emotion regulation strategies. Thus, when people with high emotional intelligence recognize that two or more strategies are appropriate under the present circumstances, they may be able to take advantage of this awareness to make an informed decision about which of the appropriate strategies they are most likely to implement effectively and thus, which of them should be chosen.

Proposition 2. Emotional intelligence is positively associated with the quality of the emotion regulation strategy that is chosen to achieve a particular emotion regulation goal.

In addition, individuals with high emotional intelligence may *implement emotion regulation strategies more effectively* than their counterparts. First, they presumably have more practice in actually performing emotion regulation strategies. We contend that people with high emotional intelligence will, on an average, have more experience and will have learned more about how to implement strategies effectively than their counterparts. Emotionally intelligent persons are thus more likely to have a precise impact on the emotion being regulated than their counterparts.

The emotion regulation of individuals high in emotional intelligence may also be more effective because it may be less conscious and more automatic than that of their counterparts. With practice, emotion regulation efforts that were controlled may become automatic. Because individuals high in emotional intelligence may have regulated emotion more frequently, their emotion regulation may be more automatic and consume fewer resources and, hence, be more effective than their counterparts' emotion regulation.

Proposition 3. Emotional intelligence is positively associated with the effectiveness of the implementation of an emotion regulation strategy.

Finally, individuals with high emotional intelligence may *adapt emotion regulation over time* better than their counterparts. First, in theory, they can recognize emotions in themselves and in others more accurately than individuals with low emotional intelligence. Therefore, they may be more likely than their counterparts to know when the emotions that are involved in a particular situation have changed.

The second reason why individuals with high emotional intelligence may adapt their emotion regulation over time better than their counterparts is that they may have a greater understanding of the nature of any new emotions that arise, including the events that were probably responsible for provoking the experience of these emotions. For example, they may recognize and use the information that can be garnered from the transition from the original emotion to the new emotion. They may recognize and use information about the *reason* that their emotions changed, what this means about how others might now feel and, in turn, whether it is appropriate to experience and show a new emotion.

The third reason why individuals with high emotional intelligence may adapt emotion regulation over time better than their counterparts is that they may be more likely to be aware of the outcomes associated with experiencing and displaying a particular emotion when the characteristics of a situation have changed. They may recognize that if the demands of the task have changed, for example, this information must be considered during any further emotion regulation.

Proposition 4. Emotional intelligence is positively associated with the flexibility of emotion regulation over time.

TESTING THE RESEARCH PROPOSITIONS

In this section, we discuss issues concerning tests of the propositions linking emotional intelligence to the four steps of the PoWER model.

Measurement of Emotional Intelligence

Several measures of emotional intelligence are currently available, presenting the researcher with an important decision. To our minds, these measures are not equally valid. One approach to measuring emotional intelligence is the *performance test* approach. Respondents are presented with emotional problems and asked to choose the best answer among a set of options (Mayer et al., 2000). The options have different degrees of correctness. Measures that employ this approach are the Mayer–Salovey–Caruso Emotional Intelligence Test (MSCEIT; Mayer, Salovey, & Caruso, 2002) and Wong's Emotional Intelligence Scale (WEIS; Wong, Law, & Wong, 2004). Measures of some of the emotional abilities encompassed by emotional intelligence include the Diagnostic Analysis of Nonverbal Accuracy (DANVA), a test of the ability to recognize emotional displays in the face and voice (Nowicki, 2000). The performance test approach is analogous to how other abilities, including the abilities encompassed by cognitive intelligence, are typically measured. For example, the Wonderlic Personnel Test contains 50 multiple choice questions. Respondents get credit to the extent that they choose the answers that have been deemed correct.

A second approach to measuring emotional intelligence is the *self-report* approach. This approach consists of measuring emotional intelligence through self-reports that use Likert-type scales. For example, the Wong and Law Emotional Intelligence Scale (WLEIS; Wong & Law, 2002) asks respondents to rate themselves on items such as "I am quite capable of controlling my own emotions." The Bar-On EQ-i (Bar-On, 2000) and the Emotional Competence Inventory (Boyatzis, Goleman, & Rhee, 2000) also employ this approach. This approach is widely used, but it is limited for at least three reasons. First, people tend to have inflated views of their abilities, with narcissism explaining approximately 20% of the variance in self-reported abilities (Gabriel, Critelli, & Ee, 1994). Second, people tend to fake responses and report having higher abilities than they believe they have (Donovan, Dwight, & Hurtz, 2003). Third, people cannot know with confidence whether their abilities are higher than their colleagues' (Paulhus, Lysy, & Yik, 1998). For these reasons, we have serious concerns about the validity of measures of emotional intelligence that adopt the self-report approach.

The third approach to measuring emotional intelligence is the *peer-report* approach. This approach consists of asking peers to provide ratings of a target individual's emotional intelligence using Likert-type scales. For example, Jordan, Ashkanasy, Härtel, and Hooper (2002) developed the Workgroup Emotional Intelligence Profile (WEIP-3) to profile the emotional intelligence of individuals in work teams. Among a large group of undergraduate students, the average level of emotional intelligence of team members was found to predict initial team performance, but not performance over time. More recently, Law, Wong, and Song (2004, Study 2, Sample 2) asked factory workers to rate the emotional intelligence of their co-workers using items adapted from the WLEIS mentioned above. The peer-report approach is limited for at least two reasons. First, peers may lack opportunities to ascertain threshold levels that determine ability levels. Second, there may be few directly observable outcomes of some emotional abilities, such as the abilities to identify and understand one's emotions. For these reasons, we have serious concerns about the validity of measures of emotional intelligence that adopt the peer-report approach.

Measurement of Wise Emotion Regulation

Several measures of emotion regulation exist, but they do not concern *wise* emotion regulation in particular. There is a need to develop measures of wise emotion regulation before the research propositions can be tested. At the moment, we believe that the emotion regulation constructs in the PoWER model may be best examined in laboratory studies because of the control that laboratory settings afford. To examine whether people choose an effective emotion regulation goal, situations could be designed in which specific emotions and specific levels of intensity could be identified as better or worse. For instance, participants might be asked to complete a task that requires creativity and in which a moderate level of happiness may facilitate performance. As we noted above, a critical challenge concerns identifying which emotions and levels of intensity are best for each task.

Laboratory studies could also be used to examine differences in the quality of emotion regulation strategies chosen by different people, given the same emotion regulation goal. A specific emotion regulation goal could be given to study participants who could be asked to achieve that goal.

The implementation of emotion regulation strategies could also be studied in the laboratory. Participants could be given a specific emotion regulation goal to achieve and asked to employ a particular emotion regulation strategy to attain that goal. The success of the implementation could be measured with assessments of the magnitude of the change in emotion following the emotion regulation efforts. Changes in facial action could be coded using the Facial Action Coding System (Ekman & Friesen, 1978), so that the more intense the change, the more effective the implementation. Changes in emotion could also be measured using psychophysiological equipment to detect changes in heart rate, blood pressure, or skin conductance (Cacioppo, Petty, Losch, & Kim, 1986). Again, the more pronounced the change, the more effective the implementation.

One alternative to laboratory studies is field studies that employ an event-contingent recording methodology (Alliger & Williams, 1993; Wheeler & Reis, 1991). For example, participants could be individuals who are completing a project in small groups over the course of several months. Key dimensions of the project such as the requirements for creative and systematic thinking and the presence of conjunctive and disjunctive tasks could be determined by the researcher. The participants would be asked to report their emotions, emotion regulation goals, and emotion regulation strategies using event contingent recording forms after significant interpersonal interactions. Each form may require the participant to report: (a) which group members were working with them at the time; (b) the emotion that they experienced at the beginning of the interaction and the extent to which it was displayed; (c) the emotion they wanted to experience and the extent to which they wanted to display the emotion; (d) the emotion regulation strategy that they employed; and (e) the emotion that they experienced at the end of the task and the extent to which it was displayed.

The end result would be a data set that would enable a researcher to determine the extent to which people regulate their emotions wisely over time, during naturally occurring events. For example, the extent to which an emotion regulation goal was implemented effectively could be determined by comparing the emotion that the person wanted to experience or display (e.g., "6" out of "7" on the display of happiness) with the amount of the emotion that they actually experienced or displayed toward the end of the interaction (e.g., "4" out of "7" on the display of happiness). This approach to studying wise emotion regulation, however, may not be possible at the moment because research must first identify when each emotion is effective and provide further knowledge about the different emotion regulation strategies and their effects. Progress in understanding basic emotions and emotion regulation processes is necessary before implementing some of the promising designs to study wise emotion regulation.

IMPLICATIONS FOR PRACTICE

Wise emotion regulation per se is an important applied outcome. For example, to the extent that wise emotion regulation consumes fewer mental resources than its alternatives, then wise emotion regulation seems to be a desirable outcome. An additional set of practical implications concerns how wise emotion regulation may impact outcomes such as well-being and performance. Research indicates that emotion regulation is related to aspects of well-being. For example, the job satisfaction of workers who amplify their displays of pleasant emotion increases from one month to the next (Côté & Morgan, 2002). There is also evidence that emotion regulation is related to job performance. For example, salespeople's emotion regulation is related to the quality of their customer service (Bagozzi et al., 2003). Taken together, these research findings suggest that organization members may enhance their well-being and performance by regulating their emotions more wisely.

If wise emotion regulation is related to outcomes such as well-being and performance, then individual differences such as emotional intelligence that may predict wise emotion regulation should have carry-over effects on the outcomes. There is a paucity of research on the mechanisms by which emotional intelligence predicts outcomes such as well-being and job performance (Côté & Miners, in press). Wise emotion regulation may represent one way in which emotionally intelligent individuals may attain such positive work outcomes. Pinpointing the emotion regulation behaviors that may mediate associations between emotional intelligence and work outcomes remains a challenge. Our PoWER model identifies some of the emotion regulation behaviors that may intervene between emotional intelligence and work outcomes.

ACKNOWLEDGMENTS

This work was supported by a research grant from the Social Sciences and Humanities Research Council of Canada (SSHRC) to the first author.

REFERENCES

Adler, N. (1997). *International dimensions of organizational behavior*. Cincinnati, OH: South-Western College Publishing.
Alliger, G. M., & Williams, K. J. (1993). Using signal-contingent experience sampling methodology to study work in the field: A discussion and illustration examining task perceptions and mood. *Personnel Psychology, 46*, 525–549.

Bagozzi, R. P., Verbeke, W., & Gavino, J. (2003). Culture moderates the self-regulation of shame and its effects on performance: The case of salespersons in the Netherlands and the Philippines. *Journal of Applied Psychology*, 88, 219–233.

Bar-On, R. (1997). *Bar-On emotional quotient inventory: A measure of emotional intelligence.* Toronto, ON: Multi-Health Systems.

Bar-On, R. (2000). Emotional and social intelligence: Insights from the emotional quotient inventory. In: R. Bar-On & J. D. A. Parker (Eds), *The handbook of emotional intelligence* (pp. 363–388). San Francisco, CA: Jossey-Bass.

Bar-On, R. (2001). Emotional intelligence and self-actualization. In: J. Ciarrochi, J. P. Forgas & J. D. Mayer (Eds), *Emotional intelligence in everyday life* (pp. 82–97). Philadelphia, PA: Taylor and Francis.

Bonanno, G. A., Papa, A., Lalande, K., Westphal, M., & Coifman, K. (2004). The importance of being flexible: The ability to both enhance and suppress emotional expression predicts long-term adjustment. *Psychological Science*, 15, 482–487.

Boyatzis, R. E., Goleman, D., & Rhee, K. S. (2000). Clustering competence in emotional intelligence: Insights from the emotional competence inventory. In: R. Bar-On & J. D. A. Parker (Eds), *The handbook of emotional intelligence* (pp. 343–362). San Francisco, CA: Jossey-Bass.

Cacioppo, J. T., Petty, R. P., Losch, M. E., & Kim, H. S. (1986). Electromyographic activity over facial muscle regions can differentiate the valence and intensity of affective reactions. *Journal of Personality and Social Psychology*, 50, 260–268.

Carroll, J. B. (1993). *Human cognitive abilities: A survey of factor-analytic studies.* New York, NY: Cambridge University Press.

Clark, M. S., & Finkel, E. J. (2004). The benefits of selective expression of emotion within communal relationships. In: L. Tiedens & C. W. Leach (Eds), *The social life of emotions.* Cambridge, England: Cambridge University Press.

Côté, S. (2005). A social interaction model of the effects of emotion regulation on work strain. *Academy of Management Review*, 30, 509–530.

Côté, S., & Miners, C. T. H. (in press). Emotional intelligence, cognitive intelligence, and job performance. *Administrative Science Quarterly.*

Côté, S., & Morgan, L. M. (2002). A longitudinal analysis of the association between emotion regulation, job satisfaction, and intentions to quit. *Journal of Organizational Behavior*, 23, 947–962.

Daus, C. S., & Ashkanasy, N. M. (2005). The case for the ability-based model of emotional intelligence in organizational behaviour. *Journal of Organizational Behavior*, 26, 453–466.

Diamond, L. M., & Aspinwall, L. G. (2003). Emotion regulation across the life span: An integrative perspective emphasizing self-regulation, positive affect, and dyadic processes. *Motivation and Emotion*, 27, 125–156.

Donovan, J. J., Dwight, S. A., & Hurtz, G. M. (2003). An assessment of the prevalence, severity, and verifiability of entry-level applicant faking using the randomized response technique. *Human Performance*, 16, 81–106.

Ekman, P., & Friesen, W. V. (1978). *Facial action coding system: A technique for the measurement of facial movement.* Palo Alto, CA: Consulting Psychologists Press.

Elfenbein, H. A. (in press). Learning in emotion judgments: Training and the cross-cultural understanding of facial expressions. *Journal of Nonverbal Behavior.*

Elfenbein, H. A., & Ambady, N. (2002). On the universality and cultural specificity of emotion recognition: A meta-analysis. *Psychological Bulletin*, 128, 203–235.

Gabriel, M. T., Critelli, J. W., & Ee, J. S. (1994). Narcissistic illusions in self-evaluations of intelligence and attractiveness. *Journal of Personality, 62,* 144–145.

George, J. M., & Zhou, J. (2002). Understanding when bad moods foster creativity and good ones don't: The role of context and clarity of feelings. *Journal of Applied Psychology, 87,* 687–697.

Grandey, A. A. (2000). Emotion regulation in the workplace: A new way to conceptualize emotional labor. *Journal of Occupational Health Psychology, 5,* 95–110.

Gross, J. J. (1998). The emerging field of emotion regulation: An integrative review. *Review of General Psychology, 2,* 271–299.

Gross, J. J. (1999). Emotion and emotion regulation. In: L. A. Pervin, & O. P. John (Eds), *Handbook of personality: Theory and research* (2nd ed., pp. 525–552). New York, NY: Guilford.

Gross, J. J., & John, O. P. (2002). Wise emotion regulation. In: L. Feldman Barrett & P. Salovey (Eds), *The wisdom in feeling: Psychological processes in emotional intelligence* (pp. 297–319). New York, NY: Guilford.

Hochschild, A. R. (1983). *The managed heart.* Berkeley, CA: University of California Press.

Isen, A. M. (1987). Positive affect, cognitive processes, and social behavior. *Advances in Experimental Social Psychology, 20,* 203–253.

Isen, A. M., & Daubman, K. A. (1984). The influence of affect on categorization. *Journal of Personality and Social Psychology, 47,* 1206–1217.

Isen, A. M., Johnson, M. S., Mertz, E., & Robinson, G. F. (1985). The influence of positive affect on the unusualness of word associations. *Journal of Personality and Social Psychology, 48,* 1413–1426.

Jordan, P. J., Ashkanasy, N. M., & Härtel, C. E. J. (2003). The case for emotional intelligence in organizational research. *Academy of Management Review, 28,* 195–197.

Jordan, P. J., Ashkanasy, N. M., Härtel, C. E. J., & Hooper, G. S. (2002). Workgroup emotional intelligence: Scale development and relationship to team process effectiveness and goal focus. *Human Resource Management Review, 12,* 195–214.

Landy, F. J. (2005). Some historical and scientific issues related to research on emotional intelligence. *Journal of Organizational Behavior, 26,* 411–424.

Law, K. S., Wong, C. S., & Song, L. J. (2004). The construct and criterion validity of emotional intelligence and its potential utility for management studies. *Journal of Applied Psychology, 89,* 483–496.

Levenson, R. W. (1994). Emotional control: Variations and consequences. In: P. Ekman & R. J. Davidson (Eds), *The nature of emotion* (pp. 273–279). New York, NY: Oxford University Press.

Locke, E. A., & Latham, G. P. (2002). Building a practically useful theory of goal setting and task motivation: A 35-year odyssey. *American Psychologist, 57,* 705–717.

Lord, R. G., & Harvey, J. L. (2002). An information processing framework for emotional regulation. In: R. G. Lord, R. J. Klimoski & R. Kanfer (Eds), *Emotions in the workplace* (pp. 115–146). San Francisco, CA: Jossey-Bass.

Mayer, J. D., Caruso, D. R., & Salovey, P. (2000). Emotional intelligence meets traditional standards for an intelligence. *Intelligence, 27,* 267–298.

Mayer, J. D., & Salovey, P. (1997). What is emotional intelligence. In: P. Salovey & D. J. Sluyter (Eds), *Emotional development and emotional intelligence* (pp. 3–31). New York, NY: Basic Books.

Mayer, J. D., Salovey, P., & Caruso, D. R. (2002). *Manual for the MSCEIT (Mayer–Salovey–Caruso emotional intelligence test).* Toronto, ON: Multihealth Systems.

Nowicki, S. (2000). *Manual for the receptive tests of the diagnostic analysis of nonverbal accuracy 2.* Atlanta, GA: Department of Psychology, Emory University.
Paulhus, D. L., Lysy, D. C., & Yik, M. S. M. (1998). Self-report measures of intelligence: Are they useful as proxy IQ tests. *Journal of Personality, 66,* 525–554.
Pennebaker, J. W. (1997). Writing about emotional experiences as a therapeutic process. *Psychological Science, 8,* 162–166.
Pugh, S. D. (2002). Emotion regulation in individuals and dyads: Causes, costs, and consequences. In: R. G. Lord, R. J. Klimoski & R. Kanfer (Eds), *Emotions in the workplace* (pp. 147–182). San Francisco, CA: Jossey-Bass.
Saarni, C. (1999). *The development of emotional competence.* New York, NY: Guilford Press.
Salovey, P., Bedell, B. T., Detweiler, J. B., & Mayer, J. D. (1999). Coping intelligently: Emotional intelligence and the coping process. In: C. R. Snyder (Ed.), *Coping: The psychology of what works* (pp. 141–164). New York, NY: Oxford University Press.
Salovey, P., & Mayer, J. D. (1990). Emotional intelligence. *Imagination, Cognition, and Personality, 9,* 185–211.
Schwarz, N., & Clore, G. L. (1996). Feelings and phenomenal experiences. In: E. T. Higgins & A. Kruglanski (Eds), *Social psychology: Handbook of basic principles* (pp. 433–465). New York, NY: Guilford.
Sutton, R. I. (1991). Maintaining norms about expressed emotions: The case of bill collectors. *Administrative Science Quarterly, 36,* 245–268.
Sy, T., Côté, S., & Saavedra, R. (2005). The contagious leader: Impact of the leader's mood on the mood of group members, group affective tone, and group processes. *Journal of Applied Psychology, 90,* 295–305.
Thompson, L. L., Nadler, J., & Kim, P. H. (1999). Some like it hot: The case for the emotional negotiator. In: L. Thompson, J. Levine & D. Messick (Eds), *Shared cognition in organizations: The management of knowledge* (pp. 139–161). Hillsdale, NJ: Lawrence Erlbaum.
Totterdell, P., & Parkinson, B. (1999). Use and effectiveness of self-regulation strategies for improving mood in a group of trainee teachers. *Journal of Occupational Health Psychology, 4,* 219–232.
Triandis, H. (1983). Dimensions of cultural variations as parameters of organizational theories. *The International Executive, 35,* 513–524.
van Kleef, G. A., De Dreu, K. W., & Manstead, A. S. R. (2004). The interpersonal effects of emotions in negotiations: A motivated information processing approach. *Journal of Personality and Social Psychology, 87,* 510–528.
Wheeler, L., & Reis, H. T. (1991). Self-recording of everyday life events: Origins, types, and uses. *Journal of Personality, 59,* 339–354.
Wong, C. S., & Law, K. S. (2002). The effects of leader and follower emotional intelligence on performance and attitude: An exploratory study. *Leadership Quarterly, 13,* 243–274.
Wong, C. S., Law, K. S., & Wong, P.-M. (2004). Development and validation of a forced choice emotional intelligence measure for Chinese respondents in Hong Kong. *Asia Pacific Journal of Management, 21,* 535–559.
Zeidner, M., Matthews, G. M., & Roberts, R. (2004). Emotional intelligence in the workplace: A critical review. *Applied Psychology: An International Review, 53,* 371–399.

CHAPTER 2

THE IMPACT OF EMERGENT LEADER'S EMOTIONALLY COMPETENT BEHAVIOR ON TEAM TRUST, COMMUNICATION, ENGAGEMENT, AND EFFECTIVENESS

Vanessa Urch Druskat and Anthony T. Pescosolido

ABSTRACT

The purpose of this paper is to help clarify the actions of effective emergent leaders in self-managing work teams (SMWTs). Multiple methods were used to test hypotheses that leader's behaviors consistent with the development of emotionally competent team norms (interpersonal understanding, caring behavior, creating an optimistic environment, and proactive problem solving) would be more strongly linked to team trust, open communication, personal task engagement, and team effectiveness than traditional task-focused leader's behaviors (directive statements, using questions). Most hypotheses were supported. Directive leader's behaviors were for the most part negatively associated with team trust, open communication, and personal task engagement. It is argued that in SMWTs that have a history and a future together, emergent leaders who engage in behaviors that build

Individual and Organizational Perspectives on Emotion Management and Display
Research on Emotion in Organizations, Volume 2, 25–55
Copyright © 2006 by Elsevier Ltd.
All rights of reproduction in any form reserved
ISSN: 1746-9791/doi:10.1016/S1746-9791(06)02002-5

emotional competence in the team are more likely to create team effectiveness than emergent leaders focused on directing team members.

INTRODUCTION

Surveys show that a growing number of organizations are implementing self-managing teams in order to lower costs and improve decision making (Lawler, 1998). Self-managing work teams (SMWTs) are defined as teams that monitor and manage their own performance, make decisions related to their work, and take collective responsibility for meeting their own goals (Hollander & Offermann, 1990). While implementing SMWTs is often productive for organizations, the most common reason for failure is poor leadership (Beyerlein, Johnson, & Bcyerlein, 1996; Cohen, Chang, & Ledford, 1997; Wageman, 2001).

Leading a *self-managing* team sounds paradoxical and, in fact, the unclear nature of the role makes over- and under-management by the leader, common problems (Manz & Sims, 1984; Druskat & Wheeler, 2003; Walton, 1977). Getting the leadership role "right" is particularly difficult because so little research has helped clarify the role. Yet, researchers have consistently found that effective leadership of SMWTs is pivotal for their success (Kirkman & Rosen, 1999; Wageman, 2001). This leadership can come from two sources: external leaders who reside outside the team (see Druskat & Wheeler, 2003; Manz & Sims, 1987), and emergent or informal leaders who emerge from inside the team (see Bales, 1950; Wolff, Pescosolido, & Druskat, 2002).

The purpose of this chapter is to investigate and identify the actions of effective emergent leaders in SMWTs. Most research on emergent leaders has focused on identifying the leadership behaviors that predict one's emergence into the leadership role. That research has, traditionally, suggested that group members who emerge as informal leaders exhibit two types of behavior: task-focused and socio-emotional (Bales, 1950; Smith & Foti, 1998; Taggar, Hackett, & Saha, 1999).

Recently, research and theory have suggested that emergent leader's socio-emotional skills may be most necessary for team effectiveness (Pescosolido, 2002, 2004; Wolff et al., 2002). Wolff et al., (2002) argued and found that leader's empathy, defined as the ability to recognize and understand the feelings and emotions in one's team, is the basis for identifying and employing the task-focused and/or socio-emotional behaviors that are most appropriate to a situation; their findings suggest that empathic skill is critical to leader emergence. Pescosolido (2002, 2004) also argued that team effectiveness is contingent on an emergent leader's ability to manage the team's emotions, and that because of an emergent leader's status; he or she is in the unique position to be able to effectively influence emotions as they arise in the team.

In a related theory, Druskat and Wolff (2001) have argued that for groups who have been working together for a long period of time awareness and management of emotion are critical to team effectiveness. They specifically argue that because emotion is ubiquitous in groups (see Kelly & Barsade, 2001), a group's ability to develop emotionally competent norms (defined as norms that acknowledge, recognize, monitor, discriminate, and respond constructively to emotion and emotional challenge) leads to group effectiveness (Druskat & Wolff, 2001). It is important to note that research has revealed that emergent team leader's socio-emotional skills predict whether a team develops emotionally competent norms (Druskat, Wolff, & Dyck, 2001).

In this chapter, our objective is to use recent theory and research to develop and test hypotheses about effective emergent leader behavior and its link to team effectiveness. Specifically, we use parts of Druskat and Wolff's (2001) socio-emotional theory of group effectiveness, Pescosolido's (2002) theory of emergent leaders as managers of emotion, and previous research findings on the role of the leader's task-focused behaviors (Lord, 1977; Taggar et al., 1999) to develop hypotheses about the emergent leader behaviors significantly lined to the development of group trust, open communication, task engagement, and team effectiveness.

We will use the terms group and team interchangeably in this paper. Also, we define a group or team as "made up of individuals who see themselves and who are seen by others as a social entity, who are interdependent because of the tasks they perform as members of a group, who are embedded in one or more larger social systems (e.g., community, organization), and who perform tasks that affect others (such as customers or coworkers)" (Guzzo & Dickson, 1996, p. 308).

EMERGENT TEAM LEADERS

Group researchers have long known that certain influential group members emerge as leaders in groups (see Bales, 1950). These emergent leaders have been formally defined as team members who exhibit initiative and have influence over group members (Hollander, 1961; De Souza & Klein, 1995).

They hold no legitimate authority or power. Instead, they acquire authority from group members who give them control because they believe these individuals provide value to the group. In fact, emergent leaders have been found to be more responsive to followers' needs, more interested in the task, and more competent than appointed leaders (Yammarino, 1996).

Two distinct trends of thought have emerged over the past few years regarding the behavior of emergent leaders. The first, exemplified by Taggar et al. (1999), suggests that individuals emerge as leaders primarily because of their knowledge of and focus on the team's task. Consequently, these individuals use their influence to create task-focused roles and strategies to assist team performance.

The second, exemplified by Pescosolido (2002) and Wolff et al. (2002), and emphasized in our present study, suggests that the primary role of emergent leaders within an empowered or self-managing team context is to create a team environment that allows for understanding of differences, expression of emotion (positive and negative), and trust among team members. The assumption underlying this premise is that, in an empowered team environment, most team members are already competent at the task, therefore, building a trusting team, member participation, and communication and engagement of member talent and energy becomes a primary leadership responsibility. Schein (1980) supported this view in his argument that a relational style of leadership, as opposed to a task-focused style, becomes increasingly important as employees take on increasing responsibility. Therefore, what may be most needed in SMWTs are emergent leaders who can build the trust, communication, and task engagement necessary for the success of an SMWT. We now turn to an explanation of the socio-emotional theory of group effectiveness to identify emergent leader's behaviors that might build trust, open communication, and task engagement.

THE SOCIO-EMOTIONAL THEORY OF GROUP EFFECTIVENESS

The socio-emotional theory of group effectiveness (Druskat & Wolff, 2001; Wolff & Druskat, 2003) contributes to current theory on group effectiveness by clarifying how emotion and relationships influence group effectiveness. As shown in Fig. 1, the theory proposes that engagement of team members in the group's task and in effective task-focused processes (e.g., communication), are supported by group social capital, defined as

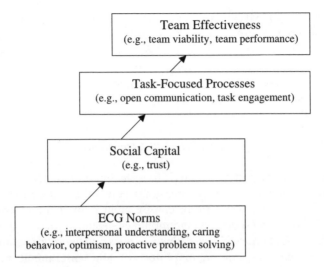

Fig. 1. Simplified Socio-Emotional Model of Group Effectiveness.
Source: Druskat and Wolff (2001).

constructive group member relationships (e.g., trust), which, in turn, is supported by emotionally competent group norms (ECG norms). The cornerstone of the theory is a set of emotionally competent norms that a team must develop. Important to the thesis in this paper is Druskat and Wolff's (2001) proposal that emergent leaders play a role in the development of ECG norms. Their research has also found that emergent leader's socio-emotional skills predict whether emotionally competent norms get developed (Druskat, Wolff, & Dyck, 2001). However, no research has examined whether emergent leaders enacting emotionally competent behaviors enable team effectiveness. In the next section, we explain the socio-emotional theory and how emotionally competent behaviors influence team effectiveness.

An Emotional Structure

The interpersonal interactions and behaviors that are at the core of group work are the source of many emotions, e.g., joy, contentment, fear, anger, and embarrassment (Kemper, 1978). However, the emotional dynamics (i.e., exhibition of emotion and the way emotion is dealt with) that occur in groups are not random; they emerge through member interactions, which are restricted by the social context and the range of actions considered admissible by contextual and cultural factors (Morgeson & Hofmann, 1999). Over time, group member back-and-forth interactions cause certain emotional dynamics to become routine and to emerge as a collective emotional structure or a set of norms about how emotion is exhibited and dealt with in a group. The status of emergent leaders enables them to play an influential role in determining which dynamics will emerge as group norms (Bales, 1950).

Group Emotional Competence

According to Wolff and Druskat (2003), the emotional structure a group adopts determines its level of emotional competence. Group emotional competence is defined as a group culture created by a set of norms that facilitate a productive social and emotional environment that leads to group effectiveness. "ECG norms" are defined as rules and expectations that foster acknowledgment, recognition, monitoring, and discrimination among emotions, and constructive responses to emotion and emotional challenge (see Holmer, 1994; Huy, 1999).

In the present field study, because of resource constraints, we chose to examine only four of the nine emotionally competent norms defined by Druskat and Wolff (2001). The first of the norms we examined is "interpersonal understanding," defined as the expectation that members will work to understand the feelings, interests, concerns, strengths, and weaknesses of team members. It is akin to demonstrating empathy or sympathy, the latter of which is defined as understanding someone's emotions without necessarily feeling those emotions oneself. The second norm is "caring behavior," defined as the expectation that members will take actions to communicate appreciation, respect, and possibly affection for others. The third norm is "creating an optimistic environment," defined as the expectation that members will take actions to produce positive group effect and an optimistic outlook within the group. The fourth norm is "proactive problem solving," defined as the expectation that members will work to anticipate problems before they occur or to take immediate ownership and control of a problem.

Trust, Open Communication, and Task Engagement

As shown in Fig. 1, socio-emotional theory of team effectiveness proposes that emotionally competent norms lead to group social capital (defined as the value added by the structure and quality of social relationships, e.g., trust, group identity – see Nahapiet & Ghoshal, 1998), and effective task processes, all of which are proposed to lead to group effectiveness. Therefore, we also chose to examine constructs from each of these categories including trust, which has been defined as the most fundamental element of social capital (Coleman, 1990; Putnam, 1993), open communication, a task process that is fundamental to group interaction and effectiveness (Steiner, 1972), and task engagement, which is central to the effort required for group task effectiveness (Hackman, 1986; Kahn, 1990). These constructs will be defined below.

Team Effectiveness

We agree with those who argue that long-term effectiveness in SMWTs requires that teams focus on two aspects of team effectiveness: (a) perform-ance, defined as the degree to which the team's product or service meets the needs of customers, and (b) team viability, defined as the degree to which members of the team are able to continue working together in the future (see Hackman, 1986). In teams that work together for long periods of time, a singular focus on performance would eventually harm member well-being, group viability, and eventually, customer satisfaction (Sundstrom, De Meuse, & Futrell, 1990). Therefore, we also include measures of team per-formance and team viability to examine team effectiveness in this study.

TASK-FOCUSED LEADER BEHAVIORS

As previously discussed, two distinct trends of thought about emergent leader behavior have emerged. Some theorists (e.g., Lord, 1977; Taggar et al., 1999) suggest that the primary role of emergent leaders is to focus the team on its task. These theorists argue that emergent team leaders are most effective when they use their influence to encourage and demand task-focused norms and behavior. Leader behaviors recommended by these the-orists include directing and questioning team members to increase their participation and task focus. Such behaviors optimize efficiency and productivity (Bales, 1950; Lord, 1977; Stein & Heller, 1979; Taggar et al., 1999). We examine task-focused behaviors in our study because research emphasizing task-focused emergent leader behavior has been primarily conducted in short-term student groups. Thus, as presented below in our hypotheses, we propose that task-focused behavior can have a negative influence on motivation and team effectiveness in SMWTs that work together for long periods of time and have a history as well as a future together. Here, task-focused behaviors may be perceived as controlling and might have a negative influence on trust, communication, and task engagement (see Ryan, 1982; Tetrick, 1989).

STUDY HYPOTHESES

We begin by hypothesizing that specific emergent leader behaviors will predict team trust, open communication, task engagement, and the group effectiveness constructs of team viability and team performance. Then, using the socio-emotional theory of team effectiveness, we hypothesize that some of the relationships between leader's emotionally competent behaviors and team performance will be mediated by trust, open communication, and task engagement.

Emergent Leader Behaviors and their Link to Trust, Communication, and Task engagement

Team Trust

Trust involves the willingness to make oneself vulnerable to the actions of others because of the expectation that those actions will be favorable to one's interests (Mayer, Davis, & Schoorman, 1995). Trust can grow out of positive affect displayed between individuals (i.e., reciprocal care and concern) and/or out of calculus-based cognitions (i.e., I believe you will do what you say) (Rousseau, Sitkin, Burt, & Camerer, 1998). Group member trust is particularly important in SMWTs because it reduces member opportunism and increases participation that is cooperative, altruistic, and extra-role (Fukuyama, 1995). Research also indicates that trust can improve the enactment of task-related activities by improving the coordination of actions (Dirks, 1999).

The behavior of leaders sets the tone for relationships among team members and influences the quality of those relationships (Bass, 1990; Kirkpatrick & Locke, 1996; Shamir, Zakay, Breinennn, & Popper, 1998). Consistent with the ideas of Mayer et al. (1995) suggesting that trust involves the expectations that others' actions will be favorable to one's interest, we propose that two types of emergent leader behavior will influence the level of trust among members of a SMWT. First, trust is enhanced when leaders exhibit behaviors consistent with "interpersonal understanding" because they increase team members' sense of being understood and valued. Second, trust is hurt when emergent leaders are directive and direct member behavior can be interpreted in the SMWT environment as attempting to assume control of a collectively managed team. We offer the following hypothesis:

Hypothesis 1. Trust in team members is positively associated with emergent leader display of: (a) interpersonal understanding and (b) negatively associated with leader directive statements.

Open Team Communication
Communication is the major ingredient by which a SMWT is held together (Steiner, 1972). Open team communication refers to honest and full participation in the communication and exchange of information among team members. Open communication norms invite candor and dissent. In fact, communication does not need to be agreeable to be effective; even when a dissenting viewpoint is wrong it often improves group decisions (Nemeth & Staw, 1989). Open communication is considered particularly important in SMWT environments because jobs and decisions are more complex than they are in traditional teams, and breadth and depth of member input is critical to team decisions and problem solving (Pearce & Ravlin, 1987).

Although research indicates that the complex nature of the task drives members of self-managing teams to openly communicate more than members of traditional teams (LePine & Van Dyne, 1998), we argue that emergent leaders in SMWTs influence the extent and openness of that communication. We believe that team members will be more apt to take the risks inherent in speaking openly in an environment where leaders listen to and work to understand members and make them feel that their presence is essential to the team (see Edmondson, 1999). We also believe that the task-focused behavior of using questions will increase communication simply by virtue of its intent being to get members to participate and share ideas and opinions. On the other hand, Morrison and Milliken (2000) argue that leaders can easily close down communication and honesty when they engage in authoritative or directive behavior because it signifies that member input is unnecessary. We offer the following hypotheses:

Hypothesis 2. Open team communication is positively associated with emergent leader's display of: (a) interpersonal understanding, (b) using questions, and negatively associated with (c) leader directive statements.

Task Engagement
Task engagement implies involvement, commitment, and the application of one's "full self" to one's work. Theory and research suggest that engagement

of member energy and commitment is linked to SMWT effectiveness (Pearce & Ravlin, 1987) and should be a fundamental leadership objective (Bass, 1990). According to Kahn (1990), leaders influence the degree to which individuals either become engaged or alienated from their work. His research revealed that engagement increases in an environment experienced as psychologically safe, that is, where individuals feel accepted, supported, and able to participate without negative consequences (Kahn, 1990). We propose that by virtue of their respect and influence in the group, emergent leaders are in a position to behave in ways that help to create such an environment and to increase member involvement in the task and in the team's self-management. Thus, we believe that a psychologically safe environment that facilitates task engagement is likely to be created through interpersonal understanding, which lets members know that their input is valued, and through caring behavior, which helps create the type of supportive environment discussed by Kahn. We also believe that task engagement will be reduced if members feel that leaders are indirectly *pushing* them to engage through the use of tactics like "using questions." We offer the following hypotheses:

Hypothesis 3. Member-task engagement is positively associated with leader display of: (a) interpersonal understanding (b) caring behavior, and negatively associated with leader display of (c) using questions.

Emergent Leader's Behaviors and their Link to Team Effectiveness: Team Viability and Performance

Research indicates that team leaders influence team performance (see Bass, 1990). One of the most robust predictors of individual performance is a sense of efficacy or belief in one's capability to perform a task (Gibson, Randel, & Earley, 2000). A growing body of research suggests that team efficacy, or a team's belief in its capability to perform well is also a strong predictor of task performance (Campion, Medsker, & Higgs, 1993; Gibson, 1999; Guzzo, Yost, Campbell, & Shea, 1993, Pescosolido, 2001). Positive expectations seem to stimulate behavior that makes them self-fulfilling (Darley & Fazio, 1980; Lindsley, Brass, & Thomas, 1995). We, therefore, argue that team-leader behavior that creates optimism about the team's ability to be successful will be associated with team performance. We also believe that leader behavior that encourages members to manage their negative emotions through proactive problem solving will be associated with team performance. Recent research examining the socio-emotional theory of group effectiveness reveals that a norm of proactive problem solving is strongly linked to team performance (Druskat, Wolff, Messer, & Stubbs, 2003). We offer the following hypotheses:

Hypothesis 4. Team performance is positively associated with emergent leader's display of: (a) creating an optimistic environment and (b) proactive problem-solving.

Team viability is defined as a group's ability to continue working together effectively in the future. Viable teams are healthy teams in which members feel they are valued by the team, feel optimistic about the future, and feel that when they work together the team is strong and effective. Therefore, we argue that leader interpersonal understanding and creating an optimistic environment will increase team viability. We also believe that leader's behavior aimed at overtly directing members' behavior will reduce the team's sense of strength and have a negative influence on team viability. We offer the following hypotheses:

Hypothesis 5. Team viability is positively associated with emergent leader display of: (a) creating an optimistic environment (b) interpersonal understanding, and negatively associated with leader's display of (c) directive statements.

Mediation of the Effects of Leader's Emotionally Competent Behavior on Team Effectiveness

The socio-emotional theory of group effectiveness proposes that the link between emotionally competent behaviors and team effectiveness is mediated by social capital and task processes (Wolff & Druskat, 2003). Thus, using ideas from the socio-emotional theory of group effectiveness (see Fig. 1) and the logic provided in the above hypotheses, we propose three mediating relationships.

First, we propose that the link between leader's interpersonal understanding and team performance will be mediated by the socio capital variable of trust. Second, we propose that the link between leader's interpersonal understanding and team performance will also be mediated by the group-process variable of open communication. Finally, we propose that the link between leader's caring behavior and team performance will be mediated by task engagement. Therefore, we offer the following hypotheses:

Hypothesis 6. The effects of interpersonal understanding on team performance will be mediated by trust.

Hypothesis 7. The effects of interpersonal understanding on team performance will be mediated by open communication.

Hypothesis 8. The effects of caring behavior on team performance will be mediated by task engagement.

METHOD

Setting

The research site was a Fortune 500 chemical-processing manufacturing plant with 2000 employees and 150 self-managing production teams. Teams had undergone the change from manager-led to self-managing approximately five years prior to data collection. The manufacturing operation was a continuous process, running for 24 h, seven days a week. Teams rotated their four-day, 12 h shifts so that all teams eventually worked all shifts. Team members belonged to one team.

Data Collection and Procedures

Data were collected as part of a larger study of norms and processes in SMWTs. A sample of 20 teams out of the 150 was selected for in-depth study. To select the sample we obtained nominations from managers, team members, and performance data. Teams were selected to represent all areas of the plant, to be conducting comparable production tasks, and to be considered at least average performers. According to plant management, this latter criterion meant teams were fully self-managing and a primary research objective was to study self-managing teams. All teams in the sample were responsible for running large manufacturing equipment with the objective of achieving high production quantity and quality through the management of time, coordination, equipment breakdowns, and frequent product changes. Teams ranged in size from 6–13 members ($M = 9.75$).

Emergent-Leader Behavior
Emergent-leader behavior was assessed by coding leader behavior on videotapes of each team. Coding leader behavior enabled us to get a measure of emergent-leader behavior in the context of their team without subjecting the study to the biases and inaccuracies inherent in self-reports or other reports (e.g., ratings from peers). Videotapes were obtained from 2.5 h

videotaped team-interviews conducted with each team. The interview format was the critical incident interview (Flanagan, 1954) adapted for use with a full team. The interviewer asked the team to discuss two types of events: (a) events in which the team worked well together and felt effective as a team and (b) events in which members did not work together well and felt less than effective as a team. The role of the interviewer in a critical incident interview is to say as little as possible so as not to lead the interviewees. In a team critical incident interview, the interviewer asks questions and lets the interviewees tell their story and come to consensus on issues with as little interruption as possible. The full interview consisted of going back and forth between the two types of events and discussion among group members.

Interview-Data Processing and Analysis

Of the twenty teams included in the study, four teams were eliminated leaving a final sample of sixteen teams. Two teams were eliminated because technical errors made the videotapes difficult to code. Two more teams were eliminated because they had elected a team coordinator who was unable to attend the interview. Field observations suggested that in this plant, election meant that a member was respected and influential within the team. Consequently, we felt that the absence of these elected leaders would have significantly impacted our ability to study emergent leaders within the group. These elected leaders missed the interviews because they were members of the plant-paramedical team, which was undergoing training at the time of the interviews. Field notes were examined to determine if there were other missing team members who stood out as being highly influential on the plant floor; no cases of this were discovered.

Team member participation in interviews ranged from 57% to 100% ($M = 83\%$, Mdn $= 82\%$), with 3 teams falling below 75% participation and 5 teams achieving 100% participation. Absences were in most cases due to illness, or conflicting meetings. Given the size of the teams (range $= 6$–13 members, $M = 9.8$), the percentage of members in each team who participated in the team interviews was high. This was most likely because team members were either given time off the production line or paid overtime wages to participate. Total participation included 130 team members.

Identification of the Emergent Team Leaders

To identify emergent team leaders we used the definition cited in previous research: team members who take initiative and have influence over other team members (De Souza & Klein, 1995; Wheelan & Johnston, 1996), which led us to use two criteria for leader selection. The first was election by the team into the role of team coordinator. Team coordinators had no formal authority in the team. They worked on the production line and received the same pay as other members, but had time-off of the line each day to: monitor the daily "line—up" (i.e., ensure team members knew their daily positions on the line), get supplies, take product samples to labs, keep daily records, and act as a contact person for external management. Teams decided whether to rotate this position or to elect one coordinator. Eight of the sixteen teams in our final sample chose to elect a coordinator. Our use of election as a criterion was based on field notes suggesting that election signaled that an individual had influence in the team and that his or her ideas were respected by team members. As a validity check for the use of this criterion, the researchers watched these members on the videotapes and using the criteria outlined below for selection of emergent leaders in the remaining eight teams, determined that these members acted as emergent leaders during the session. In all eight cases this was true. This check also reinforced the validity of our leader-selection criteria outlined below.

Our second criterion for leader selection was selection by a panel of four judges who independently viewed the videotapes to select team members who showed initiative and had influence, which was operationalized as: (a) when this individual talks, others take notice and listen, (b) the individual's statements and ideas have influence over the statements and actions of other members, and (c) the individual shows initiative by suggesting topics and sharing ideas; importantly, consistent with point (b), these initiatives must be accepted by team members (as opposed to rejected or ignored).

Over the years, research has repeatedly found that more than one emergent leader emerges in most teams (see Bales, 1950; Burke, 1971; De Souza & Klein, 1995; Neubert, 1999; Wheelan & Johnston, 1996). Thus, our first task was to determine the number of leaders emerging in the SMWTs in our sample. Four members of our research team used the criteria outlined above while independently and repeatedly watching the sixteen videotapes. There was consensus that two emergent leaders emerged in these teams. Previous researchers have also found that two leaders emerge in groups the size of those we were studying (Bales, 1950; Bales & Slater, 1955; Neubert, 1999; Wheelan & Johnston, 1996); thus, we decided to code the leadership behaviors of the two emergent leaders in each team.

After we viewed the tapes to determine the number of leaders, four independent judges proceeded to independently review the tapes (using the criteria outlined above) to select the two leaders in each team. They achieved an inter-rater reliability (James, Demaree, & Wolf, 1984) of .98 (range for all leaders = .89–1.0). It is worth noting that we conducted a post-hoc analysis (e.g., after data were analyzed) and found no significant differences between the frequencies of each coded behavior exhibited by the leaders in our sample who had been elected as coordinators and those who were selected by the judges. We also found no significant differences between those exhibited by the two leaders in each team.

Content Analysis of Leader Behaviors

Our research questions ask about the specific behaviors exhibited by the emergent leaders of SMWTs. Consequently, we created a behavioral code to describe and operationalize the individual leader's behaviors examined in this study. The behavioral code was created by the authors through a careful process of examining the research literature and the videotapes to ensure that our descriptions of leader behaviors were relevant to the types of behaviors seen in the SMWTs. Table 1 presents the final codes, their definitions, and examples of the statements coded for a behavior. This list served as a codebook.

Coding Leaders and Determining Code Reliability

At this point, two new coders joined our research team to code the behavior of each emergent leader in the 16 teams (32 leaders). The coders underwent a training process to learn the codes by iteratively coding clips from four training videotapes (clips not used in the final analysis) and meeting with the researchers to clarify applications and code definitions. Once the coders reached an inter-rater reliability of .75 on each code using the training tapes, they independently coded three 15-min clips from each of the 16 tapes (coding the two leaders on each tape for a total of 45 min per tape). The first 15-min clip occurred 0.5 h into the interview, the second clip occurred 1 h into the interview and the third clip occurred 1.5 h into the interview. The timing of these clips was selected to capture representative sections of the tape that did not involve the early warm-up or winding down phases of the interview.

Coding involved marking a code on a scoring sheet and indicating the timing on the tape when an emergent leader exhibited the behavior as it was described in the codebook. Coding-videotaped critical incident interviews allowed the codes to be applied in three ways: (a) to non-verbal behaviors exhibited during the team interview (e.g., a head nod to signify affirmation of a member idea), (b) to statements made during the interview (e.g., the leader stating that she agrees with a member's idea), and (c) to leader

Table 1.   Emergent Leader Behaviors, Definitions, Sample Quotes and Examples.

Emergent Leader Behaviors	Definitions	Sample Quotes and Examples
Emotionally competent behaviors		
1. Interpersonal understanding	(a) Demonstrating insight into a member's personality or personal situation, or (b) Expressing empathy or the ability to hear and understand the thoughts, feelings, needs and concerns of others	"That recognition made her light up like a light bulb" "You can tell when she's smiling inside. She's smiling inside right now"
2. Caring behavior	(a) Supporting members in the conversation by affirming their ideas or input through statements or body language (e.g., affirmative nods) (b) Praise comes from the leader and goes to specific individuals (c) Verbal or non-verbal support, affection, or warmth	"Exactly" "What she just said" "Most of the time [Pam] was right" The leader made coffee for another team member and gave it to her before getting his own coffee The leader touches team member in a caring way
3. Creating an optimistic environment	Explicit comments demonstrating optimism about the team's ability to handle problems and to manage itself	"We knew what (the external leader) expected of us. We knew what we wanted to do and what was needed to do a good job" "I think we could have made that decision" "We don't need a supervisor to do a good job"
4. Proactive problem solving	Statements made to influence the team to think proactively about a problem	"You have to give people in the creel time to catch up" "We just had to do whatever we could
Task-Focused Behaviors		
5. Using questions	(a) Using questions that involve/invite team members into the conversation, or (b) Using questions to confirm own assessment or	"How long did it take?" "Sally, you were there ... what did you think had happened?" "Is that not right?"

Table 1. (*Continued*)

Emergent Leader Behaviors	Definitions	Sample Quotes and Examples
	interpretation of the situation	
6. Directive statements	(a) Intervening to direct conversation or member conversation (e.g., stepping in to define what happened or has to happen), or (b) Directive questions The difference between this code and no. 5 (Using questions) is the tone involved. Here, the question is in the form of a directive or command	"What happened is this ... " "No. No, you were there then ... " "Can't you tell some things about that meeting?" "How do you think we are going to tell them if you don't want to bring it up so we can talk about it?"

behaviors that occur within the critical incident being described (e.g., as part of the critical incident, a member describes how the leader supported her ideas). The leader was the unit of analysis and the number of times a code could be applied was unlimited.

When coders completed a tape, they made a frequency count of the number of times each code had been applied to each leader. When all tapes had been coded, coding reliabilities were calculated for each separate code as the percent agreement across all tapes between both coders (Boyatzis, 1998). Coders achieved a mean reliability of .88 (range for all 13 codes = .75–.99). To determine the final frequency count for each code for each leader, we averaged the code applications of the two coders. The end result was a frequency count of the number of times a leader exhibited each of the seven behaviors. Table 2 presents the means and standard deviations for exhibition of each behavior by the 32 emergent leaders and intercorrelations among the behaviors. Because team self-evaluation occurred so infrequently ($M = .22$, SD $= .49$), we chose to drop it from all further analyses.

Trust, Communication, and Task Engagement
Trust in group members was measured using seven items from Cook and Wall's (1980) interpersonal trust at work survey; sample items include, "Most of my teammates can be relied upon to do as they say they will do," and "I can rely on the other workers in my team not to make my job more difficult by careless work." Cronbach's α estimated scale reliability was .73.

Table 2. Descriptive Statistics for Emergent Leader Behaviors and
Intercorrelations among Behaviors ($N = 32$).

Leader Behaviors	Mean	SD	1	2	3	4	5	6
Interpersonal understanding	1.06	1.76	—					
Caring behavior	14.4	9.44	0.38*	—				
Optimistic environment	1.50	2.45	0.20	−0.03	—			
Proactive problem solving	3.78	4.36	−0.02	0.14	0.30	—		
Directive statements	7.75	5.94	0.44*	0.39*	0.03	0.14	—	
Using questions	2.59	3.59	−0.04	0.09	−0.09	0.31	0.31	—

*$p < .05$.

Item anchors for this and all other scales used in the study were 1 = *strongly disagree* to 7 = *strongly agree*.

Open group communication was assessed using Seashore, Lawler, Mirvis, and Cammann's (1982) four item open group process scale; example items include, "My teammates are afraid to express their real views" (R), and "In my opinion everyone's opinion gets listened to." Cronbach's α scale reliability was .86.

Task engagement was measured using six task engagement items from Hackman and Oldham's (1980) Job Diagnostic Survey; sample items include, "Whether or not this job gets done right is clearly my responsibility," and "I feel a very high degree of personal responsibility for the work I do on this job." Cronbach's α scale reliability was .79.

Scale Aggregation
Individual responses to the scales (including the three listed above and the team viability scale listed below) were aggregated to the team level because aggregation was consistent with Rousseau's (1985) suggestion that the level of analysis be based on the focal unit of the study. We were interested in the influence of emergent leader's behavior on the team as a whole, thus the focal unit of the dependent measures was the team. To determine if aggregation was empirically justifiable we performed the intraclass correlation coefficients (ICCs) test (Shrout & Fleiss, 1979). The ICC test has been discussed as difficult to pass because significance requires both high within-team agreement and low between-team agreement (see James et al., 1984). Our ICC analyses showed that all of our scales were significant at the $p < .05$ level. Overall, we felt these analyses supported our conceptual argument for aggregation, and the scales were aggregated.

Team Effectiveness

Because production tasks varied slightly, interviews were conducted with managers to determine the objective data most representative of each team's performance. Data type included: Amount of top quality product produced per "person hour," average amount of time taken for product changes, and average amount of waste produced. Daily performance data were collected for a mean of 10 weeks. To enable comparisons of performance data across teams conducting different tasks, data were standardized using z-scores. This resulted in a score for each team showing how far above or below the mean its performance stood relative to all other teams in the plant doing the same work. For all teams included in the study, tasks and equipment were considered of comparable difficulty to perform and operate.

Team viability was measured using items from the group viability scale from Hackman's (1990) Flight Crew Survey; sample items include, "There is a lot of unpleasantness among people in this team (R)," and "Sometimes one of us refuses to help another team member out." Cronbach's α scale reliability was .79. Table 3 shows descriptive statistics and intercorrelations among our various dependent variables.

RESULTS

To test our hypotheses, we conducted a series of regression analyses using trust, communication, task engagement, team viability, and team performance as the dependent variables and entering the hypothesized emergent leader behaviors as the independent variables. Table 4 shows the results.

Table 3. Descriptive Statistics, Reliability Estimates, and Intercorrelations among the Dependent Variables ($N = 16$).

Variable	M	SD	1	2	3	4	5
Trust	5.63	0.38	(0.73)				
Open communication	5.08	0.74	0.55*	(0.86)			
Task engagement	5.84	0.38	0.43	0.19	(0.79)		
Team performance	0.26	0.90	0.48	0.40	0.24	—	
Team viability	5.10	0.81	0.64**	0.73**	0.13	0.18	(0.79)

Notes: Cronbach's α reliability estimates are shown along the diagonal in parentheses. Scales ranged from 1 = strongly disagree to 7 = strongly agree. Team performance is reported as z-scores.
*$p < .05$,
**$p < .01$.

Table 4. Results of Regression Analyses Used to Test Hypotheses about Leader Behaviors that Predict Trust, Communication, Task Engagement and Team Effectiveness ($N = 32$).

Independent Variables	Dependent Variables			Team Effectiveness	
Emergent leader behaviors	Trust	Open communication	Personal engagement	Team viability	Objective team performance[a]
Interpersonal understanding	0.56**	0.40*	0.06	3.27	
Caring behavior			0.35*		0.38*
Optimistic environment				0.13	
Proactive problem solving					−0.27
Directive statements	−0.35	−0.50*	−0.51**	−0.57*	
Using questions		0.38*			
F	5.13	3.08	5.45	4.02	2.67
P	<0.01	<0.05	<0.01	<0.05	<0.10
R^2	0.26	0.25	0.37	0.30	0.17
Adjusted R^2	0.21	0.17	0.30	0.23	0.10
Df	2, 29	3, 28	3, 28	3, 28	2, 27

Notes: Standardized regression coefficients are shown.
** $p < 0.01$,
* $p < 0.05$,
[a] $N = 30$.

Trust, Communication, and Task Engagement

Hypothesis 1 predicted that team trust would be positively associated with emergent leader's display of: (a) interpersonal understanding and negatively associated with leader (b) directive statements. The overall regression model was significant ($F = 5.13$, $p < .01$) indicating that together these behaviors significantly predicted trust and accounted for 26% of the variance in trust. Hypothesis 1a was supported; leader exhibition of interpersonal understanding was a positive predictor of trust ($\beta = .56$, $p < .01$). Hypothesis 1b was not supported; however leader's exhibition of directive statements was almost a significant negative predictor of trust ($\beta = -.35$, $p < .10$).

Hypothesis 2 predicted that open team communication would be positively associated with emergent leader's display of: (a) interpersonal understanding and (b) using questions, and negatively associated with leader's (c) directive statements. The overall regression model was significant ($F = 3.08$, $p < .05$) indicating that together these behaviors significantly predicted open communication and accounted for 25% of the variance in open communication. Hypothesis 2a was supported; interpersonal understanding was a significant predictor of open communication ($\beta = .40$, $p < .05$.). Hypothesis 2b was also supported; leader's "using questions" was a significant predictor of open communication ($\beta = .38$, $p < .05$). Hypothesis 2c was also supported; leader's directive statements were a significant negative predictor of team responsibility ($\beta = -.50$, $p < .05$).

Hypothesis 3 predicted that task engagement would be positively associated with emergent leader's display of: (a) interpersonal understanding (b) using questions, and negatively associated with (c) using questions. The overall regression model was significant ($F = 5.45$, $p < .01$) indicating that together these behaviors significantly predicted task engagement and accounted for 37% of the variance in task engagement. Hypothesis 3a was not supported. Interpersonal understanding was not a significant positive predictor of task engagement ($\beta = .06$, n.s.). Hypothesis 3b and 3c were both supported. Caring behavior was found to be a significant positive predictor of task engagement ($\beta = .35$, $p < .05$). Using questions was found a significant negative predictor of task engagement ($\beta = -.51$, $p < .01$.).

Team Effectiveness

Team Performance

Hypothesis 4 predicted that team performance would be associated with emergent leader's display of: (a) creating an optimistic environment and

(b) proactive problem solving. The overall regression model was not significant ($F = 2.67$, $p < .10$), however, it approached significance. This indicated that together these leader behaviors did not significantly predict team performance. However, it is encouraging that creating an optimistic environment was a significant predictor of team performance ($\beta = .38$, $p < .05$). We were surprised to find that not only was proactive problem solving an insignificant predictor of team performance, it was also negatively related to team performance ($\beta = -.27$, n.s.).

Team Viability
Hypothesis 5 predicted that team viability would be positively associated with emergent leader's display of: (a) interpersonal understanding, and (b) creating an optimistic environment, and negatively associated with (b) using questions. The overall regression model was significant ($F = 4.02$, $p < .05$) indicating that together these behaviors significantly predicted team viability and accounted for 30% of the variance in team viability. Hypotheses 5a and 5b were not supported. Interpersonal understanding was neither a significant positive predictor of viability ($\beta = .27$, n.s.), nor was creating an optimistic environment ($\beta = .13$, n.s.). Hypothesis 5c was supported as leader's directive statements ($\beta = -.57$, $p < .01$) was a significant negative predictor of team viability.

Tests for Mediation
To assess the degree to which trust, communication, and task engagement mediate the relationship between leader behavior and team performance, we used the multi-step analysis suggested by Kenny, Kashy, and Bolger (1998). Three relationships must be investigated to demonstrate mediation: (1) the proposed mediator must significantly predict the dependent variable, (2) the independent variable must predict the mediator, and (3) the contribution of the independent variables must drop considerably for *partial* mediation and must become insignificant for *full* mediation, when entered into the model together with the mediating variable.

Hypothesis 6 predicted that trust would mediate the relationship between leader's interpersonal understanding and team performance. As shown in Table 5, the degree of team trust is strongly related to team performance (step 1), interpersonal understanding predicts team trust at an acceptable level ($p < .10$; Kenny et al., 1998) (step 2), and interpersonal understanding drops to insignificant when entered into the model simultaneously

Table 5.   Mediating Effects of Trust on the Link between Interpersonal Understanding and Team Objective Performance.

	β	t	
Step 1			
Predicting: team objective performance			$R^2 = 0.10$
Independent variable			P
Team trust	0.48	2.86	0.008
Step 2			
Predicting: team trust			$R^2 = .23$
Independent variable			P
Interpersonal understanding	0.31	1.80	0.08
Step 3			
Predicting: team objective performance			$R^2 = .24$
Independent variables			P
Interpersonal understanding	−0.14	−0.79	0.43
Team trust	0.52	0.30	0.007

with trust (step 3). Thus, Hypothesis 6 is supported. Trust fully mediates the relationship between leader's interpersonal understanding and team performance.

Hypothesis 7 predicted that open communication would mediate the relationship between leader interpersonal understanding and team performance. As shown in Table 6, the degree of open communication is strongly related to team performance (step 1), interpersonal understanding does not predict open communication at an acceptable level ($p = .36$) (step 2), however Kenny et al. (1998) state that this association does not need to be significant. Finally, the relationship between interpersonal understanding and performance drops (but not significantly as it was not significantly related to open communication in the first place) when it is simultaneously entered into the model with open communication (step 3). Thus, Hypothesis 7 is partially supported. Open communication partially mediates the relationship between leader's interpersonal understanding and team performance.

Hypothesis 8 predicted that task engagement would mediate the relationship between leader's caring behavior and team performance. As shown in Table 7, the degree of task engagement is not significantly associated with performance. Thus, we never go beyond step 1. Thus, Hypothesis 8 is not supported. Task engagement does not mediate the relationship between leader caring behavior and team performance.

Table 6.   Mediating Effects of Open Communication on the Link between Interpersonal Understanding and Team Objective Performance.

	β	t	
Step 1			
Predicting: team objective performance			$R^2 = 0.16$
Independent variable			p
Open communication	0.40	2.30	0.03
Step 2			
Predicting: open communication			$R^2 = 0.03$
Independent variable			p
Interpersonal understanding	0.17	0.92	0.36
Step 3			
Predicting: team objective performance			$R^2 = 0.16$
Independent variables			p
Interpersonal understanding	−0.04	−2.1	0.84
Open communication	0.40	2.3	0.03

Note: Standardized regression coefficients are shown.

Table 7.   Mediating Effects of Task engagement on the Link between Caring Behavior and Team Objective Performance.

	β	t	
Step 1			
Predicting: team objective performance			$R^2 = 0.05$
Independent variable			p
Task engagement	0.23	1.23	0.22
Step 2			
Predicting: task engagement			$R^2 = 0.08$
Independent variable			P
Caring behavior	0.33	1.90	0.07
Step 3			
Predicting: team objective performance			$R^2 = 0.07$
Independent variables			P
Caring behavior	−0.29	−1.54	0.13
Task engagement	0.32	1.69	0.10

Note: Standardized regression coefficients are shown.

DISCUSSION

Since the mid-1980s there has been a steady increase in the number of SMWTs implemented at all levels of organizations (Cohen & Bailey, 1997; Lawler, 1998). However, despite the knowledge that leading SMWTs is more complex than leading traditional teams (Hackman, 1986) and that leadership is pivotal to their success, (Cohen et al., 1997; Kirkman & Rosen, 1999) little research has examined the leadership role in these teams (Druskat & Wheeler, 2003). For the present study, we chose to examine closely the efficacy of emergent team leader's behaviors on team behavior and effectiveness because we believe emergent leadership is fundamental for SMWT effectiveness. Unlike external leaders of SMWTs, emergent leaders are continuously present and, thus, have continuous influence over team behavior.

Our study makes several contributions to current knowledge. First, as predicted, our results indicate that emergent leader behavior consistent with emotionally competent norms has a positive influence on team trust, open communication, task engagement, and on team effectiveness. This suggests that emotionally focused emergent leader's behavior influences positively the experience of working in an SMWT and influences the bottom line. A second contribution to knowledge is the finding, as predicted, that in the SMWT context, task-focused leader behavior generally has a negative influence on the team experience, particularly when it is directive behavior. It is important that we stress that these results are very likely due to the types of teams we studied. That is, self-managing teams that have a five-year past and a long future in front of them. Recent research (Robert, Cheung, & Trembath, 2004) has found that team task has a strong influence on the emergent leader's traits that influence team effectiveness. It may be that when an SMWT is in a start-up phase, or if team members do not know each other well, that task-focused leader behavior is most effective. This is a question for future research.

Our results also contribute to the knowledge about specific emergent leaders' behaviors and the routes through which they influence team performance. The first and perhaps most powerful behavior we studied was interpersonal understanding. This behavior involved taking actions to fully understand team members – even to the point of empathizing with them. This behavior linked significantly to the exhibition of leader trust and open communication and linked strongly to team viability. Moreover, the behavior also linked to objective team performance through the mediating relationship of trust and open communication. This suggests that one of the most important ways an emergent leader in a well-established SMWT can impact team performance is by making members feel emotionally understood and validated. Such behaviors create a climate of trust and open communication, which increases performance.

Another leader behavior we examined was "caring behavior," which is linked significantly to members' task engagement. We found that when members feel supported and cared for it enables them to fully engage in the task at hand. This finding is consistent with Kahn's research on caring behavior in organizations (1990). In a strange twist, task engagement was not found to be related to team performance. This may have been due to our small sample size and clearly needs to be examined again in future research.

Creating an optimistic environment was another leader behavior we examined. Because of its link to team efficacy, which has consistently been found to be associated with team performance (see Gibson, 1999), we hypothesized and found that the optimistic leader's behavior was linked to objective team performance. This suggests that emergent team leaders have an influence on this critical climate variable. It also suggests that managing emotion so that the outlook in the group is positive may be a fundamental part of the emergent leader's role.

We predicted that the leader's behavior of "proactive problem solving" would have a positive influence on objective team performance since the norm of proactive problem solving has previously been linked to team effectiveness (Druskat et al., 2003), however, this prediction was not supported. It may be that this behavior, which is hypothesized in the socio-emotional theory of group performance to manage group anxiety and emotion, was perceived as too task-focused in an environment where leader task-focused behaviors were not helpful to the team.

Although we found that the task-focused behavior of "directive statements" was consistently negatively related to team trust, open communication, and viability, we did find that, as predicted, the task-focused behavior of asking questions had a positive impact on open communication. It may be that when task-focused behaviors are directly related to improving the group emotional climate, they have a positive effect on the team climate.

Finally, our study provides some support for the socio-emotional theory of group effectiveness. As shown in Fig. 1, the theory proposes that emotionally competent norms link to group effectiveness through their influence on trust and task processes like open communication. We tested whether trust and open communication mediated the relationship between leader's interpersonal understanding (an emotionally competent norm) and objective team performance. Results supported our hypotheses. It appears that the socio-emotional theory of group effectiveness has some promise and should be studied further.

STUDY LIMITATIONS

There were a number of limitations in our study that must be noted. First, we had a small sample of emergent leaders. Second, and perhaps most important, we coded leader behavior during one team meeting that was, in fact, an interview. We cannot guarantee that when these emergent leaders and these teams are on the shop floor that leader behaviors will be the same. On the plus side, however, despite the fact that we used multiple methods in this study (coded leader behavior, questionnaires, and objective perform-ance), many of our predictions were supported. This suggests that the coded interviews were demonstrating behaviors of importance to the team.

CONCLUSION

In 1998, three organization scholars predicted that if someone could crack the code on how to effectively lead SMWTs – they would fare well in the new millennium (Maertz, Morgeson, & Campion, 1998). By no means have we yet cracked that difficult code. Much more research is needed on the leadership of SMWTs. However, we do believe that we have added to current knowledge and thus taken one more step closer to cracking the SMWT leadership code. Specifically, our research suggests that emergent leaders have an important influence on SMWT climate and performance. One of the most useful skills an emergent leader can bring to an SMWT is an awareness of emotion and its influence on the team.

ACKNOWLEDGMENTS

This research was funded by a research grant from the Weatherhead School of Management at Case Western Reserve University. We thank the members of our research team: Leonard B. McKendrick, Jaye Goosby Smith, Velvet Weems-Landingham, and Esther Wyss for their assistance with interview coding and analysis. We are also grateful for the insights and helpful feedback of Eric H. Neilsen, Steven B. Wolff, Richard Klimoski, and Stephen J. Zacccaro.

REFERENCES

Bales, R. F. (1950). *Interaction process analysis: A method for the study of small groups.* Cambridge, MA: Addison-Wesley.

Bales, R. F., & Slater, P. E. (1955). Role differentiation in small decision-making groups.In: T. Parsons & P. E. Slater (Eds), *The family, socialization and interaction processes* (pp. 259–306). Glencoe, IL: Free Press.

Bass, B. M. (1990). *The Bass & Stogdill handbook of leadership* (3rd ed.). New York: Free Press.

Beyerlein, M. M., Johnson, D. A., & Beyerlein, S. T. (1996). Introduction. In: M. M. Beyerlein, D. A. Johnson & S. T. Beyerlein (Eds), *Advances in interdisciplinary studies of work teams*, (Vol. 3, pp. ix–xv). Greenwich, CT: JAI Press.

Boyatzis, R. E. (1998). *Transforming qualitative information: Thematic analysis and code development.* Thousand Oaks, CA: Sage.

Burke, P. J. (1971). Task and socio-emotional leadership role performance. *Sociometry, 34,* q22–40.

Campion, M. A., Medsker, G. J., & Higgs, A. C. (1993). Relations between work group characteristics and effectiveness: Implications for designing effective work groups. *Personnel Psychology, 46,* 823–850.

Cohen, S. G., & Bailey, D. E. (1997). What makes team works: Group effectiveness research from the shop floor to the executive suite. *The Journal of Management, 23,* 239–290.

Cohen, S. G., Chang, L., & Ledford, G. E., Jr. (1997). A hierarchical construct of self-management leadership and its relationship to quality of work life and perceived work group effectiveness. *Personnel Psychology, 50,* 275–308.

Coleman, J. S. (1990). *Foundations of social theory.* Cambridge, MA: Belknap Press.

Cook, J., & Wall, T. (1980). New work attitude measures of trust, organizational commitment and person need non-fulfillment. *Journal of Occupational Psychology, 53*(1), 39–52.

Darley, J. M., & Fazio, R. H. (1980). Expectancy confirmation processes arising in the social interaction sequence. *American Psychologist, 35,* 867–881.

De Souza, G., & Klein, H. J. (1995). Informal leadership in the group goal-setting process. *Small Group Research, 26,* 475–496.

Dirks, K. T. (1999). The effects of interpersonal trust on work group performance. *Journal of Applied Psychology, 84,* 445–455.

Druskat, V. U., & Wheeler, J. V. (2003). Managing from the boundary: The effective leadership of self-managing work teams. *The Academy of Management Journal, 46,* 435–457.

Druskat, V. U., & Wolff, S. B. (2001). Building the emotional intelligence of groups. *Harvard Business Review, 79,* 81–90.

Druskat, V. U., Wolff, S. B., & Dyck, L. R. (2001). Using group member skills and abilities to predict emotionally competent group norms. Presented at the annual meeting of the Academy of Management, Washington, DC.

Druskat, V. U., Wolff, S. B., Messer, T., & Stubbs, E. (2003). Emotionally competent group norms and group effectiveness. Presented at the Annual Academy of Management Conference, Seattle, August.

Edmondson, A. (1999). Psychological safety and learning behavior in work teams. *Administrative Science Quarterly, 44,* 350–383.

Flanagan, J. C. (1954). The critical incident technique. *Psychological Bulletin, 51,* 327–358.

Fukuyama, F. (1995). *Trust: The social virtues and the creation of prosperity.* New York: Free Press.

Gibson, C. B. (1999). Do they do what they believe they can? Group efficacy and group effectiveness across tasks and cultures. *Academy of Management Journal, 42,* 138–152.

Gibson, C. B., Randel, A. E., & Earley, P. E. (2000). Understanding group efficacy: An empirical test of multiple assessment methods. *Group and Organization Management, 25,* 67–97.

Guzzo, R. A., & Dickson, M. W. (1996). Teams in organizations: Recent research on performance and effectiveness. *Annual Review of Psychology, 47,* 307–338.

Guzzo, R. A., Yost, P. R., Campbell, R. J., & Shea, G. P. (1993). Potency in groups: Articulating a construct. *British Journal of Social Psychology, 32,* 87–106.

Hackman, J. R. (1986). The psychology of self-management in organizations. In: M. S. Pallack & R. O. Perloff (Eds), *Psychology and work: Productivity, change, and employment* (pp. 89–136). Washington, DC: American Psychological Assoc.

Hackman, J. R. (1990). *Flight crew survey.* Unpublished Survey. Harvard University, Cambridge, MA.

Hackman, J. R., & Oldham, G. R. (1980). *Work redesign.* Reading, MA: Addison-Wesley.

Hollander, E. P. (1961). Emergent leadership and social influence. In: L. Petrullo & B. Bass (Eds), *Leadership and interpersonal behavior* (pp. 30–47). New York: Holt, Rinehart and Winston.

Hollander, E. P., & Offermann, L. R. (1990). Power and leadership in organizations: Relationships in transition. *American Psychologist, 45,* 179–189.

Holmer, L. L. (1994). Developing emotional capacity and organizational health. In: R. H. Kilmann, I. Kilmann, & Associates (Eds), *Managing ego energy: The transformation of personal meaning into organizational success* (pp. 49–72). San Francisco, CA: Jossey-Bass.

Huy, Q. N. (1999). Emotional capability, emotional intelligence, and radical change. *Academy of Management Review, 24,* 325–345.

James, L. R., Demaree, R. G., & Wolf, G. (1984). Estimating within-group inter-rater reliability with and without response bias. *Journal of Applied Psychology, 69,* 85–98.

Kahn, W. A. (1990). Psychological conditions of personal engagement and disengagement at work. *Academy of Management Journal, 33,* 692–724.

Kelly, J. R., & Barsade, S. G. (2001). Mood and emotions in small groups and work teams. *Organizational Behavior and Human Decision Processes, 86,* 99–130.

Kemper, T. D. (1978). *A social interactional theory of emotions.* New York: Wiley.

Kenny, D. A., Kashy, D. A., & Bolger, N. (1998). Data analysis in social psychology. In: D. T. Gilbert, & S. T. Fiske (Eds), *The handbook of social psychology* (4th ed., Vol. 2, pp. 233–265). New York, NY: McGraw-Hill.

Kirkman, B. L., & Rosen, B. (1999). Beyond self-management: Antecedents and consequences of team empowerment. *Academy of Management Journal, 42,* 58–74.

Kirkpatrick, S., & Locke, E. (1996). Direct and indirect effects of three core charismatic leadership components on performance and attitudes. *Journal of Applied Psychology, 81,* 36–51.

Lawler, E. E. (1998). *Strategies for high performance organizations.* San Francisco, CA: Jossey Bass.

LePine, J. A., & Van Dyne, L. (1998). Predicting voice behavior in work groups. *Journal of Applied Psychology, 83,* 853–868.

Lindsley, D. H., Brass, D. J., & Thomas, J. B. (1995). Efficacy performance spirals: A multilevel perspective. *Academy of Management Review, 20,* 645–678.

Lord, R. G. (1977). Functional leadership behavior: Measurement and relation to social power and leadership perceptions. *Administrative Science Quarterly, 22,* 114–133.

Maertz, C. P., Morgeson, P., & Campion, M. A. (1998). How to make a million in the new millennium. *The Industrial–Organizational Psychologist, 35,* 97–99.

Manz, C. C., & Sims, H. P., Jr. (1984). Searching for the 'Unleader'': Organizational member views on leading self-managed group. *Human Relations, 37,* 409–424.

Manz, C. C., & Sims, H. P., Jr. (1987). Leading workers to lead themselves: The external leadership of self-managing work teams. *Administrative Science Quarterly, 32,* 106–128.

Mayer, R. C., Davis, J. H., & Schoorman, F. D. (1995). An integrative model of organizational trust. *Academy of Management Journal, 20,* 709–734.

Morgeson, F. P., & Hofmann, D. A. (1999). The structure and function of collective constructs: Implications for multilevel research and theory development. *Academy of Management Review, 24,* 249–265.

Morrison, E. W., & Milliken, F. J. (2000). Organizational silence: A barrier to change and development in a pluralistic world. *Academy of Management Review, 25,* 706–725.

Nahapiet, J., & Ghoshal, S. (1998). Social capital, intellectual capital, and the organizational advantage. *Academy of Management Review, 23,* 242–266.

Nemeth, C. J., & Staw, B. M. (1989). The tradeoffs of social control and innovation in groups and organizations. *Advanced Experimental Social Psychology, 22,* 175–210.

Neubert, M. J. (1999). Too much of a good thing or the more the merrier? Exploring the dispersion and gender composition of emergent leadership in manufacturing teams. *Small Group Research, 30,* 635–646.

Pearce, J. A., & Ravlin, E. C. (1987). The design and activation of self-regulating work groups. *Human Relations, 40,* 751–782.

Pescosolido, A. T. (2001). Informal leaders and the development of group efficacy. *Small Group Research, 32,* 74–93.

Pescosolido, A. T. (2002). Emergent leaders as managers of group emotion. *Leadership Quarterly, 13,* 583–599.

Pescosolido, A. T. (2004). Managing emotion: A new role for emergent group leaders. In: C. E. J. Härtel, W. J. Zerbe & N. M. Ashkanasy (Eds), *Emotions in Organizational Behavior* (pp. 317–334). Mahwah, NJ: Lawrence.Erlbaum Associates, Inc.

Putnam, R. (1993). *Making democracy work.* Princeton, NJ: Princeton University Press.

Robert, C., Cheung, Yu Ha, Trembath, J. R. (2004). Conscientiousness and performance: Negative relationships with a creative group task. Paper presented at the Annual Meeting of the Society for Industrial & Organizational Psychology, Chicago, IL.

Rousseau, D. (1985). Issues of level in organizational research: Multi-level and cross-level perspectives. In: L. L. Cummings & B. Staw (Eds), *Research in organizational behavior,* (Vol. 7, pp. 1–37). Greenwich, CT: JAI Press.

Rousseau, D., Sitkin, S., Burt, R., & Camerer, C. (1998). Not so different after all: A cross-discipline view of trust. *Academy of Management Review, 23,* 387–392.

Ryan, R. M. (1982). Control and information in the intrapersonal sphere: An extension of cognitive evaluation theory. *Journal of Personality and Social Psychology, 43,* 450–461.

Seashore, S., Lawler, E., Mirvis, P., & Cammann, E. (1982). *The Michigan organizational assessment questionnaire.* Ann Arbor, MI: Institute for Social Research, University of Michigan.

Schein, E. H. (1980). *Organizational psychology* (3rd ed.). Englewood Cliffs, NJ: Prentice-Hall.

Shamir, B., Zakay, E., Breinennn, E., & Popper, M. (1998). Correlates of charismatic leader behavior in military units: Subordinates attitudes, unit characteristics, and superiors' appraisals of leader performance. *Academy of Management Journal, 41*, 387–409.

Shrout, P. E., & Fleiss, J. L. (1979). Intraclass correlations: Uses in assessing rater reliability. *Psychological Bulletin, 86*, 420–428.

Smith, J. A., & Foti, R. J. (1998). A pattern approach to the study of leader emergence. *Leadership Quarterly, 9*, 147–160.

Stein, R. T., & Heller, T. (1979). An empirical analysis of the correlations between leadership status and participation rates reported in the literature. *Journal of Personality and Social Psychology, 37*, 1993–2002.

Steiner, I. D. (1972). *Group process and productivity*. New York: Academic Press.

Sundstrom, E., De Meuse, K. P., & Futrell, D. (1990). Work teams: Applications and effectiveness. *American Psychologist, 45*, 120–133.

Taggar, S., Hackett, R., & Saha, S. (1999). Leadership emergence in autonomous work teams: Antecedents and outcomes. *Personnel Psychology, 52*, 899–926.

Tetrick, L. E. (1989). The motivating potential of leader behaviors: A comparison of two models. *Journal of Applied Social Psychology, 19*, 947–958.

Wageman, R. (2001). How leaders foster self-managing team effectiveness: Design choices versus hands-on coaching. *Organization Science, 12*, 559–577.

Walton, R. E. (1977). Work innovations at Topeka: After six years. *The Journal of Applied Behavioral Science, 13*, 422–433.

Wheelan, S. A., & Johnston, F. (1996). The role of informal member leaders in a system containing formal leaders. *Small Group Research, 27*, 33–55.

Wolff, S. B., &Druskat, V. U. (2003). A socio-emotional theory of workgroup effectiveness. Paper presented at the annual meeting of the American Psychological Association, Toronto.

Wolff, S. B., Pescosolido, A. T., & Druskat, V. U. (2002). Emotional intelligence as the basis of leadership emergence in self-managing teams. *Leadership Quarterly, 13*, 505–522.

Yammarino, F. J. (1996). Group leadership: A levels of analysis perspective. In: M. A. West (Ed.), *Handbook of work group psychology* (pp. 89–224). New York: Wiley.

CHAPTER 3

LEADERSHIP AND THE DRIVING FORCE OF SHAME: A SOCIAL CONSTRUCTIONIST ANALYSIS OF NARRATIVE

Erika Sauer and Arja Ropo

ABSTRACT

This article uses a social constructionist approach based on ethnography and narrative analysis to understand emotions in leadership. The empirical context of the study is leadership of a theater ensemble's rehearsal process. The study shows that a creative process, such as in a theatrical setting, involves emotional paradoxes. Specifically, the study points out how shame can be used as a leadership tool to increase organizational performance and professional development, rather than for purposes of manipulation as may be typically assumed.

INTRODUCTION

During the past decades, researchers in the organizational and leadership fields have paid attention to the undeniable role of emotions in leadership as well as followership (Hochschild, 1983; Ashkanasy, Härtel, & Zerbe, 2000;

Individual and Organizational Perspectives on Emotion Management and Display
Research on Emotion in Organizations, Volume 2, 57–80
Copyright © 2006 by Elsevier Ltd.
All rights of reproduction in any form reserved
ISSN: 1746-9791/doi:10.1016/S1746-9791(06)02003-7

Fineman, 1993, 2003; Brundin, 2002). Yet researchers disagree on the nature of that role. Fletcher (2004), for example, has claimed that positive emotions are key to leading an expert team and developing a creative atmosphere. Brundin (2002), in contrast, states that creativity needs confrontation and tension. Our research, carried out in the context of a theater ensemble, suggests that emotional tensions, especially tensions that can be traced to the feeling of shame, are present, powerful, and positive.

Leadership in an Artistic Organization

Theater work is often described as Janus-faced: on the one hand, it can be viewed as a nest of positive feelings representing acceptance of the unifying role of the leader as sole visionary, one who miraculously finds the inner capacity of the actors to be creative. Yet on the other hand, it can also be seen as a chaotic group unable and unwilling to cooperate. Rather than adopt only one of these viewpoints, we find it more fruitful to consider leadership in this context as a mutual relationship, something that is constructed together, sometimes painfully, in the presence of emotional tensions in the everyday work processes of the ensemble.

The work of a theater ensemble typically involves a number of phases: the play is chosen, the director is appointed, and the ensemble is formed. Usually, within 6–8 weeks after the start of an intensive rehearsal period, the play is ready for the opening night. In the event that the director is visiting, as opposed to permanently employed by the theater, he or she then moves on to another theater to direct another play.

The leadership provided by the director him/herself can be seen as paradoxical. Ideally, the performing arts are thought to be independent, free of structures and conventions. And art is usually not thought of as done to gain profit, at least not solely. Thus, the intrinsic motivation of an artist to perform and the task of the leader to organize the work to gain profit and to be as financially effective as possible seem to clash. In the case of a director and an actor or a group of actors, the case is even more complex. Whether or not there are concerns about profit, the ways that actors and directors think about their art can be very different, especially in the case where the director comes from outside the organization to direct one play before moving on again. These differing motivations and styles may give rise to strong emotions.

Emotions can be contagious (Hatfield, Cacioppo, & Rapson, 1994) whether transmitted intentionally or unconsciously. This is especially relevant in the case of high-activation emotions such as anxiety, frustration, and anger (Bartel & Saavedra, 2000), which are easily recognized by others. It has also been found that negative emotions are more contagious than positive ones (Joiner, 1994) and that this collective emotion can influence group behavior (Barsade, 2002).

Ethel Brundin (2002) undertook an extensive examination of emotion and strategic leadership in boardrooms. She points to the possibility of negative emotions giving fuel to creativity.

> The very confrontations involving emotions carry a lot of energy, which promote the course of events, whereas without such confrontations there seems to be a lack of creative energy (p. 310).

For example, what should we make of the production of a play, where the director is described as a "diabolic torturer", where the actors suffer physically and mentally, and the end result is both artistically and financially successful?

It is not our intention to promote practices that hurt people or their feelings. Rather, we wish to facilitate discussion on the dimension of leadership, where "negative" and "positive" emotions and "good" and "bad" leadership get mixed. Leadership is understood here as a social process where emotions play a key role. The borders between black and white of negative and positive as well as good and bad get blurred. Emotions are a crucial part of the humanity of leadership where imperfection, edges, and controversies become visible. In artistic organizations, this area of leadership may be more present than in business organizations. However, we think that studying emotions in a theater gives insights also into leadership practices in other kinds of innovation-seeking and creative organizations.

Do creative people need emotional tensions to be creative? Difficult and enervating processes might be needed for contrast and learning purposes. The sense of having gone through something, or having survived an ordeal, may be important for organizational members and the success of the organization itself. We think that while positive leadership skills are a way to build coherence and congruence, contributing to a desire for synthesis, leadership for innovation and creativity, is also about tensions. Occasionally the leadership process may become very concrete, ugly, smelly, and even frightening. We think that the outcomes of an artistic process and the leadership process that are embedded in emotions, are interrelated. Against the common understanding that a good, trusting process will result in great outcomes, our study suggests that sometimes a very ugly process can result in a masterpiece (see also Wright & Staw, 1999; Jing & George, 2001). A special emotion, shame, is the focus here. It seems that shame can be constructed as a liberating and empowering emotion in an artistic process.

STUDYING EMOTIONS AND LEADERSHIP

Interest in emotions has grown exponentially during the last two decades, making emotions a recognized subfield in organization studies (e.g. Eriksson & Parviainen, 2005). Organizations are now generally recognized as emotional arenas (Hochschild, 1983; Ashkanasy et al., 2000; Fineman, 1993, 2003) as well as behavioral and cognitive ones. This surge in attention to emotions in organizations began with discussion of emotional labor and management (e.g. Hochschild, 1983). Even more recently, emotional intelligence (Salovey & Mayer, 1990; Goleman, 1995; Mayer & Salovey, 1997) has become an active area for study generally and more specifically with respect to leadership in organizations. Emotional intelligence is based on the idea that emotional capabilities are important in social and business life. Researchers have developed scales to measure emotional aspects in leader traits and behaviors and investigate how these influence leadership effectiveness.

Some authors have expressed concern that research on emotions has been impregnated with biological and psychological determinism, with little room for social interactive processes (Eriksson & Parviainen, 2005). (For example, studies on emotions and leadership often involve a laboratory or a test setting, such as where facial expressions and emotions are combined with leadership perception and impressions (Newcombe & Ashkanasy, 2002; Dasborough & Ashkanasy, 2002)) This deterministic presupposition can more often be seen by reading between the lines than literally in the text. Fineman (1996) suggests that a more sociological eye be taken that includes historical dimensions, social context, roles, and experiences. Most of the work on emotions that has taken an organizational psychology perspective has concentrated on correlations between emotions outcomes such as perceived job satisfaction. Similarly, studies on emotions and leadership often concentrate on the correlations between leadership styles and traits and emotions (e.g. Wolff, Pescosolido, & Druskat, 2002) as well as emotion management (e.g. Pescosolido, 2002), perceptions of leaders and emotional displays (e.g. Newcombe & Ashkanasy, 2002). The findings of such studies suggest that emotions are related to several key issues in leadership: that empathy predicts leadership emergence, that management of group members' emotions is an important part of the leadership process, and that leaders who successfully manage group processes can influence performance (Humphrey, 2002).

Historically, research on the general topic of leadership has tended to focus on exchange relationships, in which the role of emotions was minimized or ignored. More recent approaches have acknowledged the role of emotions within leadership, especially transformational and charismatic leadership theories (e.g. Conger & Kanungo, 1998; Bass, 1985). Transformational leadership has been found to include communication of enthusiasm and vision, a positive outlook, intuitive insight, and emotional competency (Ashkanasy & Tse, 2000). The literature on empowerment related to motivation and participative leadership also suggests that emotional leadership behaviors and relations facilitate empowerment (Yukl, 2002). Nevertheless, leadership based on emotions can have a "dark side" (Conger & Kanungo, 1998; McIntosh & Rima, 1998) although Yukl (2002) has noted that despite possible adverse consequences, not even a negative charismatic leader is necessarily doomed to failure.

From a methodological point of view, some authors have argued that the study of emotion is at odds with the "myth of rationality" in organizational analysis (Putnam & Mumby, 1993) and with the cognitive paradigm in organization studies (Fineman, 1996). Thus, and in contrast to traditional positivist and realist perspectives, emotions have been studied from the social constructionist (e.g. Hochschild, 1983), and ethnographic and feminist perspectives (e.g. Abu-Lughod, 1993; Abu-Lughod & Lutz, 1990).

The approach we take here attempts to make space for other understandings of leadership and emotions than the modern rationality allows. This means seeing leadership not only as individual traits, skills, and characteristics, but more like a social, relational process. We wish to advance the thinking of leadership as a shared, ongoing relational process instead of as focused on the traits and behaviors of one heroic individual (Yukl, 2002; Hosking, 2002; Pearce & Conger, 2003). We also draw inspiration from charismatic leadership research, where leadership is typically understood as an individualistic phenomenon (Shamir, 1995; Conger & Kanungo, 1998; Fineman, 2003; Boje, 2001). This is consistent with leader–member exchange theory, social exchange and group processes (Jacobs, 1970; Graen & Uhl-Bien, 1995) as well as transformational leadership (Bass, 1996).

ONTOLOGY AND METHODOLOGICAL CHOICES

The following sections describe in detail the methodological approach and the findings of our study. We focus on leadership of a rehearsal process, especially on the relationship between the director and the actor(s). The

research method used is social constructive, based on ethnography and
narrative inquiry (Hosking, 1999; Koivunen, 2003), narrative and experiential writing (Connelly & Clandinin, 1990, 2000; Richardson, 1994). A
narrative was assembled following a period of participant observation by
the first author, during which the first author was employed by the theater.
The narrative was constructed by synthesizing the connections and situations that came up in interviews, observations, and during the work process
(Berger & Luckmann, 1995). The method was influenced by the works of
Koivunen (2003), Katila (2000), and Czarniawska (1999). We hold the position that the story we tell here is only one of many possibilities (Hosking,
2002). As we expect that many readers are unfamiliar with narrative inquiry,
before presenting the narrative we begin with a description of its foundations in ethnography, and of our assumption that the reality of leadership is
socially constructed.

Methodology: Social Constructionism, Ethnography, and Narrative Inquiry

Academic discourse is based on communication through writing. Since the
Renaissance, the world of writing has been divided into literary writing and
scientific writing. Literature has since been associated with fiction, rhetoric
and subjectivity, whereas scientific writing has been associated with fact,
plain language, and objectivity, fiction being "false" and science "true",
since it only "objectively reported" the reality. Nevertheless, beginning in the
nineteenth century, the social sciences have crossed this dualism, by applying
the language of science to literature and vice versa (Richardson, 1994).

Researchers employing qualitative approaches in social sciences strive for
thick, rich description and good writing, but at the same time they are
constrained by the scientific method and influenced by traditions of models
stemming from quantitative tradition. The meaning of the qualitative work
is in the reading and in the postmodern, poststructuralist tradition, where
the writing is a method of knowing.

When it comes to evaluating the quality of qualitative research in general
and constructionist research in particular, there is a great deal of debate. The
discussion ranges from opinions in favor of preserving the traditional positivist criteria of validity and reliability to demands to abort all those criteria
(Bryman, 2001; Denzin & Lincoln, 1994; Lincoln & Guba, 1985). Agar
(1986) suggests that qualitative researchers should abandon concerns about
validity and rather concentrate on intensive personal involvement, abandon
scientific control and focus on flexibility and improvisation instead. Feminist

researchers underline democracy, empathy, ethics, education, and emancipation as a set of criteria for quality of research (Roman & Apple, 1990).

Guba and Lincoln have offered both a conservative set of trustworthiness criteria, related to the traditions of validity and reliability and an authenticity criterion, which is rooted in constructionist research. Authenticity refers to the democratic positioning of research participants, the growth and development of researcher's thinking, and empowering and educating the subjects of the the study (Lincoln & Guba, 1985).

According to Smith (1990), there is an infinite number of constructions of the world, without no single, privileged construction. This makes qualitative constructionist research idealistic and anti-foundational, whereas the judgement of good and bad is foundational by definition, thus such judgments are difficult to apply to constructionist research, according to Smith. Later, Smith has acknowledged that quality characteristics can be applied to constructionist research as long as the quality characteristics are kept open-ended and evolving (Smith & Deemer, 2000).

There are several opinions about the concept of ethnography and what it includes. It can mean broadly a study of explorative nature, where the data were unstructured, and where the researcher is case oriented and interested in meanings (Alvesson, 2003, p. 171). Silverman (1985) defines it as any study referring to naturally occurring events. Typically, an ethnographic study means a study involving a long period of fieldwork, as the researcher tries to get close to the community he or she studies. The researcher relies on the accounts through informal listening or through more formal interviews, and his/her own observations perhaps in the role of participant in the setting and also on other material as documents and material artifacts. Interviews or less formal, more spontaneous talks between the researcher and informants are an important complement to the participant's observation. Without the accounts of the people, it gets very difficult to say anything about the practices and situations the researcher has witnessed. Interviews may also provide better understanding as the researcher gets more deeply familiar with the informants and is better able to formulate the questions (Alvesson, 2003, p. 172).

Crucial to ethnography is the element of thick description, which means careful, detailed, and insightful accounts of social processes and the ways meanings are expressed. Ethnography is looked upon as it involves more than just interviews. The experience of "having been there" often offers a better and informed understanding.

The second major element in ethnography follows the process of fieldwork and is the writing of the text (Van Maanen, 1995). In narrative inquiry, the ethnographic representation is thus "fictional"; the writer defines his\her work as fiction, using dialogue, internal monologue, and other literary styles to encase the story, where cultural norms are explored through the characters.

Narrative inquiry is a process of gathering information and describing situations through stories. Field notes, interviews, journals, letters, autobiographies, and stories are all methods used in narrative inquiry. After gathering the data, the researcher constructs her/his own narrative, using conventions of storytelling such as scene and plot. Thus, the research becomes a collaborative document. Narrative captures and investigates experiences as human beings live them in time, in space, in person, and in relationship (Connelly & Clandinin, 1990, 2000).

When constructing the narrative for this study, we were influenced by the postmodern technique of experiential writing (Richardson, 1994). Experimental genres deploy literary devices, try to re-create lived experiences, and evoke emotional responses in the reader. Katila (2000), for example, provides an excellent demonstration of narrative inquiry, in whose study ethnomethodology, ethnography, interviews, and written documents were presented to the reader in the form of life histories of farms and the farmers in order to explore the moral order of country life.

Writing a Story of Emotions and Leadership

The story of leadership and shame is presented here in a form that helps the reader understand the variety of roles that emotions play in constructing leadership, the different places where leadership and emotions are intertwined, and finally how emotions are an organic and inseparable dimension of leadership. The data on which our story is based was collected, in part, in the role of a "native". The first author worked in various positions in the theater from 1989 until 1995, and participated in the rehearsal process in the position of dress designer in autumn 2004. During that time, she was deeply immersed in the life of the theater group. All members of the ensemble were aware that she was doing research on the rehearsal process.

In addition to these observations, she interviewed members of the ensemble, including actors and the director. During the interviews, discussions turned often into performances in their own right, where the discussion partner dramatized a story or personal experience. The interviews were often characterized by humor and tragedy and represented, in many ways, stories in themselves. When talking about their experiences, both directors and actors often told small stories, illustrating and exemplifying their work. Very often these examples were taken of extreme processes, which had been physically and emotionally demanding.

Stories are central to our experience of organizations. Much of organizational life is spent hearing or reading stories already told, and interpreting them within a set of already existing rules, or routines. Sense making, or the activity of attributing meaning to previously meaningless cues, also occurs; storytelling is a never-ending process constructing meaning in organizations. Stories simplify the world, and are thus useful as guides. Notably, stories simplify organizations far less than conclusions about organizations drawn from the formal models provided by the logico-scientific theories (Weick, 1995).

The role of emotions in leadership became clear during the reading of notes of observations, thinking about the period during which the first author worked as a member of the group, and the re-reading of transcribed interviews. People often explained the situations and actions through telling about their emotions or others' emotional behavior and made a contrast to current events with tales of their opposite or controversial experiences. Through this process of reflection the narrative that is presented below began to take form, particularly as the theme of an ordeal recurred again and again. The ordeal was most often linked to leadership, which was experienced as almost cathartic, controversial, and as a depressing or enraging process.

Even though the empirical context of the study is theater, we chose not to employ a dramatological analysis, because of the risk of concept confusion: the metaphors of theater would have been used simultaneously with the concepts describing the actual work at the theater, which would have caused a double-layer structure in the text. We felt that this double interpretation, i.e. separating what took place at the theater and what takes place in the analysis, would have distanced the reader from fully understanding the rehearsal process as any work process that requires close collaboration of several people. Because we wish to promote the innovative use of the narrative method in doing qualitative research on emotions, we chose to use a less obvious form of analysis.

This analysis has been influenced by the Foucauldian tradition of ontological constructionism, where the subject of the study is not language alone, but there are non-discursive worlds beside texts. This means that the analysis can sometimes be impossible to derive back to exact words, but the description of the moment should make the analysis understandable. This kind of research aims to analyze how different worlds are discursively built in different language-related practices and/or how non-discursive and discursive worlds relate to one another. Thus, it questions self-evident and unquestioned truths, power relations, and hierarchies. At the same time, ontological constructionist research constructs counter-discourses and opposing positions (Jokinen, Juhila, & Suoninen, 2000). In the analysis, we aimed to reveal controversial emotional tensions, which, in this narrative, are constructed mainly in terms of the experience of shame. This is a re-told combination, a fictional narrative of these stories, and incidents, and our own experiences (Rhodes & Brown, 2005; Patient, Lawrence, & Maitlis, 2003).

THE STORY OF POWERFUL SHAME

Erkki had been called by a theater manager, who offered him a job. Erkki was slightly confused. He had been asked if he would be interested in coming to direct a play in this small theater, a two hour drive north from the capital city where Erkki lived. His financial situation having been better, he would never have seriously considered this offer: in his opinion, all theater worth seeing was done in Helsinki. His colleagues would never travel outside the city to see his work, no matter how good it would turn out. And what was worse, the whole town would soon be gossiping that he was no longer a hot theater director who had critical and controversial ideas. He was proud of having been a rebel, but being a rebel did not pay the bills. He had compromised and made two predictable but best-selling plays where the cash machines in the ticket office were singing as loud as the choir on the stage. But somehow the work offers stopped coming. He had not directed anything in Helsinki during the last 18 months. However humiliating this thought was, he knew he needed a job ... any job.

The theater itself has stood by the town square for the last 100 years, in the heart of this small provincial city of 200,000 people. The theater had a regular audience who came to be entertained. The biggest hits of the theater had been "West Side Story" in the 1960s and "Sugar" (The Musical version of "Some Like It Hot") in the 1980s. After that, the theater had struggled with financial problems beginning with the Finnish economic downturn in the early 1990s, and after that the partial downsizing of the publicly subsidized cultural sector.

The daily rhythm in the theater was rigorously constructed. The morning rehearsals would usually start at 10.00 am and end by 2.00 pm, although sometimes they would run from 11.00 am to 3.00 pm. In the middle of the rehearsals, there would be a coffee break. The evening rehearsals would start at 5.00 or 6.00 pm and end by 10.00 pm. If there were a show in the evening, the staff would be expected to arrive about an hour before the curtain went up.

As Erkki stepped into the room for the first time, he raised his voice to announce that he would say a few words after which it would be possible for the actors and other people to introduce themselves. He described how in this theater, his texts had been misunderstood to be comedies, whereas they actually were subtle criticism of modern society. Erkki became quite passionate in his speaking: he used his strong rhetorical skills and his loud voice to describe his view of the present state of mankind, to paint pictures of slow suffocation of civilization and the inevitable and complete decline of the western hemisphere and the crucial role of theater in revealing this degradation. This took about two and a half hours. Erkki's performance had paralyzed the listeners, two actresses and two actors, which he took as a proof of how overwhelmingly more profound his analysis had been compared to those of his predecessors. Content, he sat down, closed his eyes and made a small gesture with his hand to signal that someone should start the introductions. This did not take more than a couple of minutes. People could barely utter their names. Erkki opened his eyes and stared at the actors for a few seconds, as if he had just seen them for the first time and then turned angrily away. He could not believe his ears: he had loudly and clearly told the manager of the theater precisely which actors he wanted to have into his production. Two actors, he specifically had asked for, were missing. Instead, there was a male and a female actor he had never even seen before. He marched out into the manager's office complaining in a vociferous manner about the material he had been given: there were only two actors in this theater he approved of, but neither of them was assigned to his production. He felt he had been humiliated and betrayed. The manager tried to make the director understand the complex system caused by the necessity of keeping up a good repertoire, meaning the other plays performed simultaneously on other stages of the same theater. His favorite actors were currently assigned to those plays, since some other female actors were on maternity leave. The theater director had the aspiration to rotate all the actors of the theater, to give everyone a chance to perform, but explaining these things to Erkki seemed to be in vain.

Anyway, the manager was not too worried about Erkki. He knew Erkki was one of those hard-to-handle, unpredictable freelancers with few opportunities anywhere. However, once or twice he had succeeded quite nicely in interpreting a classic in a modern way. That had been a while ago, though. Since then, his style had altered to a more rebellious direction. The critics had praised him as a modernizer of the Finnish theater. Originally, however, the manager had hired him because the previous director became ill. Besides, bursts of anger were not unheard of in theater ... there was nothing to worry about: Erkki had already signed the contract to direct this play.

Everybody was happy that the rehearsals could be started directly on the stage, however the atmosphere was nervous. The director had bargained to get his own visual designer. She would be responsible for the set design, dresses, and all printed material. All in all, the whole visual image was in her hands. Erkki and the set designer, Anna, sat side by side in the audience, while the actors went through the scenes on the stage. Eva, an actor, was a little uneasy. She often felt the scornful eyes of the director on her back, but tried to forget about that. She knew he was an experienced professional, but so was she. Eva was at her best in witty snappy comedies. She had the sense of rhythm the author had in his texts and she was looking forward to this hallmark play of his.

Next morning, the director went up to the stage, asked the actors to gather around him, and to sit down. He wanted to make something very clear: they obviously had not understood or perhaps even consciously ignored the guidelines he personally had given in the first meeting: he explicitly wanted this play to be a criticism of modern man. This play was not a comedy! He did not want to see any of the old school "running in the stairs, banging of the doors, getting in a wrong room" stuff. This play was about the shallowness of the middle class, so it was not written to please the middle class! They should forget about conventionality and pleasing! The clue would be the awkwardly modernist and ultrastylish set design against which the cruelty and egotism of man would come out. Erkki's voice increased in volume … soon he was shouting his lungs out. His blue eyes almost burst out of their sockets as he yelled:

> Don't expect this to be easy! I expect you to reach further than you ever even thought you could think!

The second week of rehearsals was coming to an end. They had not made much progress. The director stood on the stage staring at the actors with his mean eyes. He did not get out of these actors what he wanted. They did not understand at all what was going on! For 2 h now he had been trying to get Rina, a younger female actor, to say one sentence as he wanted to hear it. She repeated it over and over again without him accepting any version. In the end he shouted to her:

> How dare you come and stand here like some idiot! You should be ashamed to be coming here and bothering your colleagues, experienced professionals, with your beeping!

She wept in shame and anger. She offered to leave the production if she was not good enough. Erkki told her to stop acting like a child and told her that clearly she was no professional, and he had his doubts if she ever would become one. But he would not let her leave. He told her to shut up for the rest of the week and learn. He would take away some of her lines in order not to let her ruin them.

Eva could not stand still any more:

> Can you please leave her alone? As a director you should know that when it does not come it does not come! Leave it! Try again tomorrow! Sweet Jesus ...!

Erkki turned to her:

> Shut up and concentrate on what you are saying! You should be learning your lines instead of mixing into this! How can it be that you are so slow learning them by heart?

Later, in the Green Room,[1] Rita could not help bursting into tears again. She wept openly on the corner of the couch. The other actors in the work group gathered around to comfort her. They were as confused as she was. The good thing was that this director never came into the Green Room. He stayed on the stage and prepared the next scene.

The bar across the street, called "The Brick", was the place where the artistic work group met after hours. The people working at the theater office, the ticket salespersons, or marketing people did not hang out with the artistic staff, but often the bar was full of hangers-on, people who wanted to see and be seen with the celebrities of a small town. The work groups sat together in big tables, had vivid conversations, laughing. People would come and go. As Erkki and Anna did not actually live in town, the theater had rented apartments for them. In the evening, they also dropped into the bar but, acting as if they had not recognized the people with whom they just a couple of hours ago had shared the same room, they walked through the place, did not greet anyone, and sat down in a corner table, being completely absorbed with each other. Their work group grew suddenly very silent. This was unheard of. As if it had not been humiliating enough that the director did not have coffee with them during the rehearsal breaks.

One morning, arriving at the theater through the staff entrance, Rina felt physically sick at the thought of having to work with Erkki. She spent more time than usual in the lobby, taking her coat off and checking her mail. On her right, there was the janitor who buzzed the door open to everybody. To her left, there was a white board with everybody's names. As she stared at the board to see if Erkki was in already, she realized that not all names were listed: there were all the actors, a few technical staff, nobody from the ticket office, nor the doorman, nor anybody else she knew was working inside the theater building. Beside the name on the white board there was a green button. As you pushed the button, it turned red, which meant that you were inside the building. She could see that the director was in already ... she felt her stomach turn upside down ... she had to make it to the restroom ...!

The rehearsal was tougher than ever before. The four actors were already sweating after 1 h. But the atmosphere was euphoric. The actors were almost in a trance playing the scenes. As Erkki stared at them, his face turned milder, his eyes almost loving and tender.

> "Wonderful, just wonderful ..." he sobbed.

Anna, the visual designer was the one talking to the technical staff. As Erkki had enough to do with the actors, she did not want to expose him to another group constantly asking questions and seeking guidance. It would ruin his concentration. Mostly, when Erkki was trying to explain himself to the actors on the stage, Anna stood by the curtains in the dark. The sides and the back of the stage were painted black. There were some light spots here and there to guide the steps. You had to go through the dark backstage to get into each of the Green Rooms. Anna preferred the actors' Green Room. The technician's Green Room was not that cozy. She thought it was a fusion of the worst bachelor's pads she had seen: empty pizza boxes, large television, dirty kitchen sink with unwashed cups, constant smoke in the air, an old spotty sofa, and black brick walls. Besides, she felt nude every time she stood there. The men were looking at her with unfriendly eyes. She saw that they wished her out of the room. Her presence meant work .... Well, she was not planning to make it easy for them.

The next day Erkki had told Anna he was going to try something new on the actors. They were sitting together in the dark in the eighth row of the audience seats. "Watch me make her hysterical", Erkki whispered. He took the megaphone and shouted to Rina on the stage:

> What is wrong with you today? How dare you go up there as if you had never seen the script before? What do you think you are? We have practiced for three weeks and you still look like you do not know what you do up there? You should come and see yourself from here ... you look pathetic!!

She turned red, and started shaking. She had to sit down on the floor, otherwise she would have fallen. She tried to explain, but the director shouted:

> I cannot hear you! Please try to speak up! What are you whining about up there!

The other actors moved slowly closer to Rina. Eva took her by the shoulder and squeezed. She gave the director a murdering glimpse. Erkki was satisfied: after the incident, Rina did better. Her expression was free. When shame was too hard to handle, it disappeared completely.

For the fifth week in a row now they had exceeded all the limits set by the Working Hour Restriction Act ... they were tired, sweaty, and smelly. Erkki was the only one who seemed to have all his energy left: he shouted and flailed around his arms, gesticulating the positions and gestures. His blue mean eyes rolled around as he strode off round the stage. Suddenly Eva realized how Erkki was like an ancient shaman, hypnotizing everybody with his terrifying and yet magical appearance. The actors stared at him through their own blurred eyes and tried their best. Once again, Eva could not get a line straight ... she had tried and tried for the last 90 min. The others were lying around by the walls on the stage. Suddenly they heard Erkki sob:

> "My God ... I did not know I'd ever live to see this ... this was the Perfection!"
> Eva: "But ... what did I do?"

The fleeing thought in Eva's head:

> "I will most certainly die if he asks me to do that again".
> Erkki sighed: "Just do not EVER even TRY to imitate that"

And he continued:

> "It will just ruin the beauty of this moment!"

As the rehearsals finally came to an end toward midnight, the actors were too tired to even talk to each other. They had lost weight. They had not been downstairs to "The Brick" since Erkki had been there with Anna. It was not that they would somehow have contaminated the place, it was just that they were squeezed completely empty ... they barely had the energy left to go home. As Eva shut the door behind her, she felt the hunger and nausea. Yogurt was the only food she possibly could hold inside her: no need to chew ... just the lovely feeling of having something in the stomach.

The last week of rehearsals was about to begin. Eva and Rina were terrified. They were expecting Erkki any second now and had the thankless task of telling him the two other actors had caught the flu. Thank God it was still six days until the premiere. They would make it there. Finally he came and received the news. He marched to the first row of audience seats, sat down, and started yelling at Eva and Rina. He was furious ...

> They are sick just to annoy me ... just to ruin my work .... How dare they get sick in the situation like this?

He could not stop these thoughts from popping up. They had to rehearse without them. Toward the night his anger grew. He could not help nagging and complaining about the work on the stage ... but the actors were too tired to take it personally. Erkki stood up and started mimicking their mannerisms. He strutted back and forth on the stage. Eva stared at him

> "Whatever you say ..."
> "See, see, this is how you look", Erkki mocked them.
> "OK, whatever, you are the boss ..."

Eva knew Erkki just tried to build up a good fight with her. He would have wanted to work his anger and stress off on her, but Eva was just too tired. She could not have cared less. Finally, Erkki gave in and furiously stopped the rehearsals for the day.

The press performance before the opening night was a huge success. All the papers in the country seemed to be interested in this particular play. Erkki was known as a controversial director and on top of this it was his own script on the stage. The press was used to seeing a few short scenes of a play, to have a photo-opportunity, and a possibility to interview the work group. Now it was different. Erkki made them watch half of the second act, and instead of accepting any questions, he made them watch it over again. After that he only took a few questions in all of which he underlined the talent and great working morale of his work group. Directly after the press performance, he demanded that the actors would stay and go through the ending. This was done again and again. After 2 h, Rita asked if they could have a pause to go to bathroom. Erkki said no. The last scene had to be fixed before anyone would go anywhere. Eva could not believe her ears:

> Come on ...! This is insane! You have to give us a break, now!

A 10-min break was announced. After the break they continued until two o'clock in the morning.

Two days after the opening night it became clear that the play was a hit. The director was praised, the script was described as genius, and the performance of the actors as unmatched. In the only interview Erkki agreed to give, he underlined the self-sacrificing work of the actors. The performance continued to draw full audiences for 3 years, and would have continued to do so if changes in the theater staff had not forced the play to be withdrawn from the repertoire.

Once in a while, Eva was surprised to catch herself thinking it would do her good to work with Erkki again ....

EMOTIONAL TENSIONS IN THE LEADERSHIP PROCESS

The paradoxical nature of theater work can be recognized in this story. It can be seen at an intrapersonal as well as interpersonal level. The contradictory, emotionally shaking, and abusive actions of the leader evoke emotional reactions in others. The director is both a bully and a humble admirer, and the actress Eva is at the same time a frightened coward and a knight in shining armor (see Table 1). They both move easily from one role to another, depending on the moves of the other party. The director used shame to achieve his goals. The group as a whole was shamed by the humiliation of individuals. Such humiliation in front of colleagues was often described by actors as a mortifying experience. Shame (Poulson, 2000), especially shared, collective shame (Parrot & Harré, 1996; Taylor, 1996), led the actors to the state of complete freedom to do whatever the director wanted: the bottom had been already reached, so there was no risk of betraying anyone's expectations or any pressure to keep up the façade anymore.

Table 1 shows the subject–object nature of the communication between Erkki and Eva and the paradoxical tensions in their interpersonal relationship. Erkki is the trigger and Eva reacts to his behavior. His insults and pressure evoke her fear and shame.

In Erkki and Eva's relationship, there is also an equal, subject–subject level (see Table 2). Of the work group, Eva is the one who speaks up and the

Table 1. Tensions at Interpersonal Level: Subject–Object Relationship.

Erkki	Eva
Hates the expected mediocre, ordinary achievement	Dreads the inadequacy in oneself
Attacks	Surrenders
Insults others by "admiring" one actor	Despises herself for being used as a dummy in hurting colleagues

Table 2. Tensions at Interpersonal Level: Subject–Subject Relationship.

Erkki	Eva
Admires the talent of an actor	Admires the uncompromising, visionary director
Demands a diligent work ethic	Demands human work ethic
Visionary leader	Professional actor
Lonely rider	Defender of a team

director occasionally gives in. She seems to have an insight into Erkki's
turbulent shifts in mood. She also understands and values the inspiring and
visionary sides of him. She even seems to choose when and how to react to
Erkki's roller coaster-like changes of mind.

At the individual level, the paradoxes become obvious (see Table 3). Erkki
is at the same time the gentle admirer of art and talent, but can turn into a
bully when demonstrating his discontent. He demanded total commitment
and concentration by actors in the rehearsal process, but sometimes he
unscrupulously tore down their self-respect and their spirit as autonomous
artists. He could be extremely interested, interesting and inspiring, and in
the next moment turn completely inward.

Eva's rehearsal process was of walking the tightrope between the joy of
admiration and the fear of shame (see Table 4). She missed collegiality and
loyalty, but criticized the director within the work group by openly opposing
the decisions and demands of the director. During the rehearsal process,
leadership was constructed through emotions within the work group. This
director stepped out of the expected role into a gray area. He behaved
paradoxically, shaking the ground under the work group. The director and
the work group led each other to their psychological and physiological
limits. The actors found themselves in a turbulent atmosphere of being the
target of humble admiration and the source of disappointment. They felt
misused. The controversy between expectations and the experiences evoked
paradoxical emotions and interaction. Eva was set into the position of an
intermediary person. She was the buffer between the director and the rest of
the group, because she was, on the one hand, the most admired by the
director, and again on the other, the one whom he was most disappointed
with. Still, they were able to have a dialogical working relationship.

Table 3.   Tensions at Intrapersonal Level: Erkki.

Admires the talent in an actor	Hates and accuses the same actor of mediocre, ordinary achievement
Demands a diligent work ethics	Attacks and insults the members of the work group
Inspiring group leader	Lonely rider

Table 4.   Tensions at the Intrapersonal Level: Eva.

Admires the uncompromising, visionary director	Dreads the inadequacy in oneself
Demands collegiality	Criticizes the director
Actor, defender of a team	Surrendering, passive reactor

In the background, the previous experiences and the expectations stemming from artistic training, professionalism, and the organization culture within the theater strengthened the autonomous position of the actors while simultaneously giving full artistic freedom to the director. Actors did not want to give in, however humiliating and hard the work was. The director forced the actors to leave behind their mannerisms and the familiar, safe way to do their job.

The uniting factor within the work group was the norm of professional respect guided by absolute commitment to their art, which does not tolerate compromises, but demands that everybody work to their full potential to prepare the play. Despite personal insults and other difficulties, the mutual desire to learn from each other and to be ambitious within the art form remained strong. Through Eva, the actors understood that the director did not use his hierarchical position to transform or reinforce power structures within the theater or the group, since he was only a visiting director. After all, they saw that despite his bad behavior as a leader, he wanted to achieve something extraordinary within the theater art. Somehow, as Eva did, the actors may have seen themselves as the chosen ones to participate in fulfilling this task.

CONCLUSIONS: SHAME AS AN EMPOWERING EMOTION?

Leadership is an emotionally demanding relationship. The use of the so-called negative or unpleasant emotions, such as fear and shame, is common (Eriksson & Parviainen, 2005). We have described and analyzed one social process of leadership from the perspective of emotions. Despite the advances made into the direction of thinking of leadership as a relational process, within leadership studies the rational, transaction-driven paradigm has been dominant where emotions and rationality are understood as contradictory forces. Rationality represents the objective, calm, and desirable state of affairs. Emotions are thought of as the annoying behavior of subordinates that leaders need to control. The emotions of charismatic leaders are paradoxically seen as something mystical and seductive, as something that elevates them above the gray, dull mass. Instead of such a trait and role approach that emphasizes the individual heroic leader, we call for understanding leadership as a social process. This brings the thick web of emotions back to the everyday life of organizations and leadership, where we think it belongs and can play\s a major role in our understanding.

The interplay of emotionality and rationalization was crucial in this study, where the actors, especially Eva, tried to re-frame the insulting behavior of director so as to make it understandable. Eva acted here as the mediator between the director and the group. She rationalized the abuse and considered it useful for their professional development. As a result, they perceived that the director did not use these extreme emotions as a method of manipulation, but as a genuine way of working. In this way, they could free themselves of the guilt of professional insufficiency as they thought the insults were simply how this director worked: it became much more about the director himself than about the actors.

Actors took the objectives of the director as ultimately altruistic: he insulted them in order to whip the best out of them, which, in the end, would benefit everybody. The work group saw themselves growing in their profession, which, in turn, gave the audience an artistic and entertaining experience. As a result, critics were praising the actors and the director. Their professional achievement was publicly acknowledged, which finally legitimized the method of the director. Together with the audiences, the process re-affirmed the positions of the director and the actors inside the theater, and even inside the theater field in Finland. The results of the ordeal made its miseries worthwhile.

In this study, we have tried to make room for the multiple voices of emotions, to the development of the situations and to the context (Fineman, 1996; Hosking, 2002). This study is an example of how the rational and emotional intertwine within leadership and how emotional performances influence outcomes. It raises as many questions as answers. Is the use of shame emotional exploitation? Do the actors do emotional labor, defined as displaying wanted emotions as part of the work role (Hochschild, 1983), just by virtue of being actors? Or does acting become emotional labor only in circumstances like this case where the situation evokes powerful contradicting emotions? Is this the worst kind of manipulation? The use of shame to make people perform better definitely sounds like manipulation, but then again, the actors did not talk about themselves as an oppressed group of people. They saw themselves as well-educated experts, who can take care of their own rights. The director was a visitor, and they were permanent staff.

The shifting, temporal nature of the leadership of the director may have been an advantage in this creative process, which took a limited, previously determined amount of time. The routine ways to work were being challenged. The artistic nature of theater work intrinsically embraces change and renewal, even though human nature tends to prefer standardization and routines. The excessive use of shame caused people to lose touch with ordinary ways of measuring progress, which is often done through trying to please and to gain acceptance from the director. The actors felt forced to work outside normal, customary ways. The unfamiliar situation of not being able to follow known codes of accepted emotion makes people free of self-judgments. People are lost in their work, the feelings are "of me but not about me" (Csikszentmihalyi, 1977; Frese, Fritz, & Stolte, 1991). An overload of shame made them free and open to new ways of being on the stage.

This suggests that difficult and even cruel processes may enhance creativity and new paradigms, which are measures of success in an arts organization. This approach opens up an area that definitely calls for further research. Afterward, people felt proud of having gone through an ordeal, a suffering that has pushed them toward a better future, which may even sound like being a member of a very discriminating club.

METHODOLOGICAL CONTRIBUTIONS

Organizational narratives as a mode of knowing and communicating can be of great value to organizational researchers. Narrative forms of reporting can enrich organization studies by complementing, illustrating, and critiquing traditional forms of research. By creating distance from the perceived necessity to be absolutely factual to exactly match theory and practice, organization studies can enter into a dialogical relationship with the organizations. Narratives are by nature not tightly prescribed as might be with specific models or methodological blueprints. They are there for everyone to use, to re- and deconstruct according to need. The difference between make-believe and reality is a fluid one, as is the difference between theater and real life. Organizational narratives are both inscriptions of past performances and script and staging instructions for future performances. Narrative approach in its all varieties offers vast possibilities for emotion and leadership researchers.

NOTES

1. A Green Room is an informal area for actors to spend time between performances or during rehearsals and performances while not on the stage. Technical staff may have their own Green Room.

REFERENCES

Abu-Lughod, L. (1993). *Writing women's worlds : Bedouin stories.* Berkeley: University of California Press.

Abu-Lughod, L., & Lutz, C. (1990). Introduction: Emotions, discourse and the politics of everyday life. In: C. A. Lutz & L. Abu-Lughod (Eds), *Language and the politics of emotion.* Cambridge, UK: Cambridge University Press.

Agar, M. H. (1986). *Speaking of ethnography.* Thousand Oaks, CA: Sage.

Alvesson, M. (2003). Methodology for close up studies – struggling with closeness and closure. *Higher Education, 46*(2), 167–193.

Ashkanasy, N. M., Härtel, C. E. J., & Zerbe, W. J. (2000). Emotions in the workplace: Research, theory and practice. In: N. M. Ashkanasy, C. E. J. Härtel & W. J. Zerbe (Eds), *Emotions in the workplace: Research, theory and practice.* Westport, CT: Quorum Books.

Ashkanasy, N. M., & Tse, B. (2000). Transformational leadership as management of emotion: A conceptual review. In: N. M. Ashkanasy, C. E. J. Härtel & W. J. Zerbe (Eds), *Emotions in the workplace: Research, theory and practice* (pp. 221–235). Westport, CT: Quorum Books.

Barsade, S. G. (2002). The ripple effect: Emotional contagion and its influence on group behavior. *Administrative Science Quarterly, 47*(4), 644–675.

Bartel, C. A., & Saavedra, R. (2000). The collective construction of work group moods. *Administrative Science Quarterly, 45*(2), 197–231.

Bass, B. M. (1985). *Leadership and performance beyond expectations.* New York: Free Press, Jossey-Bass.

Bass, B. M. (1996). *A new paradigm of leadership. An inquiry into transformational leadership.* Alexandria, VA: U.S. Army Research Institute for the Behavioral and Social Sciences.

Berger, P. L., & Luckmann, T. (1995). *Modernity, pluralism and the crisis of meaning.* Gütersloh: Bertelsmann Foundation Publishers.

Boje, D. (2001). *Toward a narrative ethics for modern and postmodern organization science.* Retrieved September 13, 2005, from New Mexico State University, College of Business web site: http://cbae.nmsu.edu/~dboje/papers/toward_a_narrative_ethics_for_mo.htm

Brundin, E. (2002). *Emotions in motion. The strategic leader in a radical change process.* JIBS Dissertation, Series no. 012, Jönköping International Business School.

Bryman, A. (Ed.) (2001). *Ethnography.* London: Sage.

Conger, J. A., & Kanungo, R. (1998). *Charismatic leadership in organizations.* Thousand Oaks, CA: Sage.

Connelly, F. M., & Clandinin, D. J. (1990). Stories of experience and narrative inquiry. *Educational Researcher, 19*(5), 2–14.

Connelly, F. M., & Clandinin, D. J. (2000). *Narrative inquiry: Experience and story in qualitative research.* San Francisco, CA: Jossey-Bass.

Csikszentmihalyi, M. (1977). *Beyond boredom and anxiety.* San Francisco, CA: Jossey-Bass.

Czarniawska, B. (1999). *Writing management: Organization theory as a literary genre.* Oxford: Oxford University Press.

Dasborough, M. T., & Ashkanasy, N. M. (2002). Emotion and attribution of intentionality in leader–member relationships. *The Leadership Quarterly, 13*(5), 615–634.

Denzin, N. K., & Lincoln, Y. S. (Eds) (1994). *Handbook of qualitative research.* Thousand Oaks, CA: Sage.

Eriksson, M., & Parviainen, J. (2005, May). Management by fear in expert organizations. Paper presented at the EURAM conference, Munich.

Fineman, S. (1993). Organizations as emotional arenas. In: S. Fineman (Ed.), *Emotions in organizations* (pp. 9–35). London: Sage.

Fineman, S. (1996). Emotion and organizing. In: S. Clegg, C. Hardy & W. R. Nord (Eds), *Handbook of organization studies* (pp. 543–564). London: Sage.

Fineman, S. (2003). *Understanding emotion at work*. London: Sage.

Fletcher, J. K. (2004). The paradox of postheroic leadership: An essay on gender, power and transformational change. *The Leadership Quarterly, 15*(5), 647–661.

Frese, M., Fritz, A., & Stolte, W. (1991). Psychological aspects of the work of software developers. In: M. Frese, S. Kasten, C. Skarpelis & Zang-Seucher (Eds), *Software for the work of tomorrow*. Bonn: Institut Arbeit und Technik.

Goleman, D. (1995). *Emotional intelligence*. New York: Bantam Books.

Graen, G., & Uhl-Bien, M. (1995). Relationship-based approach to leadership: Development of leader–member exchange (LMX) theory of leadership over 25 years: Applying a multi-level multi-domain perspective. *The Leadership Quarterly, 6*(2), 219–247.

Hatfield, E., Cacioppo, J. T., & Rapson, R. L. (1994). *Emotional contagion*. New York: Cambridge University Press.

Hochschild, A. (1983). *The managed heart: The commercialization of human feeling*. Berkeley: The University of California Press.

Hosking, D. M. (1999). Social construction as a process: Some new possibilities for research and development. *Concepts and Transformation, 4*(2), 147–166.

Hosking, D. M. (2002). E-communications and relational constructionism: Distributed action, distributed leadership, and ecological possibilities. In: L. Holmes, D. M. Hosking & M. Grieco (Eds), *Organizing in the information age: Distributed technology, distributed leadership, distributed identity, distributed discourse* (pp. 27–44). Aldershot: Ashgate.

Humphrey, R. (2002). The many faces of emotional leadership. *The Leadership Quarterly, 13*(5), 493–504.

Jacobs, T. O. (1970). *Leadership and exchange in formal organizations*. Alexandria, VA: Human Resources Research Organization.

Jing, Z., & George, J. (2001). When job dissatisfaction leads to creativity. *Academy of Management Journal, 44*(4), 682–696.

Joiner, T. E., Jr. (1994). Contagious depression: Existence, specificity to depressed symptoms, and the role of reassurance-seeking. *Journal of Personality and Social Psychology, 67*(2), 287–296.

Jokinen, A., Juhila, K., & Suoninen, E. (2000). *Diskurssianalyysin aakkoset*. Tampere: Vastapaino.

Katila, S. (2000). Moraalijärjestyksen rajaama tila: maanviljelijä-yrittäjäperheiden selviytymisstrategiat. Acta Universitas Oeconomicae Helsingiensis. A-174. Helsinki School of Economics and Business Administration.

Koivunen, N. (2003). *Leadership in Symphony Orchestras: Discursive and aesthetic practices*. Tampere, Finland: Tampere University Press.

Lincoln, Y., & Guba, E. (1985). *Naturalistic inquiry*. Beverly Hills, CA: Sage.

Mayer, J. D., & Salovey, P. (1997). What is emotional intelligence. In: P. Salovey & D. Sluyter (Eds), *Emotional development and emotional intelligence: Implications for educators* (pp. 3–31). New York: Basic Books.

McIntosh, G. L., & Rima, S. D. (1998). *Overcoming the dark side of leadership: The paradox of personal dysfunction*. Grand Rapids, MI: Baker Books House.

Newcombe, M. J., & Ashkanasy, N. M. (2002). The role of affect and affective congruence in perceptions of leaders. An experimental study. *Leadership Quarterly, 13*(5), 601–614.

Parrot, G. W., & Harré, R. (1996). Embarrassment and the threat to character. In: R. Harré & G. W. Parrot (Eds), *The emotions: Social, cultural and biological dimensions* (pp. 39–56). London: Sage.

Patient, D., Lawrence, T. B., & Maitlis, S. (2003). Understanding workplace envy through narrative fiction. *Organization Studies, 24*(7), 1015–1044.

Pearce, C. L., & Conger, J. A. (2003). All those years ago: The historical underpinnings of shared leadership. In: C. L. Pearce & J. A. Conger (Eds), *Shared leadership: Reframing the how's and why's of leadership* (pp. 1–18). Thousand Oaks, CA: Sage.

Pescosolido, T. (2002). Emergent leaders as managers of group emotion. *The Leadership Quarterly, 13*(5), 583–599.

Poulson, C. (2000). Shame and work. In: N. M. Ashkanasy, C. E. J. Härtel & W. J. Zerbe (Eds), *Emotions in the workplace: Research, theory and practice* (pp. 250–271). Westport, CT: Quorum Books.

Putnam, L., & Mumby, D. K. (1993). Organizations, emotions and the myth of rationality. In: S. Fineman (Ed.), *Emotion in organizations* (pp. 36–57). London: Sage.

Rhodes, C., & Brown, A. D. (2005). Writing responsibly: Narrative Fiction and Organization Studies. *Organization, 12*(4), 467–491.

Richardson, L. (1994). Writing: A method of inquiry. In: N. K. Denzin & Y. S. Lincoln (Eds), *Handbook of qualitative research* (pp. 516–529). Thousand Oaks, CA: Sage.

Roman, L., & Apple, M. (1990). Is naturalism a move away from positivism? Materialist and feminist approaches to subjectivity in ethnographic research. In: E. Eisner & A. Peshkin (Eds), *Qualitative inquiry in education* (pp. 38–73). New York: Teachers College Press.

Salovey, P., & Mayer, J. D. (1990). Emotional intelligence. *Imagination, Cognition and Personality, 9*(3), 185–211.

Shamir, B. (1995). Social distance and charisma: Theoretical notes and exploratory study. *The Leadership Quarterly, 6*(1), 19–47.

Silverman, D. (1985). *Qualitative methodology and sociology: Describing the social world.* Gower: Aldershot.

Smith, J. K. (1990). Goodness criteria: Alternative research paradigms and the problem of criteria. In: E. G. Guba (Ed.), *The Paradigm Dialogue.* London: Sage.

Smith, J. K., & Deemer, D. K. (2000). The problem of criteria in the age of relativism. In: N. K. Denzin & Y. S. Lincoln (Eds), *Handbook of qualitative research,* (2nd ed.) (pp. 877–896). Thousand Oaks, CA: Sage.

Taylor, G. (1996). Guilt and remorse. In: R. Harré & G. W. Parrot (Eds), *The emotions: Social, cultural and biological dimensions.* Sage: London.

Van Maanen, J. (Ed.) (1995). *Representation in ethnography.* Thousand Oaks, CA: Sage.

Weick, K. (1995). *Sensemaking in organizations.* Thousand Oaks, CA: Sage.

Wolff, S. B., Pescosolido, A. T., & Druskat, V. U. (2002). Emotional intelligence as the basis of leadership emergence in self-managing teams. *The Leadership Quarterly, 13*(5), 505–522.

Wright, T. A., & Staw, B. M. (1999). Affect and favorable work outcomes: Two longitudinal tests of the happy-productive worker thesis. *Journal of Organizational Behavior, 20*(1), 1–23.

Yukl, G. (2002). *Leadership in organizations* (5th ed.). Upper Saddle River, NJ: Prentice-Hall.

CHAPTER 4

BENEATH THE MASKS: A CRITICAL INCIDENT FOCUS ON THE EMOTIONS EXPERIENCED IN THE WORKER/SUPERVISOR RELATIONSHIP

Fleur Piper and Nanette Monin

ABSTRACT

Worker perceptions of their emotional response to a supervisor, during an incident identified as of critical significance, are described and analyzed in this study. We invited 14 participants, aged from 39 to 56 years to share their stories with us in semi-structured interviews. The organizations represented by the workers' stories included private business government and educational institutions. A grounded-theory approach was adopted to allow key themes to emerge (Locke, 1996). We encouraged participants to allow "buried perspectives" (Hochschild, 1983) to surface: as they interpreted the relational effects of "what happened" in retrospective sense making. As they explored their perceptions of these interactions, participants revealed the complex and disturbing array of emotions and frustrations that lay beneath the veneer of rationality and control they chose to present during the incident. Felt emotions, whether expressed, repressed or edited, were overwhelmingly negative; and awareness of power

Individual and Organizational Perspectives on Emotion Management and Display
Research on Emotion in Organizations, Volume 2, 81–105
Copyright © 2006 by Elsevier Ltd.
ISSN: 1746-9791/doi:10.1016/S1746-9791(06)02004-9

issues emerged as a key driver in the "feeling rules" (Hochschild, 1983) workers perceived as needing to be observed. Worker tension was seen to be exacerbated by adherence to these rules because "the rules" conflicted with their own personal values and beliefs. Emotional dissonance resulted from this. The role of the organizational community within which workers coped with their experience, and subsequent emotional response, was also explored.

INTRODUCTION

That feeling of being completely powerless, of being invisible, not listened to, unvalued .... It's like realising that the light is on the other side of the window and that you're just a moth to the candle flame battering yourself against the glass and the only person getting damaged is you (crying) ... (Clare, Law Lecturer, 44 years).

Clare, the moth in this metaphor, is describing her feelings of powerlessness and extreme frustration as she recalls the intransigence and stonewalling she experienced during a critical incident with her supervisor. Her words serve to highlight both the emotional tensions associated with the power differential implicit in the worker–supervisor relationship, and also the inescapable centrality of interpersonal communication within organizational life. This centrality is acknowledged widely in management literature, and indeed interpersonal health within the worker/supervisor relationship has been identified as a crucial factor in improving organizational relationships and productivity (Kamp, 1999; Maclean, 2002).

Our chapter explores a particular aspect of this relationship: workers' perceptions of their emotional response to a critical incident with a supervisor, and their experience consequent to it. Although interpersonal ethics theory requires supervisors to be real, to pay attention to equality, and to recognize the dimensions of compassion and truth in the treatment of workers (Maclean, 2002), in critical interpersonal situations organizations are still being experienced as emotionally unhealthy. We have placed Clare's story, and the stories of the other participants in this study, in the chasm that seems to stretch between the theory of supervision and supervisory practice: between espoused theory and theory in use (Senge, 1994). The emotional tensions arising from this gap as experienced by workers, have already been identified as the most frequently cited sources of intense emotion and conflict in the workplace (Frone, 2000; Waldron, 2000) but we do not yet have a rich picture of the outcomes, individual and organizational, of this emotional experience. We asked a group of workers who had experienced a critical incident with a supervisor to reflect on what had happened, and the relational effects of this, by using a retrospective sense-making technique. We aimed to allow "buried perspectives" to emerge (Hochschild, 1983), and from this sense-making to better understand the emotional component of the workers' experience.

Following a grounded-theory approach we invited 14 workers, who were aged from 39 to 56 years and who represented business, government and educational institutions, to share their stories with us in semi-structured interviews. In the interviews we encouraged participants to interpret the relational effects of "what had happened" and as they explored their perceptions of these interactions, participants revealed the complex and disturbing array of emotions and frustrations that lay beneath the veneer of rationality and control they chose to present during the incident. Felt emotions, expressed, repressed or edited, were overwhelmingly negative; and their awareness of power issues emerged as a key driver in the "feeling rules" (Hochschild, 1983) workers perceived as needing to be observed. We found that because "the rules" conflicted with their own personal values and beliefs, the rules exacerbated worker tension. Emotional dissonance resulted from this, therefore we also explored the role of the organizational community within which workers coped with their experience, and their subsequent emotional responses.

LITERATURE REVIEW

While historically significant interest has been shown in the unique relationship which exists between supervisor and worker (Jablin, 1979), the focus on the emotional dimensions of the worker/supervisor relationship is relatively new. Throughout the 1980s and 1990s researchers focused on a diverse range of aspects of worker/supervisor interactions, including the use of arbitrary and punitive power (Fulk & Wender, 1982), worker perceptions of appropriate use of supervisor power (Hofstede, 1984), dominance and responsiveness in supervisor style (Darling, 1991) and the relationship between worker satisfaction and supervisor behavior (Page & Wiseman, 1993). More recently focus on the worker/supervisor relationship has centred on communication accommodation theory (McCroskey & Richmond, 2000; Willemyns, Gallois, & Callan, 2000), the impact of social support (Yoon & Thye, 2000) and conditions of psychological safety (May, Gibson, & Harter, 2004). However, within these studies emotions were not focused on as an explicit dimension of worker/supervisor interactions, prompting Callahan's call to future researchers not to limit themselves to studying the symptoms of emotion, and emotion work (such as stress and job satisfaction in the workplace), but instead to "explore the existence, expression, and consequences of emotions themselves" (Callahan, 2000, p. 247).

As noted above, to date only limited research has explored the intersection of emotion and worker/supervisor relationships. The first of these was Waldron and Krone (1991) who used a written questionnaire to ask participants to recall an emotional interaction with co-workers or supervisors which had an emotional impact on them. They found that some employees actively attempted to express, repress or edit emotion charged messages as a means of maintaining work relationships. Tiedens, Ellsworth, and Mesquita, (1998 cited in Ashkanasy, Härtel, & Zerbe, 2000) further found, in laboratory and questionnaire studies, that the social status positions of supervisors and assistants influenced emotional perceptions of agency feedback appraisals. They concluded that social status can influence which emotions people experience, and that emotions influence perceptions of social status, and in this way seem to have the potential to reinforce one another. Tiedens, Ellsworth, and Mesquita (2000) confirmed these findings in three vignettes which were designed to examine people's stereotypes of the emotions that accompany social status positions. They went on to signal as an area of future research the actual emotional reactions in social hierarchies, a challenge our study addresses.

Fineman and Sturdy (1999) investigated management of emotions through an examination of the emotions of control, and found that in the interactions between inspectors and local managers "social-structural rules of regulatory events and their ambiguity and tensions, shape and are shaped by the emotions of control" (pp. 640–641). Interview findings revealed that the process of controlling for the regulatory inspectors involved many essentially emotionalized conceptions such as: assumptions about themselves and those they were interacting with in regard to status, role security, and professional competence.

In previous studies, retrospective critical incident focus has also been used to explore aspects of the worker/supervisor relationship. As we understand it, to be considered critical an incident must occur in a situation where its purpose can be interpreted by the observer and its consequences leave little doubt about its effect (Gundry & Rousseau, 1994). Angelides (2001, p. 430) defined a critical incident as a "surprise or problematic situation, which stimulates a period of reflection or a problematic solution". Crucial to the concept of the critical incident is that its criticality is based on the significance and meaning attributed to it by those involved. "Incidents happen, but critical incidents are produced by the way we look at a situation: a critical incident is an interpretation of the significance of an event" (Tripp cited in Angelides, 2001, p. 431). Significantly Conville (1991) cited in Stewart and Logan (1998) states that in a relationship experiencing a critical incident or turning point of some kind, disintegration of the prior relationship occurs when the old relationship has ceased to work in some way. Alienation then resynthesis follow as the relationship is redefined and a positive spiral of growth or negative spiral of disintegration ensue.

Critical incidents in the communication of culture to newcomers have been explored by Gundry and Rousseau (1994). They asked participants to relate their experiences of formative events and the messages derived from them. They did not explicitly focus on emotions in relation to these, but participants cited supervisor/worker conflict as the most frequently occurring type of critical incident. Critical incidents in this context were also perceived by workers to be a significant turning point in the life of a relationship.

An investigation of emotions during a critical incident linked to injustice was undertaken by Harlos and Pinder (2000). They sought to investigate emotions as causes of injustice, emotions that accompanied injustice, and emotions as consequences of injustice, and they found that cases of interactional justice "consisted exclusively of unjust treatment between employees at different hierarchical levels with the aggressor or perpetrator occupying positions of greater power" (p. 272). They identified anger and fear and along with this "rage, desire for revenge, shame, guilt and hopelessness, and cynicism", as the predominant emotions experienced in relation to "powerful others" (p. 265). They concluded that "emotions precede, accompany and are a consequence of injustice experiences" (p. 270), that most participants' emotional responses in the context they described were felt rather than displayed, and that the two emotions most predominant were anger and fear.

Clearly the interpretation and perceptions of emotions experienced at times of critical significance are part of a sense-making process (Weick, 1995) that can profoundly impact on the worker/supervisor relationship. In this sense it is the emotional rather than the legal, financial or geographical bonds which are the strongest connections between individuals and which thus create both visible and invisible organizational realities (Rafaeli & Worline, 2001). Yet these invisible organizational realities, in relation to emotions and critical incidents, have only rarely been explored.

THE STUDY

Our study sets out to lift further the masks of workers as "corporate actors" (Flam, 2000) by providing opportunity for them to reflect on the complexity and relational consequences of their emotional response in choosing to share or withhold their public (expressed) versus private (felt) responses during an incident considered to be of critical significance. In addition to this we asked them to examine their perceptions of the role, and emotional impact on them, of others in the organizational community who helped them make sense of their experience subsequent to the incident. A key difference between most previous studies and this research is that instead of asking participants to respond to a laboratory vignette or a questionnaire, or to write about an incident, we allowed workers to tell their own stories within the context of a 30–40 minutes interview. Additionally, we did not direct participants as to whether the incident should be positive or negative; we did suggest that it must in some way reflect a turning point in the relationship because of the way the supervisor managed it. Above all we intended our study to be an exploration of actual emotional reactions in a social hierarchy (Tiedens et al., 2000) reflecting Callahan's (2000) exhortation to future researchers, to investigate the existence, dissonance and consequences of emotions.

In the pursuit of these objectives the focus of our study became the exploration of a "single event memory narrative" (Singer & Salovey, 1993) recalled in an interview situation. In this type of narrative "a sequence of actions or images, identifiable as a unique occurrence and located in a discrete moment of time in an individuals life" is shared (Singer & Salovey, 1993, p. 96). We asked participants to identify the emotions associated with the experience of a critical event with a supervisor in an organizational context, mindful that stories that are noteworthy within organizations are those that depart from the expected in four key ways.

> The actions described are difficult, the situation poses a predicament that cannot be handled in a routine manner, unexpected events happen in an otherwise normal sequence of events and something about the situation is unusual in the narrator's experience (Robinson, 1981 cited in Weick, 1995, p. 127).

In the creation of the remembered self, emotionally evocative experiences are more likely to be remembered because the arousing nature of these implicitly demands further processing (Singer & Salovey, 1993). Regardless of the positive or negative tone of information shared, it is that which can be described as affectively intense which is best remembered (Dutta &

Kanungo, 1975 cited in Singer & Salovey, 1993, p. 48). Thus the focus on events described as critical incidents in this study allowed for an exploration of the short- and long-term impact of the emotions experienced on supervisor/worker relationships.

Weick (1995) affirms this approach from the perspective of the ongoing sense-making that occurs in organizations using stories.

> Actions are fleeting; stories about action are not. If organizations are social norms distinguished by their capability for coordinated action and if the distinguishing character of those forms disappears the moment it occurs, then we must be concerned with what persists when actions keep vanishing (Weick, 1995, p. 127).

Focusing on how workers remember and filter their description of the emotional impact of a particularly significant interaction helped provide insight into the complexity of organizational relationships. The sense-making process was also abetted by the role they described as being played by others within the organizational community as they helped the worker to interpret and understand the treatment they had experienced within the larger context.

PARTICIPANT PROFILES AND METHODOLOGY

In our study, we conducted semi-structured open-ended interviews with 14 participants from a large (22,000 student) tertiary institution. The sample was comprised of 14 university lecturers, seven men and seven women from a range of departments within the institution. Their ages ranged from 39 to 56 years and all had worked at the university for a three year minimum time period. Selection of this age bracket enabled us to draw on the professional background and experience of those interviewed as they reflected on past events.

Only half of the sample chose to talk about a situation within their current organization. The industries represented by the seven others included business, government and other educational institutions. The most recent incident had occurred three months ago and the most distant in time was 14 years ago. All those who shared their experiences chose to focus on what they identified as a negative event at the time: however one of the fourteen stressed strongly that positive relational outcomes arose from this. Particular attention was made in the analysis to expressed, as opposed to felt, emotions (Hochschild, 1983) and the reasons underlying the decision to share or not to share these emotions.

Also of importance was the participant's evaluation of the long-term consequences of their action in deciding to share or repress their emotions at the time of the interaction. As Harlos and Pinder found in their investigation of injustice and emotion, whether the emotion occurred the day, month or year before the interview "emotional intensities were easily recalled and their emotional arousal during interviews was focused on specific individuals, decisions, processes and systems" (cited in Fineman, 2000, p. 257).

All interviews were tape recorded and held in the interviewer's office or in the offices of the participants. Labov's (1972, 1982 cited in Riessman, 1993) framework for interpretation was used to guide prompts in the interviews. Tompkins and Cheney (1983) maintain that interviews of retrospective accounts do not necessarily reveal with true objectivity what happened but do uncover what people value. What is certain is that the feelings experienced and remembered have an involuntary character that cannot be produced at will and as a result generate a sympathetic or antipathetic change that informs the substance of a relationship (Gundry & Rousseau, 1994).

Tapes were fully transcribed using the modified version coding key outlined by Boje (2001). Following the transcription of the tapes a grounded-theory approach was adopted to allow key themes to emerge (Locke, 1996). In this way the development of themes was part of an iterative process using categories identified by the participants in the analysis (Boje, 2001).

DISCUSSION

Nature of the Critical Incidents and Relational History

The context of the critical incidents described by workers ranged across five "one on one" meetings, to both formal and informal meeting situations involving others. While in some encounters the supervisor and worker interaction was directly confrontational to a greater or lesser degree, there were also instances where a single action observed by the worker resulted in a dramatic shift in how the supervisor was perceived. Two such situations involved the worker hearing a lie being told by the supervisor. In both these situations the interpretation of the worker was based on the way in which what had been said was historically situated (Fineman & Sturdy, 1999). In two further situations a comment blocking the worker's suggestions in a dismissive way in a meeting was identified as the critical incident. In another, the unusually cold and aloof body language of a supervisor, indicating the worker was being ignored, was perceived as an indicator of a dramatic change in treatment. A summary of the contexts and nature of each incident can be seen in Table 1. The table also indicates the time frame

Table 1. Participant and Incident Outlines.

Pseudonym	Age	Gender of Supervisor	Time Working with Supervisor	How Long Ago the Incident Occurred	Nature of the Critical Incident
Stephanie (female)	53	Male	5 years	3 years ago	Following a long and unpleasant work dispute a lie was told in a formal meeting situation (3 people present)
Scott (male)	50	Female	3 years	9 months ago	One-on-one meeting responding to a request related to overseas conference travel that had been "deliberately" left unresolved till the last moment
Brian (male)	39	Female	2 years	10 years ago	A telling off occurred in front of others at the end of a staff meeting. "10 to 15 people were milling around"
Clare (female)	44	Female	10 years	3 months ago	In a staff meeting situation Clare having talked for 20 min, was responded to by her supervisor with "no I don't like it" and ignored
Max (male)	45	Female	4 years	3 years ago	One-to-one meeting in which terms and conditions of employment were discussed
Anna (female)	52	Male	4 years	5 years ago	Business lunch situation with the participant, one other person and the supervisor
Jim (male)	46	Male	5 years	5 years ago	Meeting of eight people to solve a dispute about the supervisor and another staff member

Table 1. (*Continued*)

Pseudonym	Age	Gender of Supervisor	Time Working with Supervisor	How Long Ago the Incident Occurred	Nature of the Critical Incident
Robyn (female)	"40–50"	Male	14 months	1 year ago	Rang the participant in the middle of a meeting to express his anger and dissatisfaction with her work
Bill (male)	50	Female	4 years	10 years ago	Participant was totally ignored in an informal meeting group
Susan (female)	45	Male	6 months	14 years ago	Reprimanded in one-to-one meeting
Steve (male)	51	Male	4 years	3 years ago	Reprimanded in a meeting in front of a small group of staff he was responsible for
Sally (female)	49	Female	18 months	6 years ago	One-to-one meeting to reprimand S on the actions she had taken
Mary (female)	56	Female	5 years	4 months ago	In a meeting situation with three others trying to resolve reporting arrangements
Ben (male)	47	Male	3 years	10 years ago	One-to-one meeting criticizing the design abilities and competency of the participant

in which each individual's recall of the critical incident experience takes place.

As was anticipated, the incidents which were most recent were also those most vividly and intensely described. The seven incidents which occurred up to three years ago belonged to this category. Two of the participants cried as they remembered various aspects of their experience. For all of the workers recalling incidents within the three-year time bracket, aspects of what happened still appeared to be unresolved to a greater or lesser extent. By contrast, the seven participants who described their experience as occurring five to fifteen years ago were more philosophical in their approach and "removed" in their analysis. Particularly notable was the tendency these people had to laugh about aspects of their experience. Harlos and Pinder (2000) found in their study of emotions and injustice, that though those whose experience had taken place more than a year ago may still consider it aversive, it was also viewed as transformative in a number of cases.

Thirteen of the 14 incidents focused on sharing the experience and consequences of a negative incident. However one "story" of interaction with a supervisor was distinctly different from the rest as it had a positive outcome and the worker–supervisor relationship was enhanced. In this situation Jim, a 46-year-old tertiary education manager, relayed his mediation role in what he described as "the most difficult meeting" he had ever chaired with his supervisor and colleagues. As Jim states, "this story had the veneer of disruption but what actually came out of it was a positive thing".

Undoubtedly, previous experience of the relationship whether positive or negative, strongly shaped and influenced perceptions during the time of the encounter retrospectively described. Five participants outlined a positive relationship history with their supervisor, but of these only Jim experienced a growth and enhancement of the original relationship following the critical incident.

> I think the level of trust went deeper ... it changed in terms of depth but not in terms of breadth. We already had quite a good relationship before that but it was because it showed the cards in practise what happened was there was a greater sense of who each person was.

The remaining four participants with a history of a previously positive relationship all maintained that their feelings of disillusionment and dissatisfaction were heightened by the previous condition of health. The remaining nine participants had a previous history of supervisor relationship which had been distant at best, or toxic and longstanding in negativity at worst. For Ben, a 47-year-old graphic designer, the treatment he received in the critical incident he described was like reaching a final summation of all that had gone before.

> Him saying those few words was like putting a heading on the top of all the other things ... it's like putting the heading title on a folder which I had kept in my mind for the previous three years, a folder of all the quips or asides, or seeming criticisms of my work.

Nature of Emotions Experienced/"Felt"

Of the 13 participants who experienced a negative incident with their supervisor, a complex range of emotions was experienced and "felt". These included the following: anxiety, embarrassment, disappointment, fear, hurt, shock, intimidation, humiliation, anger, indignation, powerlessness, frustration, resentment, confusion and disbelief. For the workers who had previously regarded their supervisors positively, their initial feelings were of shock and disappointment. Emotions of confusion and disbelief also arose as they tried to reconcile what was happening with their previous experience and expectations of what they believed constituted appropriate personal and professional behavior. Feelings of shock and disbelief were intensely experienced as is evidenced by Stephanie, a 53-year-old lecturer, describing the emotions she felt when her supervisor lied about her actions in a formal legal meeting.

> Gutted ... just disbelief I can see your need to do that, I mean there are sort of issues that have to be protected here but hell this is me.

For five of the participants the initial emotions of shock and the perceptions of the actions of the supervisor as unjust served to energize their resolve to deal with the situation. By contrast, for others the predominant emotions remained those of intimidation, hurt and intense feelings of vulnerability. For most participants, whether their previous relationship with the supervisor was positive or negative, subsequent feelings of anger with the treatment received were linked strongly with feelings of powerlessness and impotence.

Emotions Shared or Masked During the Incident

While the range and nature of emotions felt in the encounter varied among individuals, none of the 14 participants elected to share all emotions experienced. Four participants decided to share some of their emotions at the time of the interaction while the remaining 10 shared none. The small group who decided to share some of the feelings experienced at the time of the incident were made up of Max, Scott, Sally, and Jim.

The reasons for this decision to share varied between these four participants. Scott, a 50-year-old commerce lecturer, had no choice but to share his anxiety because this was so immediately obvious in a situation two days before needing to leave for an overseas conference and still waiting on his supervisor's final permission to actually go. The other primary emotion Scott felt but decided not to share was anger. He saw this repression as a necessary part of political life in an organization whereby workers have to keep under control their negative feelings in order to protect the long-term relationship between worker and supervisor in the hierarchy. Like Scott, another participant chose to share his feelings of concern but also consciously decided to submerge his anger. His two key reasons for this were concern about "losing his head" and sense of control if he did begin to truly share his feelings, and also a profound lack of trust in his supervisor.

> I think if I'd become angry I think she would have used that as a perfect excuse to go
> back. My manager is very deceptive, she's like a crocodile, she smiles but behind her
> smile she can be very dangerous and I sensed the danger.

One participant, Sally a 49-year-old administrative manager is noteworthy in that she maintains she shared most of her feelings during the one-to-one meeting with her supervisor because she saw this as being reflective of her own personality and the degree of comfort she felt with being assertive ... "if you want to be assertive you have to say what you feel". However what she did not decide to share were feelings of "hatred".

The final participant to share some of the emotions he felt during his encounter was Jim, the only participant to relate a positive incident. He explained that during the meeting his emotions ranged from

> a sense of feeling confident to feeling very disabled to feeling reliant on something that
> wasn't physical and then to feeling hopeful at the end.

However he chose to share only the emotion of feeling hopeful during the meeting and explained this as resulting from the responsibility he felt in his mediation role. He maintained that within this role it would have been inappropriate to express any personal fears or concerns of his own.

The remaining 10 participants decided to share none of the emotions they felt at the time and instead chose to mask their true feelings. Hochschild (1983) describes this process as transmutation, which is when those involved try to act out what they perceive is needed in the particular situation so that the emotional tone of the social encounter is created. Directly aligned with a desire to self protect was the recurrent theme of not sharing emotions, which was considered to be the best strategic move possible in the circumstances. It was perceived as a way of regaining control in a situation that was potentially unsafe, and where any sharing might be misunderstood. This was indicated by comments such as "I didn't think any of them were capable of dealing with my feelings" or "I didn't share any because he was a closed sort of person".

In addition, not sharing emotions at the time of the incident provided an opportunity for personal reflection on events. It was also viewed as strategic not to share because there was concern that once anger was unleashed the consequences on the worker's long-term future in the organization, and more particularly with that supervisor, could be dire.

Many of those who decided it was inappropriate to share any emotions also discussed the context as being inappropriate. For example, Steve received his "blasting" in a meeting full of others, as did Brian and Robyn. In these and a number of other situations, participants were extremely conscious of power issues and what would be appropriate behavior in terms of their roles. Others (Clare and Mary) stated that they were silenced by disbelief and shock and that meetings were cut short by their supervisor overriding them. Clearly, within all the situations discussed the deliberate masking of strong, unpleasant and socially "inappropriate" emotions within the work context was seen as a means of survival.

Causes of Feelings of Dissonance

The sources of the dissonance experienced by all participants, with the exception of Jim who relayed a positive critical incident, stemmed from one key area of conflict. This was the substantial gap present between the supervisor's behavior and the personal and professional values and expectations of the workers. This gap in expectation was reflected in how workers would prefer to have been treated at the time of the critical incident. The desire for their supervisor to show increased professionalism was common to participants, the lack of which resulted in workers expressing both disenchantment and disillusionment. Sally was "amazed that somebody so senior could do something so wrong".

Workers were also disgruntled with the behavior of their supervisor because of the deep inconsistency they viewed as existing between this and their own personal values. The telling of a lie resulted in feelings of unease and mistrust for two of the participants. In both situations it was perceived that a lie had been told to justify the supervisor's own actions and as a form of self-protection, thus resulting in a breakdown of trust between the worker and supervisor.

> He lied and I started to think if he lies about that what else does he lie about and that was the point that I realised that manager was there for himself (Anna, 52 years, social agency worker).

Feelings of Powerlessness

Feelings of powerlessness and the experience of the supervisor as using "power over" and/or "power from" tactics (Hollander & Offerman, 1990) played a significant role in workers deciding not to share felt emotions with their supervisors. As Hochschild (1983) states, power and authority play a key underlying role in the feeling rules workers perceive must be observed. In this study the worker's experience of either a supervisor exhibiting hierarchical power over them, or of power derived from the tactics the supervisor employed in controlling the situation, resulted in feelings of intense powerlessness, vulnerability and frustration.

The intimidation felt at the experience of having personal power removed or undermined was responded to actively by all participants with the exception of three workers, two of whom had experienced particularly devastating treatment by supervisors known to others in the organizations as "bullies". As a result of this and the high position of the supervisor within the hierarchy, their feelings of professional confidence were severely undermined.

For the remaining participants power was sought back in a variety of ways. Six of the participants sought to exercise their own power covertly and decided to leave the organization, and until opportunity for this arose decided to submerge their own personal response. A common theme that emerged as they reflected on their supervisor's behavior was that they perceived it as irrational.

> I began to view her not so much as someone that was unbalanced but someone that was a little bit irrational ... and as a result of that my need to get positive affirmation from her decreased and it almost got to the point that when I got negative affirmation from her I felt quite positively about it because I thought she was slightly imbalanced anyway (Brian, 39 years, secondary teacher).

The remaining group of participants chose to dispute the issue over which they were in conflict with their supervisor. For them this involved seeking official redress through formal channels in the hierarchy. Significantly, with the exception of Jim, none of the ways these participants chose to deal with the critical incident resulted in it being resolved positively in terms of the health of the relationship.

Impact on the Supervisor/Worker Relationship

A number of common themes arose as the 13 participants discussed the emotional impact of a negative incident on their relationship. The first was that as a result of the treatment they received they experienced a loss of respect for their supervisor.

Allied closely to this was the concern that the supervisor could no longer be trusted. One participant commented that her supervisor never noticed how the lie he had told impacted on the relationship because having decided as a result of what happened to leave, she "cloaked herself in the hierarchy of the organization" observing him covertly and always feeling "at any time there could be a knife in my back".

The most typical response to the ongoing relationship with the supervisor described by workers was to avoid contact. Clare described herself as withdrawn and Ben as becoming "even more retiring", while Brian, Robyn, Mary, and Susan avoided interaction with the supervisor. When this did inevitably occur, sometimes feelings of unresolved tension remained, for example, Scott stated it was not possible to have a "normal conversation ... when you try and have a normal conversation it's reduced to a win–lose situation".

Of the 13 people interviewed who discussed the experience of a negative incident, six left the organization, or in the case of Clare, remained within the organization but severed any connection with the supervisor and her department. The sentiments expressed by Bill were typical of this group: "I left because I couldn't see it getting any better".

The five who currently have the same supervisor with whom they had experienced the critical incident all have unresolved feelings from the treatment they received. This is despite the fact that for three of them the incident occurred three years ago. Max spoke about the nature of the toxic relationship between himself and his supervisor and the impact of this in triggering intense feelings of disillusionment.

> In many ways I think I have lost my innocence .... I think the people who really can survive are people who are unethical, who are dishonest, and these are the people who are actually going to be successful. The people who are honest and people who are innocent are the people who always get hurt.

Like others with unresolved emotions, Max's current relationship with his supervisor was described as "compounding on itself ... I feel like any time we see each other the relationship gets worse". Most frequently the intensity of the initial emotional response had grown rather than diminished. Despite now working "years on" from the incident, with the same supervisor, Stephanie says that while the human resource aspects of the issue are resolved "the relationship thing stayed ... like an open sore".

For the final participant remaining in an ongoing relationship with the supervisor involved, the incident occurred only four months ago. Like other participants, Mary, a 56-year-old manager within a tertiary organization, rationalized the possibility of being able to raise the issues of concern but felt unable to.

> It completely broke down ... we don't talk ... except she saw me here and I walk by her door and I think ooh I hope I don't see her and the other thing I think is I really ought to go and knock on her door and say can't we sort this out and then I think why don't I because I'm too bloody frightened.

Jim, who was the only participant to describe a positive incident, experienced growth in the relationship with his supervisor. It is important to note a number of the key factors in this situation that differentiate it from the experience of other workers in this study. Firstly, Jim took on the role of a mediator in a meeting situation of colleagues to resolve a sensitive issue about the supervisor's behavior towards another staff member. In this sense he was not confronting the supervisor directly but rather acting in a facilitation and buffer role for others. Secondly, as the facilitator of the meeting he was in a position of unique power which he chose to share to allow issues and concerns to emerge. In this sense the power he demonstrated was "power to" or empowerment as explained by Hollander and Offerman (1990).

The Role of the Organizational Community for the Worker at the Time of the Experience

In seeking to both understand the critical incident experienced and also deal with the emotional aftermath of this, 11 of the 14 participants chose to talk to someone in their organization about the experience. Of the eleven, five talked openly with their immediate supervisors while six discussed what had happened with colleagues. A key issue to emerge from this was that sharing with others resulted in them feeling emotionally supported to a greater or lesser extent. This confirms the findings of Karabanow (1999) and Abraham (1998) who both highlight that strong relationships between co-workers and social support can mitigate the effects of dissonance. Sharing also helped to enable them to rationalize what had happened, as highlighted by Clare.

> It's such a relief being able to share my reaction (with colleagues) and have it kind of mirrored back shock, horror, what's going on here ... it diffuses it ... was that so out of line that it just got shot down in flames and buried ... to have the legitimacy of the point and the reaction confirmed (Crying at this point).

Sharing was not however perceived as a universal panacea that resolved the situation. Sally expressed reservations about the value of sharing, voicing her concern that this could result in the co-worker/s she talked to about the situation "taking ownership" or becoming involved in the situation and heading off in a different direction.

However the overall sentiment expressed by those who did share with colleagues and immediate supervisors was that they took this action because they could trust them and that the sense of friendship and affirmation they received played a significant healing role. Mary stated it was good to "burst into tears and have someone realise this is really important". For Jim, being able to talk with his colleague about the tensions of the meeting he mediated affirmed that his efforts were valued.

> I went away feeling like there was a kind of arm around my shoulder, that it was OK to make mistakes, that there was no perfect right answer in the thing and that essentially it was OK to come up with a human answer to a human situation that didn't tick all the boxes all the way through but came out feeling OK at the end.

The other crucial advantage experienced by those who shared with others in the organizational community was to learn from and compare their own experiences of the supervisor to that of others in the wider context of organizational life. By communicating their experience to others, many found that the supervisor's reputation for poor relationships was known throughout the organization – as highlighted by Brian

> these sorts of incidents she was infamous for ... she was the kind of person who blew people up and moved on and thought that everything was fine.

Three participants decided not to share their experience with anyone within the immediate organization. Steve was already aware that colleagues knew what had happened because the "blasting" he had received occurred within the context of a meeting. He felt uncomfortable about raising this issue because of the humiliation he had experienced, and also out of a desire to forestall any rumours. He instead chose to share what happened with his partner at home which allowed him some feeling of relief because "in sharing something like that you are letting some of it go". Stephanie chose not to share her experience with any work colleagues because it accelerated quickly into a legal dispute and this escalation meant that she did not consider it appropriate to discuss. In her overseas posting Susan's decision not to share was impacted by feeling isolated in a small overseas office because of the intensely political climate.

ANALYSIS

Within their workplace encounters, men and women must continually adjust to a complex array of changing relational experiences. The emotional component of these experiences is often submerged, hidden away from the glare of organizational scrutiny. It is nonetheless formative, sometimes destructive, and certainly significant for both individuals and organizations. Our research has uncovered elements of this experience, and in the analysis that follows we highlight four key elements of emotional experience that emerged from participants' attempts to make sense of the critical incidents they described. Whether positive or negative, the nature and quality of the worker's previous relationship with their supervisor contributed to the adverse outcomes of the incident. Felt emotions, whether expressed, repressed or edited, were overwhelmingly negative and remained so despite the passage of time; and emotional tension was exacerbated by the workers perceived need to play an organizational or professional role which conflicted with their personal values and beliefs. Finally, we describe and explore the role of collegiality in emotional support and its connection to worker survival.

Contribution of the Nature of Previous Relationships to Outcomes

Emotional experiences, as highlighted in this study, frequently spill over the neat boundaries and traditional expectations set by assigned roles (Selznick, 1957). As the workers we interviewed sought to make sense of the treatment they received, the nature of the previous relationship with the supervisor played a significant role in the degree of emotional intensity with which the worker reacted to the critical incident. Those who, for example, had experienced a positive relationship previously, or a highly toxic one, were most affected; feelings of disillusionment were frequently described by those who enjoyed a positive relationship previously; and those whose relationship was already toxic spoke of the incident as representing a key turning point in the disintegration and downward spiral of the relationship (Conville, 1991 cited in Stewart & Logan, 1998).

All participants of the study sought to establish how what happened was "historically situated" (Fineman & Sturdy, 1999), and for this reason chose to outline previous events in the relationship in an overview before specifics of the critical experience were described. Clearly this innate desire to link the previous experience of the relationship with the new behavior was crucial to the retrospective sense-making process (Weick, 1995). This also emphasized a desire by the workers to rationalize their experience by attempting to understand what had happened within a larger context. This proved crucially important because almost all cases involved an emotionally traumatic event where the supervisor's behavior appeared to them irrational and unpredictable. In this sense, placing it historically frequently provided participants with an opportunity to view the incident in terms of the larger organizational picture and match it to existing patterns of how this person related to and treated others.

Consequences of Submerged Negativity

In all the incidents relayed which focused on a negative critical incident, a complex range of negative emotions were "felt", and the nature of the previous worker/supervisor relationship emerged as a factor in these

feelings. For those previously positive in their relationship, shock and disbelief were most common. In all negative incidents, what also inevitably
emerged were feelings of anger, powerlessness and impotence. These findings link to those of Harlos and Pinder (2000) who found that when workers
experience injustice one of the predominant emotions experienced is anger.
Like the current study, a complex array of other emotions were also outlined. The key difference between this study and that of Harlos and Pinder
(2000) is that the latter focused specifically on issues of injustice whereas this
research allowed workers to have any incident of emotional impact as their
key focal point. In this sense, the wider range of emotions identified in the
current study was to be expected since incidents ranged from telling lies to
public reprimands. The nature of these events themselves have potential for
further individual exploration, for example exploring exclusively the responses of workers who experienced a public reprimand.

In choosing to actively "express, repress or edit emotion" as described by
Waldron and Krone (1991), participants sought in all cases to choose a
response that would allow them strategic leeway. The decision also reflected
feelings of perceived lack of political safety and awareness of the inappropriateness of the context and nature of the relationship to be able to fully
express themselves. It is significant that though a small number chose to
share some of the emotions felt, none of the 14 participants chose to share
all emotions felt at the time of the critical incident encounter. As also found
by Harlos and Pinder (2000), participants responded to the higher status of
the supervisor by suppressing their feelings of anger.

All participants experienced changed perceptions of the relationship, as
also found by Waldron and Krone (1991). This was evident particularly in the
way workers with previously positive relationships altered the definition of
their relationship (Waldron & Krone, 1991). The changes provided disturbing
images of disillusionment and frustration. With the range of time lapsed
having occurred from fourteen years to three months, between the event to
the present, it seemed most likely that these buried emotional perspectives
(Hochschild, 1983) were unlikely to ever be shared with the supervisors.

Worker Masking of Dissonance

A key factor determining change in worker perceptions of supervisors was
the experience of dissonance between their own personal and professional
values and expectations. The personal conflict this created for individuals
was intense as they reflected on the difference between their organizational
experience and their own beliefs about how people should be treated and

responded to by others within the workforce. The gap in expectations was frequently discussed by them in terms of the moral and ethical issues present.

The outwardly "passionless environments" Jim refers to "where people are so dishonest with how they feel that they backstab" represented for those in this study a reflection of the response sometimes adopted in an environment where it was unsafe to express genuine emotional responses. Beneath the veneer of rationality and control that participants chose to present to supervisors lay a complex and disturbing array of emotions and frustrations. This issue of dissonance lies at the heart of the emotional concerns and frustrations expressed by workers.

On one level this is due to workers having to deal with intense personal feelings of discontent at their supervisor's behavior. However, at a deeper level they were also wrestling with their own sense of incongruity because of their need to perform as corporate actors (Flam, 2000). As a result they were unable to be true to their own beliefs and values since sharing these would bring them into further conflict with their supervisor. In this way tension was clearly evident between the espoused values they discussed and the frustration they felt in terms of their own theory in practice (Senge, 1994). May, Gibson, and Harter (2004) state that workers experiencing an unsafe environment which is ambiguous, unpredictable and threatening are likely to disengage from this in a self-protective response. This was evident in our study in the masking of emotions, with the human cost of this incongruence and lack of authenticity reflected in the levels of distress many expressed.

Feelings of Powerlessness

As participants shared their experience with others in the retrospective sense-making process, it was frequently revealed that many of the supervisors belonging to the upper hierarchy were "known" for the unfair treatment of many staff. This extends the image of the powerless individual to that of a network of many workers experiencing treatment they perceive as unjust with limited avenues of recourse. The decision to challenge the supervisor using the hierarchical structures of redress available was adopted by only three participants. All other participants, with the exception of Jim who described a positive critical incident, explained that the choice to avoid such confrontation was implicitly based on the fear that negative consequences might arise as a result of challenging their supervisor. This sense of fear was intrinsically related to the feelings of powerlessness experienced and can be viewed as legally, hierarchically and materially framed (Fineman & Sturdy, 1999). The ongoing result of these feelings of powerlessness was a sense of existing in a stalemate situation where any progress forward could potentially jeopardize their future career plans.

Hidden Organizational Outcomes

Our exploratory study raises key questions about the development of health in organizational relationships. We suggest that if the climate discourages workers from communicating genuine concerns, then many individuals will leave situations that have become untenable without ever revealing the true reasons for their departure. The subtext of their decision to leave is that they desire to work in an environment that allows them to be treated in a humane and civil way. The absence of this was interpreted as demonstrating both a lack of respect and value for them as workers and fellow human beings.

Despite the bleak picture which has tended to emerge of the relationships between these workers and their supervisors in the upper hierarchy of organizations, support was experienced by many from their immediate supervisors and colleagues. The most significant aspect of this was that workers who chose to share what happened to them experienced an increased sense of emotional connection with others. Sharing also resulted in workers developing an increased understanding of patterns of behavior in terms of how the supervisor had responded in other situations. This typically led to reduced feelings of isolation, and recognition that what they experienced was not unique to them. This collegiality demonstrates that organizational learning progresses when emotional experiences are acknowledged and discussed.

CONCLUSION

Our research suggests that while management and supervision theory promotes positive communication strategies and ethical guidelines for developing the worker/supervisor relationship, an examination of the workers' stories and their emotional experiences within this study suggests that there is a marked discrepancy between this theory and workplace practice. It appears that when workers experience what they perceive as negative emotional incidents with supervisors, they most often feel powerless to redress their concerns. The foremost emotions expressed in relation to this are those of powerlessness and frustration, as described in Clare's metaphor: she saw herself as a moth, a fragile creature battering hopelessly at the glass through which she could see, but not communicate with, the flame of her supervisor. In her hopeless struggle she sees herself as damaging only herself, but our study shows that where secrets of deep discontent are perceived as too unsafe to share and redress using official channels, the emotional battering the moth endures also undermines the health of the organizational community.

However one positive outcome in critical incident handling emerged from Jim's story. This single case highlights both hope and the prospect of learning, and signals that the organizational community has the potential to assist workers in resolving the emotional stalemates faced. In this incident a meeting between a devastated worker and a supervisor known for bullying was led by an objective, humane and skilled facilitator who assumed the role of negotiator and reconciler. Clearly a dire need exists for the leadership of such individuals within contemporary organizations. Only then is there the possibility that masks may be lifted, real perceptions and emotions revealed, and interpersonal health restored.

LIMITATIONS

In reviewing this research a number of key factors could potentially be considered limitations. The first of these is the narrow age group and occupation of the workers, since all were middle aged, highly educated professional individuals. While in depth interviewing provided rich texts and enabled complex responses to emerge, a broader picture of worker experience would also emerge from an extended sample size. This would be particularly helpful in potentially providing opportunity for an increased number of positive experiences.

One aspect of the research methodology that could benefit from redesign is the use of a more iterative process in the actual interview process. By this we mean that following the first interview and analysis of this, participants could return for further clarification of key issues raised. The difficulty associated with this is the time factor for both the participants and workers. One further key limitation is evident in not setting a time limit on how far back in time the critical incident occurred. The incident described in this study most distant in time was 14 years. In retrospect it may have been more helpful to set a five-year-time limit on the interval since the incident occurred, which may have ensured a more accurate focus in recall detail.

FUTURE RESEARCH

As discussed in the limitations in this research, an important area of further investigation lies in exploring and comparing the emotional experience of workers in different age groups within organizations. This could be insightful in terms of not only revealing differences in how participants express emotions, but might also reveal how the role of the organizational community is utilized in the retrospective sense-making process. The possibility of focusing on lower socio-economic groups could also be considered in potential future research directions.

In the completed study, participants were free to choose either a positive or negative incident. All chose to discuss a negative incident and only one of these had a positive outcome. Carrying out a further study asking participants similar questions about the emotional impact of a supervisor handling a positive critical incident would be a beneficial complement. This would be potentially useful in learning what supervisors "do right" and exploring the emotions and relational aftermath associated with happiness and satisfaction in the work context. However, a cautionary note must be sounded in that a study with such a focus would be effective only if it captured the complexity of the emotions and circumstances present. This is clearly because authentic voices can be best heard when the dialectical tensions present in the untidy and sometimes contradictory nature of our experience within the organizational context are allowed to emerge.

REFERENCES

Abraham, R. (1998). Emotional dissonance in organizations: Antecedents, consequences, and moderators. *Genetic Social and General Psychology Monographs, 124*(2), 229–246.

Angelides, P. (2001). The development of an efficient technique for collecting and analysing qualitative data: The analysis of critical incidents. *Qualitative Studies in Education, 14*(3), 429–442.

Ashkanasy, N., Härtel, C., & Zerbe, W. (2000). *Emotions in the workplace.* Connecticut: Quorum.

Boje, D. M. (2001). *Narrative methods for organizational & communication research.* London: Sage.

Callahan, J. L. (2000). Emotion management and organizational functions: A case study of patterns in a not – for – profit organization. *Human Resource Development Quarterly, 11*(3), 245–267.

Darling, J. R. (1991). Improving communication in organizational leadership. *Psychology, 28*, 1–14.

Fineman, S. (2000). *Emotion in organizations.* London: Sage.

Fineman, S., & Sturdy, A. (1999). The emotions of control: A qualitative exploration of environmental regulation. *Human Relations, 52*(5), 631–663.

Flam, H. (2000). *The emotional man and the problem of collective action.* Frankfurt: Peter Lang.

Frone, M. R. (2000). Interpersonal conflict at work and psychological outcomes: Testing a model among young workers. *Journal of Occupational Health Psychology, 5*(2), 246–255.

Fulk, J., & Wender, E. R. (1982). Dimensionality of leader-subordinate interactions: A path – goal investigation. *Organizational Behavior and Human Performance, 30*, 241–264.

Gundry, L. K., & Rousseau, D. M. (1994). Critical incidents in communicating culture to newcomers: The meaning is the message. *Human Relations, 47*(9), 1063–1078.

Harlos, K., & Pinder, C. (2000). Emotion and injustice in the workplace. In: S. Fineman (Ed.), *Emotion in organizations* (2nd ed., pp. 255–276). London: Sage.

Hochschild, A. R. (1983). *The managed heart*. USA: University of California Press.

Hofstede, G. (1984). *Cultures consequences: International differences in work related values*. Beverley Hills: Sage.

Hollander, E. P., & Offerman, L. R. (1990). Power and leadership in organizations. *American Psychologist, 2*, 179–189.

Jablin, F. M. (1979). Superior-subordinate communication: The state of the art. *Psychological Bulletin, 86*, 1201–1222.

Kamp, D. (1999). *The 21st century manager*. London: Kogan Page.

Karabanow, J. (1999). When caring is not enough: Emotional labour and youth shelter workers. *Social Service Review, 73*(3), 340–357.

Locke, K. (1996). Rewriting the discovery of grounded theory after 25 years? *Journal of Management Inquiry, 5*(3), 239–245.

Maclean, A. (2002). *The heart of supervision*. Wilmington, NC: Topdog Publishing.

May, D. R., Gibson, R. L., & Harter, L. M. (2004). The psychological conditions of meaningfulness, safety and availability and the engagement of the human spirit at work. *Journal of Occupational and Organizational Psychology, 77*, 11–27.

McCroskey, J. C., & Richmond, V. P. (2000). Applying reciprocity and accommodation theories to superior/subordinate relationships. *Journal of Applied Communication Research, 28*(3), 278–289.

Page, N. R., & Wiseman, R. L. (1993). Supervisor behavior and worker satisfaction in the United States, Mexico and Spain. *Journal of Business Communication, 30*(2), 161–169.

Rafaeli, A., & Worline, M. (2001). Individual emotion in work organizations. *Social Science Information, 40*(1), 95–123.

Riessman, C. K. (1993). *Narrative analysis*. Newbury Park, CA: Sage.

Selznick, P. (1957). *Leadership in administration, a sociological interpretation*. New York: Harper & Row.

Senge, P. (1994). *The fifth discipline*. Australia: Random House.

Singer, J. A., & Salovey, P. (1993). *The remembered self: Emotion & memory in personality*. New York: Free Press.

Stewart, J., & Logan, C. (1998). *Together: Communicating interpersonally*. USA: McGraw-Hill.

Tiedens, L. Z., Ellsworth, P. C., & Mesquita, B. (2000). Stereotypes about sentiments and status: Emotional expectations for high and low status group members. *Personality and Social Psychology Bulletin, 26*(5), 560–574.

Tompkins, P., & Cheney, G. (1983). Account analysis of organizations: Decision making and identification. In: L. L. Putnam & M. Pacanowsky (Eds), *Communication and organization: An interpretive approach* (pp. 123–147). Newbury Park, CA: Sage.

Waldron, V. R. (2000). Relational experiences and emotion at work. In: S. Fineman (Ed.), *Emotion in organizations* (pp. 64–82). London: Sage.

Waldron, V. R., & Krone, K. J. (1991). The experience and expression of emotion in the workplace. *Management Communication Quarterly, 4*(1), 287–309.

Weick, K. E. (1995). *Sensemaking in organizations*. USA: Sage.

Willemyns, M., Gallois, C., & Callan, V. (2000). Accommodating powering supervisor/supervisee communication. *Australian Journal of Communication, 27*(1), 129–142.

Yoon, J., & Thye, S. (2000). Supervisor support in the workplace. *Journal of Social Psychology, 140*(3), 295–316.

CHAPTER 5

CARE IN ORGANIZATIONS: A CONCEPTUAL LENS TO STUDY EMOTIONS AND CAPABILITY

Dorthe Eide

ABSTRACT

This paper explores and elaborates on emotions and capability in organizations through the phenomenon of care. Drawing upon multi-disciplinary theory, as well as empirical material from a case study in the hotel industry (involving four organizations), a theoretical framework is offered for understanding the multidimensional, dynamic, social relational nature and role of care in organizations. This is shown through the suggestion of a conceptual framework of four ideal types of practices in frontline work. In the practice of care, emotions are one of the vital parts in a larger whole. Regarding the role of care in organizations, it is suggested that what, and how, one cares for, are continually created, tested, negotiated and/or re-constructed. This paper suggests that the claims regarding care also provide implications for the study and understanding of emotions and capability in organizations.

INTRODUCTION

Recently, the notion of care has been brought into the discussion about leadership, including the role of managers in caring for their employees to

Individual and Organizational Perspectives on Emotion Management and Display
Research on Emotion in Organizations, Volume 2, 107–143
Copyright © 2006 by Elsevier Ltd.
All rights of reproduction in any form reserved
ISSN: 1746-9791/doi:10.1016/S1746-9791(06)02005-0

facilitate learning and knowing in organizations (Von Krogh, 1998). Care for employees is also one of the key concepts in relational management (e.g. Spurkeland, 1998). In the health sector, the phenomenon and concept of care versus cure is rather well known, and now this distinction seems to have relevance to other sectors. Studies from the private service sector describe frontline work as including emotional labor and as being new forms of care work (Forseth, 2001). While others question practitioner's claims about being care workers, claiming that care is not a part of private service, it is mainly rhetoric (Wray-Bliss, 2001). In my own research undertaken in the context of the hotel industry, care has shown up as a returning phenomenon, showing different and intricate sides. For example, hotel receptionists often claim to be care workers for healthy people and indicate that care is vital in the frontline. On the other hand, room cleaners often describe the high risk of becoming careless due to the high degree of routine in their work. At the same time, both employees in the frontline and in the backline describe how their ability and will to care can be threatened and reduced through their interactions with others. Surprisingly the 'other' in such cases, is seldom customers, rather they are often people inside the organization working in other communities of practices (CoPs),[1] i.e. interactions across CoPs and hierarchical levels, particularly managers.

This chapter offers a theoretical framework for understanding aspects of emotions and capability in organizations, through the phenomenon of care in organizations. In doing so, I seek to participate and contribute to the ongoing discourses exploring and elaborating the diverse sides of emotions, rather than viewing them as something irrational that should be avoided or as something to instrumentally utilize as an invisible asset (Ashkanasy, 1995; Fineman, 1993, 2000, 2003; Weick & Westley, 1996). As argued by Sjöstrand (1997), the continued presentation of management and strategy as something highly rational is a blind spot, which continues to obscure how such practices take place in organizations.

> To put it simply, managers do not cope with uncertainties simply by maximizing utility, making logical analyses ex ante, and by aiming to achieve known and specific goals ... . Strategic actions often involve a *mixture of analytical thinking (cognition), feelings, habitual behavior and intuitive or aesthetic considerations* (p. 194).

Our understanding of emotions as part of human practice and of knowing, remain limited. I suggest that we can gain an increased understanding of work, emotions and capability through exploring, elaborating and using the phenomenon and concept of care. In this chapter, as part of exploring and elaborating care, I address the following research questions: (1) What does (can) care mean? (2) What are (can be) the core dimensions of care in work, and how do they interrelate? (3) How can care be created and re-constructed? To do this, I begin with a brief introduction of the ontological and theoretical point of departure and then describe the methodology used in the research. In the remainder of the chapter, I explore the research questions by first illustrating and elaborating on how care in customer-interactions (CI) involves a combination of emotion, cognition and action (and much more) and second, by discussing the notion of care in hotel work in comparison with studies of care in other contexts. The chapter concludes with a discussion of the theoretical and practical implications.

ONTOLOGICAL AND THEORETICAL ISSUES

This chapter draws largely upon philosophy scholars inspired by Aristotle such as Heidegger and Taylor. Aristotle viewed emotions as a vital and integrated part of being human, whereby if a person lacked emotions he or she was seen as 'inhuman' (Aristotle, n.d./1998). Both Heidegger (1996)[2] and Taylor (1995) show that emotions are not something we can 'step in and out of', rather emotions run deeply through human existence and activities. Heidegger (1996) set out with the ambition of overcoming the traditional dualism, and suggested a relational, situated and practice-based ontology. This approach shares many of the ideas central to an interpretive–constructionist paradigm, not least the vital role of meaning and meaning constructions; and seeing meaning constructions as having both personal and socio-cultural (collective) sides where the two sides largely meet and take place in relations with others. What is further unique to Heidegger's approach is that he did not see meaning, interpretation or understanding/ knowing as purely cognitive, and he therefore gives a vital contribution toward rethinking emotions and capability (knowing in practice).

A Broad Situated-Relational Ontology

Below, I briefly introduce some of the main assumptions of the ontology used in this research (a more detailed elaboration of some of the aspects can be found in Eide, 2005). First, human beings are ontologically situated in four fundamental and intertwined ways: in body (with the head, as a living whole bodily being); in and across relations with others, things/objects and self, as a relational being; in and across contexts (physical and socio-cultural); and in and across time (past, present and future). Second, human

beings are whole persons, and as such encompass all the primary domains of
cognition, emotions and action. Therefore, individual, interrelational and
collective practices also potentially include all of the three primary domains.
In order to simplify this, we can say that human beings are fundamentally
emotional and thinking beings but what a person feels or thinks in a situated
time and place, or how people tend to express feelings or thoughts must be
studied empirically as it varies and is at an ontic level. Third, it follows from
the ontological structuring that human beings always find themselves situated in the world and relations as attuned and within a horizon (historical,
socio-cultural) of understanding: "Attunement always has its understanding, even if only by suppressing it. Understanding is always attuned" (Heidegger, 1996, p. 134). It can be argued that we are somehow always emotional and understanding, where other activities are influenced by and intertwined with these two fundamental ways of being and becoming in the
world, which again originate from the broader situatedness. A further fundamental way of being that is elaborated by Heidegger is care. This is
particularly relevant to the discussion in this chapter and will be elaborated
on in the next section. Finally, since the situatedness of human beings tends
to change, human beings, including emotions and capability, largely (not
only) are dynamic, emerging and hence a matter of becoming and not
mainly something which we have as objects.

What can Care Mean? A First Introduction

Heidegger (1996) claims that care is a fundamental mode of being and
elaborates three main concepts of care, namely care for things, care for
others and care for self. It should be noted that the latter two concepts were
argued as being fundamentally different from the care for things.

The first concept of care I will discuss is care of things. This mode of
caring is characterized by taking care of things, situations or problems
through finding out about them, discussing them and accomplishing them.
Furthermore, when neglecting, omitting and even resting, Heidegger (1996)
claims we are still somehow taking care of things, but to a very low degree.
Such kind of being and care was not Heidegger's main concern.

> In contrast to these prescientific ontic meanings, the expression "taking care" is used in
> this inquiry as an ontological term (an existential) to designate the being of a possible
> being-in-the-world. We do not choose this term because Da-sein[3] is initially economical
> and "practical" to a large extent, but because the being of Da-sein itself is to be made
> visible as care .... Ontically, as well as ontologically, being-in-the-world has priority as
> taking care (Heidegger, 1996, pp. 53–54).

Within Heidegger's 'taking care' lies the notion that when being in the world, we are not relating only or mainly by staring at it in a distanced and objective way, rather we are more engaged in the world, which is shown in and as care.

The second concept of care I will discuss is care (concern) for others. There is a vital difference between things and human beings, hence also of relating with and caring for things versus human beings. Humans are not "useful things at hand; it is itself Da-sein. This being is not taken care for, but is a matter of concern" (Heidegger, 1996, p. 114). This point also has relevance for the understanding of care (concern) for self. When relating with another being, directly or indirectly, we are more or less practicing ways of care (concern). If we are passing-one-another-by, without mattering and caring for one another, then we practice low concern. Relating with low concern for others has similarities with a low care for things, however there is a vital ontological difference. One can argue that relating with others as if the other does not matter, results in the other being made into an almost invisible object. As two passing ships not noticing each other, or more as an I–it (and not I–You) relation as described by Buber (1992, 1993). Since everyday being with others often can be a 'passing-one-another', one not only risks missing meeting or limiting the care for the other, but also limiting the care for and relation with self. Such passing also includes concealing oneself, which tends to misrepresent self (Heidegger, 1996), i.e. getting to know one's self is hampered when being concealed. This line of argument follows from Heidegger's view of knowing/understanding (including empathy), as not being something originating from cognition, but from being in the world through relating with it, i.e. one can argue he takes a relational and practice-based view on knowing. Care, as well as the getting to know, depends upon being with others in a more open and understanding way: "Being-with-one-another that understands[4] ... provide the first *ontological bridge* from one's own subject, initially given by itself, to the other subject, which is initially quite inaccessible" (Heidegger, 1996, p. 117). The relation with and understanding of the other is, however, partly dependent on one's understanding of own being, which is argued a projection and therefore tends to be incorrect. The accuracy of understanding partly depends upon how well the persons knows themselves, which depends upon being with others in a way that makes the knowing of self more transparent.[5]

There is an array of different modes of concern, spanning from two extreme alternatives. The first extreme, a *dominating way*, takes the care away from the person, i.e.: "take the other's "care" away from him and put itself in his place in taking care, it can leap in for him ... the other is thus displaced" (Heidegger, 1996, p. 114). Such care is argued as being similar to the taking care of things; it can be a manipulative, cure-like and determinant care. One can argue that the others are abandoned into a role of being a passive observer (e.g. as an audience for the service employee), an object without right to speak and interact as another subject. The others are not seen as one who knows. One takes the responsibility and care away from the others; as such the others become less able to care for themselves. Put differently, what seems as a concern can instead be doing the other a disservice. The second extreme, *authentic care*, is where one: "does not so much leap in for the other as leap ahead of him" (Heidegger, 1996, p. 115). This point has similarities with Søren Kierkegaard's notion of 'the art of helping others'.

> In order to truly succeed in leading a human being to a certain goal, you first have to meet the human being, where it is and start there. The one that does not do that, fools him self if he believes he can help anyone. In order to help anyone, I must certainly understand more than he does him self, but first and foremost I must understand what he understands (Søren Kierkegaard, 1859).

Heidegger (1996) further argues that being with one another is often based upon a sort of 'taking care of together'. Taking care together, does not however, mean doing the same thing (i.e. symmetry of doing, for example in the assembly line in a mass-producing factory), as the latter can become a relation with distance, which can increase mistrust. Heidegger further claims that taking care of food, clothes or other things for others (e.g. when being a nurse, parent or cleaner), is not the same as taking care of things, and that it should rather be seen as part of being concerned for others. One can argue that such relation with things at the same time involves a direct or indirect relation with the other, which is to eat the food or use the clothes or other things. If it is so, this opens an interesting altered understanding of the relations with things, such that, for example, cleaning not only is about care for the things, but also for the users of the things.

The third concept of care I will discuss is care (concern) for self. In addition to the fundamental relations of being-in-the-world addressed so far, Heidegger elaborates a third form of care, namely care for self. Care for self is about being one's self, which has to do with 'who to be?', 'who to become?', and 'how to reach ones potentials?'. It means not remaining closed, nor only doing and being what others, things and everyday life expect of us. It originates like a call for care not coming through words or being willed, it can come in the form of, for example, being guilty. This chapter focuses mainly upon the care for others and for things, while acknowledging that the three forms are blurred and intertwined. Later in this chapter I will suggest more concrete examples of how this may take place.

How to Conceptualize Emotion and Capability?

Humans experience unique emotions compared to animals, since human experiences tend to be infused with meanings, and the emotions these evoke are vital when judging (Taylor, 1995). Judging is central in knowing/understanding in practice (a view rooting back to Aristotle). Both Heidegger (1996) and Taylor (cf. Nyeng, 2000) show how emotions have at least three main roles, i.e. making us attentive, representing and creating understanding, and motivating us toward action. One can further argue that emotions are seen as vital in moral and ethical matters, both of which are closely linked to phronesis.[6] Ethical matters, along with other aspects linked to phronesis, such as social and emotional understanding and capability in practice, are not something that can be learned at school or once and for all, rather they are dynamic and infinite and therefore need to be continually re-learned and further developed throughout life – as an art (Aristotle, cf. Vetlesen & Nortvedt, 1996).

Based upon Taylor's emotional ontology, Nyeng (2000) suggests a simplified conceptual framework for emotions, including attunement, affect, feeling, desire and sensations, which I will briefly describe. (1) *Attunement* refers to emotions rooted in our personal and social existence as a human being (Heidegger, 1996). These are the most basic, immediate, often dim and less conscious emotions. Examples of these emotions include anxiety (existential angst threatening the existential and ontological security of the person, see, e.g. Giddens, 1991) and mood (e.g. good/uplifted, bad/dejected). (2) *Affect* refers to strong, surprising, often rapidly coming and rapidly dissipating emotions. These emotions are at the other end of the spectrum compared to attunement, i.e. the wave crests of emotions.

(3) Feelings are processed (mediated) experiences that are emotionally loaded, which tend to be conscious and easier to articulate. For example, one either does or does not experience or express such as friendliness, care, love, trust, compassion and commitment. Nyeng (2000) describes how the feeling of fear[7] differs from anxiety, as fear originates from and is related to something more specific in the world (e.g. a spider falling down from the roof). When the object or situation disappears, the fear disappears. When articulating our feelings, we may alter how we feel (Taylor, 1985). I further suggest using two sub-terms, i.e. *feelings experienced/felt* and *feelings expressed*. It is not easy to hide feelings being felt in interactions with others, nor is it easy to manipulate in highly instrumental ways the expression or experiences of feelings. Conversely, we can express feelings that we do not feel – perhaps in combination with what we feel. Sometimes we can be rather good at

managing both feelings expressed and even partly what we feel. Sometimes expectations from others or self about what and how to feel and express can be in disharmony with feelings felt, such emotional dissonance can be alienating, stressing or in other ways be harmful for the involved persons (see e.g. Ashforth & Tomiuk, 2000), also it can reduce the quality of work and interactions (see Eide, 2005). This may be a situation where the situatedness in a specific context and relation in a specific time does not harmonize with other sides of the situatedness, which has colored the attunement and some of the feelings felt. Feelings felt and feelings expressed are two different aspects of feelings, operating at two different levels that are intertwined.

(4) *Desires* can be both biologically/chemically and socially constructed. (5) *Sensations* are inner body experiences and outer expressions based upon emotional experiences and knowing. They could be deemed to be similar to both attunement and feelings. Sensations are also part of intuition and emotions in judgments in practical tacit knowing.

This categorization of the emotions framework is a theoretical simplification; attunement, affect and feelings can be seen as the primary concepts, while desires and sensations are intertwined in one or more of the others. In particular, feelings can be further elaborated into a large array of different feelings felt and expressed. At this point, it should be noted that I do not use the term emotions in a narrow way, capturing only limited kinds of feelings, for example as done by Salovey and Mayer (1990). Rather, I use the concept of emotions in a broader way. The three fundamental domains (cognition, emotions and actions) are not distinct; rather they are interdependent and partly intertwined. My understanding of emotions involves the two most common conceptual approaches to emotions in organizational studies, i.e. the social constructional and the psychoanalytic (see Fineman, 1993). I share with social constructionists the view that emotions are not mainly a phenomenon originating within an isolated individual, however, I do not concur with the social constructionist's view on emotional labor (e.g. Sturdy & Fleming, 2001; Van Maanen & Kunda, 1989) or other human phenomenon (e.g. Gergen, 1994) that emotions are mainly about expressing emotions at the surface or emotional managing/engineering, i.e. an instrumental use of own and other's surface expressions. This also means that the more unconscious, deeper and personal (history and bodily) sides, which are the focus of the psychoanalytical view, are also an equally important part. And I share the more recent warning about addressing emotions as an invisible asset, even if emotions seems re-discovered, emotions still often seem mainly approached in traditional instrumental ways (Fineman, 2000; Taylor, 1995). Being human,[8] and human emotions, is more than the surface level. How one feels is more or less dependent upon the broader situatedness and at-tunedness, and generally not something easily managed in instrumental ways. This follows from the situated-relational ontology (Heidegger, 1996). One can argue it is partly determined, and partly based upon one's own meaning constructions and coping. A high desire to care for/in the work increases the will and commitment and hence also moves one toward caring activities, although these aspects are not enough alone. Even a highly ex-perienced and usually capable employee or manager, may either temporarily or more permanently become less capable, due to the situatedness at work. For example, the insecurity following an altered situatedness can change the person's approach when working, and hence their attention ('see', sensiti-vity), tacit knowing, feelings, judgment and other aspects of co-operating, so that their capability is reduced.

In this chapter, capability is conceptualized building upon the views of human understanding/knowing elaborated above. As far as I see there are at least three philosophers who have contributed here, i.e. Polanyi (1958, 1966, 1969) (and with Polanyi & Prosch, 1975), the late Wittgenstein (1953) and Polkinghorne (1988); and hence elaborators (e.g. Bruner, 1990; Johannes-sen, 1988, 1989; Strati, 2001). Central key words characteristic of these views are tacit knowing, intimacy understanding/knowing, know-how and narra-tive knowing, in addition to the more traditionally addressed terms of knowledge about or explicit knowledge. This means that explicit knowledge is only a part of a larger frame characterizing human knowing and capa-bility in practice, similar to the tip of an iceberg constituting only a smaller yet integrated part of something much larger.

This is illustrated in the quote of Finne below:

> Much I just know, it cannot be described with words, because then it becomes so beggarly or counterfeited (Ferdinand Finne, painter).

METHODOLOGY

This chapter presents research findings focusing on CI, using data from frontline employees and managers (i.e. particularly receptionists), and to a lesser extent backline employees and managers (i.e. particularly cleaners) in the hotel industry. As the employees and their work are situated within a wider organizational context, the elaboration not only explores the role of the personal side, but also the role of the 'others' they interact with including their colleagues and managers, and hence also relational and collective sides of practices. When choosing methods and data, the empirical study has given priority to rich and varied data instead of traditional validation. The study seeks to understand the meaning of the data and to develop theory with the main focus at 'what' and 'how', and not mainly to explain 'why' (e.g. why a dependent variable varies one way or another). The data are constructed through a hermeneutical case study of four small/small-medium (i.e. SME)-sized hotels in Northern Norway, building mainly upon internal informants, but supplemented by external informants. Since the hotels were small, the employees and managers usually did more varied work than those employed at larger hotels. For example, receptionists were usually alone on their shift in the reception, and they were responsible for multiple tasks, not only traditional receptionist's work. They were also involved with such things as conference host tasks, chatting with business travelers, making and serving coffee/drinks. Some even organized the breakfast and performed cleaning duties, invoicing and answered (orally and written) requests. The hotels catered for different markets including (1) hosting courses and conferences, (2) business travelers, as well as (3) local, regional, national and international leisure and tourism. Further information about the organizations can be found in the appendix. (Please note, the organizations are given fictitious names including Arctic, Business, C&C and Diversity.) The hotels and the service workers were influenced by the local culture and history, including the wild nature, climate and fishing traditions. Most of the people (managers and employees) in these hotels had little formal education and except for one of the hotels (hotel Business) there were minimal written (explicit) rules guiding their work. This seems to be common not only in this industry, but also in SMEs more generally in Norway, not least in rural districts.

The empirical study used method and data triangulation primarily building upon data methods, such as participant observation combined with interactions and ongoing conversations (individual and group), as well as semi-structured interviews (Spradley, 1979, 1980). It was critical to try to follow processes in their natural contexts, which made events, breaks, narrations/narrating and other ways of coping with events particularly interesting to study. The study of meaning constructions was central (Agar, 1986). The data collection in each of the organizations involved approximately two–three intensive weeks (working from the morning until late night, in three of them even sleeping). The study tried to use some of the methods and ideas of ethnography, however, neither the time spent in the organizations nor the descriptions provided here (i.e. they are not enough thick) satisfy the ambition of ethnography. The data were supplemented with secondary data such as written materials as well as newspaper articles and internal notes/memos. All the main groups in these hotels were followed in order to get an understanding of their work (in a broad sense). Interviews were not taped rather responses were written down during the interviews, and usually supplemented soon after. The interview notes and observation logs were later transcribed into digital files. Data analysis began during the period of field research, and continued in a more systematic fashion post-data collection. The interpretations took place as iterative moves between parts and wholes (Agar, 1986; Alvesson & Sköldberg, 2000; Czarniawska, 1998; Thompson, 1996).

CORE DIMENSIONS OF CARE IN FRONTLINE WORK

In this section, I attempt to show how the practice of care in work is a multi-dimensional practice where at least all of the three fundamental domains (emotions, thoughts and actions) are parts of a larger whole. A frame of four main ideal types of practices is suggested, i.e. 'natural-careless', 'stand-ardized-tasks', 'standardized-play' and 'situated-care'. These four main types of ideal practices are discussed below. The degree of care is highest in 'situated-care', and this ideal type tends to be the most capable.

What does it Means to Work in the Front Line?

During the early stages of data collection in the hotels, I was particularly keen on 'testing' the literature assumption that frontline work is mainly to express positive emotions. Surprisingly most receptionists and even managers denied this assumption; instead they argued that *being natural, relational* and *caring* is vital in frontline work. Such practicing I have elaborated further and termed 'situated-care'. This study differs to Ashforth and Tomiuk (2000) in that most informants only in more exceptional situations experienced having to 'put on a mask'. There are a variety of potential reasons for this difference. One is that both managers and employees explicitly addressed skepticism and distancing from actors, contexts and ideologies taking more instrumental service approaches (e.g. distance from air crews, from the American service culture and literature), while they also distanced themselves from careless, grumpy and incapable service employees. Instead they identified with traditional care workers. Partly this finding seemed to be due to the more informal culture in the SMEs and in more local rural contexts, e.g. there are few traditions with formal training, particularly on the inter-personal relationship side of work. Still they were influenced by the more global ideas of customer service and relational marketing. In such they seemed as though they had gone through a rather similar learning and naturalizing process regarding the importance of customers and CI.

The main reason participants argued for being natural, relating and caring was: work, capability knowing and learning are situated within unique personal beings and within unique, dialogical,[9] and ongoing interactions with customers. CI can, therefore, only in a limited way be standardized through formalization. Some examples illustrating this are

> When it is natural, one feels comfortable and it *shows in your eyes* (hotel employee).
>
> In the relation between me and the guest there are no standards, because all the time you have to *size up* the guest *to know how to meet the guest*. It is perhaps possible to a certain degree to have standards in customer-interactions, but it is hardly the best way to do it, considering that *people are so different*. One must be able to *see what the guests are after*. The relations between me and the customer are important, and then *communication* is important (receptionist).

To be '*natural*' is seen as the opposite of false and highly standardized behavior; it is broader and more flexible and develops in the situation. One can argue that working as a frontline employee in CI is situated in at least the following ways: within the employee (as whole bodily person), the customer (as whole bodily person), the ongoing situation and time, and not least the relation between the two. In addition to that, also involved are different levels and partly overlapping socio-cultural contexts inside and outside the organization. When the work is highly standardized, the pressure is to ignore such broad and dynamic situatedness. I argue that the presentation of, and focus on the, differences (uniqueness and not only similarities) between employees, customers and their situations, is vital when preparing for (i.e. organizing and learning) and actually doing the work. As indicated in the second quote above, it is important that the employees are willing and able to 'see', 'read', understand and interact with different customers and situations. This also includes the ability and will to learn and interact on the spot, and to choose among and even develop (tailor) solutions and relations on the spot, through relating in dialogic ways with customers. Such an approach in CI is claimed to be impossible to learn through lectures or reading in courses, from colleagues or through direct formal management. The will and ability instead comes through a conscious hiring policy, good work environment (e.g. social and professional support), and not least through autonomy and flexibility for the employees when in CI; so they can use and develop their personal experience and judgments, create solutions and learn on the spot when interacting without having to ask the manager. The capability and will to care is not only a personal practicing, but also a relational and collective practice being constructed and reconstructed, involving also collegues and managers.

The term *natural* is not meant to refer to something mainly being inborn, static or within the sphere of natural science. Rather what is described as natural tends to be something learned, dynamic and situated both within the persons, the relations, context and time – in a broad combination. One can argue that what we see, feel and relate to as natural and self-evident tends to result from experiences and constructions depending on the person, relation, time and context. Even what is experienced as unique and personal is often socio-culturally embedded and embodied (see Bourdieu, 1998). How it is situated in contexts may not be recognized, and often what seems natural in one context can be seen as unnatural and even inappropriate in another context.

Identifying and Distancing: To be Capable in Caring Ways or not

Smiling has been argued by my informants as being a minor aspect of service-work. One can argue that smiling or not smiling is like other activities and expressions, part of a larger complex whole. In certain situations smiling can be quite inappropriate, and in most situations it is far from enough to interact in a capable way. As briefly introduced, the receptionists (and other informants) in this study often presented themselves and their work by *distancing themselves from* two main groups of other service employees, those being too professional and experienced by others as false and taking a 'cure' approach, and those being seen as careless. What do such practices mean?

Practicing *'standardized-play'* (cure) is an ideal type of practicing, which seems to have increased sufficiently in the modern climate of customer-orientation, where simple surface training (smiling, lip service and proverbs) is provided and emotional labor tends to be standardized. It can be glimpsed in the example below involving a guest and two receptionists (freely retold by a guest, after staying at hotel Business).

> One of the receptionists had an overwhelming friendly tone toward me. I was in the reception to pay my bill, not to do the final check-out. A colleague stood close by, thinking I was about to check out and asked for the key. She misunderstood the situation. Then the first receptionist turned to the colleague, when I listened, and addressed her in a highly growling, non-respectful, tone.

One can argue that at least three things are problematic in this situation. First, the first receptionist is perceived by the customer as false (inauthentic) when interacting with the customer (i.e. too friendly). Second, the customer experienced the first receptionist's way of interacting with the colleague as being intolerant, hostile and negative. Third, the switching between the two ways of interacting was experienced as odd and as an inconsistent way of being, which increased the negative experience of the customer. In the example, the receptionists did not seem to approach the others with a positive basic attitude, really seeing the other, and meeting the other, which are key elements when being natural and caring (i.e. the situated-care approach). Instead, the positive attitude and service-mindedness operated as a standard mask and behavior put to use in an instrumental and superficial way, which was not embodied (and could therefore seem false) and not sufficiently situated (embedded) in the relation. It had a larger risk of failing to match the situation and the 'other'. Even though hard working and service-minded, the receptionist seemed less able and willing to see, understand, respect, adapt to – and really meet – the other as a unique subject. If the 'other' differed from the receptionist's expectations of how they should be, this was not noticed, given importance or coped with in a capable way. If this professional practice did not match the customer and the situation, it was a larger risk that their more standardized approach became visible (revealed) and problematic. Such practice can be argued to be more in accordance with cure logics[10]: 'I will do all I can to help you ... but in my/ our way'. It seems more one-sided, static and closed, as if the receptionists lived in a world designed and orchestrated by them, where customers have to accept their 'game'. Paradoxically, both employees and customers often seemed to be successful players of social service games.

It is however risky, because it is all too easy to step over 'the line' of what is perceived as natural and appropriate in the specific situation. There can be different reasons for crossing such lines. A person or collective may not know 'the lines'; they are too consumed and veiled by the social role. Anyway it is not so easy to know lines that are vague, dynamic and depended upon situations. A further reason could be that the employee may play humorously with the service roles and routines, as a way to cope with work experienced as meaningless due to standards, or as a way to put theatrical talents to use. Independent of the reason, there is at least one large problem with such line crossing; if customers experience it as too false there are few chances that they are going to feel comfortable with and experience being related within a caring capable manner. As far as I can see, there seems to be at least two reasons hampering development of comfortable feelings in such line-crossing events. One seems to be that customers are turned into an audience of a standardized play, and then are not really being met and interacted with as unique persons; they are not given access to being real participants (subjects) either. To use the vocabulary of Heidegger, it is more as if they are related with and cared for as a thing (object). Second, interacting with the other so that one is experienced as being false and standardized (not authentic) tends to discredit also the other, limiting *trust* in what the other (including the organization) is willing and capable of doing in the interactions.

Receptionists and other organizational members *also distance themselves* from receptionists and hotels where the frontline employees are described as *careless* about the customers and CI. Carelessness can take the form of either being grumpy and only a wage-earner, i.e. practicing the ideal type of '*natural-careless*'; or only focusing on and caring for administrative backstage tasks and machines/things, such as being an office-clerk, i.e. practicing the ideal type of '*standardized-tasks*'. Both these ideal types were seen as incompetent or less competent ways of interacting with customers and working in the frontline. In such practices there is a low degree of customer-orientation and thereby also of care, as customers and CI tend to be seen as disturbing self or other tasks, as being problematic, and as 'a necessary evil': "There are receptionists that only see customers and occasions as more work, and they are sulky. They do not see it as a possibility to help customers, that it is a positive challenge" (receptionist). The main attention, desire and capability is then not in regard of customers and CI, but of back office tasks, routines and things (this practice is termed ideal type 'standardized-tasks'). It can also take place when the frontline employees tend to have their attention on and care for other internal members and not least self,[11] (being inner and self-oriented) instead of attention and care for the present customer and CI (this practice is termed ideal type 'natural-careless'). In both these latter ideal types the employees hardly or only to a limited extent see, really meet and care for the single customer (or user). The example below illustrates 'natural-careless' practice, and is taken from my observation log (hotel Diversity).

> Two guests stand by the reception to check out. They look like musicians leaving after a job stay. The receptionist utters a pronounced sigh when the phone rings. Two potential guests are the next in line; and they also have to wait for a long time. They want to rent a group room, and receive information about prices. The receptionist is sulky and discouraging; there is little smiling, service or interest. She does nothing to sell the room. They take it after some discussion between themselves; they have no alternative, but are evidently irritated and despondent.

This small scene illustrates an interaction approach that I interpret as low in capability and customer-orientation, as it contributed to low service quality.

One can argue this receptionist is a 'bad case', and that she differed from the experienced and regular receptionists in this hotel. From a customer point of view, this observation became a negative surprise even before talking with the person involved. The receptionist is the initial contact for most customers/potential customers and is responsible for creating the atmosphere, which in this case was negative.

Surprisingly, most of the receptionists generally *identified with* care workers in the health sector: "You must like people and enjoy relating with them in a work context and like to give service. In a way, this is like care-work for healthy people". As part of this identity, they also claim to identify with the customers, sometimes even more than with the organization. It seems that the customers are central in nurturing such an identity, as well as benefiting from this, thus creating a positive spiral. The identification with care and customers was coupled with a strong *will* (including desire and commitment), and often also a *capability*, to care for the individual guests and their situation when interacting. Statements relating to being a care worker were usually coupled with claims on being natural and relating; together this makes up the ideal type of practice that I termed '*situated-care*'. Their notion of care includes one that is to meet and relate with the customers in a way that is natural, in the meaning of situated as argued above. Most informants described their CI-work as positively challenging, most of the time it feels right, meaningful and energy generating (not only drawing). They both feel and express a genuine interest in helping and relating with guests. There can be exceptions to performing at an optimum level that includes not feeling 100%, or when interacting with particularly difficult situations/guests, precipitating the need to put on a 'mask'.

> It is dangerous to become *too professional*, in that it becomes a dressed smile. Sometimes if I am not in shape, it becomes a mask. But the guests notice. You can smile as much as you like with your mouth, but *then you do not smile with your eyes* (receptionist).

It seems that identifying plays a vital role in how employees meet and relate with customers; also it seems to have a vital role for their ongoing knowing and learning. The customer's situation and problem is met and related with as if it is a unique and mutual problem that is *to be taken care of together*, through a more or less mutual process where both are involved. Such an approach seems to be a care (concern) for others, and is opposite to more standardized and instrumental (cure) approaches or careless approaches. Also situated-care practice has elements of routines and standardizing, but in a different mode and degree. It shares similarities with playing music or games. Even jazz is not only improvising, as even such practices have more stable elements (like the drums). Even note playing in, for example classical music, permit and can depend upon improvising and personal touches in order to reach high quality. So it is also when experts play chess or do their daily work (Dreyfus & Dreyfus, 1986; Tsoukas & Vladimirou, 2001; Tsoukas & Chia, 2002).

When first facing the arguments about care as part of frontline work in hotels, it appeared to be just one of many dimensions. Now it is suggested that there are more fundamental differences in the broader practice, as if there are two more fundamentally different logics of practice (grounded assumptions about rationality and human nature) in CI. A first simplified construction of practices in the frontline centered on the notions of care versus cure as the dominating logics when preparing for and actually meeting and interacting with customers (first presented in Eide, Lindberg, & Jensen, 1997).

The two preliminary ideal types of practices can shortly be explained as the practice of *care*; 'let me help you in your way'; versus the practice of *cure*, 'let me help you in my way'. When elaborating the notion and terms we found inspiration in health research (e.g. Martinsen, 1989) and not least the study of Olsen (1997) who found the two patterns of practices (care and cure) when studying nurse's ways of relating with patients. The term cure refers to a dominating logic of practice based on instrumental action, mainly in the control of the service organization and employee, and similar to relations with and care for things. Care involves more than only action, emotions or thought. I suggest that care is a broader practice when it comes to focus and rationality and involves deeper and more genuine inner and outer involvement and activity. Additionally, it tends to involve all three primary domains of cognition, emotions and action. Not least, it is more dialogic (two-way) and involves relations with another subject. Listening and sensitive attention are just as important as telling or doing, and the customers' opinions are just as important as the employees. The cure approach can be performed in service occupations, and often comes with a smile and simple proverbs as part of the uniform and standard routine, but whom the 'other' is, seems not to really be 'seen', understood or appreciated/respected.

In the literature on emotions in organizations and emotional labor, customer experiences are seldom included. This is also the case in my study, however customers also argue that care, personal dimensions and dialogue are vital in private service. In research involving hotels and tour operators, Jensen (1997) found that the 'personal element' (i.e. the care and the personal dimension) is important in tourists' traveling experiences. The *care dimension* is argued to be a traditional part of the hospitality industry (including hotels), which includes friendliness, generosity and the personal treatment of customers, e.g. to be taken care of (a human and warm feeling), and the feeling of getting positive personal contact and communication. In this notion of care, the emotional side is particularly evident, and this also shows that care and emotions are relational. The *personality dimension* refers to the uniqueness of the people involved, and is often expressed in the personal relations between the hotels and the tour operators, or the hotels and the customer. In Jensen's (1997) study, tour operators argued that hotels in Northern Norway are more often characterized by a 'natural charm'. Natural charm means the opposite of hotels characterized as 'cold and professional' and 'machine operators' or mass-producers. Mass-producers tend to be highly standardized and rationalized with little autonomy for tailoring (flexibility) and taking care of the individual guests. One can argue they tend to relate with customers as if they are one homogeneous group — a 'faceless crowd of cows'. Similarly, Simarud and Titlestad (1997a, 1997b) suggest the role of personal and caring relations within the conference market, claiming that the main competitive advantage of smaller hotels compared to larger ones tends to be their capability to cope with the relational aspect, both in regard to the single guest being a conference participant and in regard to the re-building of business-to-business relations and loyalty with conference organizers.

> That the conference host or others that follows up, has their *attention on what goes on so that things are taken care of*, one feels the *trust and care* rather than having to run around the hotel to find the person or to ask for what should have been foreseen and done by the hotel (e.g. cream for the coffee, enough cookies, bulb for the overhead).

From these brief examples we see that care is not only something claimed by employees and managers within private service, it is also claimed by customers.

Four Ideal Types of Practices: Toward a First Summarizing

I propose that the practices in CI can be constructed as four ideal[12] types: (1) 'natural-careless', (2) 'standardized-tasks', (3) 'standardized-play' and (4) 'situated-care'. They seem to differ with regards to several facets: (1) identity, (2) degree of customer-orientation, (3) degree of standardizing (versus being natural), (4) degree of care (high versus lower), (5) attention (focal attention), (6) communication, (7) knowing, and (8) learning. The core aspects and facets in the four ideal types are summarized in Table 1 below.

Table 1. Four Ideal Types of Practices in Front Line Work.

Core Aspects	Ideal Types			
	Natural-careless	Standardized-tasks (cure)	Standardized-play (care-cure)	Situated-care
	Wage-earner	*Office-Clerk*	*Professional service-provider*	*Care-worker*
(1) Identity; identifying/distancing				
(2) (A) Degrees of customer-orientation and (B) assumptions about customers.	A) Low/absent, careless B) Stable, homogeneous. Customers are a problem.	A) Low/absent, careless B) Stable, homogeneous. Customers disturb, often a problem.	A) Rather high B) Partly dynamic and relative, within pre-defined categories. To be sized, categorized and then provided with solutions by the receptionist/organization.	A) High B) Unique, complex, changing. Partly sized and categorized based on experience, partly to be learned and developed in action in a mutual process.
(3) Degrees of standardizing	Low, accidental	High	Rather high	Low-medium, natural (≅situated)
(4) Degrees of care (concern) for the customers.	Careless about work tasks and CI (unmotivated, mindless).	Cure logic (technical–instrumental rationality) on some work areas, careless on others (the relational).	*Let me help you in my/our way.* Limited carefulness, mainly through cure logic (technical–instrumental rationality) on task and relational aspects.	*Let me help you in your way.* Domination of care rationality: mindful, situated, reciprocal relations.

Table 1. (Continued)

Core Aspects	Ideal Types			
	Natural-careless	Standardized-tasks (cure)	Standardized-play (care-cure)	Situated-care
(5) Attention	Inward, self-centered	Prescribed, administrative/back office tasks, routines, things/tools.	Standardized responses, routines, norms, surface.	Present customer and ongoing situation, tries to 'read' and understand. Empathy, perspective taking.
(6) Communication	Negative non-verbal, closed/inward. Unmotivated, grumpy.	Information supply. Sub(ob)ject–object.	Managed two-way, pretended to be joint management. Conducted conversation/play. Customer is the audience.	Open sensitive dialogues. Capable, spontaneous, improvising. Mutual participation, reciprocal interaction, Subject–subject.
(7) Knowing/capability	Accidental, low/incapable.	'Head': systemized. 'Hands': perform tasks through implementing rules, generalized knowledge.	'Head': systemized. 'Hands': perform through drawing on formal and/or informal service scripts/standards.	Continually created, situated, personal, tacit, relational. Perspective making.
(8) Learning	Low	Low–Medium in regard of standard tasks.	Low–Medium in regard of standards.	High

It seems that a person or a community in their daily life practice a pattern mainly in accordance with one of these types, and only practices other types more rarely and temporarily (e.g. depending on the person's mood or well-being, events taking place within other relations in the organization). One may also imagine that one person, community (unit) or organization can move from mainly practicing within one of the ideal types to another ideal type, depending on such factors as attunement, tacit knowing, attention, formal and informal organizing, learning and recruitment. Likely move patterns are: from 2 to 3 or 4 to 3 if an organization starts to focus largely on service standardizing and quality controls. Such movements are however only speculations, they have not been observed, and are yet to be studied empirically. There are, however, brief glimpses in the data in this study (including stories) that a person, or almost the whole frontline, in a whole hotel can move from being highly capable to becoming less capable. The degree of care (concern) for self and the experience that self and customers are being cared for or not, by others, not least managers, seems vital in the nurturing of the practice that dominates.

One may argue that carelessness and carefulness are the two ends of the continuum, with cure existing somewhere in the middle, as cure in the form of 'standardized play' includes some will to help and handle both the tasks and the relation with customers, although it is more restricted than in situated-care. 'Standardized-tasks' can have elements of care for the backstage things and tasks, but a combined carelessness and cure approach when relating with customers. These are only suggested interpretations and constructed patterns of practices, and not strategies for employees or managers to willfully choose between, manage and implement through quick-fixes.

What Characterizes the Highly Capable?

Simplified, the core sub-processes involved in capable knowing and inter-acting are developing some overview, control and confidence; being caring in broad and situated ways through being open and sensitive (attention and attuned) toward others; being engaged and dialogic in broad ways (physical, emotional, intellectual and oral), responsible, improvising and creating on the spot when interacting. Together these activities make up a conceptual frame of capable knowing and learning in (more complex) customer-inter-active work, based on the ideal type of situated-care. Among other things, such sub-processes depend upon certain kinds of identifying and gaining access to really participate as an involved, engaged and capable person. This also has to do with power and organizing.

Social interactions, more than relations with things, are like ongoing 'polyphonies' (creative co-play) that are complex, spontaneous and depend upon multifaceted, improvising and learning persons. The other's facial expressions, gesticulation or other bodily or verbal activities interfere with the other actor (Fog, 1994). They are in a flux that is not planned in another time or space. The participants have a different starting point (different background and intentions), but they also share and create (improvise, negotiate) together on the spot. One can therefore argue that the work of the frontline or other work being intensive on interactions with different kinds of other human beings in different kinds of situations, hardly can or shall be calculated and planned within the same technical–instrumental logic as in the production of things, and this has implications also for knowing, learning and doing. The sensing–judging–coping 'on the spot' when interacting is a way of knowing and doing where there is no or little time to stop and think, and then later start to act. One has to sense, think, feel, act and relate (a) simultaneously; (b) on the spot in interactions; and (c) its result is often highly visible for the other (external word). The activities of employees in CI, I will argue, give the work a character of irrevocability (Weick, 1995). Molander (1996) claims that practical work and knowing often is palpable and definitive in nature, as it is different from only thinking as an inner activity, where one can recreate over and over again, without anyone noticing.

The ideal type of situated-care is not a technique but a broader practice that also includes such factors as attunement, tacit knowing, attention, attitudes, values, respect, trust, tasks/action and relations to and as whole bodily and multi-dimensional beings. One can argue that capable employees are able and willing to read situations and emotional tones and to understand and interact with and through their own and others' emotions and body, i.e. they are capable as whole bodily persons in relations. How? Capable frontline employees seem similar to capable nurses with the 'clinical look' (intimate knowing), they often are able to read and understand the situation of the other and then know-how to interact. Studies have shown the importance of attention, sensitivity – being attuned toward the other – and of empathy (see, e.g. Ickes, 1997; Frost, Dutton, Worline, & Wilson, 2000). Küpers (1997) further suggests that service quality depends on the 'incarnational meeting' where the people involved are 'situated body subjects'. In understanding service quality this embodied meeting process between employee and guest are seen as critical. One can argue that it is only as whole bodily, relating and cultural beings that are sensitive, feeling, 'reading', acting and capable beings. This is particularly vital when work involves high degree of interactions and care (concern) for other human beings. The oral language or more aesthetic sides being expressed, cannot do the work alone, but are a part of the interaction. Strati (2001) shows that aesthetic knowing is more than expressing, also it is about sensing, emotions, meaning construction and other embodied and embedded intertwined aspects. In this way a more holistic practice-based approach seems more promising than approaches only focusing at the surface or only the unconscious. One can conclude that the narrative of situated-care also brings insight into the interdependency of *emotions–cognition–interaction* (*actions and relations*), instead of mainly the dominating focus on cognition or cognition-action.

The Four Ideal Types Compared to other Frames

If comparing the four ideal types with other suggested constructed ideal types of services, 'situated-care' seems to be closest to Ritzer and Stillman's (2001) 'person-oriented service', while a high degree of standardizing seems close to what they term 'system-oriented service'. System-oriented can be practiced as 'McDonaldized' or 'Systemized'. In the latter, all or most social interaction is reduced and machine interaction is implemented instead. Traditional person-oriented service is described as requiring experience-based know-how and a willingness to help and understand customers. Customers and the nature of service are then seen as more dependent upon the service employee being capable (including attentive), but also dependent upon the employee being more patient and spending more time with the customers. This can be seen as too costly and insufficiently controllable (risky in that it depends upon the persons) within the logic of system-oriented service. I have also shown that the instrumental cure approaches can be risky. According to Ritzer and Stillman (2001), the dominating trend has long been, and still is, to move toward more instrumental rational models for organizing service instead of more authentic relational approaches. If it is so, the logic of cure is increasing, and care is decreasing. However, my study indicates that caring relations within organizational and market contexts still can have vital contributions for service quality, customer satisfaction and work quality, which are arguments for moving in the direction of care instead of cure.

Compared to my suggested framework, Gutek's (1995) 'encounters' appear to be similar to the two 'standardized' approaches suggested in this study due to the high degree of standardization and instrumentality they possess. Her 'relationship' is closest to 'situated-care' being more unique personal and relational. She argues that most encounters are characterized by

(1) each provider has the same knowledge or expertise and (2) only this knowledge or expertise is necessary to perform the expected task or to deliver service. Any provider

who acquires the knowledge to perform the provider role through proper training (or who already has the experience) can handle an encounter equally well – which is why, from the customer's point of view, each provider is functionally equivalent. The training required for providers in encounter organizations is very often minimal and the scope of the services or goods offered is relatively small ... they are characterized entirely by instrumental behaviour on the part of both parties (Gutek, 1995, pp. 40, 260).

On the other hand, Gutek's ideal type seems to assume that an extremely high degree of standardizing of human beings, interactions, work, knowing and learning are possible. I disagree with this assumption. Who can be sure that only the same knowledge or expertise is used or needed? Would the person be able to interact if such extreme manipulation were possible? Would not that be to assume that human beings could be programmed like a robot? Managers, trainers or other organizational actors may assume that this rather high degree of standardizing is possible, but in my view there are always limitations on what can be prescribed and standardized, as neither humans nor organizations are machines. Both humans and organizations can however be seen as such, and be approached as such, as exemplified by McDonaldization. But that does not mean that humans or organizations are machines, or only use the standardization when knowing or interacting. Furthermore, Gutek expects an increase of encounter-like practices, and addresses how service work tends to be deskilled, which can reduce life and work quality. One can also argue that this probably also includes an increased risk of reduced service quality. One further difference between my framework and Gutek is that her framework (i.e. ideal type, issues and consequences) has not been studied empirically. However, one point that I do agree with is her suggestion that the framework can reveal more veiled practices and contribute to a decrease of unintended consequences.

DISCUSSION: CARE AS PART OF WORK

In this section, I discuss the role of care in work and particularly in private service work.

Is Care Just a Myth and Bad Metaphor within the Private Sector?

One can ask: Is receptionists' claims about being and identifying as care workers and the role of care is only a way to present their work as more complex and themselves as more capable and important than they are? Partly this may be so, since it is reasonable that receptionists, like other people, try to present themselves and their own work in a favorable light focusing on the most complex and meaningful aspects of it. *Who wants to be seen as false, just performing simple standards or being an underdog?* However, since the points of being natural and caring are also argued by other internal members and even customers, these empirical claims seem to have both functional and symbolic meanings and anchoring. *Who wants to interact with a rude, grumpy or otherwise careless, or highly instrumental service employee?* Also one can argue that such employee discourses about work and identity can contribute to meaning, autonomy and empowerment, as it restricts the planning and control of management. Identifying, constructing and practicing as a care worker can also be argued to be important functionally and symbolically, as a fruitful way of crafting work as suggested by Wrzesniewski and Dutton (2001).

That hotel and other service employees view themselves (identity) as careworkers has been recognized earlier. Lund (1996, p. 22) found in a hotel study that more than 50% of female informants identified themselves as care-workers and emphasized the importance of caring qualities/competence: "Women have a natural competence in dealing with people, and to care about others ... Women fulfilled the care-role ... We have more to give ... Women can better give the guests a home-feeling". Lund also claims in this quote that there is a significant gender[13] dimension involved, where women can tend to have a comparative advantage. Smith (cf. Forseth, 2001, p. 49) argues that both nurses and flight crews do care and emotional labor as both are expected to work with users' (patients or customers) emotions and their own emotions, so that they 'appear to care'. I do not disagree that the superficial appearance of care can take place, however it seems that many of the informants in my study really care and not only appear to do so.

Wray-Bliss (2001) suggests three critical interpretations of employees' (informants) claims about being caring and responsible in service interactions (giving tailored/personal service). First, they can suffer from indirect management control: the employees have internalized the rhetoric and logic of the service management literature and the managers about the significance of the customers, and have thereby become entrapped instead of empowered. They are seen as being in indirect control of management through the service culture, identifying (too) strongly with this ideology and being (too) motivated for doing CI and emotional labor. They even experience meaning and realizing of self through this work. I find this interpretation surprising and odd. Is it a problem if such work is meaningful and identified with? Is it so difficult to see that such interactive work can be fun, educational and meaningful? One might suspect there is a portion of snobbery in operation, hampering the ability to understand and appreciate such work. Second, Wray-Bliss (2001) contended employees contribute partly to their own oppression when presenting and constructing self with descriptions about being caring, responsible and giving personal service. Such presentation is interpreted as employees attempting to resist the tendency by managers to focus on quantity instead of quality, and of masculine values instead of feminine. Wray-Bliss (2001) questions their self-understanding and claims that CI and service as care are an illusion and only a way for the managers to manipulate their employees and customers. This interpretation I only partially sympathize with. While it can be a resistance and battle on how to organize and what is important, if managers or others push toward quantification and instrumentalism, I do not share the view that care within the private sector is impossible and only manipulative. Third (and final interpretation, where he draws heavily on Bauman), the informants present service work as a moral challenge. If the employees experiences a high degree of instrumental and distanced (bureaucratic) approaches and norms, the employees can try to resist by pointing at the moral responsibility and thereby the significance of values such as care, responsibility and qualitative service for the single customer, since customers are actually persons. This point I agree with, one can argue it shows that private service can include care and ethical concerns.

How to Understand the Nature and Role of Care in Work?

Weick and Roberts (1996) illustrate the meaning of care in high reliability teamwork as dependent upon being attentive, relational and hence caring toward others/things. If not being so, one is termed careless. This notion of care has similarities with my elaboration of situated-care. They however, elaborate care versus carelessness as mainly a matter of cognitive attentiveness and joint action: "… to act with care does not mean that one plans how to do this and then applies the plan to the action. Care is not cultivated apart from action. It is expressed in action and through action" (Weick & Roberts, 1996, p. 349). I share the view that action and joint action are central in care, and not only thinking, feeling or planning about care. However, I miss the presence and role of emotional aspects. Instead of drawing upon research in the army context, I will turn to more traditional care work as well as philosophy, which may also be seen as a turn from a rather traditional and masculine world toward a more feminine or androgynous world.

   That intimacy relations and care can represent a fundamentally different practice (including knowing and ethic) compared to more cure-like practices seems rather well-known within traditional care work and relational ethic (e.g. Buber, 1992, 1993; Levina, Løgstrup and Gilligan quoted in Vetlesen & Nortvedt, 1996; Martinsen, 1989). The point of relating (meeting) with the other as another subject, and not as a thing to be approached instrumentally, shows the ethical but also fundamental aspect of emotions and interpersonal relations.

> Approaching other human beings on the basis of pure technique means that one manipulates them, and if one approaches them on the basis of pure dynamic it means that one makes them a thing, that is, makes human beings only a *thing*. And these humans feel and recognize immediately the manipulating quality or the thing-making tendency (Frankl, 1994, p. 12, my translation, his italic).

Situated-care as shown in Table 1 seems to include the care ethic and care rationality, which is a kind of ethic and rationality brought forward largely by feminist writers. Trust, appreciation, respect and empathy have been argued as being central in care rationality (Martinsen, 1989), because the relations are equally as important as the tasks/actions. These are characteristics more often argued as vital in present working life, not least in inter-disciplinary teamwork, learning and relational leadership (see, e.g. Spurkeland, 1998; Von Krogh, 1998). Care rationality is often understood as morally and emotionally motivated action in interaction based on mutual involvement and focus on the other subject (e.g. patient or child). The relation must be influenced and engraved by the perspectives of both the involved parties. If the relation becomes a one way perspective, it can become engraved by strategy, control, mistrust and a power domination, i.e. an instrumental and cure rationality (Martinsen, 1989). Care includes empathy in the meaning of experiencing and understanding the other person's situation (thoughts, feelings, actions), but often this alone is not enough, as the interaction also calls for respect, responsibility, action and other relations. It does not mean to force upon others one's own feelings and solutions without really seeing, respecting and relating with the other.

> The sensitivity is not a sentimental care, subjectivism or intimacy. Then my participation in the situation of others is narrowed down to my own emotions. The situation is gone. The objectivity of empathy means concretely to find out how the other at best can be helped, where the key is appreciation and sympathy (Martinsen quoted in Nortvedt, 1993, p. 127, my translation).

> The intellect must interact with emotional abilities and abilities to imagine, such abilities must be practiced throughout an inter-human life and experience (Vetlesen & Nortvedt, 1996, p. 33, my translation).

Further, quote one with the point about finding out about the other, has clear similarities with the point of both Kierkegaard and of Heidegger in the beginning of this chapter. One may say that emotions are not sufficient alone; yet emotions remain a central part of care practice and of being capable. Nortvedt (1993, p. 131, my translation) elaborates on how emotion can contribute in knowing and particularly in care work, claiming that: "Emotions gives us access to and make us sensitive toward the patients' unpleasant and ambivalent expressions. Emotions, together with reflection, constitute the basis for an adequate judging of the situation". Emotions are here seen as having cognitive and moral functions; this resonates well with the theoretical ideas elaborated in the theoretical introduction. If the emotions are only at the surface and not experienced and felt, emotions do not seem to get an orienting, judging and hence knowing role in the interactions, knowing and learning. Human and inter-human issues are often complex and dynamic, also within service enterprises, in such situational practical judging, ethic and emotions can be vital. These sides of human life differ from general knowledge, handcraft and technical skills. The latter three are easier to learn through training as they are more general and rule-based, and episteme can often be learned through intellectual learning. While the inter-human issues are situated, dynamic and have to be learned continually (lifelong) through practice-based approaches. If seen in regard to the concepts of empathy and of care, one can argue that a cognitive and distanced empathy is not enough. In order to see, understand, act and relate one also needs emotional empathy, as this also increases the likelihood of moving the person into activity (Vetlesen & Nortvedt, 1996).

Care as Part of Work also in other Hotel Occupations

I suggest that care in and for work is not limited to the frontline, rather care (and the core dimensions) can be a more or less vital part of most, if not all, kinds of work and capability – be it in the frontline, backline, or in management. The practice and meaning of care can however differ depending upon the specific work, as what is to be related with varies, and what is experienced as carefulness within different occupational, organizational, trade and geographical contexts probably varies, still some core dimensions can probably be relatively similar. So far the phenomenon of care has been seen in relation to work where relations between people are a central part of the work. In other kinds of work, attentiveness and relations with machines, other things and tasks may be the critical issue, and as long as the relations are not with other human beings the notion of care somehow alters. For example, in performing work relating with things how can cleaners' work be practicing more or less care? When studying the work, knowing and learning of room cleaners it was rather easy to see the difference between careful and highly capable cleaners, compared to the more careless. The highly capable were aware of the high risk of becoming less careful due to the high degree of routine tending to slow their ability and willingness to 'see', relate and in other ways clean and do the work with a high degree of attention, tempo, perseverance, pride, responsibility and hence care.

> If you do not make an effort, are *careless* and lazy, this is not the place to be (cleaner in hotel Diversity).

> The work demands that we are working with precision, but there is lots of routine and one *becomes 'blind'* and does not see what is dirty and needs to be done. One grows listless and then it is easy to become *careless*, that is human. The control system is good to prevent this (team leader and cleaner, hotel Business).

None of the cleaners in this study presented themselves as care workers; yet one may still argue that they practice care, at least in the mode of care for things. Put differently, also cleaners' work can be like a 'careful dance'. Cleaners (like people at home when cleaning) participate in an indirect social relation with the guest and other colleagues in the organization. Both cleaners and other hotel staff can be well aware of that: "If the rooms are not properly cleaned, then the rest does not help" (cleaner). They relate mainly with the guests indirectly, since it is the guests that live in the rooms, they benefit most directly from cleaners doing their work with care, and they suffer if the work is performed carelessly. Also colleagues, managers and owners can benefit or suffer from how cleaners practice their work, such as through positive feedback and customer loyalty or negative feedback and exit. Here we begin to see the more complex relational web of how the practicing of care (or carelessness) can be produced and can far more wide-reaching consequences than dirty rooms or rooms with unreliable appliances (e.g. phone, TV, lamp, shower). While within the service management logic, it is the frontline and the dyad between the frontline and customers that often receives the main attention as the critical point in the chain, this study (re-)shows that cleaners and managers are also central facets of the larger teamwork and web of performing the tasks and nurturing care and quality in a hotel organization (this is not the place to elaborate further on care practices of cleaners and managers). This research shows how 'parts', i.e. individuals and units caring, or being careless, can have vital consequences for other parts and for the larger whole.

CLOSING REMARKS

Can the phenomena of situated care in work also have relevance more widely as an ideal case in order to gain a deeper understanding of capability, emotions and their interconnectedness? I suggest yes, but not in the meaning of showing all possible sides.

Theoretical and Methodological Implications

First, this study suggests that emotions can be part of being, knowing and interacting in capable ways. Such knowing and capability in practice should be seen as multidimensional, where at least all three fundamental domains of cognition, emotions and action can and often are a part of a larger integrated whole. This conclusion is not extraordinary in itself, it is a view that is becoming increasingly more recognized and accepted, but is seldom present in theories about knowing and learning, and it is more often claimed than shown. The phenomena and concept of care elaborated and illustrated here can provide a window not only into emotions and relations in organizations, but also demonstrate how knowing and learning in practice can involve emotions and relations as parts in a larger whole. Emotions are not only experienced or expressed; they can also be vital in our capabilities to orient, judge, understand, move and act/interact.

Second, care and hence also emotions and capability in work and organizations, can largely be seen as situated, relational, constructed (including negotiated) and dynamic, without excluding the personal side in the meaning of human beings as the ones that know, feel, relate and learn. It makes these phenomena less static and general characteristics of an individual, as they are not independent upon where, when and who one relates with. This may have rather thought-provoking implications for the theoretical understanding, methodology and for practice. Since emotions, capability, including such as emotional intelligence, or whatever term one uses, are then not something that one has, nor are they general and static in the meaning of independent of the broader situatedness and the relations with others, things or self. For example, it means that in certain contexts and relations I care, feel and am seen as capable, in others I am not. It means that my ability and will to care is not only dependent upon my self, but also my continual relations with others. In sum, care, emotions, and capability, can be tested (i.e. questioned by others or self, tried out), negotiated and constructed across relations making up webs of interactions. This multi-relational argument is a view shared by writers such as Gergen (1994) and Burkit (1999).

Practical/Managerial Implications

If being and relating in caring ways are as important as suggested here, it is paradoxical that one of the main trends within service is to increase standardizing, formalizing and use of machines, instead of more caring interactions. One central aim of standardizing is to save money, however this can be costly both in money and other values. I have indicated that instrumental approaches can structure practice so that people may become less capable and learning, and perhaps alienated. Walsh (in Strannegård, 2003, p. 19) addresses this point in regard to academic life by adding a caution about guidebooks: "A prescribed life is not a lived life". The narrative about situated-care I suggest shows that '*To meet, is to be changed*', because when one really meets one touches each other, emerges and develops (becomes) together.

The practice of care depends upon and includes access to participating more broadly in the organization than just performing orders and standard routines. Not least access in the meaning of some autonomy (a) to draw upon personal experiences, emotions and fore-understanding; and (b) to improvise and construct (negotiate and create) together with the other (customer, colleague, manager) during interactions. Such broader access seems to make employees more capable and willing, since they get the opportunity to learn, and to draw upon experiences, emotions and other aspects, and not only to express standards. Such access symbolizes appreciation, inclusion, respect, being seen as knowing and important, in short, being cared for by others. One may argue it creates a positive spiral of increased desire, will and ability to care, relate and work in capable ways. Also one can argue that employees have a responsibility to be able and willing to care. Becoming more able and willing to care for and involve others and self is perhaps my best practical advice. It seems obvious, while it also seems to be far too easily forgotten, and easier to tell than to do. To practice care in organizations, not only depends upon employees' identity, ability and will, it depends also upon the identity, care and other features of managers' practices.

LIMITATIONS

Simplifications were made to accommodate practical constraints, and accordingly I focused mainly upon frontline employees, and only briefly addressed concerns relating to other employees and hierarchical levels. What it means and takes to care in a particular occupation in a particular context, time and even relation, is variable and while I hope this point has been sufficiently illustrated, this must be studied empirically and not assumed a priori. The exploration and elaboration of care, and emotions and capability as part of that, has only concentrated on data from one industry, one country, a small number of organizations and mainly as seen from the perspective of employees. As a result, the suggested frames and arguments need to be further studied in order to compare and develop the concept further through studies of other kinds of contexts and relations with.

NOTES

1. An introduction of the phenomenon 'community of practice' can be found in, e.g. Wenger (1998).
2. This book was first published in 1927.
3. Da-sein, i.e. the human being.
4. Such understanding is often termed empathy by others.
5. One may argue the logic here has parallels to the point argued in the JOHARI-window model, where disclosure can follow from feedback (see e.g. http://www.augsburg.edu/education/edc210/johari.html).
6. *Phrónesis* is the intellectual activity related to *práxis* (Flyvbjerg, 1991), simplified it means practical wisdom and moral knowledge.
7. Heidegger (1996) however elaborates on fear as a mode of attunement, being a more defined kind than anxiety or other moods.
8. The discussion is limited to working adults and does not extend to the mentally ill.
9. Dialogical in the meaning of a reciprocal and multi-dimensional 'social dance', which is not one way, nor is it only oral.
10. This was also found in a study of nurses (Olsen, 1997).
11. This does not mean that employees' care for self are a problem more generally. Care for self are important for many reasons such as to prevent violence, to process strong emotional experiences after a CI, or to draw borders in regard of what is acceptable in CI. However when being in CI, the main focus should be on the other and the mutual relation.
12. Ideal types can be argued stereotypic and too dichotomic. They can also be seen as different interpretations (ideal second-ordered constructions) of front line work based upon both accounts constructed during my empirical study and literature review.
13. Also other studies have shown that people often assume (rather stereotypically) that women are more capable of doing service work (Amble et al., 2003). Also my study shows that both frontline and backline works are gendered (e.g. there are significantly fewer men, the wages are low and activities and abilities are often seen as more feminine). However, there is nothing in my observations indicating that the frontline men are less able or willing to care or in other ways less capable, than the female.

ACKNOWLEDGMENTS

I would like to acknowledge (1) the vital role of the informants in the hotel industry, who let 'me get a glimpse of their working life'; (2) the financial support of the research project of which this paper is a part, not least by NFR (The Research Council of Norway), and Bodø Graduate School of Business; (3) the financial support provided by Bodoe Regional University to allow me to participate at the EMONET conference in London; and (4) helpful comments from the blind reviewers, my colleague Frank Lindberg, as well as the book editors, not least Charmine Härtel.

REFERENCES

Agar, M. H. (1986). *Speaking of ethnography*. London: Sage.

Alvesson, M., & Sköldberg, K. (2000). *Reflexive methodology: New vistas for qualitative research*. London: Sage.

Amble, N., Enehaug, H., Forsth, U., Gjerberg, E., Grimsmo, A., Hauge, T., & Winther, F. (2003). Arbeidsmiljø og mestring hos frontlinjearbeidere i flytransporttjenesten, *AFI-rap*, 6, Oslo: AFI.

Aristotle. (1998). The Nicomachean ethics (D. Ross, Trans.). Oxford: Oxford World's Classics.

Ashforth, B. E., & Tomiuk, M. A. (2000). Emotional labour and authenticity: Views from service agents. In: S. Fineman (Ed.), *Emotions in organizations* (pp. 184–203). London: Sage.

Ashkanasy, N. (1995). Organizational culture: Emotion or cognitions. *Managerial and Organizational Cognition Interest Group Newsletter (Mocig News)*, 5(2), 1–2.

Bourdieu, P. (1998). *Practical reason*. Oxford: Polity Press.

Bruner, J. (1990). *Acts of meaning*. USA: Harvard University Press.

Buber, M. (1992). *Jeg og Du [You and I, 1923]*. Gjøvik: Cappelens Forlag AS.

Buber, M. (1993). *Dialogens Väsen [Zwiesprache-Traktat von dialogischen Leben, 1932]*. Falun: Dualis Förlag AB.

Burkitt, I. (1999). *Bodies of thought. Embodiment, identity & modernity*. London: Sage Publications.

Czarniawska, B. (1998). *On the absence of plot in organization studies*. Paper, Gothenburg Research Institute/School of Economics and Commercial Law.

Dreyfus, H. L., & Dreyfus, S. (1986). *Mind over machine: The power of human intuition and expertise in the era of the computer*. New York: Free Press.

Eide, D. (2005). Emotions: From 'ugly duckling', via 'invisible asset' toward ontological reframing. In: C. E. J Härtel, W. J Zerbe & N. M. Ashkanasy (Eds), *Emotions in organizational behavior* (pp. 11–44). Mahwah, NJ: Lawrence Erlbaum Associates, Inc.

Eide, D., Lindberg, F., & Jensen, Ø. (1997). Care or cure? Exploring the nature of service interactions, proceedings. *EIASM workshop on quality management in services VII*, Kristiansand: Agder College.

Fineman, S. (1993). *Emotion in organizations*. London: Sage.

Fineman, S. (2000). *Emotions in organizations*. London: Sage.

Fineman, S. (2003). Emotionalizing organizational learning. In: M. Easterby-Smith & M. A. Lyles (Eds), *The Blackwell handbook of organizational learning and knowledge management* (pp. 557–572). Oxford: Blackwell.

Flyvbjerg, B. (1991). *Rationalitet og magt: Bind I. Det konkretes videnskab.* Odense: Akademisk Forlag.

Fog, J. (1994). *Med samtalen som udgangspunkt: Det kvalitative forskningsinterview.* København: Akademisk Forlag.

Forseth, U. (2001). *Boundless work: Emotional labor and emotional exhaustion in interactive service work.* Doctoral dissertation. Trondheim: The Department of Sociology and Political Science, The Norwegian University of Technology and Natural Science.

Frankl, V. E. (1994). *Vilje til mening [The will to meaning].* Oslo: Aventura.

Frost, P. J., Dutton, J. E., Worline, M. C., & Wilson, A. (2000). Narratives of compassion in organizations. In: S. Fineman (Ed.), *Emotion in organizations* (pp. 25–45). Thousand Oaks, CA: Sage.

Gergen, K. (1994). *Realities and relationships.* Cambridge, MA: Harvard University Press.

Giddens, A. (1991). *Modernity and self-identity.* Cambridge, MA: Polity Press.

Gutek, B. A. (1995). *The dynamics of service.* San Francisco, CA: Jossey-Bass.

Heidegger, M. (1996). *Being and time.* Albany: State University of New York Press.

Ickes, W. (Ed.) (1997). *Empathic accuracy.* New York: Guilford Press.

Jensen, Ø. (1997). *Kjøper-selger-relasjoner innenfor internasjonal reiselivsnæring: En studie av samspillet mellom bedriftene ut fra ønske om utvikling av varige konkurransefortrinn.* Doctoral dissertaton.. Institut for Markedsøkonomi, Århus: Handelshøjskolen I Århus.

Johannessen, K. J. (1988). Tanker om tyst kunskap. Dialoger, no. 6, Stockholm.

Johannessen, K. J. (1989). Intransitiv forståelse – En fellesnevner for filosofisyn, språksyn og kunstsyn hos Wittgenstein. In: K. J. Johannessen & B. Rolf (Eds), *Om tyst kunskap.* Uppsala: Uppsala Universitet.

Kierkegaard, S. (1859). Fragments of a plain message, page unknown.

Küpers, W. (1997). Embodied and symbolic service organization and the question of a service quality leadership. Paper presented and in proceedings of Quality Managment in Service VII, Kristiansand, Norway, April 28–29.

Lund, E. (1996). *Kvinner i etterutdanning og ledelse.* Stavanger: NHRF-rapport.

Martinsen, K. (1989). *Omsorg, sykepleie og medisin: Historisk-filosofiske essays.* Otta: Tano A.S.

Molander, B. (1996). *Kunskap I handling.* Göteborg: Daidalos.

Nordtvedt, P. (1993). *Følelser, omsorg og fornuft, in Kirkevold, Nortvedt & Alvsvåg (red), Klokskap og kyndighet.* Norway: as Notam Gyldendal.

Nyeng, F. (2000). *Det autentiske menneske – med Charles Taylors blikk på menneskevitenskap og moral.* Oslo: Fagbokforlaget.

Olsen, R. (1997). *To act for or with the patient (Å handle for eller med pasienten).* Unpublished working paper. Bodø: Nordland University College.

Polanyi, M. (1958). *Personal knowledge.* Chicago, IL: University of Chicago Press.

Polanyi, M. (1966). *The tacit dimension.* Gloucester: Massachusetts Peter Smith.

Polanyi, M. (1969). *Knowing and being.* Chicago, IL: University of Chicago Press.

Polanyi, M., & Prosch, H. (1975). *Meaning.* Chicago, IL: Phoenix.

Polkinghorne, D. E. (1988). *Narrative knowing and the human sciences.* Albany: State University of New York Press.

Ritzer, G., & Stillman, T. (2001). From person – to system-oriented service. In: A. Sturdy, I. Grugulis & H. Willmott (Eds), *Customer Service.* London: Palgrave.

Salovey, P., & Mayer, J. D. (1990). Emotional intelligence. *Imagination, Cognition and Personality, 9*(3), 185–211.
Simarud, L. B., & Titlestad, C. (1997a). Hvordan dannes kundetilfredshet blant arrangører av kurs og konferanser på hotell? Unpublished student dissertation at graduate level (Siviløkonom oppgave) in marketing. Bodø: Bodø Graduate School of Business.
Simarud, L. B., & Titlestad, C. (1997b). Referat fra intervjuer til Siviløkonomoppgave. Confidencial report with the interview transcripts. Bodø: Bodø Graduate School of Business.
Sjöstrand, S. E. (1997). *The two faces of management: The Janus factor.* London: International Thomson Business Press.
Spradley, J. P. (1979). *The ethnographic interview.* New York: Holt, Rinehart & Winston.
Spradley, J. P. (1980). *Participant observation.* New York: Holt, Rinehart & Winston.
Spurkeland, J. (1998). *Relasjonsledelse.* Otta: Tano Aschehoug.
Strannegård, L. (2003). Att leda och bli ledd. In: Strannegård, L. (Ed.), *Avhandlingen: Om att formas till forskare.* Lund: Studentlitteratur.
Strati, A. (2001). Aesthetics, tacit knowledge and symbolic understanding: Going beyond the pillars of cognitivism in organization studies. Paper presented at 17th EGOS Colloquium, 5–7 July, Lyon, Group: Knowing as Desire.
Sturdy, A., & Fleming, P. (2001). Talk as technique – a critique of the words and deeds distinction in the diffusion of customer service cultures. Paper presented at 17th EGOS Colloquium, 5–7 July, Lyon Conference paper presented at EGOS, Lyon.
Taylor, C. (1985). *Human agency and language: Philosophical papers (Vol. 1).* Cambridge, MA: Cambridge University Press.
Taylor, C. (1995). *Identitet, frihet och gemenskap.* Göteborg: Daidalos.
Thompson, C. J. (1996). Caring consumers. Gendered consumption: Meanings and the juggling lifestyle. *Journal of Consumer Research, 22,* 388–407.
Tsoukas, H., & Chia, R. (2002). On organizational becoming: Rethinking organizational change. *Organization Science, 13*(5), 567–582.
Tsoukas, H., & Vladimirou, E. (2001). What is organizational knowledge? *Journal of Management Studies, 38*(7), 973–993.
Van Maanen, J., & Kunda, G. (1989). Real feelings: Emotional expression and organizational culture. In: L. L. Cummings & B. M. Staw (Eds), *Research in organizational behavior,* (Vol. 11, pp. 43–104). Greenwich, CT: JAI Press.
Vetlesen, A. J., & Nortvedt, P. (1996). *Følelser og moral.* Oslo: AdNotam Gyldendal.
Von Krogh, G. (1998). Care in knowledge creation. *California Management Review, 40*(3), 133–153.
Weick, K. E. (1995). *Sensemaking in organizations.* Thousand Oaks, CA: Sage.
Weick, K. E., & Roberts, K. H. (1996). Collective mind in organizations: Heedful interrelating on flight decks. In: M. D. Cohen & L. S. Sproull (Eds), *Organizational learning* (pp. 330–358). London: Sage.
Weick, K. E., & Westley, F. (1996). Organizational learning: Affirming an oxymoron. In: S. R. Clegg, C. Hardy & W. R. Nord (Eds), *Handbook of organization studies* (pp. 440–458). Thousand Oaks, CA: Sage.
Wittgenstein, L. (1953). *Filosofiske undersökningar.* Stockholm: Basil Blackwell Ltd.
Wray-Bliss, E. (2001). Representing customer service: Telephones and Texts. In: A. Sturdy, I. Grugulis & H. Willmott (Eds), *Customer service: Empowerment and entrapment* (pp. 38–59). London: Palgrave.
Wrzesniewski, A., & Dutton, J. (2001). Crafting a job: Revisioning employees as active crafters of their work. *Academy of Management Review, 26,* 179–201.

APPENDIX: AN OVERVIEW OF THE HOTELS

Table A1. Key Aspects Characterizing the Four Hotels Chosen.

	Arctic	Business	C&C (Creative&Cosy)	Diversity
Size (full-time positions) about	13	20	11	26
Location	Rural small village	City	City	Rural small village
Main markets	All three	Individual business travelers	Individual business travelers and small conferences	All three
Rooms and beds (approximately)	65/125 plus summer hotel (70/140)	75/110	50/93 plus summer hotel expansions planned	80/180 (not all traditional hotel rooms)
Facilities	Breakfast buffet, bar facilities (in the reception), meeting rooms/smaller conferences (max. 150). Restaurant (outsourced but in the building as if it is part of the hotel)	Breakfast buffet, waffles and free simple supper. Bar facilities (in the reception). Refreshment room, meeting rooms (small conferences). Activities for guests	Breakfast buffet, waffles and free simple supper. Bar facilities (in the reception). Simple refreshment room, meeting rooms (small conferences about 60). Lunch/dinner only for closed conferences (parties)	Full service hotel (conference hall, meeting rooms, café, restaurant(s), bar, disco, refreshment room). Different overnight facilities/rooms

	Primary owner is also CEO	Employed CEO	Employed CEO (offered a small share percent, the primary owner is the board manager and he helps with operative tasks)	Employed CEO combined with an active main owner/board manager (also involved in operative decisions)
CEO/daily top management				
Field organizing	Locally owned, voluntary membership in national chain	Chain member and owned by chain	Locally owned and run (no chain membership)	Locally owned and run (no chain membership)
Middle/team management (TL) and staff-functions	TLs for receptionists and for cleaner's section. The former is also conference host; the latter is also housekeeper and cleaner. A marketing/sales person	TLs for receptionists and for cleaning staff. The former is also conference host and key person on marketing/sales. The latter also cleaner and housekeeper	A marketing/sales person. The conference host also completes clerk tasks, purchasing, and functions as the TL for receptionists, cleaners and waiters. Some TL tasks done by informal leaders in the operative section	TLs in each section. The TL for receptionists works nearly full time in reception, besides also being the conference host and sales/marketing person. TL for cleaners, cleans almost full time and does housekeeper tasks

CHAPTER 6

EMOTIONAL AFFECTS – DEVELOPING UNDERSTANDING OF HEALTHCARE ORGANISATION

Annabelle Mark

ABSTRACT

This paper looks at the current portrayal of emotion in healthcare as delivered within formal organisational settings, notably the UK National Health Service (NHS). Its purpose is to set out some examples of the problems and suggest new ways of conceptualising issues that will assist healthcare organisations in gaining a better understanding of the role of emotion and its impact, using appropriate examples. Developing understanding of the location of emotion and its differing constructions indicates that interdisciplinary and interpersonal boundaries differentiate interpretations of emotion, often for instrumental purpose as examples drawn particularly from the Public Inquiry into Paediatric Cardiology at Bristol Royal Infirmary (The Kennedy Report) demonstrate. The privileging of rationality over emotion as part of the dominant paradigm within the healthcare domain is shown to affect outcomes. However, the boundaries between organisations and individuals are changing, so are the location, access, technologies and timing of activities, and these are reconstructing healthcare organisation and the patient's experience of

Individual and Organizational Perspectives on Emotion Management and Display
Research on Emotion in Organizations, Volume 2, 145–166
ISSN: 1746-9791/doi:10.1016/S1746-9791(06)02006-2

healthcare at both rational and emotional levels. It is suggested that in healthcare it is the patients' journey through their lives (the macro context), as well as their individual encounters with the system at different times of need (the micro context), that iteratively constitute the construction of the emotional terrain. The conclusions drawn could have wider implications for the development of emotional understanding, across organisations that are subject to similar changes.

INTRODUCTION

The organisation of healthcare provides a unique context in which to explore the role of emotion, which is often referred to, in this domain, as affect. Affect combines the roles of both feelings that are taken to be individual internal experiences and emotions that are generated through interactions and relationships between individuals, groups and organisations. What follows is an attempt to consider this context, what is unique to it and what it shares with other organisations.

Developments in knowledge around emotion and the individual within the wider cultural, scientific and social and managerial contexts are the subject of contemporary study (Evans, 2001; Massey, 2002; Oatley & Jenkins, 1996). The need to explore the emotional challenge found in organisations is moving to the forefront of concern (Ashkanasy & Daus, 2002; Fineman, 1993, 2000; Gabriel, 1999; Hassard, Holliday, & Willmott, 2000; Obholzer & Roberts, 1994; Payne & Cooper, 2001; Rafaeli & Sutton, 1989); healthcare too is now attempting to identify its application to individuals, the workforce and organisations more generally (Hinshelwood & Skogstad, 2000; Mark, 2000; Styhre et al., 2002).

Although the terrain of healthcare has always dealt with the consequences of emotion or affect, for example, in the doctor–patient relationship (Balint, 2000; Heath, 2003), it is not seen as part of the explicit activity of the organisation. However, the use of the metaphor of narrative (Czarniawska, 1997; Greenhalgh & Hurwitz, 1999), in the delivery of care, is a notable exception, showing as it does that "Emotion words and emotion talk are key ingredients" (Fineman, 2003, p. 16). These narratives rest on both social and cultural expectations constructed through roles and scripts that are understood through appropriate language and its interpretation. Such attempts to understand these relationships began with Titchener's (1909) work on empathy as a way of describing how it is possible to "feel ones way into" the experience of another. This work has continued notably through the insights of the psychologist Carl Rogers (1975) in the development of the therapeutic relationship. In relation to medical care, Reik (1949) describes empathy as a process of two phases in the clinical encounter with patients; the first of which we recognise as the "merging relationship" but the second involving the highly cognitive process of subsequent detachment to neutralise this emotional encounter. Halpern (2001) has more recently confirmed these two aspects of empathy within clinical encounters but emphasised that it starts with the more risky emotion-guided activity of imagination. Utilising this information in ways that develop greater understanding within the health domain can also improve patient outcomes (Blasi & Ernst, 2001). This also confirms the assumptions behind Weiss and Cropanzano's (1996) seminal work on affective events theory (AET) that links the impact of affective events in the workplace to positive and negative organisational outcomes. This may have wider implications for professions, health organisations and other organisations that deal with the person as a product.

Emotions – Individual and Organisational

A growth in understanding of the emotional challenges that are posed by new ways of working and new processes of healthcare, are becoming essential (Scherer, 2001). Emotion is often recognised by the meaning it gives to actions and thoughts and is usually divided into two groups that are described as primary and secondary emotions. Primary (Kempner, 1987) or basic emotions, can be distinguished by their clinical and physical manifestations and are multicultural (Ekman, 1992). Secondary or higher emotions (Evans, 2001) are often basic emotions modified into a cultural context, or combinations of basic emotions in a response to these differing contexts.

In general, the study of emotions is concentrated largely on the individual (Lupton, 1998); this is in part due to the concentration of effort in identifying the location and purpose physiologically, and the domination of the personal over the social in the field of psychology. Scientific study has also been dominated by a concern for the individual, and rather less concern to the relationships between individuals and groups and their context within organisations. Such an approach has influenced the direction of many other fields (Summers-Effler, 2002), and much less is known about the dynamics of emotion within the organisation, except perhaps within the study of the culture and climate of organisations (Cartright, Cooper, & Earley, 2001).

The need to develop understanding in an organisational context must now consider the interplay between emotions and the impact they have. For example, it has been suggested that the interplay between the expression and management of emotion may mask the need for cultural change (Callahan, 2002) in organisations. This negative impact, through this control over emotions, also highlights the differing views of rational and emotional responses and their acceptability in organisational life. Furthermore it draws attention to the research emphasis placed so far on expressed emotion, rather than those that are hidden. Yet such emotional containment is a significant factor in the stress and burnout experienced by individuals (Grandey, 2000).

Organisational Narratives

The role of emotion is embedded within the organisational narratives, an example of this in healthcare is the use of the term 'operating theatre' expressing the dramatic nature of the activities, and the roles played by those involved. Role-playing as part of this dramaturgy (Downing, 1997), is also at the heart of the relationship between patients and professionals, as identified by Goffman (1959). More recent work by Hochschild (Hochschild, 1983) has given us the concept of emotional labour, which involves the act of expressing organisationally desired emotions (Morris & Feldman, 1996), including role-play with emotions to achieve professional and organisational goals. This management of emotions for a wage (Grandey, 2000) also incorporates the notion of what are termed 'surface' and 'deep' acting. Surface acting requires the regulation of emotional expression; for example, the doctor does not express views about a patient's injuries and how they may have been acquired. Whereas in deep acting, feelings are consciously modified in order to convincingly express the desired emotion; for example, the nurse who shows sympathy for patients while on duty but can switch off when the shift is finished. Both are strategies with a twofold purpose: to maximise patient confidence and co-operation, and minimise staff stress. Role-play is thus a critical activity of healthcare provision but is also crucially derived from the 'display' (Goffman, 1959) or 'feeling' (Hochschild, 1983) rules for the organisation as a whole. Such strategies may have other purposes, such as a political or cultural component; however, for the purpose of immediate and observable interactions, the role and purpose of surface and deep acting has provided a useful insight into what is happening, particularly for nurses (Smith & Gray, 2001). Problems, however, can occur when there is confusion or a lack of clarity about what constitutes the 'display' or 'feeling' rules of the organisation. This will interfere with the construction and maintenance of role identity (Larson & Yao, 2004). This confusion is further aggravated when there are frequent organisational changes, which have increasingly been a feature of the UK healthcare environment (Webster, 2002). The NHS, which has existed since 1948, is subject to government intervention, and the organisations that make up the NHS have, in recent years, been distinguished only by their instability (Mark, 2003). More importantly, the emergence of these new rules becomes critical to the continuation of successful relationships, because as communication theory suggests, emotion is constructed on-line as part of the developing relationship emerging from a real-time encounter between people (Parkinson, 1995). These must be contrasted with individual feelings, which are subjective internal experiences, and may or may not be on display during these encounters, depending on whether surface or deep acting is in play.

EXPERIENCES FROM THE UK NHS

The attention given to the effect on the individual of changing roles or jobs within healthcare is more significant than the attention given so far to the organisation as a whole and the part it plays in encapsulating and transmitting rules, especially during times of change. However, the effect on both individual and organisational outcomes is a reflection of both the emotional and aesthetic identity constructions of the organisation (Hatch & Schultz, 2002); the health of these health organisations is determined by the congruence between the way the organisation is viewed externally and internally. Where this differs significantly, problems arise. The most notable recent example of this from the UK NHS is the public inquiry into children's heart surgery at the Bristol Royal Infirmary (Kennedy, 2001). This notorious case arose because of the alarming number of children who died when admitted for cardiac treatment, and the questions that arose about the failure of the organisation both locally and nationally to take action to prevent these inappropriate and inept clinical interventions. The situation described in the report also demonstrates the catastrophic results that occur when the congruence between internal experiences and external realities are ignored.

The failure to make congruent the links between internal experiences and external realities thus suggests that affect and effect must be more instrumentally linked across boundaries and groups. The history of the NHS, however, does seem to show that a lack of attention to such important links has indeed presented problems that could well be repeated in the continuing rapid changes to role and organisational boundaries. The need to develop emotional collectivity rests upon a need for joint commitment (Gilbert, 2002) and separates the issue from one of purely physiological derivation.

Indeed, such shared experiences are the access points to organisational knowledge and sense-making (Snowden, 2002). They look at the history of both action and emotional efforts (Reddy, 2001), and such an approach aids a more general need to reincorporate or re-balance the mind and heart in bureaucratic organisations (Rogers, 2001).

Historical Evidence

Historically, emotion was at the heart of the organisational narratives that describe the development of UK healthcare after the Second World War (Beveridge, 1942). It had less to do with economic considerations than the political belief that removing the fear of ill health and infirmity was the mark of a civilised society. Self interest was best served by a shared community interest in the provision of healthcare. Like many such visions, a rational justification had to be found, and this appeared through the development of economic analysis at both national and international levels (Rivett, 1998). This constant and explicit resort to economic and scientific rationality then displaced the role that emotion played in both the political justification for and subsequent delivery of healthcare. Such neglect, it is now suggested, may not only increase the potential workload in healthcare (Stewart Brown, 1998) but also ignores the original purpose of the NHS, which was to reduce fear and increase happiness through better health. In spite of this, the purpose of emotion and healthcare organisations remains very much the same, as both in their different ways provide protection and fulfilment for individuals and communities; this relationship is therefore important. The problem however is that in research terms this importance has been hindered by the methodological imperatives inherent to the practice of healthcare (Baker & Kirk, 1998) and its organisation (Mark & Dopson, 1999). This has excluded and often derided the role that emotion plays in researcher and researched (Hubbard, Backett, & Kemmer, 2001).

A more recent acknowledgement of the need to learn (Expert Group on Learning from Adverse Events in the NHS, 2000) from past mistakes has focussed attention on a more systematic approach to such problems. These methods and approaches, while appealing to both the medical and managerial communities, continue to miss the messier dynamic of emotion that is central to an understanding of such failures. Parents of the children who died in the tragedy surrounding the provision of paediatric cardiology in Bristol (Kennedy, 2001) were distressed not only by the events themselves but also how these events were being justified by the organisations and professionals concerned, who seemed disconnected from the emotional consequences. This disengagement with the emotional consequences of action in healthcare can be contrasted with the utilisation of emotion to deceive as practiced by Dr Harold Shipman; this was the general practitioner (GP) convicted at about the same time as the Bristol Inquiry, of the mass murder over time of many hundreds of his patients. In contrast to the lack of emotional engagement in Bristol, it was the very deception of Shipman's emotional role-play as a caring doctor that facilitated his actions (Kaplan, 2000). So understanding both the use and abuse of emotion, as well as its absence, as part of the emotional labour process (Larson & Yao, 2004) can be important in determining what is going on.

Emotions thus play a role in the most negative as well as the most positive activities and therefore an approach to healthcare based on a rational systems approach alone, although necessary, is not sufficient to the task ahead (Vince, 2001). This was summed up in Bristol with the statement, "we can no longer overlook those elements of the service that go beyond technical skills and competence and beyond the systems in which they are practised" (Kennedy, 2001, p. 258).

Further barriers to progress relate to the continued analysis of emotions through the cognitivist approach (Carr, 2002). For example, the focus taken by much of the emotional intelligence literature which rests on the idea of managing one's self and one's relationship to others through the key components of empathy, self awareness, self regulation, motivation and social skills (Goleman, 1996). This approach assumes that knowing alone will resolve the issues, without accounting for how identity and moral diversity implicitly influence this emotional landscape. An example of this is the different cultural responses or secondary emotions that manifest in the delivery of effective healthcare to different ethnic groups (Consedine & Magai, 2002).

Conceptualising the Relationships

What the history of the NHS as an organisation highlights, is a failure to connect the organisation to the unique task it performs within society, and the emotional as well as rational consequences of this. Perhaps, this is because there is some confusion about what that task is, or should be in the future; meanwhile, patients continue to feel disempowered by the system as currently provided (Department of Health, 2000). Understanding these connections, at both rational and emotional levels, will be critical to the future success of the organisation, as well as the people it serves.

The patients' journey is a way of conceptualising these issues (Kennedy, 2001), but it is argued here, must not be confined alone to specific encounters with the health system. Patient experience exists within a context of lifetime as well as individual encounters with health providers.

Both aspects must be at the core of the UK government policy objective of putting the patient at the centre of policy. Scientific advances in both medicine and the wider organisation of healthcare are predicated on the assumption of improving both. What is argued here is that the development of these dual strategies is also currently responsible for the loss of some of the intervening relationships essential to success, damaging both current and future utilisation of the system. Developments in telemedicine and telecare are examples of this, as their use has led to a reduction in the role of the senses and emotions in the provision and organisation of care (Mark & Shepherd, 2001). However, the anonymity of this new environment is beneficial for some patients who might not otherwise use the system, and is one of the benefits of what Fineman describes as virtual emotions (Fineman, 2003) now operating in organisations.

Healthcare in the UK at the beginning of the 21st century is comparable to much of the rest of the world, no longer just about meeting needs but also about the new boundaries between the provision of health and the improvement of lifestyle for individuals and communities. Identifying where these boundaries are and how the health budget should be allocated between products and treatments that provide for both is a key challenge. Much of the discussion around them is also emotionally based, so rational solutions alone will no longer suffice in providing answers. However, history and current practice within healthcare continue to pursue the empirical view that self-evident propositions are the basis of all knowledge (Locke, 1690). Its current manifestation in evidence-based medicine (EBM) (Gray, 1996) reiterates a focus on the external world and not the world of feeling and emotion, and in this way it fails to account for other aspects of the clinical role (Larson & Yao, 2004). Challenges to this view are increasing as EBM is revealed as more social construction than scientific fact (Fitzgerald, Ferlie, Wood, & Hawkins, 1999), however, the focus of this challenge, while identifying the problems, may not have grasped why EBM is a necessary but insufficient response.

It is not a question of either rationality or emotion for patient care or organisational arrangements, but rather a need to understand these distinctive worlds of meaning and experience that constitute the practice of medicine (Good, 1994), and how they influence each other in a 21st century organisational context. This will enable a better understanding of health organisation, costs and outcomes (Blasi & Ernst, 2001; Taylor-Gooby, 1998) to be found as, for example, in the relationship between the development of good human resource management policies and positive patient outcomes (West et al., 2002). Inherent within all these aspects is the notion of trust, that is itself a feeling or emotion (Lahno, 2002) through which vulnerability is revealed (Korczynski, 2000). As such trust is at the heart of healthcare where the patient is vulnerable to both the interpersonal and organisational context in which they are placed. As Lahno (2002) suggests, if we want to promote trustful interactions we must first form our institutions in ways that allow individuals to experience their interests and values as shared, and this has been notably lacking in some instances (Kennedy, 2001). Health, however, is not alone in marginalising emotion, for example, business ethics privileges reason over emotion as the source of moral action (Bos & Wilmott, 2001) providing further justification for the managerial adoption of this limited perspective (Learmonth, 1999) within healthcare organisations. The success or failure of an intervention or innovation, either medical or managerial, is therefore being marred by a lack of appropriate attention to the barriers that exist at both sensory and emotional levels (Fiol & O'Connor, 2002), making both individual and organisational processes dysfunctional and outcomes less reliable.

TWO CONTEXTS

Looking at the effect of emotion requires two perspectives of the patients' journey, experienced as both an emotional as well as a rational process. These perspectives are the journey through life or the macro context for patients; each encounter with healthcare provision will affect their responses to future encounters. Additionally, the micro context that is each individual journey through the system in times of need, is experienced according to influences from the macro context. Both are being restructured by new organisations and technologies, for example, in the UK the micro context of the technologically guided conversation of NHS Direct, which is the evidence-based decision support software system, that now allows individuals to access help and information about health 24 hours, seven days a week in the UK. What this also represents is a more general move in society away from relationships to encounters (Gutek, 1997) where trust is substituted by risk-sensitive technology, and different emotional responses are required (Mark & Shepherd, 2001). It is justified as a method for both managing demand in a low risk context (Mark & Elliott, 1997), and for providing appropriate care to meet patient needs. In its more developed settings (Mark & Shepherd, 2001), the patient accesses both advice and out of hours doctors by telephoning NHS Direct. Within this system, however, much sorting into priorities is undertaken in the interests of patients' needs and risks; yet, little explanation is given to patients who are waiting for this telephone response to their needs. Much of the response depends on the aural clues picked up by professionals through the telephone conversation with patients, because of the absence of other sensory information. The intervening waiting period, which can start with electronic queues to get through, means the patients must be patient when even beginning their journey; and may be difficult to manage when fear and anxiety are integral to much health-seeking behaviour in the first place. This can lead to frustration (at this micro patient encounter) and a failure to use the system when next required as part of the patients' macro journey. This can result in reducing demand for NHS Direct, but perhaps for the wrong reasons, especially if this results in increased demand in other areas, for example, accident and emergency services. These technological barriers are somewhat ameliorated by the role of the nurse in interpreting both the emotional and social contexts for the patients (Mark & Shepherd, 2001), where fear and frustration can also reduce or interfere with the information that needs to be provided (Grudin, 2001).

Professional barriers are also predicated on emotion, as it is often the emotional distancing developed by some staff as part of both the process of developing empathy (Halpern, 2001) and the use of the emotional labour process (Larson & Yao, 2004), which compounds anxiety. This is confirmed in evidence from the public inquiry in Bristol "The [medical] profession are removed from the needs of the users on an emotional level and because of the very difficult job they do, communication often only stays at a clinical level" (Kennedy, 2001, p. 292). This can precipitate a crisis of trust in both the individuals and their organisations, especially when the instrumental use of emotion is increasingly understood by patients in their daily lives (Mestrovic, 1997). This crisis of trust can result in a culture of aggression and violence, for example, in accident and emergency departments, unless the patient's perspective is more appropriately understood and managed (Garnham, 2001) by the organisation as much as by the individual professionals involved.

Such micro patient journeys, when they falter, also damage the trust between the patient citizen and the healthcare system, and influence the patient's macro context for the future. Trust is the feeling at the heart of healthcare, yet evidence from contemporary alternative practice (Kaptchuk, 2002) suggests that the distances being created between doctors and their patients, through a lack of attention to emotion, are dysfunctional in enabling recovery. Increasing this attention will indeed improve the quality of provision (Davidoff, 2002; Larson & Yao, 2004). This will also be important to the changing shape of the macro journey as it is interpreted through new clinical specialities, such as psychoneuroimmunology (PNI), which acknowledge the links between the rational and emotional worlds (Kiecolt-Glaser, 2002). The developments in genetics will also increasingly influence the macro context of the healthcare journey providing patients with both rational and emotional choices not previously encountered. The patient may have no outward signs or symptoms and therefore has to accept the doctor's word on trust that a problem will occur in an unspecified future. This scenario implies a higher reliance on the emotions and more particularly the emotional intelligence of clinicians, who may already suffer from emotional exhaustion caused by stress, much of which is generated by organisational rather than individual activities (Mayor, 2002).

The focus on emotional intelligence together with emotional labour in influencing healthcare is still largely concerned with only the interactions between individuals from the professionals' perspective, rather than a wider organisational context as postulated by affective events theory (AET). Indeed, some colonisation of the two currently dominant aspects of emotion has also taken place; the medical and managerial perspectives look to emotional intelligence, while nurses have largely colonised the emotional labour discourse with its concern to change outcomes through an understanding of context (feeling rules) and role-play (surface and deep acting) and their influence on interactions.

Dealing with the doctors' own emotional competence may be relatively new to medical training, but lessons can perhaps be learned from medicine's own methods of dealing with patients' fear, through the use of, for example, a placebo (Evans, 2003). The use, or in the case of placebo, perhaps abuse, of trust as part of what is the emotional labour process has its own cost to the professions involved. These include stress and burnout (Mayor, 2002) and may even be implied in more serious disorders of personality (Phillips et al., 2001). Such pressures not only affect staff but also simultaneously increase the risks to the patient. This is because where decision-making is under pressure, emotions dominate (Gordon & Arian, 2001; LeDoux, 1998), thus bringing primary emotions into play. This marginalizes, and sometimes obliterates rationality, thus destabilizing the process and interplay between these two key areas.

Two Approaches

New approaches to the effect of emotion need to be understood and enacted within organisations. The first is to make more explicit the role that emotion plays in the delivery of healthcare by staff to patients within professional training and development (Larson & Yao, 2004), including as Larson and Yao suggest rewards for being empathetic. The second is the significance of emotion at different points in the patient's journey. Conceptualising these in the context of the macro and micro journeys requires something more than a two-dimensional medium can easily express, because the impacts of these factors on each other are multidimensional, variable and complex (Snowden, 2002).

Current deficits in awareness of role-play by all professionals will need to incorporate a greater explanation and awareness of the "backstage" (Goffman, 1959) activity where roles are prepared and relinquished, the role sometimes clothing emotion or alternatively the emotion being generated through the role-play. An example of this is the contrast between the routine nature of work for the clinical professionals, and the alarm sometimes experienced by those who witness it as lay observers. Expectations and outcomes sought between patients and healthcare professionals differ, as a review of the problem of what are termed "heartsink" patients in UK General Practice suggests (Butler & Evans, 1999). These patients, in seeking attention and support through the presentation of problems, produce the opposite response from their doctors so that the whole encounter becomes emotionally counterproductive for both parties, even though the superficial encounter is located within a biomedical framework. Differentiating and separating the two experiences overlooks the essential link between the two, as the report of the Public Inquiry in Bristol points out, "Medical practice is essentially an intellectual pursuit. Being ill is a highly emotional experience" (Kennedy, 2001, p.281).

Clinical Training

The clinician's primary concern is directed at defining the problem and the effects of treatment: has it made the patient better; while the patient's first concern is that they should feel better. The bridge between such disparity is the trust of the patient, and the assumption that the professional will seek to move these disparate points closer together (Tudor, 1996). Where this fails to happen, because training of the professional has been inadequate, outcomes can be compromised; for example, patient compliance with treatment may be jeopardised. Where such trust is damaged alternative ways of managing the future for organisations are often sought via some form of monitoring or control, recently encapsulated within a systems approach in healthcare (Berwick, 1996). However, such approaches fail to account for the fact that the essence of the problem often lies outside such devices. If trust is to be regained, what is required is not just a way of dealing with an unknowable future, but furthermore a demonstration that the organisation can help to deal with the emotional detritus of the past experience. This is confirmed in the organisational response at Bristol Royal Infirmary where parents found that "once their child had died, the hospital ceased to behave as if it had any other responsibilities by way of care" (Kennedy, 2001, p. 223), which led the Inquiry to conclude "we were struck by a strong theme that emerged consistently from parents' evidence in Phase One: that they felt abandoned, both in the hospital and later, after the discharge, or the death of their child (Kennedy, 2001, p. 294).

The Macro Journey

The example from Bristol links into the second strategy that is more complex for healthcare to engage with, and relates to the macro journey of patients. Significant encounters with healthcare, among other things, influence future expectations and behaviour as the cognitive theorists suggest (Frijda, 1988), where physical reactions based on past experience dominate. A first step in understanding this can be made by looking at the significance given to emotion at different stages of the journey: identifying which emotions are important, how they can be identified, where they appear, why they appear, how they are dealt with, and what can be done to ensure that this process of developing these multiple perspectives is embedded as an aspect of this complex organisational activity. Such activities are, however, context dependent and cannot be transferred across from one organisation to another, although the process employed may be transferable. In healthcare, innovation in the approach to professional learning and development may facilitate this. An example is provided at the new Peninsula Medical School based in South West England, where the education of students is for the first time in UK medicine based on the patient lifecycle, starting training with prenatal work and proceeding through the lifecycle of individuals. This approach has been implemented in an attempt to encourage a more holistic perspective by doctors towards patients, assisting the identification of patients as individuals.

Organisational Context

In a wider context, the structural and cultural changes in the organisation of healthcare in the UK during the 1980s and 1990s, led by politicians moved away from a public service ethic towards a more commercial internal market for healthcare. This effectively cast aside attempts to provide a caring organisational context, and set up emotive dissonance (Hochschild, 1983) for many of those giving and receiving healthcare. This dissonance, or mismatch, between what is experienced and what is desired and expected, is the emotional impact of redrawing the political map of healthcare policy without considering the emotional and behavioural consequences. Such changes have also affected the macro context of the patient's journey, so the checking of expectation (Tudor, 1998) is now a key issue at each new encounter between patient, professional and the organisation.

The need to understand the interplay between emotional states, as manifested physically and psychologically, and emotional action is also important in understanding lay perceptions of health, but the transition process remains unclear between both the individual and the organisations involved. For example, what makes people worry enough to seek advice, then get angry when there is a delay in receiving it, as the previous example in the use of NHS direct has demonstrated? Some of this will be learnt behaviour as described by the social constructionist's approach, some will be based on physical responses and the use of past experience to understand the present, as in the cognitive theory approach, but much will depend on the individual attitude to risk. This has so far been a neglected area of study in relation to emotion; especially if, as Lupton suggests, risky behaviour increases in response to the intensification of control and predictability of modern life (Lupton, 1999). All these responses involve the interplay between rational and emotional processes. Sorting these factors is complicated because the patient and organisational perspectives have also been disrupted by some corruption of emotions as a signalling device (Mestrovic, 1997) across society in general. This understanding of the utilisation of emotions for instrumental purposes that takes place within the wider society is carried by the patient between the external world and the health system. The consequences of this can contribute to the breakdown of trust between the public and those seeking to persuade and influence them (Beck, 1992).

The mistake for the health system has been adopting general managerial methods for healthcare organisations, without really thinking through their interpretations and consequences either at an emotional level within the organisation, or at the interface with patients. The culture of blame that has dominated the managerial domain for so long in the UK (Mark & Scott, 1991) became apparent with the arrival of managerialism, based as it is on control. This engendered a climate of fear for many who were used to the consensual service ethic that had underpinned the NHS since 1948, and the results often seemed negative for those both working in and using the system. Current attempts to change this are predicated once again on the need to change aspects of medical culture (Roland, Campbell, & Wilkin, 2001). Meanwhile the managerial domain remains locked in such behaviours often for very instrumental reasons based on fear (Faugier, 2002) as the study by Faugier, of managerial failure to listen to concerns about abuse of patients, reveals. Further areas of concern that have also influenced the way healthcare organisations must now respond are the international and scientific context of healthcare – the former changing expectations for provision, and the latter changing expectations for intervention. Fear, as well as a desire for happiness and fulfilment, drives both types of expectation. These emotions are simultaneously utilised to advantage by commerce and by professional groups in promoting their own agendas. Healthcare organisations in comparison may find it more difficult to use emotion to promote what are, by their very nature, more mixed agendas, often involving patients in shared decisions. These decisions could result in negative outcomes unless handled with emotional sensitivity, because as the Public Inquiry in Bristol found, it "calls for the ability to convey uncertainty without fearing that it will appear weak" (Kennedy, 2001, p. 326). These issues also require an increased acceptance of risk and uncertainty, if we are to avoid a population divided only between the chronically ill and the worried well (Brashers, 2001).

FUTURE PERSPECTIVES

New perspectives that look at the differing primary and secondary emotions vested simultaneously by and within the organisation, those working in it and those using it, must now match the emphasis on the individual. Ignoring emotions or marginalizing their relevance, given the feelings of patients, may add to alienation if it separates emotion and action and redefines the latter in only rational terms. Rationality does appeal to management, the scientific community of the NHS and the fiscal interests of the taxpayer, as it provides what are seen as independent justifications for action or inaction. In addition the fear generated by increasing and often unpredictable changes to the organisation now threatens the NHS through the emotional dysfunction of many of its key players (Williams, Michie, & Pattani, 1998). The emotional health of the organisation is jeopardized. Yet patients start from the implicit assumption (Hatch & Schultz, 2002) of a state of well-being in organisations providing care. This is the basis of the trust relationship essential to their participation through their own bodies in the delivery of healthcare. These issues require effective emotionally intelligent leadership from both the clinical and managerial domains (George, 2000; Goleman, McKee, & Boyatzis, 2002) if such participation is to continue in a more uncertain future. A future where, for example, diagnosis through the use of genetic information is separated over both time and space, disconnecting the emotional impact from the decision process involved in treatment.

Barriers that exist to these changes in the culture of healthcare are therefore now being joined by changing roles within and between all participants in the healthcare process. The organisation itself will need to reflect these changes, and the cultural and technological changes that accompany them (Scherer, 2001). Where emotion is accepted as a driving force of the organisation, as the Bristol Public Inquiry says it must be, "The quality of healthcare can only meet levels of which the NHS can be proud, if healthcare first encompasses the notions of respect for and honesty towards patients. It must recognise the emotional as well as the physical needs of patients" (Kennedy, 2001, p. 258). Thus these positive advantages can increases motivation, improve understanding, enrich job performance, reduce stress and enhance relationships. Whereas ignoring it will increase stress (Styhre et al., 2002) and reduce the quality and quantity of acceptable patient outcomes. Furthermore, the integration of rationality and emotion also involves acceptance of the idea that knowledge based on reason is also implicitly valued in the organisation for its emotional role, as essential to the maintenance of trust between patient and professional. Reason is, in this context, the third party agent used as a justifiable tool to persuade both organisations and individual patients to set aside potentially negative emotional responses such as fear, in order to allow extraordinary interventions to occur.

Neglecting the emotional impact may place even the rational elements of this process in jeopardy if it is seen as just a matter of defence against criticism. The capacity to manage emotion positively is developed implicitly through the socialisation processes and the informal organisation, and awareness of the impact of these needs to become commonplace among those working within it. A greater ability to understand and characterise emotion explicitly within organisations will also have ethical and legal benefits, as Kennedy suggested "the way forward lies in a review by an expert group of the entire system of clinical negligence litigation, with clear terms of reference to consider alternatives to the current arrangements. The review must also address needs arising from harm, both financial and emotional, and how they should be compensated" (Kennedy, 2001, p. 44).

The wider social context of healthcare in society is one where peer group (Mestrovic, 1997), rather than political or organisational control, is paramount; organisational structures are more transitory and there is increasing cynicism (Fineman, 1997) about the manipulation of emotion to serve organisational purposes. Professional peer groups are located through professional (Dent, 1998) rather than an organisational identity, so attempts by the organisation to challenge these professional role boundaries (Department of Health, 2000) may be doomed except in times of workforce shortages. This is because the strategies to protect these groups will be largely external. Peer groups are based on a fundamental emotional need to belong as a result of what Maslow (Maslow, 1954) termed our affiliation needs. Peer groups are therefore relatively impervious to organisational attempts to control them. Likewise attempts to manage emotions for organisational purposes are not paramount, as the focus of the organisation is its impact on the patient. The paradox being, as Rafaeli and Worline (2001) point out, that as emotion is more and more organisationally managed, the less it will feel truly emotional.

CONCLUSIONS

Emotion is a dynamic but fundamental process for both the organisation and the individual; its explicit incorporation is now essential to the future success of healthcare. In more general terms what is revealed in considering aspects of healthcare organisation in this example from the UK, is the need to consider the interplay between the individual and the organisation in emotional terms, and how that is shaped and reshaped by experiences. It also involves understanding how this forms part of the organisational knowledge as it interacts with task and context, and how failure to understand this will marr both organisational change and innovation. However, the definition and location of emotion and the differing constructions of it in healthcare, indicates that interdisciplinary and interpersonal boundaries differentiate interpretations of emotion, often for instrumental purpose; as the Public Inquiry at Bristol found. "The cardiac surgeons took the view that the development of the medical service, was a better use of resources than meeting the emotional and psychological needs of families" (Kennedy, 2001, p. 221).

These perceptions so far have rested upon the explicit privileging of rationality over emotion as part of the dominant paradigm. In spite of this, a number of emerging issues are altering these differing perspectives, for example, the boundaries between organisations and individuals are changing, and so are the location, access, technologies and timing of activities, and these are reconstructing healthcare. Patients' journeys through their lives (the macro context), as well as their individual encounters with the system at different times of need (the micro context), can constitute the construction of the emotional terrain that will enhance the ability of the organisation to respond appropriately. Approaching this at an organisational level requires developing awareness for individuals and organisations, developing multiple perspectives and understanding the limits to transferability of people, ideas and processes. The conclusions drawn within healthcare will have wider implications for the development of emotional understanding, across organisations subject to similar changes, especially perhaps those where an individual rather than an object is viewed as the product or outcome of the organisation's purpose. Therefore, the hope implicit in the policy purpose of putting the patient at the centre of healthcare, will be achieved only when the emotional and sensory journeys that run in parallel are incorporated into developments in both healthcare provision and its organisation.

REFERENCES

Ashkanasy, N. M., & Daus, C. S. (2002). Emotion in the workplace: The new challenge for managers. *Academy of Management Executive, 16*, 76–87.

Baker, M., & Kirk, S. (1998). *Research and development for the NHS.* Oxford: Radcliffe Medical Press.

Balint, J. (2000). *The doctor, his patient and the illness.* Chichester: Churchill Livingstone.

Beck, U. (1992). *Risk society: Towards a new modernity.* London: Sage.

Berwick, D. M. (1996). A primer on leading the improvement of systems. *British Medical Journal, 312*, 619–622.

Beveridge, W. C. A. (1942). *Great Britain parliament interdisciplinary committee on social insurance and allied services.* London: HMSO.

Blasi, Z. D., & Ernst, E. (2001). Influence of context effects on health outcomes: A systematic review. *Lancet, 357*, 757–762.

Bos, R., & Wilmott, H. (2001). Towards a post-dualist business ethics: Interweaving reason and emotion in working life. *Journal of Management Studies, 38*, 769–793.

Brashers, D. E. (2001). Communication and uncertainty management. *Journal of Communication, 51*, 477–497.

Butler, C. C., & Evans, M. (1999). The 'heartsink' patient revisited. The Welsh philosophy and general practice discussion group. *British Journal of General Practice, 49*, 230–233.

Callahan, J. L. (2002). Masking the need for cultural change: The effects of emotion structuration. *Organization Studies, 23*, 281–299.

Carr, D. (2002). Feelings in moral conflict and the hazards of emotional intelligence. *Ethical Theory and Moral Practice, 5*, 3–22.

Cartright, C., Cooper, C., & Earley, C. (2001). *Handbook of organizational culture (and climate).* Chichester: Wiley.

Consedine, N. S., & Magai, C. (2002). The unchartered waters of emotion: Ethnicity, trait emotion and emotion expression in older adults. *Journal of Cross Cultural Gerontology, 17*, 71–100.

Czarniawska, B. (1997). A four times told tale: Combining narrative and scientific knowledge in organization studies. *Organization, 4*(1), 7–30.

Davidoff, F. (2002). Shame: The elephant in the room. *British Medical Journal, 324,* 623–624.

Dent, M. (1998). Hospitals and new ways of organising medical work in Europe: Standardisation of medicine in the public sector and the future of medical autonomy. In: P. Thompson & C. Warhurst (Eds), *Workplaces of the future* (pp. 204–224). Basingstoke: Macmillan Business.

Department of Health. (2000). *The NHS Plan – a plan for investment a plan for reform.* London: HMSO.

Downing, S. J. (1997). Learning the plot: Emotional momentum in search of dramatic logic. *Management Learning, 28,* 27–44.

Ekman, P. (1992). An argument for basic emotions. *Cognition and Emotion, 6,* 169–200.

Evans, D. (2001). *Emotion – the science of sentiment.* Oxford: Oxford University Press.

Evans, D. (2003). *Placebo: The belief effect.* London: Harper Collins.

Expert Group on Learning from Adverse Events in the NHS. (2000). *An organization with a memory.* London: Stationery Office.

Faugier, J. W. H. (2002). Valuing 'voices from below'. *Journal of Nursing Management, 10,* 315–320.

Fineman, S. (1993). *Emotion in Organizations.* London: Sage.

Fineman, S. (1997). Emotion and management learning. *Management Learning, 28,* 13–26.

Fineman, S. (2000). *Emotion in Organizations (2nd ed.).* London: Sage.

Fineman, S. (2003). *Understanding emotion at work.* London: Sage.

Fiol, C. M., & O'Connor, E. J. (2002). When hot and cold collide in radical change processes: Lessons from community development. *Organization Science, 13,* 532–547.

Fitzgerald, L., Ferlie, E., Wood, M., & Hawkins, C. (1999). Evidence into practice? An exploratory analysis of the interpretation of evidence. In: S. Dopson & A. L. Mark (Eds), *Organizational behavior in health care – the research agenda* (pp. 189–206). Basingstoke, UK: Macmillan.

Frijda, N. H. (1988). The laws of emotion. *American Psychologist, 43,* 349–358.

Gabriel, Y. (1999). *Organizations in depth: The psychoanalysis of organizations.* London: Sage.

Garnham, P. (2001). Understanding and dealing with anger, aggression and violence. *Nursing Standard, 16,* 37–42.

George, J. M. (2000). Emotions and leadership: The role of emotional intelligence. *Human Relations, 53,* 1027–1056.

Gilbert, M. (2002). Collective guilt and collective guilt feelings. *The Journal of Ethics, 6,* 115–143.

Goffman, E. (1959). *The presentation of self in everyday life.* New York: Overlook Press.

Goleman, D. (1996). *Emotional intelligence.* London: Bloomsbury.

Goleman, D., McKee, A., & Boyatzis, R. E. (2002). *Primal leadership: Realizing the power of emotional intelligence.* Harvard: Harvard Business School Press.

Good, B. J. (1994). *Medicine, rationality and experience – an anthropological perspective.* Cambridge, UK: Cambridge University Press.

Gordon, C., & Arian, A. (2001). Threat and decision making. *Journal of Conflict Resolution, 45,* 196–215.

Grandey, A. A. (2000). Emotional regulation in the workplace: A new way to conceptualize emotional labor. *Journal of Occupational Health Psychology, 5,* 95–110.

Gray, J. A. M. (1996). *Evidence based healthcare.* Chichester: Churchill Livingstone.

Greenhalgh, T., & Hurwitz, B. (1999). Narrative based medicine. *British Medical Journal, 318,* 48–50.

Grudin, J. (2001). Desituating action: Digital representation of context. *Human Computer Interactions, 16,* 269–282.

Gutek, B. (1997). Dyadic Interactions in Organizations. In: C. Cooper & S. Jackson (Eds), *Creating tomorrow's organizations – a handbook for future research in organizational behavior* (pp. 139–156). Chichester: Wiley.

Halpern, J. (2001). *From detached concern to empathy: Humanizing medical practice.* Oxford, UK: Oxford University Press.

Hassard, J., Holliday, R., & Willmott, H. (2000). *Body and organization.* London: Sage.

Hatch, M. J., & Schultz, M. (2002). The dynamics of organizational identity. *Human Relations, 55,* 989–1012.

Heath, C. (2003). Demonstrative suffering: The gestural (re)embodiment of symptoms. *Journal of Communication, 52,* 597–617.

Hinshelwood, R. D., & Skogstad, W. (2000). *Observing organizations: Anxiety, defence and culture in health care.* London: Routledge, an imprint of Taylor & Francis Books Ltd.

Hochschild, A. R. (1983). *The managed heart: Commercialisation of human feeling.* Berkeley: University of California Press.

Hubbard, G., Backett,, M. K., & Kemmer, D. (2001). Working with emotion: Issues for the researcher in fieldwork and teamwork. *International Journal of Research Methodology Theory and Practice, 4,* 119–138.

Kaplan, R. (2000). Murder by medical malice – the love-hate relationship between Dr Harold Shipman and his patients. *South African Medical Journal, 90,* 98–560.

Kaptchuk, T. J. (2002). The placebo effect in alternative medicine: Can the performance of a healing ritual have clinical significance. *Annals of Internal Medicine, 136,* 817–825.

Kempner, T. (1987). How many emotions are there? Wedding the social and autonomic components. *American Journal of Sociology, 93,* 263–289.

Kennedy, I. (2001). *Learning from Bristol: The report of the public inquiry into children's heart surgery at the Bristol Royal Infirmary 1984–95.* Norwich: The Stationery Office, CM5207 (1).

Kiecolt-Glaser, J. K. (2002). Emotions, morbidity and mortality: New perspectives from pscyhoneuroimmunology. *Annual Review of Psychology, 53,* 83–107.

Korczynski, M. (2000). The political economy of trust. *Journal of Management Studies, 37,* 1–21.

Lahno, B. (2002). On the emotional character of trust. *Ethical Theory and Moral Practice, 4,* 171–189.

Larson, E. B., & Yao, X. (2004). Empathy through emotional labour: An exploration of physicians identity as healers. 64th Annual Meeting of the American Academy of Management, New Orleans.

Learmonth, M. (1999). The national health service: Manager, engineer or father? A deconstruction. *Journal of Management Studies, 36,* 999–1012.

LeDoux, J. (1998). *The emotional brain.* London: Weidenfeld & Nicolson.

Locke, J. (1690). *An essay concerning human understanding.* Oxford: Oxford University Press.

Lupton, D. (1998). *The emotional self.* London: Sage.

Lupton, D. (1999). *Risk.* New York: Routledge.

Mark, A., & Elliott, R. (1997). Demarketing dysfunctional demand in the UK NHS. *International Journal of Health Planning and Management, 12,* 297–314.

Mark, A., & Scott, H. (1991). Changing Cultures – determining domaines in the NHS. *Health Services Management Research, 4*, 193–205.

Mark, A. L. (2000). Colouring the kaleidoscope – emotion in healthcare organization, 1–40. London, Nuffield Trust. Maureen Dixon Essay Series.

Mark, A. L. (2003). *Trust me I'm not a doctor*. London: Middlesex University Business School Occasional Paper Series.

Mark, A. L., & Dopson, S. (Eds) (1999). *Organizational behavior in health care – the research agenda*. Basingstoke: Macmillan Business.

Mark, A. L., & Shepherd, I. D. H. (2001). *"Don't shoot the messenger" – an evaluation of the transition from HARMONI to NHS Direct in West London*. London: Middlesex University.

Maslow, A. H. (1954). *Motivation and personality*. New York: Harper Row.

Massey, D. S. (2002). A brief history of human society: The origin and role of emotion in social life. *American Sociological Review, 67*, 1–29.

Mayor, S. (2002). Emotional exhaustion and stress in doctors are linked. *British Medical Journal, 324*, 1475.

Mestrovic, S. G. (1997). *Postemotional society*. London: Sage.

Morris, J. A., & Feldman, D. C. (1996). The dimensions, antecedents and consequences of emotional labor. *Academy of Management Review, 21*, 986–1010.

Oatley, K., & Jenkins, J. M. (1996). *Understanding emotions*. Oxford: Blackwell.

Obholzer, A., & Roberts, V. Z. (1994). *The unconscious at work: Individual and organizational stress in the human services*. London: Routledge, an imprint of Taylor & Francis Books Ltd.

Parkinson, B. (1995). *Ideas and realities of emotion*. London: Routledge.

Payne, R. L., & Cooper, C. L. (2001). *Emotions at work, theory, research and applications for management*. Chichester: Wiley.

Phillips, M. L., Medford, N., Senior, C., Bullmore, E. T., Suckling, J., Brammer, M. J., Sierra, M., Williams, S. C. R., & David, A. S. (2001). Depersonalisation disorder: Thinking without feeling. *Psychiatry Research: Neuroimaging, 108*, 154–160.

Rafaeli, A., & Sutton, R. I. (1989). The expression of emotion in organizational life. *Research in Organizational Behavior, 11*, 42.

Rafaeli, A., & Worline, M. (2001). Individual emotion in work organizations. *Social Science Information, 40*, 95–124.

Reddy, W. M. (2001). The logic of action: Indeterminacy, emotion and historical narrative. *History and Theory, 40*, 10–33.

Reik, T. (1949). *Listening with the third ear*. New York: Farrer Straus.

Rivett, G. (1998). *From cradle to grave – fifty years of the NHS*. London: Kings Fund.

Rogers, A. M. (2001). Nurture, bureaucracy and re-balancing the mind and heart. *Journal of Social Work Practice, 15*, 181–192.

Rogers, C. (1975). Empathetic: An unappreciated way of being. *The Counselling Psychologist, 2*, 10.

Roland, M., Campbell, S., & Wilkin, D. (2001). Clinical governance: A convincing strategy for quality improvement. *Journal of Management in Medicine, 15*, 188–201.

Scherer, K. R. (2001). Emotional experience is subject to social and technological change: Extrapolating to the future. *Social Science Information, 40*, 125–152.

Smith, P., & Gray, B. (2001). Emotional labour of nursing revisited: Caring and learning 2000. *Nurse Education in Practice, 1*, 42–49.

Snowden, D. (2002). Complex acts of knowing: Paradox and descriptive self awareness. *Journal of Knowledge Management, 6*, 100–110.

Stewart Brown, S. (1998). Emotional well being and its relation to health. *British Medical Journal, 317*, 1608–1609.

Styhre, A., Ingelgard, A., Beausang, P., Castenfors, M., Mulec, K., & Roth, J. (2002). Emotional management and stress: Managing ambiguities. *Organization Studies, 23*, 83–104.

Summers-Effler, E. (2002). The micro potential for social change: Emotion, consciousness and social movement formation. *Sociological Theory, 20*, 41–60.

Taylor-Gooby, P. (1998). *Choice and public policy – the limits to welfare markets.* Basingstoke, UK: Macmillan.

Titchener, E. (1909). *Experimental psychology of the thought processes.* New York: Macmillan.

Tudor, H. J. (1996). Caring effects. *Lancet, 347*, 1606–1608.

Tudor, H. J. (1998). Expectations of health care: Promoted, managed or shared. *Health Expectations, 1*, 3–13.

Vince, R. (2001). Power and emotion in organizational learning. *Human Relations, 54*, 1325–1351.

Webster, C. (2002). *The NHS a political history.* Oxford: Oxford University Press.

Weiss, H. M., & Cropanzano, R. (1996). Affective events theory: A theoretical discussion of the structure, causes and consequences of affective experiences at work. *Research in Organizational Behavior, 18*, 1–74.

West, M. A., Borrill, C. S., Dawson, J. F., Scully, J., Carter, M., & Anelay, S. (2002). The link between the management of employees and patient mortality in acute hospitals. *International Journal of Human Resource Management, 12*, 1299–1310.

Williams, S., Michie, S., & Pattani, S. (1998). *Improving the health of the NHS workforce: Report of the partnership on the health of the NHS workforce.* London, UK: Nuffield Trust.

CHAPTER 7

CULTURAL DIFFERENCES IN EMOTIONAL LABOR IN FLIGHT ATTENDANTS

Céleste M. Brotheridge and Ian Taylor

ABSTRACT

This study examines cross-cultural differences in the emotional labor performed by flight attendants working in a multi-cultural setting. There appears to be cultural variations in how workers perform emotional labor, notably in the extent to which they engage in deep acting and hide their feelings, but not in the extent to which they fake their emotional displays. The results generally suggest that collectivism, both vertical and horizontal, is associated with deep acting.

INTRODUCTION

There has been a growing interest in the study of emotions in the workplace (Bono & Vey, 2004; Briner, 1999; Lord & Kanfer, 2002; Zapf, 2002). In particular, an increasing number of studies have examined the antecedents and consequences of performing emotional labor (e.g., Brotheridge & Grandey, 2002). When employees perform emotional labor in workplace interactions, they attempt to regulate their emotional display so that they

Individual and Organizational Perspectives on Emotion Management and Display
Research on Emotion in Organizations, Volume 2, 167–191
Copyright © 2006 by Elsevier Ltd.
All rights of reproduction in any form reserved
ISSN: 1746-9791/doi:10.1016/S1746-9791(06)02007-4

are "expressing socially desirable emotions" (Ashforth & Humphrey, 1993, pp. 88, 89). Emotional labor can be accomplished by performing either surface or deep acting (Brotheridge & Lee, 2002, 2003). Surface acting involves displaying the required emotions without actually feeling them and is performed by suppressing or hiding one's personal feelings and by creating a "fake" display of emotions. Deep acting, on the other hand, involves attempting to align felt and displayed emotions by trying to feel particular emotions, for example, by psyching oneself up.

Individuals tend to behave in conformity with display rules, defined as norms for emotional expression and suppression, which may be derived from cultural, vocational, personal, and situational sources (Ekman & Friesen, 1975). Existing studies have examined vocational, personal, and situational sources of variations in the performance of emotional labor. Vocational display rules reflect expectations concerning the expression of emotions by individuals in particular occupations (Brotheridge & Grandey, 2002; Jones & Best, 1995). For example, Tracy and Tracy's (1998) 911 emergency center operators would be expected to manage their emotions in a manner that is quite distinct from Sutton's (1991) bill collectors or Yelland's (1995) nurses. Whereas personal sources of variations in emotional labor reflect personality constructs (Brotheridge, in press; Tews & Glomb, 2003), situational sources include factors such as the intensity, duration, and variety of emotions that need to be displayed in particular situations (Morris & Feldman, 1996; Tan, Foo, Chong, & Ng, 2003).

There appears to be a dearth of published studies that have examined emotions in the workplace from a cultural perspective (Earley & Francis, 2002), or the potential for cultural differences to influence how emotional labor is performed (Fisher & Ashkanasy, 2000). Emotional labor has been examined solely in within-culture studies, an approach that presupposes that study results are transferable across cultures and, thus, performing emotional labor is invariant across cultures. However, as argued by Boyacigiller and Alder (1991), and Trompenaars and Hampden-Turner (1998), the assumption that research undertaken in a single culture automatically applies to other cultures may be erroneous. This is particularly likely, given the cultural specificity of much emotional phenomena (Matsumoto, 1993).

The present exploratory study examines cross-cultural differences in the emotional labor performed by flight attendants working in a multi-cultural setting. Hypotheses are developed based on four approaches to understanding cultural variation (see Figure 1). The first perspective posits that the nature of the emotional regulation involved in performing emotional labor is invariant across cultures. According to the second approach, emotional

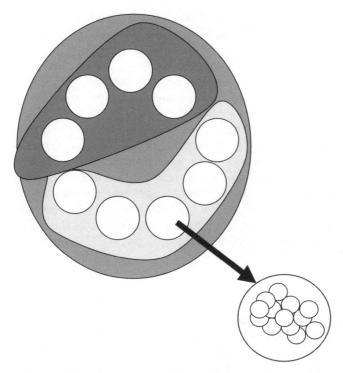

Fig. 1. Approaches to Understanding Cultural Differences. *Note:* Large Circle –
No Cultural Differences. Small Circles within the Large Circle – Country-Specific
Differences. Groupings of Small Circles – Differences Based on Hofstede's Classi-
fication. Multiple Circles within each Small Circle – Individual Differences.

labor is performed in a manner that is unique to each individual country. A
third approach employs Hofstede's framework to place countries into two
groups, individualistic or collectivist, and examines differences in emotional
labor that can be expected between these two groups. The final perspective
emphasizes the need to consider individual differences in values that may or
may not reflect the broader cultural identity or nationality of an individual.

PERSPECTIVES ON CULTURAL DIFFERENCES IN EMOTIONAL PHENOMENA

The literature that addresses cultural differences in emotions has been
dominated by two complementary theories regarding the universality of

emotional phenomena (Oatley, 1993). Universalists such as Darwin (1872) considered the experience and expression of emotions to be biologically inherited; i.e., part of an innate, prewired emotion program, and invariant across cultures. In contrast, cultural relativists argued that factors in the environment influence emotional expression (Piderit, 1925, cited in Izard, 1980) and, as such, culture-specific patterns and variations are likely to be present in emotional phenomena. Advocates of the latter perspective explained the presence of weak or inconsistent findings in attempts to find consistencies in emotional phenomena as the result of culturally learned display rules that cause individuals to adapt their emotional expressions to particular social circumstances (i.e., emotions are socially constructed; Ekman & Friesen, 1971; Oatley, 1993). Current evidence provides support for both positions depending on the facet of emotional experience and expression being examined. The following discussion examines this literature in an attempt to develop hypotheses regarding cultural differences in the performance of emotional labor.

The Universal Perspective

Existing research has found that several aspects of emotional phenomena are universally experienced (Ekman & Davidson, 1994). For example, in his study with Croatian, Gujarati, Chinese, and Japanese participants, Russell (1983) found that they employed a similar circular structure ordering for emotion words. Further support for the universality of emotion lexicons was found in the existence of consistent patterns of emotion categories across a range of languages in a dictionary study (Hupka, Lenton, & Hutchison, 1999) and in a study of emotion words used by subjects from 11 countries (Belgium, France, Switzerland, Italy, Netherlands, England, Canada, Indonesia, Japan, Surinam, and Turkey) (Frijda, Markam, Sato, & Wiers, 1995). Furthermore, research evidence indicates that individuals from a wide variety of cultures agree on the nature of the emotions portrayed in faces (Ekman & Friesen, 1971; Matsumoto, Wallbott, & Schere, 1989) and express emotions in a similar way (Ekman & Friesen, 1971). For example, Ekman (1972) found that, upon viewing films that evoked various emotions, Japanese and American subjects employed the same facial expressions for sadness, disgust, and fear.

The six basic emotions – happiness, surprise, fear, sadness, anger, and disgust – tend to be both universally expressed and recognized (see Fridlund, Ekman, & Oster's (1987) literature review), possibly because they form an integral component of human potential (Mesquita, Frijda, & Scherer, 1997).

In their study of university students located in Europe, the Middle East, the Far East, South America, and North America, Wallbott and Scherer (1988) found that most of the variance in participants' control of emotional reactions was due to the specific emotion itself rather than participants' nationality. They concluded that, "The extreme view that emotional expression and emotional experience are primarily determined by social and cultural factors would seem difficult to maintain in the face of these data" (Wallbott & Scherer, 1988, p. 55). Thus, according to proponents of the universal perspective, the national culture of workers is unlikely to influence the manner in which they regulate their emotions.

H1 (null hypothesis). No cultural variations exist in how workers perform emotional labor.

The Culture-Specific Perspective

Cultural relativists have argued that cultures socialize their members to adopt unique emotional programs (Birdwhistell, 1970) based on display rules, "norms regarding the expected management of facial appearance" (Ekman, 1973, p. 176). These are unique to a particular culture (Gudykunst & Ting-Toomey, 1988); prescribe the emotions to be expressed in particular contexts and the extent to which certain emotions should be suppressed versus expressed (Ekman & Friesen, 1975; Ratner, 2001); and are "followed by all (nonrebellious) members of a given social class, subculture, or culture" (Ekman & Friesen, 1975, p. 138). According to this perspective, workers from different cultures are likely to follow their cultures' unique display rules in regulating their emotions in the workplace. Support for this view is provided by research that indicates that socialization and social learning pertaining to emotional expression and experience begin very early in life, with its effects noticeable even in infants (Camras, Oster, Campos, Miyake, & Bradshaw, 1992).

Research that has examined cultural differences in emotional phenomena has conceptualized the notion of culture in several different ways. Traditionally, culture has been equated with one's nationality (Matsumoto, 1991), and, as a result, comparisons were made based on respondents' country-of-origin (i.e., between country comparisons). This "common and well-accepted approach to cross-cultural research on emotion ... [implies] that individuals comprising a sample from a country are relatively homogeneous with respect to each other, but relatively heterogeneous with respect to the individuals comprising a sample from another country" (Matsumoto, 1993, pp. 108, 109). Many researchers have employed Hofstede's (1991) classification of countries based on their level of individualism and collectivism to examine cultural differences in emotions. A recently developed approach examines the relationship between emotions and differences in cultural values held by individuals (Triandis & Gelfand, 1998). The following discussion examines cultural differences from each of these perspectives.

Culture as Country

Researchers have found variations across countries in a variety of emotional phenomena such as the appraisal of emotional events (Mesquita, 2001), the elicitation of emotions in interpersonal transactions (Stipek, 1998), and the frequency, intensity, and duration with which various emotions are experienced (Kitayama, Markus, & Kurokawa, 2000; Scherer, Wallbott, Matsumoto, & Kudoh, 1988; Wallbott & Scherer, 1988).

There is also support for the existence of country-based differences in emotional vocabularies (Oatley, 1993); for example, the number of words used to refer to emotions (Howell, 1981; Johnson-Laird & Oatley, 1989) and the extent to which one emotion is emphasized over another (Marsella, 1980; Nance, 1975).

A stream of research examining emotional phenomena has found that, in comparison with American subjects, Japanese subjects tended to mask their negative emotions to a much greater extent, especially in the presence of others. Ekman and Friesen (1971) found that, whereas American subjects continued to display negative emotions in response to a film, Japanese subjects masked their negative feelings with smiles in the presence of a researcher. In other research, in comparison with American subjects, Japanese subjects rated the intensity of emotions that they observed in pictures as being much lower (Matsumoto & Ekman, 1989). Also, American students tended to experience emotions, especially fear and anger, for longer durations than their counterparts in Japan and Europe (Scherer et al., 1988). This research found that Japanese students were more likely to verbalize joy, and Americans were more likely to report the experience of intense emotions, whether positive (joy) or negative (anger). Thus, it appears that the Japanese students were less expressive overall relative to the American students, and that negative emotions were more likely to be subject to control than positive emotions. This is consistent with research evidence that Japanese people tend to control their emotional reactions to situations (Ekman, 1973). Researchers have argued that these results can be explained by cultural display rules for emotional expression; i.e., "the 'inscrutable Oriental' hiding emotions between an impassive or politely smiling face, on the one hand, and the free expression, if not accentuation of emotion that seems to have become popular in at least some United States youth subcultures" (Scherer et al., 1988, p. 29).

Other research has found somewhat inconsistent results in the extent to which individuals from different countries express or hide their emotions. Research by Cosnier, Dols, and Fernandez (1986) found that individuals from Spain and Israel tended to be silent during emotional situations in contrast to those from Great Britain and West Germany who expressed their emotions. They also found that joy and anger were the least and most controlled emotions, respectively, and that the control of emotions was positively associated with the number of people involved in the social interaction. Finally, individuals from France, Great Britain, Italy, Spain, and Switzerland showed less control of verbalization than individuals from Belgium, Israel, and West Germany.

Although the foregoing suggests that there may be differences in how people from various countries experience and express emotions in a non-organizational setting, no clear patterns seem to emerge from the research. As such, no specific direction is provided in the following hypothesis:

H2. Country-specific variations exist in how workers perform emotional labor.

Culture Reflected in Groups of Individualistic and Collectivist Countries
As a result of a large-scale study of IBM employees working in over 50 countries, Hofstede (1991) identified a number of bi-polar dimensions that can be used to classify the cultural characteristics of countries. Although Hofstede's classification system has attracted criticism (McSweeney, 2002), others have argued that Hofstede's approach permits researchers to examine cultural dimensions that are theoretically useful (Matsumoto, 1991). Of the five dimensions, individualism and collectivism appear to be the most fruitful perspective from which to explore the relationship between culture and emotional labor. Oyserman, Coon, and Kemmelmeier's (2002) meta-analysis provided support for individualism and collectivism's ability to differentiate between countries and predict psychological processes such as attributional style, self-concept, and relationality. Similarly, and of particular relevance for the present study, Merritt (2000) used survey data collected from over 9,000 male international airline pilots in 19 countries to confirm the influence of national culture, and in particular individualism/collectivism, on cockpit behavior.

Members of collectivist and individualistic cultures differ in the extent to which they are group oriented and promote shared goals (Hofstede, 1991).

Group membership and affiliation in collectivist cultures serve as a major source of identity, and the focus is on duty and obligation to in-group members, thus reflecting an interdependent self (Markus & Kitayama, 1998). In individualist cultures, members emphasize their private self-identity and personal abilities and promote their own goals rather than those of society's, thus reflecting an independent self (Markus & Kitayama, 1998). This is especially evident in the self-oriented emotion terms employed by members of individualistic cultures e.g., (Dutch) versus the relationship-oriented emotion terms used by members of collectivist cultures (Semin, Gorts, Nandram, & Semin-Goossens, 2002).

However, one's emotional behavior may vary depending on the social context and, more specifically, the target of the emotions (Berry, Poortinga, Segall, & Dasen, 1992; Brewer & Kramer, 1985; Matsumoto, 1991; Messick & Mackie, 1989). Relative to people from individualistic cultures, those from collectivist cultures are more likely to attend to situational factors such as the presence of in-group and out-group members in considering their emotional behaviors (Matsumoto, 1991; Miller, 1984). Members of individualistic cultures may belong to several in-groups and, as a result, do not identify particularly strongly with any particular group. Individualistic cultures may value the open expression of emotions since this demonstrates one's separate and individual identity (Markus & Kitayama, 1994). Members of such cultures are likely to approach interactions with others in a manner that preserves their self-identity and, thus, withdraw from the relationship.

However, in self-out-group relationships (e.g., with strangers), members of individualistic cultures are more likely to suppress rather than display negative emotions because they view the interaction as one occurring between individuals and requiring harmony (Matsumoto, 1991; Triandis, Bontempo, Villareal, Asai, & Lucca, 1988). Members of collectivist cultures see less of a need to develop relationships or bonds with out-group members and, hence, will not necessarily carefully choose their displayed emotions in this context (Matsumoto, 1991). Triandis et al. (1988) found that the behavior of individuals from collectivist cultures more closely resembled that of individuals from individualistic cultures when interacting with out-group members than with in-group members.

Members of collectivist cultures may use more indirect and face-saving communication than members of individualist cultures (Triandis & Suh, 2002). The former tend to have few in-groups and tend to be highly committed to them. Since they emphasize the importance of harmony and conformity between members and in-groups, relative to members of individualistic cultures, they are more likely to expect members to display emotions in a manner that maintains this level of cohesion (Matsumoto, 1991). Members of collectivist cultures are more likely to suppress rather than display their negative emotions because they do not want to impose their emotions on others and because they find the expression of negative emotions toward in-group members to be objectionable. Collectivists may extend their identity to include customers and thus will attempt to adjust not only their self-presentation, but also their inner feelings so that they are in harmony with those expected by others. In other words, if collectivists consider customers to be part of their in-groups, they are likely to attempt to bring their inner feelings and expressed emotions into harmony. In collectivist cultures, both what is felt and expressed are culturally sanctioned and, thus, individuals with interdependent selves are more likely to "manage the expression, and even the experience, of these emotions so that they maintain, affirm, and reinforce the construal of the self as an interdependent entity" (Markus & Kitayama, 1994, p. 231). As suggested by Ashforth and Humphrey (1993, p.103), over time, complying with display rules will likely result in "an alignment between the expression of emotion and the experience of emotion." Thus, those whose identity is bound up in their roles are more likely to use deep acting. Taken together, these findings suggest the following hypothesis:

H3. Workers from collectivist cultures perform higher levels of emotional control as reflected in both surface and deep acting than those from individualist cultures.

Culture as Personally Held Values – Horizontal and Vertical Individualism and Collectivism
The previous discussion assumes that people will have certain values by virtue of their group membership; i.e., members internalize the key values of their cultures (Kitayama, 2002). This view is supported by research that identified a strong relationship between the values held by individuals and those of their cultures (see Berry et al., 1992, for a review of this literature). Others consider culture to be a loosely organized dynamic system (Kitayama, 2002) that should not be treated as the "mean value of the attributes of some aggregate of individuals" (Fiske, 2002, p. 84). Consistent with this perspective, there is research evidence that individuals from a collectivist culture describe themselves as more individualist than those from an individualist culture (Noordin, Williams, & Zimmer, 2002). Thus, despite individualism and collectivism's ability to accurately reflect the values of cultural groups, they may not necessarily characterize the individuals within these cultures (Matsumoto, 1991; Mesquita, 2001), given that individuals

may see themselves as members of a particular group but not internalize all the values associated with this group (Alvesson, 2000). If a social identity is salient, personal identity gives way to social identity, and the latter will define the self and influence behaviors (Shamir, 1991; Tajfel & Turner, 1979). In summary, we need to examine the extent to which cultural values are actually held by individuals.

Although the constructs of individualism and collectivism have been invaluable in building our understanding of cross-cultural differences in behavioral patterns, there may be differences that are not captured by these broadly defined dichotomous variables (Triandis & Gelfand, 1998). A more fine-tuned analysis is possible by considering particular attributes of these constructs that may serve to distinguish the specific nature of the collectivist values held by Korean and Japanese workers, for example. Collectivism and individualism can be further differentiated by horizontal and vertical dimensions that consider the perceived degree of similarity and equality between individuals (Triandis, 1995). Workers can hold one of four patterns of values: horizontal collectivism (HC) or individualism (HI) or vertical collectivism (VC) or individualism (VI). HC is a pattern in which individuals value equality and see themselves as being similar to each other. In contrast, people who subscribe to VC value hierarchy and see themselves as being different from each other. Although HI individuals view themselves as independent and self-reliant, they are not particularly interested in attaining a higher status than others through competition, for example, as would VI individuals (Triandis & Gelfand, 1998). Also, although both HC and VC emphasize communal sharing, in contrast to HC, VC subscribers easily submit to authority and subordinate their interests and goals for the sake of the in-group. Studies involving Korean and American students by Triandis and Gelfand (1998) found support for the convergent and discriminant validity of this four-dimensional view of culture. The foregoing suggests that:

H4. Relative to workers who hold VC, VI, and HI values, workers who value HC perform higher levels of emotional control as reflected in both surface and deep acting.

THE CURRENT STUDY

The setting for the current study is the flight attendant workforce of an international Middle East airline. The multi-cultural nature of this group of workers represents an unusual opportunity to examine the possible relationship between culture and emotional labor. The airline employs crew from 90 different nationalities who are all based at the airline's hub. As is the case for most organizations in the host country, the airline relies heavily on expatriate labor. According to the 1995 census, 75% of the host country's population were expatriate. At the time of this research, the airline employed only 46 host country nationals as cabin crew, representing about 1% of the total workforce of 3,968. The predominantly Muslim local population, language, and cultural barriers to working as a flight attendant such as serving alcohol and, for unmarried women, spending significant periods of time away from their family, exacerbate the difficulties of employing host country nationals in this role. In addition to the lack of an available local workforce, the commercial advantages of being seen as actively meeting the needs of passengers from a variety of cultures result in the airline recruiting flight attendants from a wide range of countries. Although recruiting expatriates as flight attendants is not particularly unusual in the aviation industry, the range of individuals from diverse cultures employed by this airline differentiates this organization from others. These circumstances permitted us to operationalize collectivist and individualist cultures in terms of many different countries rather than only two or three countries, as is the case in most cross-cultural research.

Working conditions also differentiate the airline from other organizations in the aviation industry. In particular, all crewmembers live in the hub city, rather than being based in their home country, and crewmembers work on all of the airline's routes rather than being utilized for language skills on specific routes only. As a result, the effects of other possible moderating or mediating variables on the relationship between culture and the performance of emotional labor, such as different working conditions, are minimized.

Finally, a single occupational grouping was selected in order to eliminate the possible effects of different levels of job-focused emotional labor (Brotheridge & Grandey, 2002). This particular occupational grouping was selected given existing research that demonstrates the high levels of emotional labor performed by flight attendants (Hochschild, 1983; Williams, 2000; Zerbe, 2000).

The flight attendant workforce in this airline is organized in a hierarchical structure. Crew members join at a level of grade 2 (G2) and work in the economy cabin before progressing to grade 1 (G1), working in business class, to first-class grade 1 (FG1), working in first class, and finally to the supervisory grades of senior flight steward(ess) (SFS), in charge of a specific cabin section, and purser in overall charge of the crew on any particular flight. The average length of tenure for flight attendants is approximately

3 years with turnover currently around 5% per annum. The workforce is predominantly female and relatively young (under 35 years of age). Since the airline is currently experiencing unprecedented growth, promotion can be rapid with new entrants becoming pursers in less than 5 years.

METHOD

Participants and Procedure

Approximately 250 questionnaires were distributed to: trainers at the cabin crew training center, ground-based cabin crew managers, crew supervisors in the preflight briefing center, and some operational supervisory crew (purser/SFS). They were asked to approach on-duty crew to complete the inventory. A total of 184 questionnaires were returned for a response rate of 73.6%. The results from 26 respondents were not included in the analyses as they either omitted key information, or were completed by participants from countries other than those defined as representing clearly individualist or collectivist cultures. Participants in this study included 158 flight attendants. Approximately 78.5% ($n = 124$) of the respondents were female; 64.6% of respondents were in the 25–30-year-old age grouping, and 65.9% had 3 or fewer years of service. Their nationality is indicated in Table 2. The study sample was broadly representative of the cabin crew population as a whole.

Measures

Data were collected using a self-report questionnaire written in the English language, given that all participants were fluent in English. Although the internal reliability estimates obtained for each of the variables were rather moderate, as argued by Hair, Anderson, Tatham, and Black (1995, p. 641), "a commonly used threshold value for acceptable reliability is 0.70, although this is not an absolute standard, and values below 0.70 have been deemed acceptable if the research is exploratory in nature."

Nationality and Cultural Values

Participants were asked to identify their personal nationality. Hofstede's (1991) individualism index and classification system (normed from 0 to 100 with a score of 100 representing a high degree of individualism) was then used to label these nationalities as representing either an individualist or collectivist culture. Whereas countries classified as having a collectivist culture were those that scored low (35 or below) on Hofstede's (1991) individualism index values (IVD), countries classified as having an individualist culture were those that scored high (60 or above) on Hofstede's IVD. "Across 40 countries, the United States, Australia, and Great Britain ranked highest on Individualism. Pakistan, Columbia, and Venezuela ranked last, indicating their strong tendency towards collectivism" (Matsumoto, 1991, p. 131).

Participants also completed Singelis, Triandis, Bhawuk, and Gelfand's (1995) measure of personally held collectivist and individualist values measured on a 5-point Likert-type scale. These included: five items measuring HI ($\alpha = .49$; sample items include: I often do my "own thing." One should live one's life independently. I enjoy being unique and different from others in many ways), seven items measuring HC ($\alpha = .64$; sample items include: My happiness depends very much upon the happiness of those around me. It is important to maintain harmony within my group. I like sharing little things with my neighbors), six items measuring VI ($\alpha = .68$; sample items include: Competition is the law of nature. Some people emphasize winning; I am one of them. It is important that I do my job better than others), and seven items measuring VC ($\alpha = .69$; sample items include: I would do what would please my family, even if I detested that activity. I usually sacrifice my self-interest for the benefit of my group. I hate to disagree with others in my group). These internal reliability estimates are generally consistent with those obtained by Singelis et al., in a homogeneous American sample. These items were subjected to two confirmatory factor analyses with Model 1 containing four factors (VI, HI, VC, and HC) and Model 2 containing two factors (individualism and collectivism). A χ^2 difference test indicated that Model 1 ($\chi^2 = 433.36$, df $= 269$, $p = 0.00$) offered a significantly better fit to the data than Model 2 ($\chi^2 = 527.67$, df $= 276$, $p = 0.00$), thus supporting the discriminant validity of Triandis's (1995) horizontal–vertical distinction. As such, the four-factor model was retained.

Emotional Labor
Participants were asked to consider how they generally feel in dealing with passengers and indicate how much they agree with the statements using a 5-point scale ($1 =$ all of the time; $5 =$ not at all). Deep acting was measured with the deep-acting subscale of Brotheridge and Lee's (1998) Emotional Labor Scale ($\alpha = .79$; items: I make an effort to actually feel the emotions that I need to display to passengers; I try to actually experience the emotions that I must show; I really try to feel the emotions I have to show as part of my job). Since Brotheridge and Lee's (1998) Emotional Labour Scale measures surface acting as a single construct, and we wanted to distinguish

between the two components of surface acting (hiding felt emotions and faking expressed emotions), we employed the relevant items from Mann's (1999) emotional labor inventory to measure surface acting. These included measures of hiding feelings ($\alpha = .62$; items: How much do you feel you hide (or try to hide) some kind of emotion from passengers? I sometimes feel positive (e.g., excited, happy, proud) because of events in my personal life or at work before dealing with passengers, but feel that I have to try to hide (or tone down) my feelings. When dealing with passengers I feel that I sometimes suppress or hide (or try to hide) positive emotions (e.g., I feel happy or excited, but try not to show it)) and faking expressed emotions ($\alpha = .55$; items: When dealing with passengers I sometimes feel that I intentionally convey (or attempt to convey) negative emotions or feelings that I do not really feel, but are appropriate at the time (I pretend to be angry, upset, dismayed, etc.). When dealing with passengers I sometimes feel a bit "fake" as if I am not really being "me." Sometimes I laugh or frown because it is expected rather than because I find something amusing or distressing). The surface-acting items were subjected to two confirmatory factor analyses with Model 1 having two factors (hiding feelings and faking emotions) and Model 2 having a single factor containing all the items. A χ^2 difference test indicated that Model 1 ($\chi^2 = 95.53$, df $= 26$, $p = 0.00$) offered a significantly better fit to the data than Model 2 ($\chi^2 = 107.02$, df $= 28$, $p = 0.00$). As a result, the two-factor model was retained.

RESULTS

Control Variables

We first examined whether or not there was a need to control for the gender of the respondent in the analyses. This step was essential, given that women have been found to be more emotionally expressive than men (Buck, Baron, & Barrette, 1982; Snell, Miller, Belk, Garcia-Falconi, & Hernandez-Sanchez, 1989; Timmers, Fischer, & Manstead, 1998). Also, other research has found that men were more likely than women to hide any feelings of hostility (McConatha, Lightner, & Deaner, 1994). One-way ANOVAs indicated that there were no significant gender differences in the mean levels of deep acting, hiding feelings, or faking emotions. As such, gender was not used as a control variable in this study. Additional ANOVAs indicated that there were no significant differences in mean levels of emotional labor across cabin crew age, tenure, or hierarchical level.

Hypothesis Testing

Mixed support was found for the hypotheses. Hypothesis 1, that no cultural variations would exist in how workers perform emotional labor, was not fully supported. As is evident in Tables 1 and 2, although there were no significant differences in the extent to which members of various cultures expressed emotions that they did not feel (i.e., "faked" emotions), there were significant differences in the extent to which they engaged in deep acting and the suppression of emotions.

Hypothesis 2, that country-specific variations exist in how workers perform emotional labor, was partially supported. A one-way analysis of variance indicated that there were significant between-country differences in the mean level of deep acting reported $(F = 1.84$ (16,141), $p = 03)$. However, Tukey post-hoc comparisons revealed no significant differences in mean levels of deep acting between pairs of countries. Finally, one-way ANOVA indicated that there were no significant between-country differences in mean levels of faking emotions and hiding feelings.

Hypothesis 3, that workers from collectivist cultures perform higher levels of emotional control as reflected in both surface and deep acting than those from individualist cultures, was not supported. Zero-order correlations indicated that, based on Hofstede's classification, membership in individualistic cultures, rather than in collectivistic cultures as expected, was associated with deep acting and hiding feelings. One-way ANOVA indicated that there were significant differences in the mean levels of deep acting reported by respondents from individualistic and collectivistic countries $(F = 13.34$ (1,156),

Table 1. Descriptive Statistics and Correlations between Emotional Labor and Cultural Values $n = 158$.

Variable	Mean	SD	1	2	3	4	5	6	7
1. Deep acting	2.65	1.04							
2. Hiding feelings	2.83	.76	.23**						
3. Faking emotions	3.06	.87	.07	.45**					
4. Horizontal collectivism	1.86	.52	.25**	.04	−.09				
5. Vertical collectivism	3.07	.77	.27**	.03	−.04	.37**			
6. Horizontal individualism	2.15	.63	−.03	.07	.07	.05	−.06		
7. Vertical individualism	3.05	.77	.05	.04	.09	.07	.24**	.16*	
8. Hofstede classification	n/a	n/a	−.28**	−.20**	.03	−.15*	−.44**	.01	−.25*

Note: Hofstede classification: $0 =$ individualistic; $1 =$ collectivist.
*$p < .05$,
**$p < .01$.

Table 2. Results from One-Way ANOVAs of Countries, Emotional Labor, and Values; Means Standard Deviations.

	N	Deep Acting	Faking Emotions	Hiding Feelings	HC	VC	HI	VI
Individualistic	96	2.89[1]	3.03	2.94[2]	1.92[3]	3.33[4]	2.15	3.21[5]
countries		1.00	0.91	0.74	0.54	0.71	0.65	0.70
Britain	32	2.95	2.98	2.91	1.88	3.39[6 7 8]	2.28	3.29
		0.90	0.95	0.63	0.58	0.55	. 0.63	0.67
Australia	29	2.48	2.84	2.98	2.00	3.24[9]	2.15	3.15
		0.91	0.81	0.73	0.50	0.73	0.72	0.58
France	5	3.40	3.10	3.00	1.94	3.34	2.40	2.97
		1.21	0.45	0.63	0.67	1.01	0.40	0.74
South Africa	15	3.27	3.47	3.11	1.92	3.10	1.96	3.31
		1.09	0.91	0.73	0.57	0.85	0.62	0.91
New Zealand	8	2.96	3.03	2.68	1.91	3.77[10 11 12 13]	1.98	3.12
		1.08	1.00	1.10	0.58	0.78	0.65	0.58
Germany	3	3.33	4.08	3.20	1.86	3.24	2.13	3.72
		1.45	0.29	1.22	0.38	0.70	0.61	0.51
Ireland	2	3.00	3.00	2.80	1.71	3.71	1.90	3.25
		0.94	1.06	0.57	0.20	0.40	0.14	0.82
Italy	2	2.50	1.75	2.40	1.71	3.57	1.70	2.00
		1.18	0.72	1.41	1.01	0.81	0.99	0.94
Collectivist	62	2.29[1]	3.09	2.64[2]	1.76[3]	2.65[4]	2.16	2.82[5]
countries		1.01	0.80	0.76	0.49	0.67	0.61	0.81
China	3	1.44	2.42	2.27	1.67	1.76[6 9 10]	2.53	2.67
		0.77	0.38	1.14	0.64	0.54	0.31	0.60
Philippines	4	2.50	3.00	2.45	1.32	3.00	2.30	3.08
		0.88	0.89	0.41	0.24	0.71	0.53	0.17
Thailand	5	2.27	3.80	3.28	1.91	2.97	2.28	3.43
		1.40	0.48	0.73	0.62	0.77	0.64	1.04
South Korea	9	2.52	2.78	2.58	1.89	2.63[11]	2.53	2.72
		0.90	0.76	0.60	0.38	0.39	0.61	0.39
Singapore	11	2.70	3.07	2.69	1.69	2.90	1.98	3.02
		1.26	1.02	0.95	0.48	0.79	0.41	0.70
Malaysia	9	2.37	3.22	2.67	1.95	2.44[7 12]	1.98	2.80
		1.02	0.75	0.51	0.40	0.81	0.50	0.87
Pakistan/	11	2.03	3.05	2.78	1.79	2.52[8 13]	2.27	2.59
Bangladesh		0.81	0.77	0.86	0.59	0.57	0.77	1.06
Kenya	5	2.27	3.40	2.48	1.77	2.66	2.16	2.87
		1.01	0.89	0.48	0.55	0.59	0.71	0.94
Indonesia	5	1.80	3.05	2.20	1.49	2.69	1.52	2.33
		0.77	0.65	0.94	0.37	0.41	0.46	0.95
Total	158	2.65	3.06	2.83	1.86	3.07	2.15	3.05
		1.04	0.87	0.76	0.50	0.77	0.63	0.77

Note: Cells with matching superscripts have significantly different mean values at $p < .05$.

$p < .001$), such that the former performed deep acting to a much greater extent than the latter. Another one-way ANOVA indicated that there were significant differences in the mean levels of hiding feelings reported by respondents from individualistic and collectivistic countries ($F = 6.18$ (1,156), $p < .01$), such that the former hid their feelings to a much greater extent than the latter. Further analyses indicated that there were no significant differences in faking emotions, given the individualistic or collectivistic classification.

Finally, Hypothesis 4, that, relative to workers who hold VC, VI, and HI values, those who value HC perform higher levels of emotional control as reflected in both surface and deep acting, was partially supported. There were significant and positive correlations between deep acting and HC ($r = .25$) and VC ($r = .27$). Deep acting was not significantly associated with either vertical or horizontal individualism. Also, neither hiding feelings, nor faking emotions were associated with any of the personally held cultural values. A one-way analysis of variance indicated that there were significant between-country differences in the mean level of VC ($F = 3.36$ (16,141), $p < .001$) and nearly significant differences in the mean level of VI ($F = 1.67$ (16,141), $p = .059$). Tukey post-hoc comparisons revealed significant differences in mean levels of VC between several pairs of countries as indicated in Table 2. One-way analyses of variance indicated that there were no significant between-country differences in HC or HI.

Post-Hoc Analysis

One-way analysis of variance indicated that there were significant differences in the mean levels of HC ($F = 3.77$ (1,156), $p = 05$), VC ($F = 37.10$ (1,156), $p < .001$), and VI ($F = 10.16$ (1,156), $p < .01$) reported by respondents from individualistic and collectivistic countries. As expected, respondents from individualist countries reported having significantly higher mean levels of VI than respondents from countries classified as collectivist. However, contrary to our expectations, they also had significantly higher mean levels of VC and HC than respondents from countries classified as collectivist.

DISCUSSION

Key Findings

The present research found mixed support for the hypothesized relationships between culture and emotional labor. There appears to be cultural variations in how workers perform emotional labor, notably deep acting and the hiding feelings dimension of surface acting, but not the faking emotions dimension of surface acting. These variations persisted regardless of the approach that was employed to measure culture. They were found in analyses that compared countries, groups of countries based on their individualism–collectivism classification, and the cultural values held by individuals. This overall result points to the need to study emotional labor in a cross-cultural context.

The values held by members of a culture appeared to be inconsistent with their particular country's individualism–collectivism classification. Respondents from individualistic countries tended to value horizontal and vertical collectivism as well as VI to a much greater extent than their counterparts from collectivist countries. As a result, the former also reported significantly higher mean levels of deep acting and hiding feelings than the latter. This is consistent with the finding that deep acting and hiding feelings are positively associated with horizontal and vertical collectivism.

In addition to demonstrating the complexities of examining the role of culture in work behaviors, these findings have several implications for future research. First, this research points to the need to avoid using a broad-brush approach in assuming that country equals culture which equals cultural values held by individuals. Rather than simply searching for between-country differences, researchers should consider individually held values as an additional reflection of culture.

These mixed results also bring into question the extent to which the collectivist and individualist construct remains a useful framework for explaining work behavior. Noordin et al. (2002) found that participants from a collectivist culture described themselves as more individualistic than those from an individualist culture. They suggested that, for example, Malaysians "are still basically collectivist in terms of their social relations, self sacrifice and family integrity but at the same time they have inculcated the elements of competition as an individualist factor at least in their working life" (Noordin et al., 2002, p. 46). Noordin et al. explained this finding in terms of the rapid economic development in Malaysia since Hofstede's initial research that linked collectivism to countries with comparatively low GDP. This would also apply to several of the collectivist countries represented in this study, particularly those that embrace Confucian values (Bond & Hofstede, 1989). These include South Korea, Singapore, and Thailand. Members of these countries and Malaysia, all relatively affluent and collectivist, accounted for over 50% of the "collectivist" sample. It appears that it was specifically in terms of VI with its emphasis on competition and inequality, rather than the autonomous self of HI, where the significant difference between the two groups emerged.

However, as argued by Kitayama (2002), it is difficult for individuals to be aware of and evaluate the features that make cultures different. For example, direct expression of preference in North America is invisible for those in that culture because it is so frequently expected and required. Additionally, what counts as independence in different groups may vary considerably. Similarly, the referent group will vary for individuals in different cultures. Individuals in collectivist cultures may describe themselves as holding strong individualist values when compared to others with collectivist values. However, we could speculate that this referent group effect (Heine, Lehman, Markus, & Kitayama, 1999) may be less prevalent in this research as the sample was drawn from a group living and working in one location with exposure to a wide range of nationalities. Various explanations can be offered for the counterintuitive result of collectivists describing themselves as holding stronger individualist values than those from individualist cultures. It may be that previously collectivist cultures are becoming more individualist with increased prosperity, or that this research sample of young people who had left their home country to work as expatriates was atypical and would hold more individualist values than others from the same country.

LIMITATIONS AND FUTURE RESEARCH

Several limitations to this research must be noted. First, although the benefits of separately considering the two components of surface acting (hiding feelings and displaying "fake" emotions) were evident, given their differential relationships with cultural variables, the measure of surface acting that was employed in this study did not perform as expected. This measure's use of fairly complex and lengthy items may have posed a difficulty for workers whose first language is not English (despite their relative fluency in English). A more reliable measure with simple items that permits the separate consideration of the two components of surface acting should be employed in future studies.

Second, other factors that influence the extent to which deep acting or surface acting is performed should be included in a future study so that the additive explanatory value of cultural factors is examined. Such factors may include, for example, employee perceptions of the frequency, duration, variety, and intensity with which they are expected to display emotions (Brotheridge & Lee, 2003), organizational display rules concerning requirements to display positive emotions and hide negative emotions (Jones & Best, 1995), and the extent to which employees identify with their organization and/or occupation. Such a study should be undertaken in a longitudinal manner so that cause–effect relationships can be established. This research would permit us to consider whether the lack of strong effects was due to the potentially distal and indirect influence of culture on individual behavior (Earley & Francis, 2002). Although the more proximal and direct influences of individual behavior, organizational culture, and job requirements were kept constant in this study, subjective perceptions of these factors may differ and, consequently, may influence the results.

Third, several writers have identified difficulties in researching cultural issues using self-report questionnaires. For example, Fiske (2002, p. 81) suggested that "there are profound cultural differences in the meaning of filling out forms ... for [the individualist] this is commonplace and boring. In some other cultures however ... the abstract, context-free questions may be confusing or meaningless." He argued that, rather than answering questions in an absolute framework, people use culturally relative frameworks to organize their experiences. The core of culture, artefacts, institutions, and relationships, including daily routines, practices, rituals, and discourses, can only rarely be translated into the verbal responses upon which rating scales rely. In addition, Semin et al. (2002) demonstrated the existence of cultural variations in how emotions are represented in language. Concrete linguistic terms such as descriptive action verbs are more likely to be used by collectivist cultures to represent emotion events. In contrast, individualist cultures use adjectives that are more abstract and that have lower contextual dependence. Self-report inventories such as the measures used in this research largely employ adjectives to describe emotions. They also use first-person statements about "what I do or believe" that are written by individualistic researchers.

Given the mixed results in this study, it may also be of value to conduct a follow-up study that qualitatively examines the behavior of flight attendants from a variety of cultures as they engage in interactions with passengers from differing cultures. This may offer an indication of the extent to which their cultural values are reflected in their behavior.

CONCLUSION

This exploratory study found that there were cross-cultural differences in the emotional labor performed by flight attendants. Those with collectivist values were more likely to engage in deep acting, a form of emotional labor that is associated with enhanced feelings of authenticity and, consequently, reduced levels of burnout (Brotheridge & Lee, 2002). In this study, the flight attendants from individualistic countries were more likely to hold collectivist values and, thus, more likely to perform deep acting. However, they were also more likely to hide their feelings, a component of surface acting that, in turn, has been associated with increased levels of burnout (Brotheridge & Lee, 2002). The foregoing suggests the need for managers to be attentive to cultural differences in the performance of emotional labor in the workplace and its attendant consequences.

REFERENCES

Alvesson, M. (2000). Social identity and the problem of loyalty in knowledge – intensive companies. *Journal of Management Studies, 378*, 1101–1123.

Ashforth, B. E., & Humphrey, R. H. (1993). Emotional labor in service roles: The influence of identity. *Academy of Management Review, 18*, 88–115.

Berry, J. W., Poortinga, Y. H., Segall, M. H., & Dasen, P. R. (1992). *Cross-cultural psychology: Research and applications*. Cambridge, UK: Cambridge University Press.

Birdwhistell, R. L. (1970). *Kinesics and context*. Philadelphia, PA: University of Pennsylvania Press.

Bond, M. H., & Hofstede, G. (1989). The cash value of Confusion values. *Human Systems Management, 8*, 195–200.

Bono, J. E., & Vey, M. A. (2004). Toward understanding emotional management at work: A quantitative review of emotional labor research. In: N. Ashkanasy & C. Härtel (Eds), *Understanding emotions in organizational behavior*. Mahwah, NJ: Erlbaum.

Boyacigiller, N. A., & Adler, N. J. (1991). The parochial dinosaur: Organizational science in a global context. *Academy of Management Journal, 16*, 262–290.

Brewer, M. B., & Kramer, R. M. (1985). The psychology of intergroup attitudes and behavior. *Annual Review of Psychology, 36*, 219–243.

Briner, R. (1999). The neglect and importance of emotion at work. *European Journal of Work and Organizational Psychology, 8*, 323–346.

Brotheridge, C. M. (in press). The role of emotional intelligence and other individual difference variables in predicting emotional labor relative to situational demands. *Psicothema*.

Brotheridge, C. M., & Grandey, A. A. (2002). Emotional labor and burnout: Comparing two perspectives of people work. *Journal of Vocational Behavior, 60*, 17–39.

Brotheridge, C. M., & Lee, R. E. (1998). On the dimensionality of emotional labor: Development and validation of the emotional labor scale. Paper presented at the first conference on emotions in organizational life, San Diego.

Brotheridge, C. M., & Lee, R. T. (2002). Testing a conservation of resources model of the dynamics of emotional labor. *Journal of Occupational Health Psychology, 7*, 57–67.

Brotheridge, C. M., & Lee, R. T. (2003). Development and validation of the emotional labor scale. *Journal of Occupational and Organizational Psychology, 76*, 365–379.

Buck, R., Baron, R., & Barette, D. (1982). The temporal organization of spontaneous nonverbal behavior in the study of emotion communication. *Journal of Personality and Social Psychology, 42*, 506–517.

Camras, L. A., Oster, H., Campos, J. J., Miyake, K., & Bradshaw, D. (1992). Japanese and American infants' responses to arm restraints. *Developmental Psychology, 28*, 578–583.

Cosnier, J., Dols, J. M. F., & Fernandez, A. J. (1986). In: K. R. Scherer, H. G. Wallbott, & A. B. Summerfield (Eds), *Experiencing emotion: A cross-cultural study* (pp. 117–128). Cambridge, UK: Cambridge University Press.

Darwin, C. (1872). *The expression of the emotions in man and animals.* London: Murray.

Earley, P. C., & Francis, C. A. (2002). International perspectives on emotion and work. In: R. G. Lord, R. J. Klimoski & R. Kanfer (Eds), *Emotions in the workplace: Understanding the structure and role of emotions in organizational behavior* (pp. 370–401). San Francisco, CA: Jossey-Bass.

Ekman, P. (1972). Universals and cultural differences in facial expressions of emotion. In: J. Cole (Ed.), *Nebraska symposium of motivation* (Vol. 19, pp. 207–283). Lincoln, NE: University of Nebraska Press.

Ekman, P. (1973). Cross-cultural studies of facial express. In: P. Ekman (Ed.), *Darwin and facial expression* (pp. 169–222). New York: Academic Press.

Ekman, P., & Davidson, R. J. (1994). *The nature of emotion: Fundamental questions.* New York: Oxford University Press.

Ekman, P., & Friesen, W. V. (1971). Constants across cultures in face and emotion. *Journal of Personality and Social Psychology, 17*, 124–129.

Ekman, P., & Friesen, W. V. (1975). *Unmasking the face: A guide to recognizing emotions from facial clues.* Englewood Cliffs, NJ: Prentice-Hall.

Fisher, C. D., & Ashkanasy, N. M. (2000). The emerging role of emotions in work life: An introduction. *Journal of Organizational Behavior, 21*, 123–129.

Fiske, A. P. (2002). Using individualism and collectivism to compare cultures – a critique of the validity and measurement of the constructs: Comment on Oyserman et al. 2000. *Psychological Bulletin, 128*, 78–88.

Fridlund, A., Ekman, P., & Oster, H. (1987). Facial expressions of emotion. In: A. Siegman & S. Feldstein (Eds), *Nonverbal behavior and communication* (pp. 143–224). Hillsdale, NJ: Erlbaum.

Frijda, N. H., Markam, S., Sato, K., & Wiers, R. (1995). Emotions and emotion words. In: J. A. Russell, J. M. Ferdandez-Dols, A. S. R. Manstead & J. C. Wellenkamp (Eds), *Everyday conceptions of emotion* (pp. 121–143). The Netherlands: Kluwer Academic Publishers.

Gudykunst, W. B., & Ting-Toomey, S. (1988). Culture and affective communication. *American Behavioral Scientist, 31*, 384–400.

Hair, J. F., Anderson, R. E., Tatham, R. L., & Black, W. C. (1995). *Multivariate data analysis with readings* (4th ed.). New York: MacMillan.

Heine, S. J., Lehman, D. R., Markus, H. R., & Kitayama, S. (1999). Is there a universal need for positive self-regard. *Psychological Review, 106*, 766–794.

Hochschild, A. R. (1983). *The managed heart: Commercialisation of human feeling.* Berkeley, CA: University of California Press.

Hofstede, G. (1991). *Cultures and organizations: Intercultural cooperation and its importance for survival.* London: HarperCollins.

Howell, S. (1981). Rules not words. In: P. Heelas & A. Lock (Eds), *Indigenous psychologies: The anthropology of the self* (pp. 133–143). London: Academic Press.

Hupka, R. B., Lenton, A. P., & Hutchison, K. A. (1999). Universal development of emotion categories in natural language. *Journal of Personality and Social Psychology, 77*, 247–278.

Izard, C. E. (1980). Cross-cultural perspectives on emotion and emotion communication. In: H. C. Triandis & W. Lonner, (Eds), *Handbook of cross-cultural psychology: Basic processes* (Vol. 3, pp. 185–220). Boston, MA: Allyn & Bacon.

Johnson-Laird, P. N., & Oatley, K. (1989). The language of emotions: An analysis of a semantic field. *Cognition and Emotion, 3*, 81–123.

Jones, R. G., & Best, R. G. (1995). A further examination of the nature and impact of emotional work requirements on individuals and organizations. Paper presented at the annual meeting of the Academy of Management, Vancouver, British Columbia.

Kitayama, S. (2002). Culture and basic psychological processes-toward a system view of culture: Comment on Oyserman et al. 2000. *Psychological Bulletin, 128*, 89–96.

Kitayama, S., Markus, H. R., & Kurokawa, M. (2000). Culture, emotion, and well-being: Good feelings in Japan and the United States. *Cognition and Emotion, 14*, 93–124.

Lord, R. G., & Kanfer, R. (2002). Emotions and organizational behavior. In: R. G. Lord, R. J. Klimoski & R. Kanfer (Eds), *Emotions in the workplace: Understanding the structure and role of emotions in organizational behavior* (pp. 5–19). San Francisco, CA: Jossey-Bass.

Mann, S. (1999). Emotions at work: To what extent are we expressing, suppressing or faking it. *European Journal of Work and Organizational Psychology, 8*, 347–369.

Markus, H. R., & Kitayama, S. (1994). The cultural construction of self and emotions: Implications for social behavior. In: S. Kitayama & H. R (Eds), *Emotion and culture? Empirical studies of mutual influence.* Washington, DC: American Psychological Association.

Markus, H. R., & Kitayama, S. (1998). The cultural psychology of personality. *Journal of Cross-Cultural Psychology, 29*, 63–87.

Marsella, A. J. (1980). Depressive disorder and experience across cultures. In: H. C. Triandis & J. Draguns (Eds), *Handbook of cross-cultural psychology* (Vol. 6, pp, 237–289). Boston, MA: Allyn & Bacon.

Matsumoto, D. (1991). Cultural influences on facial expressions of emotion. *Southern Communication Journal, 56*, 128–137.

Matsumoto, D. (1993). Ethnic differences in affect intensity, emotion judgments, display rule attitudes, and self-reported emotional expression in an American sample. *Motivation and Emotion, 17*, 107–123.

Matsumoto, D., & Ekman, P. (1989). American-Japanese cultural differences in judgments of facial expressions of emotion. *Motivation and Emotion, 13*, 143–157.

Matsumoto, D., Wallbott, H., & Schere, K. (1989). Emotions in intercultural communication. In: M. Asante & W. Gudykunst (Eds), *Handbook of intercultural and international communication* (pp. 225–246). Beverly Hills, CA: Sage.

McConatha, J. T., Lightner, E., & Deaner, S. L. (1994). Culture, age, and gender as variables in the expression of emotions. *Journal of Social Behavior and Personality, 9*, 481–488.

McSweeney, B. (2002). Hofstede's model of national cultural differences and their consequences: A triumph of faith – a failure of analysis. *Human Relations, 55*, 89–118.

Merritt, A. (2000). Culture in the cockpit-do Hofstede's dimensions replicate. *Journal of Cross-Cultural Psychology, 31*, 283–301.

Messick, D. M., & Mackie, D. M. (1989). Intergroup relations. *Annual Review of Psychology, 40*, 45–81.

Mesquita, B. (2001). Emotions in collectivist and individualist cultures. *Journal of Personality and Social Psychology, 80*, 68–74.

Mesquita, B., Frijda, N. H., & Scherer, K. R. (1997). Culture and emotion. In: J. W. Berry, P. R. Dasen & T. S. Saraswathi (Eds), *Handbook of cross-cultural psychology: Basic processes and human development* (Vol. 2, pp. 255–297). Needham Heights, MA: Allyn & Bacon.

Miller, J. G. (1984). Culture and the development of everyday social explanation. *Journal of Personality and Social Psychology, 46*, 961–978.

Morris, J. A., & Feldman, D. C. (1996). The dimensions, antecedents, and consequences of emotional labor. *Academy of Management Review, 21*, 986–1010.

Nance, J. (1975). *The gentle Tasaday*. New York: Harcourt Brace Jovanovich.

Noordin, F., Williams, T., & Zimmer, C. (2002). Career commitment in collectivist and individualist cultures: A comparative study. *International Journal of Human Resource Management, 131*, 35–54.

Oatley, K. (1993). Social construction in emotions. In: M. Lewis & J. M. Haviland (Eds), *Handbook of emotions* (pp. 341–352). New York: The Guilford Press.

Oyserman, D., Coon, H. M., & Kemmelmeier, M. (2002). Rethinking individualism and collectivism: Evaluation of theoretical assumptions and meta-analyses. *Psychological Bulletin, 128*, 3–72.

Ratner, C. (2001). Activity theory and cultural psychology. In: C. C. Moore & H. F. Matthews (Eds), *The psychology of cultural experience* (pp. 68–80). Cambridge, UK: Cambridge University Press.

Russell, J. A. (1983). Pancultural aspects of the human conceptual organization of emotions. *Journal of Personality and Social Psychology, 45*, 1281–1288.

Scherer, K. R., Wallbott, H. G., Matsumoto, D., & Kudoh, T. (1988). Emotional experience in cultural context: A comparison between Europe, Japan, and the United States. In: K. R. Scherer (Ed.), *Facets of emotion: Recent research* (pp. 5–30). Hillsdale, NJ: Lawrence Erlbaum.

Semin, G. R., Gorts, C. A., Nandram, S., & Semin-Goossens, A. (2002). Cultural perspectives on the linguistic representation of emotion and emotion events. *Cognition and Emotion, 16*, 11–28.

Shamir, B. (1991). Meaning, self and motivation in organizations. *Organization Studies, 12*, 405–424.

Singelis, T. M., Triandis, C., Bhawuk, D. P. S., & Gelfand, M. J. (1995). Horizontal and vertical dimensions of individualism–collectivism: A theoretical and measurement refinement. *Cross-Cultural Research, 29*, 240–275.

Snell, W. E., Miller, R. S., Belk, S., Garcia-Falconi, S., & Hernandez-Sanchez, J. E. (1989). Men's and women's emotional disclosures: The impact of disclosure recipient, culture, and the masculine role. *Sex Roles, 21*, 467–486.

Stipek, D. (1998). Differences between Americans and Chinese in the circumstances evoking pride, shame, and guilt. *Journal of Cross-Cultural Psychology, 29*, 616–629.

Sutton, R. I. (1991). Maintaining norms about expressed emotions: The case of bill collectors. *Administrative Science Quarterly, 36*, 245–268.

Tajfel, H., & Turner, J. (1979). An integrative theory of intergroup conflict. In: G. W. Austin & S. Worchel (Eds), *The social psychology of intergroup relations* (pp. 33–47). Monteray, CA: Brook/Coles.

Tan, H. H., Foo, M. D., Chong, C. L., & Ng, R. (2003). Situational and dispositional predictors of displays of positive emotions. *Journal of Organizational Behavior, 24*, 961–978.

Tews, M. J., & Glomb, T. M. (2003). Emotional labor and the five-factor model of personality. Paper presented at the annual meeting of the Society for Industrial and Organizational Psychology, Orlando, FL.

Timmers, M., Fischer, A., & Manstead, A. S. (1998). Gender differences in motives for regulating emotions. *Personality and Social Psychology Bulletin, 24*, 974–985.

Tracy, S. J., & Tracy, K. (1998). Emotion labor at 911: A case study and theoretical critique. *Journal of Applied Communication Research, 26*, 390–411.

Triandis, H. C. (1995). *Individualism and collectivism.* Boulder, CO: Westview.

Triandis, H. C., & Gelfand, M. J. (1998). Converging measurement of horizontal and vertical individualism and collectivism. *Journal of Personality and Social Psychology, 74*, 118–128.

Triandis, H. C., & Suh, E. M. (2002). Cultural influences on personality. *Annual Review of Psychology, 53*, 133–160.

Triandis, H. C., Botempo, R., Villareal, M. J., Asai, M., & Lucca, N. (1988). Individualism and collectivism: Cross-cultural perspectives on self-ingroup relationships. *Journal of Personality and Social Psychology, 54*, 323–338.

Trompenaars, F., & Hampden-Turner, C. (1998). *Riding the waves of culture: Understanding cultural diversity in global business* (2nd ed.). New York: McGraw-Hill.

Wallbott, H. G., & Scherer, K. R. (1988). How universal and specific is emotional experience? Evidence from 27 countries on five continents. In: K. R. Scherer (Ed.), *Facets of emotion: Recent research* (pp. 31–56). Hillsdale, NJ: Lawrence Erlbaum.

Williams, C. (2000). A pain in the neck: Passenger abuse, flight attendants and emotional labor. *Journal of Occupational Health Safety – Australia and New Zealand, 165*, 429–435.

Yelland, B. (1995). Structural constraints, emotional labor and nursing work. In: B. S. Bolaria & R. Bolaria (Eds), *Women, medicine, and health* (pp. 231–240). Halifax, NS, Canada: Fernwood Publishing.

Zapf, D. (2002). Emotion work and psychological well-being: A review of the literature and some conceptual considerations. *Human Resource Management Review, 12*, 237–268.

Zerbe, W. J. (2000). Emotional dissonance and well-being. In: N. Ashkanasay, C. Hartel & W. J. Zerbe (Eds), *Emotions in the workplace: Research and practice* (pp. 189–214). Westport, CT: Quorum Books/Greenwood.

CHAPTER 8

EMOTION WORK ACROSS CULTURES: A COMPARISON BETWEEN THE UNITED STATES AND GERMANY

Andrea Fischbach, Katrin Meyer-Gomes, Dieter Zapf and Johannes Rank

ABSTRACT

Emotion work can be defined as demands to display organizationally desired emotions regarding service-worker–customer interactions, as well as the psychological strategies necessary to regulate these emotional demands. This study applies a task-focused concept of emotion work and uses the Frankfurt Emotion Work Scales (FEWS) in a cross-cultural context to measure emotional work demands. The original German FEWS was translated into English and the extent to which the new English FEWS is equivalent to the original German FEWS is evaluated. Cultural effects on emotion work job demands are demonstrated by comparisons between a US (N = 51) and German (N = 202) travel agent sample. Cultural comparisons suggest that emotional demands in the US sales service include less emotional dissonance (i.e. the requirement to show emotions not actually felt in a situation) than in Germany. Survey results are discussed in terms of implications for further cross-cultural research.

Individual and Organizational Perspectives on Emotion Management and Display
Research on Emotion in Organizations, Volume 2, 193–217
ISSN: 1746-9791/doi:10.1016/S1746-9791(06)02008-6

INTRODUCTION: EMOTION WORK – A CROSS-CULTURAL PERSPECTIVE

The German service industry is often called a "service desert." This figure of speech is illustrated by the American Customer Satisfaction Index. In this survey customer satisfaction with service was found to be much higher in the USA than in Germany and other European countries (Fornell, Johnson, Anderson, Cha, & Bryant, 1996). US standards of service often function as models for German companies trying to overcome this unfavorable image. One of these standards results in service organizations focusing on customers' needs and wishes (Bowen & Schneider, 1988; Schneider & Bowen, 1984, 1985; Zeithaml & Bitner, 2000). In each culture there are explicit and/or implicit organizational expectations about how a service worker should interact with customers/clients (Hochschild, 1983). However, customer satisfaction surveys, such as the one mentioned above, show that these expectations might be stronger in the US than in European/German service companies. From a work-psychology perspective, emotional demands in service interactions with customers or clients are critically important. The emotional demands and psychological strategies necessary to regulate these demands are defined as *emotion work/emotional labor* (Fischbach, 2003; Zapf, 2002). An example of emotional work is when a salesperson displays friendliness and concern in order to close a sale. Even in an unpleasant service interaction with a complaining customer, the display of friendliness and concern may still be required. The requirement to display emotions not actually felt is defined as *emotional dissonance*, which from the onset of emotion work research was proposed to have negative consequences for individuals, such as physical and mental health problems (Hochschild, 1983).

Effects of emotion work on employees' well-being and satisfaction have been surveyed over the last two decades by Australian, European, Israeli, and North American research groups with corresponding samples from each region (Ashforth & Humphrey, 1993; Brotheridge & Grandey, 2002; Grandey, 2000; Hochschild, 1983; Kruml & Geddes, 2000; Morris & Feldman, 1997; Rafaeli, 1989a; Rafaeli & Sutton, 1987; Schaubroeck & Jones, 2000; Zapf, Seifert, Schmutte, Mertini, & Holz, 2001; Zerbe, 2000). How can this research be interpreted given the presence of cross-cultural differences suggested by the customer satisfaction survey example above? Are standards for positive emotional display actually higher in North American countries and lower in European countries? Do European service workers have to show emotions not actually felt (emotional dissonance) more frequently than their US colleagues? Do they suffer more as a result of this emotional dissonance?

The aim of this chapter is to examine how such questions might be answered. Beyond questions of cultural differences per se, cross-cultural research in emotion work can help integrate diverse survey results found in different cultures, leading to a deeper understanding of emotion work and its facets. This, in turn, may contribute to job design and redesign of service work.

This study uses the Frankfurt Emotion Work Scales (FEWS, Zapf, Vogt, Seifert, Mertini, & Isic, 1999; Zapf et al., 2000a, b) to study the conceptualization of emotion work (Fischbach, 2003; Zapf et al., 1999; Zapf, 2002) in a cross-cultural context. In order to answer questions about cultural differences, it is important to verify that the same conceptual framework is applied to the cultures in question. Furthermore, it is essential to determine that the instruments used to measure this conceptual framework actually measure the same thing in each culture. We will briefly describe the concept of emotion work on which this study is based, the instruments used to measure it, and general methodological issues in cross-cultural research. In this study, we evaluate cultural effects in two countries –Germany and the USA. Hypotheses will be derived based upon expected similarities and dissimilarities of service in each country. We will demonstrate the equivalence of the original German FEWS and its English translation (Meyer, 2002) –a premise for cross-cultural comparisons. Afterward, comparisons between the USA and Germany will be presented. Survey results of US travel agents ($N = 51$) and German travel agents ($N = 202$) will be discussed in terms of implications for further cross-cultural research.

EMOTION WORK AND THE FRANKFURT EMOTION WORK SCALES

In 1983, Arlie Russell Hochschild published the seminal emotion work/ emotional labor book, The Managed Heart: Commercialization of Human Feeling. Hochschild set in motion a wave of research that has resulted in a body of psychological conceptualizations of emotion work (Ashforth & Humphrey, 1993; Grandey, 2000; Morris & Feldman, 1996; Nerdinger, 1994; Zapf, 2002). The emotion-work concept used here is based on action theory (Frese & Zapf, 1994; Hacker, 2003; Zapf, 2002) and focuses on emotional tasks in service jobs. According to the behavior requirement approach of Hackman (1970), service jobs can be described in terms of behavioral demands. This connection holds regardless of whether employees actually behave according to these demands or not. Thus, behavior strategies to fulfill these job demands are clearly distinguished from the job demands that trigger them. Moreover, this concept enables researchers to relate emotional demands and employees' task-behavior strategies to consequences experienced by the service worker, service organization, and the customer. Thus, in this emotion-work concept, emotional job demands are seen as antecedents which affect strategies applied to fulfill these job demands, and result in consequences for workers, organizations, and customers (Fischbach, 2003; Zapf, 2002).

Emotional job demands can be divided into five requirements and one stressor. The five *job requirements* are the display of positive emotions, negative emotions, neutrality, sympathy, and sensitivity. The *job stressor* is emotional dissonance. The FEWS (Zapf et al., 1999, 2000a) can be used as a job analysis instrument to assess service interactions by measuring the organizational job requirements and stressor.

For the job requirements *display of positive* and *negative emotions,* separate scales were developed to accommodate the vast range of requirements to display these divergent emotions. In sales services, it is plausible that a positive display of emotions is required at all times, with no situation allowing for negative display. However, in other service–worker occupations, such as that of a preschool teacher, there is a wide variety of positive as well as negative emotion display requirements (e.g., expressing happiness toward a child who presents a nice painting, but also showing anger toward children hurting each other). The aspect of *neutrality* was added to a subsequent version of the original FEWS 3.0 based on qualitative research on job requirements in police work (Fischbach & Zapf, 2002) and is included in FEWS version 4.0 (Zapf et al., 2000a). Police officers are often required to show neither positive nor negative emotions in interactions with citizens, suspects, or witnesses. The *requirement to show sympathy* with the sorrows and problems of clients can, for example, be expected of a pediatrician – calming a hurt child in order to administer treatment. In the FEWS, *sensitivity requirements* are expected to positively correlate with the frequency with which positive and negative emotions are displayed. This is expected because the expression of an emotion during an interaction is often influenced by the emotion of the interaction partner and by the requirement to be aware of the emotions. Only in rare, short, and less intense interactions (e.g., greeting guests at a restaurant) is it unimportant to sense the emotions of the interaction partner. The job stressor, *emotional dissonance*, is present when these emotional job requirements are not actually felt. Based on *action theory* and stress research (Frese & Zapf, 1988, 1994; Zapf et al., 1999), Zapf (2002) proposed that emotional dissonance is an inherent aspect of the work role and job design, or more specifically, a job stressor leading to predictable negative consequences for the individual such as physical and mental health problems (Hochschild, 1983). Emotional dissonance occurs as a predictable work task whenever the service worker's true feelings are not in line with the feelings required to be expressed, for example when a police officer must remain neutral despite feelings of disgust and anger while interrogating a suspect about details of a brutal murder (Fischbach & Zapf, 2002).

CULTURAL DETERMINANTS OF EMOTION WORK

In this chapter, we propose that cultural variables such as display rules, organizational socialization strategies, corporate culture, and professional norms and values affect the definition of emotion work-job demands (Fischbach, 2003; Zapf, 2002).

In line with Goffman's (1959) role concept of social interaction, Hochschild (1983) used the metaphor of a drama for service-worker–customer interactions – where the work setting is seen as a stage, the customer/client is the audience, and the employee is the actor with explicit and/or implicit *display rules* governing how to interact with the customer/client (Ekman & Friesen, 1975). There is a body of literature dealing with the questions of how display rules are communicated in different corporate cultures, and how service workers are influenced by various *socialization strategies* (e.g., Ashforth & Humphrey, 1993; Hochschild, 1983; Rafaeli, 1989a, b; Rafaeli & Sutton, 1987; Van Maanen & Kunda, 1989). Sutton (1991) describes how organizations use socialization strategies such as personnel selection, training, written materials, supervisor and peer observations, and rewards and punishments to manage the emotion norms regarding interactions between bill collectors and debtors. Tsai (2001) shows that the psychological climate for service friendliness in an Asian *corporate culture* is positively related to positive emotions displayed by service workers. *Professional norms and values* are based on occupational characteristics. We propose that aspects of travel agents' work influence underlying norms and values that in turn determine which emotional display is desired and appropriate in this occupation.

A travel agent can be classified as an indirect person-related service provider (Nerdinger, 1994). The major task of travel agents is to sell travel, or more precisely, to arrange for travel consumption by customers. The service characteristics of the travel-agent occupation can be described (according to Zeithaml, 1981, citation in Nerdinger, 1994, p. 48) as both tangible and intangible. Travel quality can be evaluated by relatively objective criteria (e.g., construction noise; punctuality), and by rather subjective criteria (e.g., hotel, restaurant service). For travel agents the characteristic of inseparable service is low, as the product (travel) can be separated from product delivery. Heterogeneity of travel-agent customers can also be considered relatively low, as greater similarity in customer situations can be expected compared to other service occupations, such as teachers or medical doctors. Furthermore, the customer–service interactions can be described more in terms of encounters (Gutek, 1997) in which single, relatively short, interactions with strangers are predominant. In spite of these sales interaction realities, customer demands are often high, and travel agent–customer relationship management frequently attempts to emulate relationship characteristics of human services in order to increase sales (Gutek, 1997; Holman, 2003; Zapf, Isic, Bechtoldt, & Blau, 2003). Travel agent status relative to the customer is relatively low compared to service occupations such as teachers or medical doctors. Therefore, for travel agents there is a greater probability that customers will control the service interaction (Nerdinger, 1994; Rafaeli & Sutton, 1987).

There is no travel agent business without customers. This makes travel agents directly dependent on both customers' existence and satisfaction of their needs and wishes, which have already been described as extremely demanding. Given these characteristics, we propose that travel agents are generally expected to display mainly positive emotions – a consequence of low status and control relative to their customers (Nerdinger, 1994; Rafaeli & Sutton, 1987). "Customer is king" is the expected emotion work guideline in situations such as those of travel agents who compete for customers and collect payment only after sales are closed. Thus, it is plausible that travel agent–customer relationship management requires the expression of only positive emotions and sympathy in order to evoke trust and loyalty from the customer. Sensitivity can be expected to be part of the emotion work requirements for travel agents. It is important for travel agents to sense customers' emotional characteristics as this information assists agents in choosing appropriate sales approaches and travel suggestions leading to sales. Sensing emotional preferences of customers may also help customers commit to the agency (Nerdinger, 2001). Furthermore, we assume that negative customer events (such as impatient or complaining customers) are as likely to occur in travel agent work as in any indirect person-related occupation (Rafaeli, 1989a; Zapf, Isic, Fischbach, & Dormann, 2003). As these negative events can be intense, and may even evoke disgust and anger, it is plausible to expect a high requirement of emotional dissonance in travel agent work given the requirement for travel agents to express only positive emotions.

Cultural Similarities and Dissimilarities – USA vs. Germany

This study was conducted using a German and a US travel agent sample to examine cultural differences in emotion work requirements and the stressor – emotional dissonance. Specifically, we are interested in how these are affected by differences in display rules, socialization strategies, and corporate culture. The expression of emotions can be considered universal (Ekman & Friesen, 1975; Izard, 1971, 1980). However, cultures have different rules for displaying various emotions under different conditions, and vary significantly in their attitudes toward various emotions (Eid & Diener, 2001; Izard, 1980; Mesquita & Frijda, 1992). These differences in emotional norms can be predicted from *culture-specific value systems*. Cultural values can be defined as "shared abstract ideas about what is good, right, and desirable in a society" (Schwartz, 1999, p. 25). We propose that culture-specific value systems also affect display rules, socialization strategies, and corporate culture in the context of service work. Thus far, no study has compared the US and Germany in terms of emotion work. However, some plausible propositions can be derived from cross-cultural psychology literature and empirical findings.

In cross-cultural psychology, it is proposed that cultures are characterized by the dominance of at least five value types (Hofstede, 2001; Markus & Kitayama, 1991, 2003; Schwartz, 1999; Triandis, 1989; Triandis, Malpass, & Davidson, 1972). A strong influence on the emotion process is particularly evident for cultural differences in self-construals of independent/individualistic (e.g. USA, Germany) and interdependent/collectivistic (e.g. Japan, China) cultures (Eid & Diener, 2001; Markus & Kitayama, 1991, 2003; Triandis, 1989). However, within the individualistic cultures of the USA and Germany, differences in the emotion process can still be expected due to the countries' differences regarding other value dimensions. Based on previous findings (e.g., Argyle, 2001) and the two countries' scores on specific cultural value dimensions (Hofstede, 2001; Schwartz, 1999), differences in positive and negative emotion experiences can be hypothesized. The international happiness surveys administered by the World Values Study Group (Argyle, 2001) on about 1,000 participants in each of more than 25 countries found higher positive affect means and lower negative affect means for US respondents as compared to German respondents. Considering the cultural value taxonomy proposed by Schwartz (1999), a stronger emphasis on positive affect may be expected for Americans than for Germans, because the US is higher on the affective autonomy value (Schwartz, 1999), which reflects a cultural emphasis upon the desirability of individuals independently pursuing positive affective experience, including pleasure and excitement. Because of these differences, one may also expect that the frequency of negative emotion display requirements should be lower in the US than in Germany.

Considering Hofstede's (2001) cultural value taxonomy, the major difference between the US and Germany has been found on the uncertainty avoidance dimension (Francesco & Gold, 1998), with Germany being considerably higher on this dimension than the US. Uncertainty avoidance reflects "the extent to which the members of a culture feel threatened by uncertain or unknown situations" (Hofstede, 2001, p. 161). At least in somewhat ambiguous situations, individuals high in uncertainty avoidance may prefer to exhibit neutral behaviors to avoid acting in an inappropriate manner. Therefore, the frequency of neutrality requirements may be higher in Germany than in the US. Because individuals in high-uncertainty avoidance cultures may tend to experience negative affect if they encounter uncertain situations (Hofstede, 2001), one may also expect higher levels of negative affect in such cultures. This reasoning is further corroborated by recent findings from the GLOBE (Global Leadership and Organizational Behavior Effectiveness) study group (House, Wright, & Aditya, 1997) which found that Germany is not only particularly high on uncertainty avoidance but also comparatively low on humane orientation, a value dimension reflecting the degree of personal concern and sensitivity toward others. Low humane orientation may imply a certain indifference toward other people's emotions and may lead to lower levels of perceived responsibility for customers' affective experiences in the service encounter. Based on the empirical findings of this literature, one may expect travel agent work in the USA to place more emphasis on positive emotions, sensitivity, and sympathy requirements and less emphasis on negative emotions and neutrality than does German travel agent work.

This can also be illustrated by a study on emotion work, conducted by Rafaeli (1989a). She found that Israeli supermarket cashiers use many strategies to control demanding customers. Rafaeli speculated that this kind of control behavior would not be socially accepted in US supermarkets and is reflective of more negative Israeli service attitudes. The customer survey results presented in the introduction suggest that service attitudes in the European service sector are similar to those in the Israeli service sector. Since service quality includes quality of the interaction (e.g., SERVQUAL by Parasuraman, Zeithaml, & Berry, 1988), higher customer satisfaction in the USA than in Germany and other European countries may be partly explained by higher requirements in the US to display positive emotions and to hide negative emotions in service-worker interactions with customer/clients. Furthermore, one might expect the requirement of neutrality to be less important in USA travel agent work. Given the generally high positive emotion norm in the USA, neutrality may be seen as an undesirable or even negative response. Additionally, Germans may tend to prefer neutrality because of their greater uncertainty avoidance (Hofstede, 2001). Finally, greater emphasis on positive affect in US culture can be expected not only for service workers but also for customers. Thus, US travel agents may be exposed to less negative customer behavior than German travel agents. Due to their greater uncertainty avoidance, German customers may experience and express more negative affect and dissatisfaction because the future outcomes associated with choices between different travel options presented by travel agents can sometimes not be fully predicted. Therefore, it is plausible that emotional dissonance may be lower in US travel agent work than in German travel agent work. In the context of this study, this leads to the following hypotheses:

Hypothesis 1. The frequency of positive-emotion display requirements will be higher in the US sample than in the German sample.

Hypothesis 2. The frequency of sensitivity requirements will be higher in the US sample than in the German sample.

Hypothesis 3. The frequency of sympathy requirements will be higher in the US sample than in the German sample.

Hypothesis 4. The frequency of negative-emotion display requirements will be lower in the US sample than in the German sample.

Hypothesis 5. The frequency of neutrality requirements will be lower in the US sample than in the German sample.

Hypothesis 6. The frequency of emotional dissonance will be lower in the US sample than in the German sample.

METHOD

Cross-Cultural Research Design

Equivalence of methods is necessary for cross-cultural research (van de Vijver & Tanzer, 1997). Thus, before we can evaluate Hypotheses 1–5, we must demonstrate equivalence of the original German FEWS and the translated

English version. These two instruments are equivalent if we can show there is no construct, method, or item bias (Van de Vijver & Leung, 1997).

When translating an instrument from one language to another, it is necessary to evaluate the accuracy of the translation and demonstrate the construct validity (i.e. absence of *construct bias*) of the new instrument before using it for cross-cultural comparisons. An overview of various techniques has been presented by Hambleton (1993, 1994). On one hand it is crucial that the information collected in different cultural groups is functionally equivalent whereby the wording in the translated version should be as close as possible to the original text. On the other hand, the translation of the questions and the words used in asking these questions should appear natural for the particular setting (Pareek & Venkateswara, 1980). To make both possible, Brislin (1980) suggests using a combination of judgmental methods when translating instruments, for example, a combination of translation–backtranslation methods and committee approaches by competent bilinguals. If original and backtranslated versions are equivalent, it can be assumed that the English version accurately captures all relevant aspects of the original items. Empirically, the accuracy of translation can be evaluated by the similarity of scale reliabilities and item-total correlations in a sample of native German speakers and a sample of native English speakers (Kraemer, 1981; Van de Vijver & Leung, 1997). An additional empirical approach used here is the comparison of factor structures in each sample. Studies on the German FEWS demonstrate that emotion work is a multidimensional construct in which the emotional requirement scales are positively intercorrelated, as well as positively correlated with the job stressor emotional dissonance (Zapf et al., 1999; Zapf, 2002). An English version of the FEWS with high construct validity should reveal similar findings (Berry, 1980).

Method bias is a name for all sources of bias emanating from methodological or procedural aspects of a study. The procedure of sample recruiting, questionnaire administration, and data analysis was parallel in the German and the US survey study. While using parallel procedures prevents method bias, significant differences in means and standard deviations in demographic variables were found (see below), indicating some sample bias.

Furthermore, Van de Vijver and Leung (1997) argue that similar factor structures across cultures and the absence of method bias can only demonstrate structural equivalence. If we wish to compare scores across cultures then it is necessary to assure scalar equivalence. Scalar equivalence can be established by ruling out the presence of *item bias*. In other words, one has to demonstrate that individuals with an equal ability or attitude from different cultural groups show, apart from fluctuations by chance, the same average score on a particular item. We did find some item bias but were able to control for these while comparing scores across the German and the US survey. Procedures we used to assess scalar equivalence are described later in this chapter.

Sample

The US travel agent sample consists of $N = 51$ agents in 48 agencies (Meyer, 2002). The proportion of female subjects was considerably larger than the proportion of males (84.3% vs. 15.7%). Average age was 52 years with a range of 22–73. Work experience in the sample averaged 15 years with a range of 1–30 years. All agencies were located in California, and participation in the study was voluntary. Two hundred questionnaires were distributed and 51 were returned completed, reflecting a response rate of 20.4%.

The German travel agent sample consists of $N = 202$ German travel agents in 87 agencies (Kielhorn, 2002). Similar to the US sample, the proportion of females was considerably larger than the proportion of males (81% vs. 19%). Average age was 33 years with a range of 18–68. Work experience of the respondents averaged 10 years with a range of 0.5–42 years. Most respondents worked at agencies located in Northern Germany in cities with a population of more than 100,000 and again, participation in the study was voluntary. Of the 350 questionnaires distributed, 202 were returned completed with a response rate of 58%, substantially higher than the US response rate of 20.4%. T-tests for independent samples revealed significant differences in all of the reported demographic variables ($df_{249, 251}$; $p < 0.00$). Thus, comparisons of the German and US travel agent samples in this study are constrained by sample bias given this significant difference in response rate, sample size, and demographic variables.

MEASURES

FEWS German Version 4.0

In the German sample emotion work was measured using the FEWS German version 4.0 (Zapf et al., 2000a). For the purpose of this study, six aspects of emotion work were measured with the following six scales:

(1) *Positive emotion* – nine items measured the frequency of the requirement to display positive emotions (e.g., "How often in your job do you have to display pleasant emotions toward your clients?");

(2) *Negative emotions* – eight items measured the frequency of the requirement to display and handle negative emotions (e.g., "How often in your
job do you have to display unpleasant emotions toward your clients?");
(3) *Requirement to show neutrality* – four items measured the frequency of
the requirement to show neither positive nor negative emotions toward
clients (e.g., "How often are you required to display neither positive nor
negative emotions toward clients [i.e. showing impartiality]?");
(4) *Requirement to show sympathy* – three items measured the frequency
with which showing sympathy regarding the sorrows and problems of
clients was required (e.g., "How often do you have to express sympathy
toward clients?");
(5) *Sensitivity requirements* – four items measured the frequency of the requirement to sense the emotion of the interaction partner (e.g., "How
often is it of importance in your job to know how the clients are feeling
at a given moment?");
(6) *Emotional dissonance* – five items measured the frequency of dissonance
between felt and displayed emotions (e.g., "How often in your job do
you have to display emotions that do not agree with your true feelings?").

Each item was rated on a five-point scale ranging from very rarely/never [1]
to very often/several times an hour [5].

FEWS English Version 1.0

In the US samples emotion work was measured using the FEWS English
version 1.0 (Zapf et al., 2000b). The FEWS German version 4.0 was translated into English (Meyer, 2002), revised by a committee of bilinguals, and
altered as necessary. This preliminary English version was backtranslated
into German by two US native speakers who had been speaking German for
eight–ten years and had lived in Germany for at least two years. The comparison of the original German version with the backtranslations from the
English version revealed substantial differences in only four items. These
items were corrected based on theoretical considerations or an interview
with a native speaker to further evaluate which wording was more appropriate in the respective context. The final English version 1.0 was tested with
two US travel agents. This test did not reveal any issues pertaining to the
ability to comprehend the questionnaire. Thus it can be assumed that the
translated FEWS English version 1.0 is accurate and measures the same
content as the original version.

RESULTS

The descriptive data, correlations of all study variables, and scale properties are shown in Table 1.

Table 1. Descriptive Statistics, Correlations among Study Variables, and Scale Properties for US-American and German Travel Agent Sample.

Variable Name	Mean	SD	IC	1	2	3	4	5	6	7	8	9
1. Age (years)												
US travel agent	51.94	13.40	—	—								
German travel agent	33.47	9.81	—	—								
2. Gender (1 = female 2 = male)												
US travel agent	1.16	0.37	—	.00	—							
German travel agent	1.19	0.40	—	.23	—							
3. Work experience (years)												
US travel agent	15.25	8.24	—	.64	.03	—						
German travel agent	10.20	8.33	—	.76	.04	—						
4. Positive emotions												
US travel agent	3.96	0.59	.46–.71	.11	−.04	.04	.84					
German travel agent	3.96	0.45	.24–.56	−.07	−.16	.02	.70					
5. Negative emotions												
US travel agent	1.53	0.47	.33–.76	−.21	.12	−.16	.20	.81				
German travel agent	1.57	0.46	.38–.64	−.14	.12	−.10	−.16	.81				
6. Neutrality												
US travel agent	2.68	0.79	.36–.56	−.08	−.08	−.09	.46	.28	.70			
German travel agent	3.45	0.71	.49–.62	.10	.00	.13	.13	.12	.74			
7. Showing sympathy												
US travel agent	2.54	0.82	.38–.46	−.05	−.02	−.09	.60	.58	.48	.61		
German travel agent	2.73	0.73	.37–.56	.01	.04	−.07	.33	.31	.17	.65		
8. Sensitivity requirement												
US travel agent	3.30	0.82	.27–.65	.23	.04	.16	.33	.16	.28	.25	.74	
German travel agent	3.74	0.68	.45–.66	−.04	−.02	−.07	.34	−.16	.12	.24	.77	
9. Emotional dissonance												
US travel agent	2.92	0.82	.25–.82	−.19	.00	−.30	.29	.54	.47	.39	.36	.85
German travel agent	3.17	0.70	.21–.72	−.15	−.05	−.10	.17	.09	.27	.16	.21	.78

IC, itemtotal correlations part whole corrected (min–max); US Travel Agent, *N* (47, 50,); *p* < .01 at |r | ≥ .34; *p* < .05 at |r| ≥ .25; German Travel Agent: *N* (201,202); *p* < .01 at |r | ≥ .20. One-tailed tests. Coefficient α in *italic*.

Evaluation of the FEWS English Version 1.0

The first step in cross-cultural data analysis is to establish instrument reliability. Similar reliability coefficients, in the original and translated versions, provide evidence of measurement accuracy and, hence, the
appropriateness of the instrument for cross-cultural comparison (Kraemer,
1981; Van de Vijver & Leung, 1997). Thus, an item analysis was conducted
with the FEWS German version 4.0 and FEWS English version 1.0. This
item analysis (see Table 1) showed that four of the six scales reached a
coefficient alpha of .70–.85 in each of the two samples which was clearly
above the minimum of 0.70 recommended by Nunnally and Bernstein
(1994). Furthermore, only two items showed item total correlations (part
whole corrected) below .25 in the German sample. All other items reached
values of .27–.82, clearly above the .25 minimum recommended by Nunnally
and Bernstein (1994). The scale "showing sympathy" failed to reach this
criterion in the US (coefficient alpha = .61) and the German sample (coefficient alpha = .65). Thus, no cultural effects with respect to scale reliabilities could be observed for the data of the US and the German sample.
Therefore it can be assumed that the translation of the FEWS is accurate.

To evaluate the structural equivalence of the FEWS English version 1.0
and the FEWS German version 4.0 the cross-cultural factor structure was
compared (Van de Vijver & Leung, 1997). As expected, generally positive
first-order correlations were found, however two exceptions were identified.
Negative correlations were found between the requirement of negative
emotions and the requirement of positive emotions, as well as between the
requirement of negative emotions and sensitivity requirements ($r = -.16$ for
both) within the German sample. However, in the US sample most of the
FEWS requirement scales (positive, negative, neutrality, sympathy, and
sensitivity – see Table 1) are more highly intercorrelated than in the German
sample. The strongest effects were found for correlations with the neutrality
requirement scale. These correlations are quite different between the two
countries, being lower in the German and higher in the US sample, indicating cultural biases. Furthermore, the analysis revealed generally higher
positive first order correlations between emotional dissonance and the five
requirement scales within the US travel agent sample (range of $r = .29$–0.54)
compared to the German travel agent sample (range of $r = .09$–.27).

To evaluate scalar equivalence of the FEWS English version 1.0 and the
FEWS German version 4.0, we conducted a descriptive analysis to determine the presence of item bias by comparing the item characteristic curves
of the two cultural groups based on score level and average item score (Allen

Table 2. Items with Uniform Item Bias in both Travel Agent Samples.

Scale	Item	Question
Positive emotions	4	How often are you required to display *friendliness* when working with clients?
	5	How often are you required to display *enthusiasm* when working with clients?
	P3	How often in your job do you have to display, according to the situation, *differing positive emotions* towards clients (i.e. friendliness and enthusiasm and hope etc.)?
Negative emotions	11	How often are you required to display *aggression* when working with clients?
	V1	How often in your job do you have to display *unpleasant emotions* towards clients (i.e. strictness or anger if rules are not followed)?
Neutrality	12	How often are you required to display *impartiality/ neutrality* when working with clients?
Sensitivity	S1	How often is it necessary in your job *to empathize with the clients' emotions*?

& Yen, 1979). The item characteristic curves revealed the presence of a uniform bias in seven of 33 items in the following scales: positive emotions (three of nine items), negative emotions (two of eight items), neutrality (one of four items), and sensitivity requirements (one of four items). The items with uniform item bias are listed in Table 2.

No uniform item bias was found for the requirement to show sympathy or emotional dissonance. For all other items the item characteristic curves showed no item bias or non-uniform bias. Non-uniform bias does not, however, contradict our expectations, as differences between the samples were due to the score level of the subject group and not due to culture.

Evaluation of Cultural Effects

To determine cultural differences in the US and German samples as predicted in Hypotheses 1–5, we compared differences in the FEWS mean scaled scores between cultures. Thus, we conducted a multiple mean comparison analysis with culture (USA, Germany) as the independent variable and the six FEWS 4.0/1.0 scales (positive emotions, negative emotions, neutrality, requirement to show sympathy, sensitivity requirements, and emotional dissonance) as dependent variables. Since full score comparability is somewhat problematic, as long as the English FEWS is not free of uniform item bias (see above), we controlled for uniform item bias by

Table 3. Multiple Mean Comparisons of FEWS 1.0 (US-American travel agent) and FEWS 4.0 (German travel agent) Emotion Work Scales (ANOVA).

Sample		Positive Emotions	Negative Emotions	Neutrality	Showing Sympathy	Sensitivity	Emotional Dissonance
A	B	ΔM	ΔM	ΔM	ΔM	ΔM	ΔM
US-American travel agent	German travel agent	- −0.01 (0.02)	- −0.04 (−0.04)	- −0.77** (−0.64**)	- −0.19 (−0.19)	- −0.44** (−0.28*)	- −0.25* (−0.25*)

ΔM = mean differences in samples A, B;
*$p < .05$;
**$p < .01$ (Mean differences controlled for uniform item biases within parentheses).

computing FEWS scale scores without these biased items. Corresponding ANOVA results with full versus modified/reduced scales (Table 3) revealed similar results. Thus, we decided to report results for the full scales.

As predicted, cultural effects were revealed for the neutrality scale and the emotional dissonance scale. Thus, Hypothesis 5 – that the frequency of neutrality requirements is lower in the US sample than in the German sample and Hypothesis 6 – that the frequency of the stressor emotional dissonance is lower in the US sample than in the German sample were supported by the data. However, several hypotheses were not supported by the data. These were Hypothesis 1 – that the frequency of positive-emotion display requirements is higher in the US sample than in the German sample; Hypothesis 3 – that the frequency of sympathy requirements is higher in the US sample than in the German sample; and Hypothesis 4 – that the frequency of negative-emotion display requirements is lower in the US sample than in the German sample. Additionally, reported sensitivity requirements are significantly higher in the German travel agent sample. This finding is in contradiction to Hypothesis 2 – that the frequency of sensitivity requirements is higher in the US sample than in the German sample. Fig. 1 shows the corresponding profiles for the emotion work job demands of the US and German travel agents.

Discussion

The aim of this study was to show how cross-cultural questions in emotion work research can be answered by applying a task-focused concept of emotion work. We used the FEWS (Zapf et al., 1999, 2000a, b) to test this in a

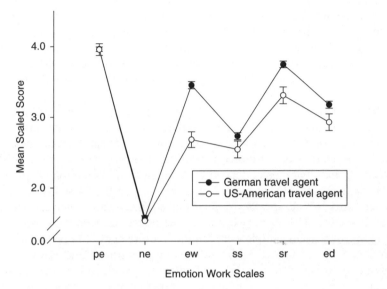

Fig. 1. Job Profiles in Emotion Work Scales for US Travel Agent vs. German Travel Agent (Solid Lines; Pe, Positive Emotions; Ne, Negative Emotions; Ew, Neutrality; Ss, Showing Sympathy; Sr, Sensitivity Requirements; Ed, Emotional Dissonance).

cross-cultural context. While interpreting and discussing the current results, it must be remembered that the results are based on a very small US sample, due to constraints in recruiting and testing US participants. This results in a considerable size difference in the German and US samples, which is somewhat problematic when estimating reliability coefficients and calculating analysis of variance. Thus, we did not use analyses of variance when estimating item bias, but instead provided a descriptive analysis of item bias and used single mean comparisons to examine cultural differences in the FEWS scales. A larger sample size would have provided opportunities for more sophisticated analysis and future studies should address this issue. However, the satisfactory reliability of the FEWS requirement and stressor scales, even in the smaller US sample, suggests that other researchers will have similar results in terms of systematic and interpretable cultural effects within an occupation.

Because equivalence of concept and methods is essential for valid cross-cultural comparisons, we translated the original FEWS German version 4.0 into English and evaluated the FEWS English version 1.0 by means of translation–backtranslation methods, reliability analysis, evaluation of structural equivalence, and item bias analysis. The results show some limitations in method equivalence but overall the final English version is accurate and largely measures the same content as the original German version. Furthermore, similar reliability coefficients in the English and German versions were found, indicating measurement accuracy in the two cultures.

The factor structure was evaluated by analyzing first-order correlations of the six requirement scales and emotional dissonance. Positive first order correlations were expected because all emotional demands (requirement of positive and negative emotions, neutrality, showing sympathy, sensitivity, and emotional dissonance) depend on frequency of interaction (Zapf et al., 1999; Zapf, 2002). This was confirmed for most of the FEWS scales in the two cultures, which speaks for factorial equivalence of the German and English version. However, two unexpected negative correlations within the German travel agent sample were found – requirement of negative emotions was negatively correlated with both positive emotions and sensitivity requirements. Because the negative correlations were found in the German but not in the US travel agent sample, this contradicts the general assumption of cross-cultural equivalence in these cases. It can be argued that frequency of interaction is not the only determinant of positive correlations between emotional demands. If these factor structure differences between cultures were also clearly found in other vocations, this would indicate a culture specific determinant leading to different factor structures for emotional demands in the US and the German cultures. Further studies should address this issue.

In the US sample, the majority of the FEWS requirement scales are more highly intercorrelated than in the German sample. These findings demonstrate that cultural differences might exist in terms of the importance of distinct emotional displays in service encounters. A general emphasis on positive emotions (see above) in the US culture might require the basis of any service encounter and situation to "be positive and friendly." It is unlikely that such a specific norm exists in the German culture and as such, service encounters and situations in Germany may result in more diverse behavior than in the US. Furthermore, the neutrality requirement scale, which measures the demand to appear impartial and exhibit a neutral affective state, emerged as a less distinguishable dimension in the US, where it was more strongly correlated with most of the other FEWS scales. This finding demonstrates that there may be cultural differences in the significance and meaning of neutrality and detachment in service interactions. Service encounters in the US might again be explained by a cultural bias to experience and express positive emotions, which prohibits a neutral stance. Therefore, construct equivalence of the neutrality scale has to be questioned. While "neutrality" was found to be a significant facet of emotion work for travel agents in Germany, future qualitative and quantitative research is needed to better understand "neutrality" in a cross cultural context. One approach to understanding this difference is the application of Hofstede's (2001) value dimension "uncertainty avoidance," as described in the introduction. Service managers and employees from countries high in uncertainty avoidance, such as Germany, may prefer neutrality in any ambiguous situation with at least moderate uncertainty regarding the appropriateness of specific emotions.

The item bias analysis shows the presence of uniform item bias in seven out of 33 items for the travel agent samples. Uniform bias implies that subjects from one cultural group have a consistently higher score on a particular item than individuals with the same score level from the other cultural group. Thus, these items have measured something different in each cultural group. In the literature, two explanations are given for uniform item bias, poor translation, and inappropriateness of the item in a given context (Van de Vijver & Leung, 1997). The first explanation suggests that uniform item bias is the result of poor translation of a specific item or inappropriateness of a specific item in a particular context. We do not find inadequate translation to be a sufficient explanation for these items since, with only one exception, the translation–backtranslations did not differ from the original items. One item of the sensitivity-requirement scale was found to be uniformly biased. This same item was also somewhat problematic in the translation process. In this item the phrase "empathize with" is used. Indeed, "empathize with" was chosen as a translation of the German "sich einfühlen" based on interviews with native speakers in the translation–backtranslation process (Meyer, 2002). The first translation was "sympathize with" but this was backtranslated to the German "sympathisieren" which was not the adequate translation to cover the meaning of that particular item. Whereas the term "sympathizing" simply expresses that an individual understands the feelings and problems of another person, "empathizing" expresses a deeper connection (i.e. entering into another person's feelings). Thus, "empathize with" was presumed to be the more adequate term and, in our opinion, is the most accurate translation. Therefore, we do not find that inadequate translation explains the discrepancy in this particular item.

The second explanation for uniform item bias – inappropriateness of an item in a specific context – is an aspect of scale homogeneity. Since items were developed to cover diverse aspects of emotional demands, including distinct qualitative facets of these demands, scales can be expected to be more heterogeneous (e.g., items measuring the requirement to display negative emotions are: "How often do you have to display unpleasant emotions?", and "How often do you have to put your clients in a negative mood?"). Thus, some items may be more dependent on cultural context than others. In US service encounters, it might be inappropriate to "empathize" if this goes beyond simple display demands. Rather, this would require a more personal, serious, and authentic relationship than is the norm in the American service context. In such situations, empathizing might be perceived as more desirable and necessary in German service encounters. This example demonstrates how item bias analyses assist in the detection and understanding of cross-cultural differences of emotion concepts in work settings. Further research should examine if the item bias found in these particular items is dependent on the cultural or vocational context.

Overall, the results show, with some exceptions, the FEWS English 1.0 version is equivalent to the German 4.0 version. The results regarding equivalence highlight the challenges of adapting an affect measurement instrument developed in one culture to another culture. However, any biases were eliminated and controlled for in an attempt to maximize equivalence.

After controlling for construct, method, and item biases, a comparison of emotion work requirements (positive and negative emotions, neutrality, sensitivity requirements, and requirements to show sympathy), and the emotion work stressor, emotional dissonance, was made among travel agents across two cultures (USA and Germany). Results show that emotion work job demands of travel agents are rather similar across both cultures for positive and negative emotions. Thus, Hypotheses 1 and 2, predicting that the frequency of positive emotion requirement is higher and the frequency of negative emotion requirement is lower for US travel agents than German travel agents, are not supported by the data. In this service profession that essentially focuses on selling, an emphasis on positive emotion display is equally required in both cultures. Therefore, the potential influence of certain cultural value differences, such as uncertainty avoidance, on these display requirements may be largely neutralized in this specific setting. Future research should examine whether this also holds true for other service professions. One might argue that in professions in which service-workers enjoy higher status (such as medical doctors, teachers) there could be greater cultural influence on job requirements.

A clear cultural effect was found for both the FEWS requirement neutrality, as predicted in Hypothesis 5, and the FEWS scale emotional

dissonance, as predicted in Hypothesis 6. Neutrality and emotional dissonance were found to be systematically higher in the German sample than in
the US sample. This can be explained by a stronger emphasis on positive
emotions in the US culture and by greater uncertainty avoidance and lower
humane orientation values in Germany, as described in the introduction. It
could be more desirable and adequate in the German culture to show neutrality in service settings than in US service settings, where a portrayal of
positive emotions is generally desired.

These considerations might also explain the lower frequency of emotional
dissonance in the US sample. If US customers are less negative than German customers, there are fewer negative situations in which positive emotions have to be displayed. Further research should explicitly examine these
propositions. It is conceivable that the difference in emotional dissonance is
somewhat more pronounced in the travel sector than in other service domains. Due to greater uncertainty avoidance (Hofstede, 2001), German
customers may express more dissatisfaction in travel agency service encounters because the future benefits and costs associated with choices between different travel options are often at least partially unknown. On the
other hand, generally higher levels of negative affect (Argyle, 2001) suggest
that German customers are more dissatisfied across service domains, as
shown in the survey studies summarized in the introduction. Given that
emotional dissonance is a job stressor, leading to predictable negative consequences for service workers (e.g. health problems), this is an important
finding. If the presence of less emotional dissonance in US sales occupations
can actually be attributed to cultural differences, then differences in display
rules, socialization strategies, corporate culture, and customer behavior
could serve as a model for German sales occupations to reduce the stress of
emotional dissonance. A further difference was also found for sensitivity
requirements, which were higher among German than US travel agents.
This finding contradicts the tenets of Hypothesis 4, which predicted more
sensitivity requirements in the US sample. As discussed for the item bias of
sensitivity items, future qualitative and quantitative research should examine the status of this requirement in a US service context.

CONCLUSION

In this chapter, we presented a task-focused concept of emotion work and
used the FEWS to compare emotion work demands between a US and
German travel agent sample. An important premise for cross-cultural

comparisons is method equivalence. In this study, sample differences, some differences in the factor structure of FEWS, and some items with uniform item bias were revealed which limit interpretation of cultural effects. However, we controlled for these limitations and we were able to show that the FEWS English version 1.0 is largely equivalent to the German version 4.0. Thus, the FEWS is an adequate instrument for studying emotional job demands and proposed effects of these job demands in US and German settings. Hypotheses about similarities and differences between emotion work demands were derived based on cross-cultural psychology findings. With regard to this research, it was expected that US travel agents would have greater customer oriented emotion displays and less emotional dissonance than German travel agents. Not all of the hypotheses were supported by the data. For instance, we found no differences between US and German travel agents in requirements to show positive emotions. This might reflect the extent to which the sales situation defines emotion work demands across cultures. However, cultural comparisons suggest that emotional demands in the US sales service include less neutrality, less sensitivity requirements and less emotional dissonance than in Germany. We hope that this study will serve as a starting point for more research regarding cultural differences associated with emotion work.

REFERENCES

Allen, M. A., & Yen, W. M. (1979). *Introduction to measurement theory*. Monterey, CA: Brooks/Cole.

Argyle, M. (2001). *The psychology of happiness* (2nd ed.). London: Routledge.

Ashforth, B. E., & Humphrey, R. H. (1993). Emotional labor in service roles: The influence of identity. *Academy of Management Review, 18*(1), 88–115.

Berry, J. W. (1980). Introduction to methodology. In: H. C. Triandis & J. W. Berry (Eds), *Handbook of cross-cultural psychology* (Vol. 2, pp. 1–28). Boston: Allyn & Bacon.

Bowen, D. E., & Schneider, B. (1988). Services marketing and management: Implications for organizational behavior. *Research in Organizational Behavior, 10*, 43–80.

Brislin, R. W. (1980). Translation and content analysis of oral and written material. In: H. C. Triandis J. W. Berry (Eds), *Handbook of cross-cultural psychology* (Vol. 2, pp. 389–444) Boston: Allyn & Bacon.

Brotheridge, C. M., & Grandey, A. A. (2002). Emotional labor and burnout: Comparing two perspectives of "people work". *Journal of Vocational Behavior, 60*(1), 17–39.

Eid, M., & Diener, E. (2001). Norms for experiencing emotions in different cultures: Inter- and intranational differences. *Journal of Personality & Social Psychology, 81*(5), 869–885.

Ekman, P., & Friesen, W. V. (1975). *Unmasking the face*. Englewood Cliffs, NJ: Prentice-Hall.

Fischbach, A. (2003). *Determinants of emotion work*. Unpublished Dissertation, Georg-August-University, Göttingen.

Fischbach, A., & Zapf, D. (2002). *Neutralität als emotionale Arbeitsanforderung (Neutrality as an emotional requirement)*. Paper presented at the 43 Kongress der Deutschen Gesellschaft für Psychologie, Humboldt-Universität, Berlin.

Fornell, C., Johnson, M. D., Anderson, E. W., Cha, J., & Bryant, B. E. (1996). The American Customer Satisfaction Index: Nature, purpose, and findings. *Journal of Marketing, 60*(4), 7–18.

Francesco, A. M., & Gold, B. A. (1998). *International organizational behavior.* Upper Saddle River, NJ: Prentice-Hall.

Frese, M., & Zapf, D. (1988). Methodological issues in the study of work stress: Objective vs. subjective measurement of work stress and the question of longitudinal studies. In: C. L. Cooper & R. Payne (Eds), *Causes, coping and consequences of stress at work* (pp. 375–411). Chichester: Wiley.

Frese, M., & Zapf, D. (1994). Action as the core of work psychology: A German approach. In: H. C. Triandis & M. D. Dunnette (Eds), *Handbook of industrial and organizational psychology* (Vol. 4, 2nd ed., pp. 271–340). Palo Alto, CA: Consulting Psychologists Press.

Goffman, E. (1959). *The presentation of self in everyday life.* New York: Doubleday Anchor.

Grandey, A. A. (2000). *The effects of emotional labor: Employee attitudes, stress and performance.* US: Colorado State University Press.

Gutek, B. A. (1997). Dyadic interactions in organizations. In: C. L. Cooper & S. E. Jackson (Eds), *Creating tomorrows organizations today* (pp. 139–156). Chichester: Wiley.

Hacker, W. (2003). *Action Regulation Theory – A practical tool for the design of modern work processes?* (pp. 1–27). Dresden: Technische Universität Dresden, Institut für Psychologie 1, Arbeitsgruppe "Wiss en – Denken – Handeln".

Hackman, J. R. (1970). Tasks and task performance in research on stress. In: J. E. McGrath (Ed.), *Social and psychological factors in stress* (pp. 202–237). New York: Holt, Rinehart & Winston.

Hambleton, R. K. (1993). Translating achievement tests for use in cross-national studies. *European Journal of Psychological Assessment, 9*(1), 57–68.

Hambleton, R. K. (1994). Guidelines for adapting educational and psychological tests: A progress report. *European Journal of Psychological Assessment, 10*(3), 229–244.

Hochschild, A. R. (1983). *The managed heart.* Berkeley: University of California Press.

Hofstede, G. (2001). *Culture's consequences: Comparing values, behaviors, institutions, and organisations across nations.* Thousand Oaks: Sage.

Holman, D. J. (2003). Call centres. In: D. J. Holman, T. D. Wall, C. W. Clegg, P. Sparrow & A. Howard (Eds), *The new workplace: A guide to the human impact of modern working practices* (pp. 115–134). Chichester: Wiley.

House, R. J., Wright, N. S., & Aditya, R. N. (1997). Cross-cultural research on organizational leadership: A critical analysis and a proposed theory. In: P. C. Earley & M. Erez (Eds), *New perspectives on international industrial/organizational psychology* (pp. 535–625). San Francisco, CA: New Lexington.

Izard, C. E. (1971). *The face of emotion.* East Norwalk, CT: Appleton-Century-Crofts.

Izard, C. E. (1980). Cross-cultural perspectives on emotion and emotion communication. In: H. C. Triandis & W. Lonner (Eds), *Handbook of cross-cultural psychology* (Vol. 3, pp. 185–222). Boston: Allyn & Bacon.

Kielhorn, K. (2002). Empirische Untersuchung zum Einfluß von Emotionsarbeit auf Burnout und Arbeitszufriedenheit bei Reiseverkehrskaufleuten (Empirical studies on the impact of emotion work on burnout and job satisfaction of travel agents). Unpublished Thesis, Georg-August-University, Göttingen.

Kraemer, H. C. (1981). Extension of Feldt's approach to testing homogeneity of coefficients of reliability. *Psychometrika, 46*(1), 41–45.

Kruml, S. M., & Geddes, D. (2000). Catching fire without burning out: Is there an ideal way to perform emotion labor? In: N. M. Ashkanasy & C. E. Härtel (Eds), *Emotions in the workplace: Research, theory, and practice* (pp. 177–188). Westport, CT: Quorum Books/ Greenwood.

Markus, H. R., & Kitayama, S. (1991). Culture and the self: Implications for cognition, emotion, and motivation. *Psychological Review, 98*, 224–253.

Markus, H. R., & Kitayama, S. (2003). Culture, self, and the reality of the social. *Psychological Inquiry, 14*, 277–283.

Mesquita, B., & Frijda, N. H. (1992). Cultural variations in emotions: A review. *Psychological Bulletin, 112*(2), 179–204.

Meyer, K. (2002). *Frankfurt emotion work scales: Construct validation in a cross-cultural context.* Unpublished Thesis, Georg-August-University, Göttingen.

Morris, J. A., & Feldman, D. C. (1996). The dimensions, antecedents, and consequences of emotional labor. *Academy of Management Review, 21*(4), 986–1010.

Morris, J. A., & Feldman, D. C. (1997). Managing emotions in the workplace. *Journal of Managerial Issues, 9*(3), 257–274.

Nerdinger, F. W. (1994). *Zur Psychologie der Dienstleistung. (On the psychology of service).* Stuttgart: Schäffer Poeschel.

Nerdinger, F. W. (2001). *Psychologie des persönlichen Verkaufs (The psychology of personal sales).* München: Oldenbourg.

Nunnally, J. C., & Bernstein, I. H. (1994). *Psychometric theory* (3rd ed.). New York: McGraw-Hill.

Parasuraman, A., Zeithaml, V. A., & Berry, L. L. (1988). SERVQUAL: A multiple-item scale for measuring consumer perceptions of service quality. *Journal of Retailing, 64*(1), 12–40.

Pareek, U., & Venkateswara, T. (1980). Cross-cultural surveys and interviewing. In: H. C. Triandis & J. W. Berry (Eds), *Handbook of cross-cultural psychology* (Vol. 2, pp. 127–180). Boston: Allyn & Bacon.

Rafaeli, A. (1989a). When cashiers meet customers: An analysis of the role of supermarket cashiers. *Academy of Management Journal, 32*(2), 245–273.

Rafaeli, A. (1989b). When clerks meet customers: A test of variables related to emotional expressions on the job. *Journal of Applied Psychology, 74*(3), 385–393.

Rafaeli, A., & Sutton, R. I. (1987). Expression of emotion as part of the work role. *Academy of Management Review, 12*(1), 23–37.

Schaubroeck, J., & Jones, J. R. (2000). Antecedents of workplace emotional labor dimensions and moderators of their effects on physical symptoms. *Journal of Organizational Behavior, 21*, 163–183.

Schneider, B., & Bowen, D. E. (1984). New services design, development, and implementation and the employee. In: W. R. George & C. E. Marshall (Eds), *Developing new services* (pp. 82–111). Chicago: American Marketing Association.

Schneider, B., & Bowen, D. E. (1985). Employee and customer perceptions of service in banks: Replication and extension. *Journal of Applied Psychology, 70*(3), 423–433.

Schwartz, S. H. (1999). A Theory of Cultural Values and Some Implications for Work. *Applied Psychology: An International Review, 48*, 23–47.

Sutton, R. I. (1991). Maintaining norms about expressed emotions: The case of bill collectors. *Administrative Science Quarterly, 36*(2), 245–268.

Triandis, H. (1989). The self and social behavior in differing cultural contexts. *Psychological Review, 96,* 506–520.

Triandis, H. C., Malpass, R. S., & Davidson, A. (1972). Cross-cultural psychology. *The Biennial Review of Anthropology, 1972a,* 1–84.

Tsai, W. C. (2001). Determinants and consequences of employee displayed positive emotions. *Journal of Management, 27*(4), 497–512.

Van de Vijver, F. J. R., & Leung, K. (1997). Methods and data analysis of comparative research. In: J. W. Berry & Y. H. Poortinga (Eds), *Handbook of cross-cultural psycholog: Vol. 1: Theory and method* (2nd ed., pp. 257–300). Needham Heights: MA, Allyn & Bacon.

Van de Vijver, F. J. R., & Tanzer, N. K. (1997). Bias and equivalence in cross-cultural assessment: An overview. *European Review of Applied Psychology, 47,* 263–279.

Van Maanen, J., & Kunda, G. (1989). "Real feelings": Emotional expression and organizational culture. In: L. L. Cummings & B. M. Staw (Eds), *Research in organizational behaviour* (Vol. 11, pp. 43–103) Greenwich, CT: JAI Press.

Zapf, D. (2002). Emotion work and psychological well-being: A review of the literature and some conceptual considerations. *Human Resource Management Review, 12,* 237–268.

Zapf, D., Isic, A., Bechtoldt, M., & Blau, P. (2003). What is typical for call centre jobs? Job characteristics, and agent–customer interactions in different call centres. *European Journal of Work & Organizational Psychology, 12*(4), 311–340.

Zapf, D., Isic, A., Fischbach, A., & Dormann, C. (2003). Emotionsarbeit in Dienstleistungsberufen. Das Konzept und seine Implikationen für die Personal- und Organisationsentwicklung (Emotion work in service jobs. The concept and its implications for personnel and organizational development). In: K. C. Hamborg & H. Holling (Eds), *Innovative Ansätze der Personal- und Organisationsentwicklung (Innovations in HR and organizational development)* (pp. 283–304). Göttingen: Hogrefe.

Zapf, D., Mertini, H., Seifert, C., Vogt, C., Isic, A., & Fischbach, A. (2000a). FEWS (Frankfurt emotion work scales, Frankfurter Skalen zur Emotionsarbeit). Version 4.0. Frankfurt am Main: Johann Wolfgang Goethe-Universität, Institut für Psychologie.

Zapf, D., Mertini, H., Seifert, C., Vogt, C., Isic, A., Fischbach, A., & Meyer, K. (2000b). FEWS (Frankfurt emotion work scales, Frankfurter Skalen zur Emotionsarbeit). English Version 1.0. Frankfurt am Main: Johann Wolfgang Goethe-Universität, Institut für Psychologie.

Zapf, D., Seifert, C., Schmutte, B., Mertini, H., & Holz, M. (2001). Emotion work and job stressors and their effects on burnout. *Psychology & Health, 16*(5), 527–545.

Zapf, D., Vogt, C., Seifert, C., Mertini, H., & Isic, A. (1999). Emotion work as a source of stress: The concept and development of an instrument. *European Journal of Work & Organizational Psychology, 8,* 371–400.

Zeithaml, V. A., & Bitner, M. J. (2000). *Services marketing. Integrating customer focus across the firm* (2nd ed.). Boston: McGraw-Hill.

Zerbe, W. J. (2000). Emotional dissonance and employee well-being. In: N. M. Ashkanasy, C. E. Härtel & W. J. Zerbe (Eds), *Emotions in the workplace: Research, theory, and practice* (pp. 189–214). Westport, CT: Quorum Books/Greenwood.

CHAPTER 9

A CONCEPTUAL MODEL OF THE EFFECTS OF EMOTIONAL LABOR STRATEGIES ON CUSTOMER OUTCOMES

Markus Groth, Thorsten Hennig-Thurau and Gianfranco Walsh

ABSTRACT

The aim of the research reported in this article was to develop a conceptual model that links emotional labor strategies performed by service employees to a number of relevant antecedents as well as to a variety of customer outcomes. We link emotional labor directly to the customer domain by examining how customers experience and react to emotional displays of service employees. Thus, we expand current emotional labor research which has predominantly focused on employee and organizational outcomes but has offered limited theoretical guidance as to how customers may be directly affected by emotional labor in the service delivery process. Specific research propositions are developed that offer insight into the antecedents and potential impact of emotional labor strategies on customer behavior. Managerial and research implications as well as avenues for future research are discussed from the perspective of emotional labor theory.

Individual and Organizational Perspectives on Emotion Management and Display
Research on Emotion in Organizations, Volume 2, 219–236
Copyright © 2006 by Elsevier Ltd.
All rights of reproduction in any form reserved
ISSN: 1746-9791/doi:10.1016/S1746-9791(06)02009-8

INTRODUCTION

Service management and marketing researchers have become increasingly interested in the role of emotions in service encounters (Lemmink & Mattson, 2002; Liljander & Strandvik, 1997; Mattila & Enz, 2002). To develop and successfully maintain relationships with customers, service employees are expected to display certain emotions (e.g., cheerfulness) and suppress others (e.g., anger) as part of their job requirements. Although such "emotional labor" (Hochschild, 1983) has been demonstrated to exert a major influence on key employee outcomes, such as job satisfaction and organizational commitment (Brotheridge & Grandey, 2002), the effects that emotional labor has on customers have only been sparingly addressed by organizational scholars. This is surprising, given that the interaction between a customer and a service provider is not only essential in the determination of customer evaluations, but often is the service itself in the eye of the customer (Bowen, 1990; Bowen, Schneider, & Kim, 2000). Thus, there is reason to believe that employees' emotion regulation in service interactions does not only affect their own well-being but also affects customer outcomes that are critical for relationship marketing success, such as customer satisfaction and retention. However, to date there has been a lack of conceptual as well as empirical research into the emotional labor–customer outcome link.

In addressing this research gap, the aim of our research is to develop a theoretical model of the antecedents of two different emotional labor strategies as well as their effects on customer outcomes in order to provide service firms with knowledge on how to achieve desirable customer outcomes through emotional labor management. The article is structured as follows: first, we review the existing literature on emotional labor strategies and their effects on employees and customers. Then, by applying a two-dimensional conceptualization of emotional labor encompassing surface acting and deep acting, we develop a theoretical model of emotional labor and its consequences and antecedents, and offer specific research propositions for future research. Specifically, we examine how the two emotional labor strategies affect customer perceptions of employees' customer orientation, customer satisfaction, social relational benefits, trust, and customer retention.

In addition, our research focuses on determinants of employees' choice of emotional labor strategy. Based on a number of organizational theories discussed below, we propose a set of individual-, dyadic-, and organizational-level antecedents on service employees' propensity to engage in either surface acting or deep acting. Finally, theoretical as well as practical implications of our conceptual model are discussed from the perspective of emotional labor theories.

Importance of Emotional Labor Strategies in Service Delivery

Recent service management research has increasingly focused on the role of emotions in service deliveries, particularly the role of emotional labor performed by service employees. Emotional labor refers to the "effort, planning, and control needed to express organizationally desired emotions during interpersonal transactions" (Morris & Feldman, 1996, p. 987). In her seminal work on service workers such as flight attendants and bill collectors, Hochschild (1979, 1983) concluded that while employees' physical, mental, and semi-motor tasks are often well documented, measured, and rewarded by organizations, emotional labor often is an unacknowledged component of their work. While the service management and marketing literatures have focused on delivering superior service quality and on the importance of courteous frontline employees delivering "service with a smile," doing so requires employees to consistently display emotions not genuinely felt by them. However, until recently, little attention has been paid to the effects such behavior may elicit. Hochschild (1983) argues that when interacting with customers under the guidance of organizational rules and regulations, managing one's emotions is not simply a private act done in a social context. Rather, emotional display is sold as labor and dictated by the organization through training, policies, and supervision.

Thus, although emotional reactions to one's organizational environment are an integral part of nearly every employee's job, emotional labor is a distinct concept in that it focuses on emotions as a requirement of the job. Organizations usually have certain explicit or implicit "display rules" (Rafaeli & Sutton, 1987), that is, norms and standards of behavior which indicate which emotions are appropriate and should be publicly expressed and which emotions should be suppressed. Early emotional labor research has primarily focused on identifying various types of emotion management strategies. Although a number of strategies have been discussed (see, e.g., Hochschild, 1983; Zapf, 2002), research has primarily focused on surface acting and deep acting as commonly adopted approaches of service employees to manage their emotions. In surface acting, employees only try to change their outward appearance without genuinely altering how they actually feel (i.e., faking). Thus, employees express feigned emotions when surface acting. In deep acting, on the other hand, employees express the desired emotion and attempt to summon those emotions. Thus, when deep acting, employees express true emotions.

Research on emotional labor has predominantly focused on the effects of emotional labor on employee well-being. Specifically, Hochschild (1983) highlighted a number of negative consequences of emotional labor, primarily psychological ill health such as stress and job burnout. Links have been shown to exist between emotional labor and emotional exhaustion (Brotheridge & Grandey, 2002), job dissatisfaction (Grandey, 2003; Morris & Feldman, 1997), and lack of organizational identity (Ashforth & Humphrey, 1993; Schaubroeck & Jones, 2000). However, empirical findings are contradictory to some extent. Wharton (1993, 1996), for example, found that the more service employees engaged in emotional labor as part of their work, the more satisfied they were. Grandey (2003) suggests that such contradictions can be explained by differentiating between acting strategies. That is, whereas surface acting has a number of negative effects on employees, deep acting may in fact be beneficial to their psychological well-being.

Emotional Labor as a Regulatory Process

In our proposed theoretical model, we conceptualize and measure emotional labor as a regulatory process. This is consistent with recent emotional labor research (e.g., Grandey, 2003) and is a significant improvement on early work in this area where emotional labor was believed to be unidimensional in terms of frequency and consequently was measured at the job level (e.g., Hochschild, 1983; Wharton, 1993, 1996). As such, survey respondents were often classified as performing high or low emotional labor based on their reported job classification. Although Morris and Feldman (1996, 1997) pointed out the limitation of this approach and proposed a model that included three dimensions of emotional labor (frequency of interaction, duration of interaction, and emotional dissonance), their model was similarly criticized for lack of content validity (Kruml & Geddes, 2000; Mann, 1999). Only recently has emotional labor been conceptualized and measured as a regulatory process involving different types of acting strategies (Brotheridge & Grandey, 2002; Grandey, 2003; Kruml & Geddes, 2000). By assessing and contrasting the effects of different types of emotion management, our study will explore the relative, comparative effects of each strategy.

Building on the identification of different alternative emotional labor strategies, our aim is to understand the consequences of alternative emotional labor strategies for customer outcomes as well as the antecedents of employees' engaging in these strategies. The great majority of empirical emotional labor research so far has exclusively focused on employee consequences (Grandey, 2003; Morris & Feldman, 1997; Schaubroeck & Jones, 2000; Wharton, 1993). To our knowledge, our model is the first attempt to systematically map the differential effects of emotional labor strategies on customers.

In addition, our aim is to examine several individual-, dyadic-, and organizational-level determinants of emotional labor strategies. Although some previous research has examined several emotional labor antecedents, most of this work has focused on task characteristics specific to the display rules of the organization (e.g., Morris & Feldman, 1996; Schaubroeck & Jones, 2000). By focusing on employee satisfaction as well as factors specific to the service delivery context, we hope to provide a better understanding of these relationships. Such an understanding will provide tools for service managers that enable them to systematically impact their employees' choice of acting strategies.

Customer-Related Outcomes of Emotional Labor

In contrast to the work on positive and negative effects of emotional labor on employee well-being, the effects of emotional labor on customers have remained largely unexplored. This is surprising, given that the effective management of service employees' emotions is an essential task for service marketers and emotional display of employees is likely to influence clients' emotions, behaviors, and attitudes, thereby influencing their buying decisions and perceptions of service quality. In fact, Bitner (1990) suggests that displayed emotions of both customers and employees are an integral part of the service delivery itself.

Existing empirical studies that address the effects of emotional labor on customers are rare (Grandey, 2003; Pugh, 2001; Mattila & Enz, 2002; Tsai, 2001; Tsai & Huang, 2002). All studies on the relationship between emotional labor and customer outcomes do not directly examine the differential effects of various emotional labor strategies. Specifically, the study by Grandey (2003) is the only one addressing the interface of emotional labor and customer outcomes directly, modeling the concept of affective delivery as an outcome of emotional labor and finding support for this impact. However, in her study, affective delivery, defined as the extent to which service delivery is perceived as friendly and warm by customers, was assessed not by customers, but by coworkers of the employee. The studies by Pugh (2001), Mattila and Enz (2002), Tsai (2001), and Tsai and Huang (2002), on the other hand, did not directly focus on emotional labor strategies, but examined the relationship between employee displayed emotions and customer emotions. Although customer assessments were gathered in all four studies from customers, employee emotions were assessed by independent observers who unobtrusively observed service employees. Obviously, such study design primarily focuses on outwardly displayed emotions but leaves unexplored underlying emotion management processes at the heart of Hochschild's (1983) definition of emotional labor. In other words, a distinction between surface acting and deep acting was not possible in these studies due to the nature of the data collection of employee emotions. In sum, a major contribution of our research is to develop a theoretical model that sheds light on a topic that has received little empirical attention to date, namely the link between employees' emotional labor strategies and resulting customer outcomes.

Antecedents of Employees' Emotional Labor Strategies

Similarly to research on customer outcomes, antecedents of employees' choice of emotional labor strategies have also received limited empirical attention, as the majority of prior research has focused on the consequences but not the determinants of employee emotional labor. Many of the existing studies tend to focus on firm and job characteristics as predictors of emotional labor, such as organizational display rules, supervision, training, and attentiveness as predictors of employees' emotional labor (e.g., Grandey, 2003; Kruml & Geddes, 2000; Morris & Feldman, 1997). In addition, some researchers have investigated dyad characteristics of employee–customer links during service interactions as factors influencing emotional labor, for example, type of service relationship (Grayson, 1998), power of role receiver (Morris & Feldman, 1997), and rapport (Bailey, Gremler, & McCollough, 2001). Recently, some of the focus has shifted to individual-level antecedents of service employees, such as affective, behavioral, and dispositional characteristics, including job satisfaction (Grandey, 2003), personality (Glomb & Tews, 2004), and cognitions (Bailey et al., 2001). The purpose of the proposed theoretical model is to expand this research stream. This will be achieved by examining additional individual-, dyadic-, and organizational-level determinants of emotional labor deemed to be important predictors of employees' choice of emotional labor strategies based on a number of organizational theories.

THEORETICAL MODEL

To understand the consequences of different emotional labor strategies on customer outcomes and to examine determinants of the two emotional labor strategies, we suggest the theoretical model illustrated in Fig. 1. Basically, we draw on the distinction of surface acting and deep acting as emotional labor strategies (Grandey, 2003; Hochschild, 1983; Totterdell & Holman, 2003). We then argue that the two strategies will have a differential impact on several customer outcome variables, which have been shown to be crucial for a service firm's economic success. Moreover, we also presume that a set of individual-, dyadic-, and firm-level factors exists that determine and influence the choice of the two emotional labor strategies. The proposed relationships of the model are discussed below.

It should be added that our model is based on the assumption that the interaction with a service employee bears the potential to be perceived as beneficial by the customer in that the service offered is interactive and individualized (e.g., hair dressers, medical services, therapists). Although some of the propositions provided might also be applicable to other kinds of services (i.e., less interactive and more standardized), we focus on individual and interactive services when discussing the consequences and antecedents of emotional labor.

Emotional Labor Strategies

With regard to emotion regulation strategies, different strategies have been suggested in the literature that can be applied by service employees to cope with organizational display rules. As discussed earlier, the most prominent distinction of acting strategies was introduced by Hochschild (1983) who distinguishes between surface acting and deep acting. This distinction has been adopted by several other researchers (e.g., Grandey, 2003; Grayson, 1998; Kruml & Geddes, 2000), although some of these authors use slightly different terminology for their constructs. As discussed, in *surface acting*, an employee tries to change only his or her outward appearance and behavior when exhibiting required emotions. For example, when dealing with an angry and annoying customer, an employee may simply put on a smile and pretend to be friendly without changing his or her inner feelings of annoyance with the customer. In *deep acting*, on the other hand, individuals express the required emotions but do so by attempting to summon these emotions within themselves. For example, Hochschild (1983) reports of flight attendants who are trained to deal with angry and annoying passengers by thinking of them as frightened first-time fliers, therefore, changing their inner feelings from annoyance to pity and empathy. Thus, surface acting can be conceptualized as a response-focused regulation strategy, whereas deep acting is an antecedent-focused regulation (Totterdell & Holman, 2003).

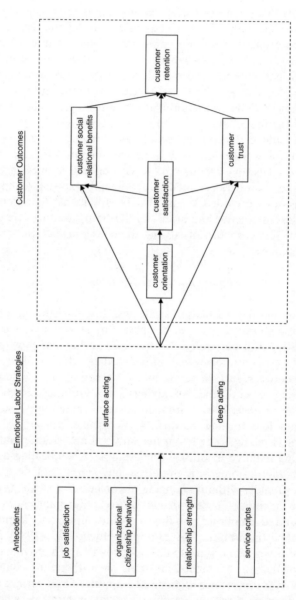

Fig. 1. Theoretical Model of Consequences and Antecedents of Emotional Labor Strategies.

Customer Outcomes of Emotional Labor

Drawing on services management research and emotional labor theory, we suggest that employees' emotional labor strategies influence customer perceptions of employees' customer orientation, customer satisfaction, customer trust in the service provider, the level of social benefits received from the relationship as well as the level of customer retention.

Emotional Labor Strategies and Customer Orientation of Employees and Customer Satisfaction

Customer orientation of the service employee is conceptualized as an employee's efforts to fulfill customer needs, combining elements such as the employee level of pampering the customer, reading customers' needs, and delivering the required service to customers (e.g., Donavan, Brown, & Mowen, 2004; Hennig-Thurau, 2004). In service industries where employees take a pivotal role for service creation and delivery, a high level of employee customer orientation usually implies that customers feel satisfied with the service provided, with satisfaction constituting a customer's cognitive–emotive appraisal of the service provision (Oliver, 1997). Indeed, research on service quality and satisfaction has confirmed that employees' customer orientation is a major determinant of customers' satisfaction with a service (Parasuraman, Zeithaml, & Berry, 1988).

Because the way that employees regulate and display emotions influences customer perceptions of the service delivery process, we expect that employees' emotional labor strategies impact the level of customer orientation of service employees as perceived by customers and consequently also customers' satisfaction with the service. Specifically, when an employee engages in surface acting, customers may question his or her motivation to provide a maximum level of service, as employees' superficiality signals to customers that employees might act according to prescribed job requirements and without a real concern for the customer's greater needs. Thus, surface acting is expected to have a negative impact on customer orientation and customer satisfaction. In contrast, when employees engage in deep acting, this behavior signals motivation and customer commitment to customers and will have a positive effect on both customer orientation and satisfaction. Thus, we propose:

Proposition 1. Surface acting (deep acting) by service employees has a negative (positive) impact on customers' assessment of service employees' customer orientation and their satisfaction with the service.

Emotional Labor Strategies and Customer Trust

Customer trust is conceptualized as customers' expectations about a firm's future behavior and their subsequent willingness to rely on the exchange partner (e.g., Rousseau, Sitkin, Burt, & Camerer, 1998). Trust is generally conceptualized as a multidimensional construct, including the dimensions of competence (or credibility) and benevolence (or integrity) (Sirdeshmukh, Singh, & Sabol, 2002).

Surface acting by employees conflicts with customer expectations of honest behavior and may be interpreted by customers as "cheating" (Grandey, 2003). Therefore, surface acting is not compatible with the benevolence dimension of trust and can consequently be expected to have a negative impact on customer trust. Deep acting, on the other hand, requires emotional investments from the employee which will be interpreted by the customer as signal that the employee is interested in a long-term relationship and does not intend to engage in opportunistic behavior, i.e., supporting the development of benevolence trust on the side of the customer. This leads us to the following proposition:

Proposition 2. Surface acting (deep acting) by service employees has a negative (positive) impact on customers' trust in the service firm.

Emotional Labor Strategies and Customer Social Relational Benefits

Customers have been shown to maintain relationships with service providers because of the social benefits associated with such relationships (e.g., Goodwin & Gremler, 1996; Gwinner, Gremler, & Bitner, 1998). Social relational benefits refer to non-functional advantages of a relationship that customers receive, such as the development of rapport, acquaintances, and "commercial friendships" with service employees (e.g., Gremler & Gwinner, 2000; Price & Arnould, 1999). We argue that the extent to which customers experience social relational benefits depends on the emotional labor strategy of the service employee.

Specifically, as social relationships require exchange partners to signal true interest in the other person, the expression of superficial and unauthentic emotions related to surface acting will have a counterproductive effect on social benefits. Moreover, surface acting stresses the emotional distance between employees and customers as employees apply standardized behavior and feigned friendliness instead of treating customers as individuals. In contrast, as deep acting involves a higher level of employee empathy and interest in the customer's well-being, it is likely to be a more appropriate and effective behavior when it comes to social relationships among employees and customers. Thus, we propose:

Proposition 3. Surface acting (deep acting) by service employees has a negative (positive) impact on customer social relational benefits.

Emotional Labor Strategies and Customer Retention

Customer retention is usually considered the key outcome variable of the relationship marketing concept (Rust & Zahorik, 1993), i.e., a company's coordinated efforts to build and maintain lasting relationships with profitable individual customers. Although we do not presume emotional labor to directly impact retention, there are reasons to believe that emotional labor handling strategies affect customer retention through the other outcome variables considered in our model. By drawing on the literature on customer orientation of service employees (e.g., Parasuraman et al., 1988) and relationship quality (e.g., Hennig-Thurau & Klee, 1997), we propose the following interrelationships among the outcome constructs of our conceptual model:

Proposition 4. Customer orientation of service employees has a positive impact on customer satisfaction.

Proposition 5. Customer satisfaction has a positive impact on customer social relational benefits.

Proposition 6. Customer satisfaction has a positive impact on customer trust.

Proposition 7. Customer satisfaction has a positive impact on customer retention.

Proposition 8. Customer social relational benefits have a positive impact on customer retention.

Proposition 9. Customer trust has a positive impact on customer retention.

Antecedents of Emotional Labor-Handling Strategies

Apart from customer-related outcomes of specific emotional labor strategies, our theoretical model also focuses on a set of predictors of employees' likelihood to engage in either surface acting or deep acting. Specifically, in our proposed model we focus on three kinds of potential antecedents of emotional labor regulation strategies, namely (a) individual-level factors, (b) dyadic factors of the service interaction, and (c) organizational factors. Although a number of antecedents can be expected to exist in each category, we focus on those variables from each category expected to have the strongest impact on employees' choice of emotional labor regulation strategies based on theoretical considerations and previous research findings.

Employee Job Satisfaction and Emotional Labor Strategy
Job satisfaction refers to the positive/negative attitude people have about their jobs (e.g., Churchill, Ford, & Walker, 1974). Findings on the impact of job satisfaction on emotional labor have been somewhat ambiguous, with some authors having found a negative relationship (e.g., Morris & Feldman, 1997) while others reported a positive relationship instead (e.g., Wharton, 1993).

These contradictory results may be due to the fact that job satisfaction has differential effects on emotional labor strategies (Grandey, 2003; Morris & Feldman, 1996). That is, employees who are dissatisfied with their jobs may have to engage in more surface acting in order to bring their displayed emotions in line with organizational display rules, but have difficulties to engage in deep acting because of the emotional investments required by that strategy. Consequently, we expect that the lower the employees' job satisfaction, the more they will engage in surface acting because it requires them to spend less effort than deep acting. Thus, we propose:

Proposition 10. Employees job satisfaction will have a positive impact on deep acting, but a negative impact on surface acting.

Organizational Citizenship Behavior and Acting Strategy Choice
Organizational citizenship behavior (OCB) is defined as behavior of individual employees that is discretionary, not directly or explicitly recognized by the formal reward system, and that, in the aggregate, promotes the effective functioning of the organization (Organ, 1988, 1990). Within the context of emotional labor, OCB has only recently received attention from researchers. Bailey et al. (2001) were the first to incorporate OCB as a variable in their model of emotional value in service encounters. These authors suggest that displaying emotions in itself may be considered as a form of OCB. Similarly, a relationship between OCB and emotional labor strategies was suggested by Totterdell and Holman (2003).

These studies suggest that employees may regard certain types of emotional labor as voluntary citizenship behavior that goes beyond organizational expectations. Building on this argument, we expect that employees with high levels of OCB will be more likely to engage in deep acting given the higher emotional effort required to deliver this emotional labor strategy. In contrast, when employees' level of OCB is low, they are more likely to prefer to engage in surface acting due to the smaller emotional efforts associated with this strategy type. Thus, we offer the following proposition:

Proposition 11. OCB will have a positive impact on deep acting, but a negative impact on surface acting.

Relationship Strength and Emotional Labor Strategy

Another potential antecedent of an employee's emotional labor strategy choice is the strength of the relationship, the employee maintains with an individual customer. In our research, we draw on a conceptualization of service relationships suggested by Gutek and colleagues (Gutek, Bhappu, Liao-Troth, & Cherry, 1999; Gutek, Groth, & Cherry, 2002) who distinguish between interactions of two people who have a shared history of interactions and expect to interact with each other again in the future (i.e., "service relationships") and interactions of people who do not know each other and do not expect to see each other again in the future (i.e., "service encounters"). This distinction can be transformed into a continuum of relationship strength, with long-term, intensive relationships defining a high relationship strength and one-time encounters with unknown customers defining low strength.

When an employee encounters a customer for the first time, he or she is likely to have difficulties in judging the appropriateness of emotional investments and therefore may be more likely to stay away from deep acting behavior, preferring surface acting instead. Surface acting is particularly likely to be applied when employees get the impression that a first-time customer will not use the service offered again in the future, e.g., because the customer is a tourist (i.e., low relationship strength). In contrast, in high relationship strength dyads, emotional investments will be considered more appropriate by the employee, based on the long-term perspective of his or her relationship with the customer. Therefore, employees will tend to apply deep acting when the strength of a relationship is high. We propose the following proposition:

Proposition 12. Relationship strength will have a positive impact on deep acting, but a negative impact on surface acting.

Service Scripts and Acting Strategy Choice

Service employees' performance is never context free, but influenced by norms and requirements of the service organization. A major organizational variable that can be expected to influence employees' choice of emotional labor strategies is the level of service scripts provided by the firm. Service scripts include formal descriptions of the way employees are expected to behave during interactions with customers (Smith & Houston, 1983). They are intended to increase the quality of service delivered through standardizing employee behavior and thereby reducing the level of service heterogeneity. Although service scripts can be found across many different types of services, empirical research on service scripts has been sparse.[1]

The extent to which service employees' behavior is regulated by service scripts is likely to impact employees' choice of emotional labor strategies. Specifically, the more service scripts restrict employee behavior, the more employees will engage in surface acting behavior because employees are prevented by rigid scripts from behaving in a natural, spontaneous way, which is part of a deep acting strategy. When service scripts are less rigid, leaving the employee sufficient space to adapt his or her behavior according to a customer's interests and needs, the employee is more likely to engage in deep acting behavior. Therefore, we offer our final antecedent-related proposition:

Proposition 13. The restrictiveness of service scripts has a negative impact on deep acting, but a positive impact on surface acting.

DISCUSSION

In this article, we developed a theoretical model that links two emotional labor acting strategies, surface acting and deep acting, to a variety of customer outcomes as well as to a number of individual-, dyadic-, and organizational-level antecedents. Given that most emotional labor research to date has focused on employee outcomes (e.g., well-being, job burnout, etc.), our research contributes to the emotions literature by drawing conceptual links between employees' propensity to engage in emotional labor and customers' attitudes and behavioral reactions to such display of emotional labor.

In short, this research focuses on the question of how the customer experience during service encounters can be managed by employing emotional labor strategies of service employees. Among service management and marketing research scholars, the interest in emotional labor is likely to surge. This research contributes to a more sophisticated understanding of the antecedents and outcomes of emotional labor and builds on previous work, which has focused on either emotional labor strategies or its consequences on employee well-being. Our conceptual model and the propositions derived from it support the notion that emotional labor is a relevant phenomenon, yet somewhat overlooked in the services literature, and has an impact on important customer outcomes such as satisfaction, trust, and loyalty behavior.

Theoretical Implications and Directions for Future Research

Our primary theoretical contribution lies in developing a model of emotional labor outcomes and antecedents. It is hoped that our proposed model will trigger some related future research. Naturally, a fruitful avenue would be an empirical test of our conceptual model. Although we focused on a number of variables deemed to be the most theoretically relevant outcomes and antecedents of emotional labor, there are other potentially important variables not included in our study. Future research may benefit from identifying additional customer attitudes, perceptions, and behaviors in regards to emotional labor that influence their service experience and ultimately affect their customer satisfaction and likelihood to remain loyal with the organization.

Our study also has implications for future research in terms of examining emotional labor strategies in a cross-cultural context. Anecdotal evidence suggests that norms and expectations regarding emotional display vary greatly among different cultures and countries among employees as well as customers. However, to our knowledge, no empirical research has examined the cross-cultural dimensions and implications of emotional labor. The advent of global markets and the fact that organizations operate across national boundaries require companies to become familiar with relevant services-related concepts (such as emotional labor) across different cultures. Thus, the relationships discussed in this article can be expected to be influenced by cultural variables. To understand the effects of culture on emotional labor, it would be especially important to examine communication patterns (verbal as well as non-verbal) as a component of culture, which is essential to any customer–employee interaction. A wealth of research has shown that cultures differ with regard to their communication styles and with regard to the importance they attach to verbally expressed messages (e.g., Gudykunst & Ting-Toomey, 1988; Guirdham, 1999; Hall, 1976). Future research may compare data collected from different cultures to explore whether emotional labor strategies and their antecedents and consequences are culture sensitive, i.e., differ across various countries and cultures.

Managerial Implications

It is hoped that by specifying the phenomenon of emotional labor, appropriate steps can be identified and taken by managers to improve service delivery. Our research advances managers' understanding of the customer experience of service delivery by showing how to strengthen customers' relationships with the service organization through increased satisfaction and retention based on a better understanding of customer perceptions of emotional display strategies of service employees. The knowledge generated by this research is not limited to service firms, but will also be of use to consumer goods companies that offer consumers interaction opportunities to increase the effectiveness of their customer-contact management.

Moving from the general to the specific, one practical implication of this research relates to employee training. Our conceptual model offers managers, implications as to how training programs need to be designed to target customers' emotional needs and improve employee performance. Our theoretical model suggests that there are benefits associated with training service employees in different emotional labor strategies as well as with a better understanding of the effects that emotional components of service delivery have on customers. For example, by applying the customer equity concept (Blattberg, Getz, & Thomas, 2001), employees could be taught that deep acting should be used when dealing with loyal and frequent customers, while surface acting is more appropriate for less frequent customers. We hope that by contributing to a better understanding of the characteristics and consequences of emotional labor among managers, organizations will be able to more effectively manage emotional demands of their employees and, consequently, create a better service experience for their customers.

NOTES

1. As a matter of fact, the authors are not aware of a single study that has empirically investigated service scripts.

REFERENCES

Ashforth, B. E., & Humphrey, R. H. (1993). Emotional labor in service roles: The influence of identity. *Academy of Management Review, 18*, 88–115.
Bailey, J. J., Gremler, D. D., & McCollough, M. A. (2001). Service encounter emotional value: The dyadic influence of customer and employee emotions. *Services Marketing Quarterly, 23*, 1–25.
Bitner, M. J. (1990). Evaluating service encounters: The effects of physical surroundings and employee responses. *Journal of Marketing, 54*, 69–82.
Blattberg, R. C., Getz, G., & Thomas, J. S. (2001). *Customer equity: Building and managing relationships as valuable assets.* New York: Harvard Business School Press.
Bowen, D. E. (1990). Interdisciplinary study of service: Some progress, some prospects. *Journal of Business Research, 20*, 71–79.
Bowen, D. E., Schneider, B., & Kim, S. S. (2000). Shaping service cultures through strategic human resource management. In: T. A. Swartz & D. Iacobucci (Eds), *Handbook of services marketing and management* (pp. 439–454). Thousand Oaks, CA: Sage.
Brotheridge, C. M., & Grandey, A. A. (2002). Emotional labor and burnout: Comparing two perspectives of "people work". *Journal of Vocational Behavior, 60*, 17–39.

A Conceptual Model of the Effects of Emotional Labor Strategies

235

Churchill, G. A., Jr., Ford, N. M., & Walker, O. C., Jr. (1974). Measuring the job satisfaction of the industrial salesman. *Journal of Marketing Research, 11*, 254–260.

Donavan, D. T., Brown, T. J., & Mowen, J. C. (2004). Internal benefits of service-worker customer orientation: Job satisfaction, commitment, and organizational citizenship behaviors. *Journal of Marketing, 68*, 128–146.

Glomb, T. M., & Tews, M. J. (2004). Emotional labor: A conceptualization and scale development. *Journal of Vocational Behavior, 64*, 1–23.

Goodwin, C., & Gremler, D. D. (1996). Friendship over the counter. In: S. B. Brown, D. Bowen, & T. Swartz (Eds), *Advances in services marketing and management* (Vol. 5, pp. 247–282). Greenwich, CT: JAI Press.

Grandey, A. A. (2003). When the show must go on: Surface acting and deep acting as determinants of emotional exhaustion and peer-rated service delivery. *Academy of Management Journal, 46*, 86–96.

Grayson, K. A. (1998). Customer responses to emotional labor in discrete and relational service exchange. *International Journal of Service Industry Management, 9*(2), 126–154.

Gremler, D. D., & Gwinner, K. P. (2000). Customer–employee rapport in service relationships. *Journal of Service Research, 3*, 82–104.

Gudykunst, W. B., & Ting-Toomey, S. (1988). *Cultural and interpersonal communication.* Thousand Oaks, CA: Sage Publications.

Guirdham, M. (1999). *Communicating across cultures.* Basingstoke: Palgrave.

Gutek, B. A., Bhappu, A. D., Liao-Troth, M. A., & Cherry, B. (1999). Distinguishing between service relationships and encounters. *Journal of Applied Psychology, 84*, 218–233.

Gutek, B. A., Groth, M., & Cherry, B. (2002). Achieving service success through relationships and enhanced encounters. *Academy of Management Executive, 16*(4), 132–144.

Gwinner, K. P., Gremler, D. D., & Bitner, M. J. (1998). Relational benefits in service industries: The customer's perspective. *Journal of the Academy of Marketing Science, 26*(2), 101–114.

Hall, E. T. (1976). *Beyond culture.* New York: Doubleday.

Hennig-Thurau, T. (2004). Customer orientation of service employees: Its impact on customer satisfaction, commitment, and retention. *International Journal of Service Industry Management, 15*, 460–479.

Hennig-Thurau, T., & Klee, A. (1997). The impact of customer satisfaction and relationship quality on customer retention: A critical reassessment and model development. *Psychology & Marketing, 14*, 737–764.

Hochschild, A. R. (1979). Emotion in work, feeling rules and social structure. *American Journal of Sociology, 85*, 551–575.

Hochschild, A. R. (1983). *The managed heart: Commercialization of human feeling.* Berkeley, CA: University of California Press.

Kruml, S. M., & Geddes, D. (2000). Catching fire without burning out: Is there an ideal way to perform emotional labor. In: N. M. Ashkanasay, C. E. J. Härtel & W. J. Zerbe (Eds), *Emotions in the workplace: Theory, research, and practice* (pp. 177–188). Westport, CT: Quorum Books.

Lemmink, J., & Mattson, J. (2002). Employee behavior, feelings of warmth and customer perception in service encounters. *International Journal of Retail & Distribution Management, 30*(1), 18–33.

Liljander, V., & Strandvik, T. (1997). Emotions in service satisfaction. *International Journal of Service Industry Management, 8*, 148–169.

Mann, S. (1999). Emotion at work: To what extent are we expressing, suppressing, or faking it. *European Journal of Work and Organizational Psychology, 8*, 347–369.

Mattila, A. S., & Enz, C. A. (2002). The role of emotions in service encounters. *Journal of Service Research, 4,* 268–277.

Morris, J. A., & Feldman, D. C. (1996). The dimensions, antecedents, and consequences of emotional labor. *Academy of Management Review, 4,* 986–1010.

Morris, J. A., & Feldman, D. C. (1997). Managing emotions in the workplace. *Journal of Managerial Issues, 9,* 257–274.

Oliver, R. T. (1997). *Satisfaction: A behavioral perspective on the consumer.* New York: The McGraw-Hill Companies.

Organ, D. W. (1988). *Organizational citizenship behavior: The good soldier syndrome.* Lexington, MA: Lexington Books.

Organ, D. W. (1990). The motivational basis of organizational citizenship behavior. In: B. M. Staw & L.L. Cummings (Eds), *Research in organizational behavior* (Vol. 12, pp. 43–72). Greenwich, CT: JAI Press.

Parasuraman, A., Zeithaml, V. A., & Berry, L. L. (1988). SERVQUAL: A multiple-item scale for measuring consumer perceptions of service quality. *Journal of Retailing, 64,* 12–40.

Price, L. L., & Arnould, E. J. (1999). Commercial friendships: Service provider–client relationships in context. *Journal of Marketing, 63,* 38–56.

Pugh, S. D. (2001). Service with a smile: Emotional contagion in the service encounter. *Academy of Management Journal, 44,* 1018–1027.

Rafaeli, A., & Sutton, R. I. (1987). Expression of emotion as part of the work role. *Academy of Management Review, 12,* 23–37.

Rousseau, D. M., Sitkin, S. B., Burt, R. S., & Camerer, C. (1998). Not so different after all: A cross-discipline view of trust. *Academy of Management Review, 23,* 393–404.

Rust, R. T., & Zahorik, A. J. (1993). Customer satisfaction, customer retention, and market share. *Journal of Retailing, 69,* 193–215.

Schaubroeck, J., & Jones, J. R. (2000). Antecedents of workplace emotional labor dimensions and moderators of their effects on physical symptoms. *Journal of Organizational Behavior, 21,* 163–183.

Sirdeshmukh, D., Singh, J., & Sabol, B. (2002). Consumer trust, value, and loyalty in relational exchanges. *Journal of Marketing, 66,* 15–37.

Smith, R. A., & Houston, M. J. (1983). Script based evaluations of satisfaction with services. In: L. L. Berry, G. L. Shostack & G. D. Upah (Eds), *Emerging perspectives in services* (pp. 59–62). Chicago: American Marketing Association.

Totterdell, P., & Holman, D. (2003). Emotion regulation in customer service roles: Testing a model of emotional labor. *Journal of Occupational Health Psychology, 8,* 55–73.

Tsai, W. C. (2001). Determinants and consequences of employee displayed positive emotions. *Journal of Management, 27,* 497–512.

Tsai, W. C., & Huang, Y. M. (2002). Mechanisms linking employee affective delivery and customer behavioral intentions. *Journal of Applied Psychology, 87,* 1001–1008.

Wharton, A. S. (1993). The affective consequences of service work. *Work and Occupations, 20,* 205–232.

Wharton, A. S. (1996). Service with a smile: Understanding the consequences of emotional labor. In: C. L. Macdonald & C. Sirianni (Eds), *Working in the service society* (pp. 91–112). Philadelphia, PA: Temple University Press.

Zapf, D. (2002). Emotion work and psychological well-being: A review of the literature and some conceptual considerations. *Human Resource Management Review, 12,* 237–268.

CHAPTER 10

CUSTOMER EMOTIONS IN SERVICE FAILURE AND RECOVERY ENCOUNTERS

Janet R. McColl-Kennedy and Amy K. Smith

ABSTRACT

Emotions play a significant role in the workplace, and considerable attention has been given to the study of employee emotions. Customers also play a central function in organizations, but much less is known about customer emotions. This chapter reviews the growing literature on customer emotions in employee–customer interfaces with a focus on service failure and recovery encounters, where emotions are heightened. It highlights emerging themes and key findings, addresses the measurement, modeling, and management of customer emotions, and identifies future research streams. Attention is given to emotional contagion, relationships between affective and cognitive processes, customer anger, customer rage, and individual differences.

INTRODUCTION: ROLE AND IMPORTANCE OF CUSTOMER EMOTIONS

Emotions play a significant role in the workplace, and employee emotions in particular have attracted considerable attention in organizational

Individual and Organizational Perspectives on Emotion Management and Display
Research on Emotion in Organizations, Volume 2, 237–268
ISSN: 1746-9791/doi:10.1016/S1746-9791(06)02010-4

research (Hartel, Zerbe, & Ashkanasy, 2005). Customers too fulfill a central function in organizations, but much less is known about their emotions. This is surprising, as emotions are frequently experienced during interactions between customers and frontline employees. These emotions can be positive or negative. Indeed, substantial media attention has been given to the display of negative customer emotions especially anger and other strong negative emotions (Mattila & Enz, 2002). Customer emotions have important practical implications, because how customers feel about a product or service impacts on customer satisfaction, repeat purchase, switching, negative word of mouth, complaining to third parties, and loyalty (DeWitt & Brady, 2003; Keaveney, 1995; Stephens & Gwinner, 1998). Customer delight, defined as a "profoundly positive emotional experience" (Oliver, Rust, & Varki, 1997) is considered critical to customer loyalty. Merely satisfying the customer is not enough as this may leave the door open for rethinking about possible alternative providers (McColl-Kennedy & Sparks, 2003).

The role of emotion is attracting greater acceptance and interest from both marketing academics and practitioners in their pursuit of a better understanding of customers and the consumption experience (Mattila & Enz, 2002; Oliver, 1997). To date, two review papers, Erevelles' (1998) "*The Role of Affect in Marketing*," and Bagozzi, Gopinath, and Nyer's (1999) paper entitled "*The Role of Emotions in Marketing*" have highlighted the importance of studying customer emotions. Erevelles (1998) summarizes research findings on affect and consumer decision making, affect and memory, post-purchase processes, product strategy, affect and advertising, retailing, services, and measurement issues and identifies 15 areas for future research. These areas are: affect and marketing strategy; role of affect in global and ethnic markets; affect and organizational buying behavior; affect, brand equity and extensions; affect and the marketing of services; affect and relationship marketing; more study across product categories; validation of product categories; altruistic, moral and gift-giving behavior; wider range of emotional appeals; effects of negative moods; multiple satisfaction processes; temporal and delayed effects of affect; measurement issues; and gender and affect.

Bagozzi et al. (1999, p. 202) argue that emotions are important in many areas of marketing, as "... they influence information processing, mediate responses to persuasive appeals, measure the effects of marketing stimuli, initiate goal setting, enact goal-directed behaviors, and serve as ends and measures of consumer welfare. Yet, we are only beginning to understand the role of emotions in marketing." The Bagozzi et al. paper highlights the importance of emotions especially for consumer behavior and focuses attention on the measurement of emotions, social bases of emotions, emotions–satisfaction relationship, and impact of emotions on behavior. The paper identifies 12 fruitful areas for future research. The areas that are particularly relevant to the study of customer emotions in service failure and recovery encounters are the following: how appraisals are conducted, identification of the key components of cognitive appraisals, and how they are influenced by marketing stimuli; the impact of emotions on post-purchase reactions and behaviors, interpersonal and group-based responses to emotions; how emotions affect information processing in consumer decision making; how emotions vary across cultures; how emotions are triggered, how distinct emotions are related to each other, and under what conditions certain emotions lead to other emotions, for example, whether frustration leads to dissatisfaction.

Liljander and Strandvik's (1997) article demonstrates the importance of negative emotions as they have a stronger impact than positive emotions on customer satisfaction. Furthermore, they showed that strong positive emotions do not influence a customer's level of satisfaction with a service. Furthermore, Liljander and Strandvik (1997) argue that emotions are multidimensional. They call for a greater understanding of customer emotions through in-depth analyses, identification of incidents that trigger negative customer emotions, and investigation into how effective service recovery can mediate the otherwise negative effect of negative emotions on customer satisfaction and loyalty.

Mattila and Enz (2002) show that even in relatively brief and mundane service transactions, customer-displayed emotions play an important role in influencing the customer's assessment of the service encounter and their overall experience with the service. Results suggest that consumers' evaluations of the service encounter correlate highly with their displayed emotions during the interaction and post-encounter mood. This finding is consistent with earlier work of Gardner (1985) that posited that mood effects are likely to be experienced in service encounters. Further, Mattila and Enz (2002) found that observations of the customer's expressed emotions as demonstrated in their eye contact, smiling, and thanking behavior can be used to predict the customer's assessment of the service provider's performance during the interaction. This finding is important as non-verbal communication is thought to comprise more than 60% of the interaction in service encounters.

Importance of Customer Emotions in Employee–Customer Interactions

Customers engage in interactions with service providers on a daily basis. Most of these encounters (direct interactions between the customer and the frontline employee) are mundane and largely inconsequential but those that are remembered, and where customer emotions are heightened, are those that "go wrong." When things go wrong with a service (defined as service failure), and during attempts by employees to fix the problem (service recovery), customers tend to experience negative emotions such as frustration, annoyance, anger, and sometimes rage (Andreassen, 2001). Indeed, studies by Berry and Parasuraman (1991) and Zeithaml, Berry, and Parasuraman (1993) suggest that customers are more involved in and more conscious of recovery attempts by employees than when the service is "normal," that is, as expected, or when it is experienced for the first time (Smith & Bolton, 2002).

Considerable attention has been given to the study of anger, demonstrating that when individuals experience anger they exhibit a tendency to want to attack the target verbally and/or non-verbally (Fitness, 2000; Deffenbacher, Lynch, Oetting, & Swaim, 2002). Sometimes this results in non-confrontational behaviors, such as exiting, boycotting, negative word of mouth, complaints to third parties; all of which have a negative impact on the organization (DeWitt & Brady, 2003; Keaveney, 1995; Stephens & Gwinner, 1998). But more overt behaviors can result in damage to the organization's property and/or persons, including frontline employee(s), other customers, and the customers themselves (Fullerton & Punj, 1993; Harris & Reynolds, 2003). Anger is one of the most commonly experienced negative emotions in service encounters. Extreme customer anger and dissatisfaction has particularly negative implications for firms including decreased brand loyalty, more customer attrition, lower return on investment (ROI), and increased negative word of mouth.

Significant resources are being spent by organizations on trying to fix problems when they arise, as happy customers are likely to stay with the firm and tell others about their positive experience, and even recommend the organization to their friends and acquaintances (Reichheld, 2003). In their 2003 article entitled *"Customer Care: The Multibillion Dollar Sinkhole – A Case of Customer Rage Unassuaged,"* the customer care alliance (CCA) compared their most recent study results with a White House-sponsored study conducted in 1976 that found effective complaint-handling practices produced high ROIs. The CCA made the following observations: This research led corporate America to invest billions of dollars in upgraded consumer affairs departments (call centers, increased remedies, Customer Relationship Management (CRM), satisfaction measurement, etc.). The good news is that effective customer complaint handling is associated with high levels of brand loyalty and profitability. This supports the conclusion of the White House study. However, ineffective policies lead to decreased levels of brand loyalty and negative ROIs. Unfortunately, the 2003 study found that most complaint-handling practices are ineffective and contribute to negative customer emotions such as anger and even customer rage.

In a similar vein, The Society of Consumer Affairs Professionals in Business Australia Inc (SOCAP), the initiator of the landmark 1995 American Express Study of Consumer Complaint Behavior (TARP), carried out the first comprehensive consumer emotions study in Australia (SOCAP, 2003) involving nine major Australian organizations and 4,000 consumers from around the nation. A key finding of the study was that very dissatisfied customers expressed negative emotions such as disappointment, anger, frustration, feeling neglected and disgusted. Only 14% of the consumers who contacted the respective organization were completely satisfied with the organization's response (SOCAP, 2003). The majority of consumers were not satisfied and expressed potentially destructive emotions such as anger, annoyance, frustration, feeling cheated, disgusted, and exasperated.

Definitions of Customer Emotions

Just as the organizational behavior researchers cannot agree on a single definition of emotion (Ashkanasy, Hartel, & Zerbe, 2000) given the different theoretical perspectives, various definitions of customer emotions exist. Bagozzi et al. (1999, p. 184) provide a broad definition of emotion as "... a mental state of readiness that arises from cognitive appraisals of events or thoughts; has a phenomenological tone; is accompanied by physiological processes; is often expressed physically (e.g., in gestures, posture, facial features); and may result in specific actions to affirm or cope with the emotion, depending on its nature and meaning for the person having it." Bagozzi et al. (1999) define "affect" as an umbrella term encompassing emotions and moods (and possibly attitudes). Erevelles (1998) defines affect as a "valenced feeling state," which encompasses mood and emotions, "mood" as "relatively low in intensity and usually unassociated with a stimulus object. Emotion, on the other hand, is defined by Erevelles as being "higher in intensity, and is usually associated with a stimulus object."

NEGATIVE CUSTOMER EMOTIONS FOLLOWING UNSATISFACTORY SERVICE ENCOUNTERS: KEY FINDINGS

Service encounters are first and foremost social exchanges where customers' (and employees') egos, sense of self-concept, self-esteem, and sense of fairness (justice) (Schneider & Bowen, 1995) are on the line. As a result, any unsatisfactory service encounter has the potential to quickly generate negative emotions and consequent behaviors. The importance of understanding and appropriately dealing with negative emotions, particularly those in the rage spectrum, has been long recognized by doctors, psychologists, and other health professionals because of the potential harmful consequences to the individual as well as others.

Drawing on the work of cognitive theorists, namely Izard (1991), Lazarus (1991), and Weiner (1985), Stephens and Gwinner (1998) argue that different types of emotions are produced from the consumer's assessments of whether the source of the negative encounter is external, situational, or internal. As such, emotion can be regarded as an outcome of a stressful cognitive appraisal (Lazarus, 1991). If blame is viewed as external, for example, the organization was to blame because they did not make a reservation even though the customer had telephoned to make the booking and the organization said they had a vacancy when the customer talked to them on the phone, anger, disgust, and contempt are likely emotions (Stephens & Gwinner, 1998; Nguyen & McColl-Kennedy, 2003). If the blame is viewed as situational, outside the organization's control, such as an electrical storm cutting off power, or failure to supply a service such as a scuba diving expedition because of bad weather, then sadness and/or fear is likely to be felt by the customer. However, if the blame is attributed to the customer (internal), then shame and/or guilt can be expected to be felt by the customer. For example, perhaps the customer did call the organization to make a reservation but made a mistake and told the person taking their phone call the wrong date. Folkes, Koletsky, and Graham's (1987) study found support for this in that airline passengers who believed that the airline was responsible for the delay in the flight felt anger at the organization and this resulted in a desire to complain to the organization responsible.

Customer Anger

Physiological changes take place when emotions are experienced. For example, anger, anxiety, and stress produce tenseness, perspiration, sweaty palms, red face, increased heartbeat, and heavier breathing (Renshaw, 2002; Scherer, 1993). Although anger is a frequently experienced emotion, anger in itself may not be that harmful. Rather, it is the way individuals express that anger initially in the anger-producing episode and subsequently in behaviors that is important (Deffenbacher et al., 2002). Intensity of the emotion is also critical because if anger is excessive, it can be harmful to the individual and may even become lethal if anger turns to rage. Intense anger and rage can result in harmful, destructive behaviors such as violence, vandalism, physical injury to one's self and/or to others and even planned retaliation (e.g., destruction, disruption, theft, psychological harassment) (Deffenbacher et al., 2002; Grove, Fisk, & Joby, 2004; Harris & Reynolds, 2003; Huefner & Hunt, 1995). Evidence of the impact of extreme anger is demonstrated by a recent rage incident in which a dissatisfied customer in Thailand (a country where open displays of emotion are shunned) destroyed his defective Toyota truck with an axe after the company continued to ignore his claims (Viriyapanpongsa & Varghese, 2005). Yet, there is also evidence that if anger is suppressed, it may produce increased tenseness, increased heart rate, and increased blood pressure (Holt, 1970).

Customer Rage

Anger and happiness are considered to be the two major basic emotions (Scherer, 2004). Anger has received particular attention as it is frequently experienced in a business setting (Scherer, 2004; Fitness, 2000) and can escalate into outrage and rage with dire consequences. However, marketing researchers and practitioners are just beginning to see the need to understand the rage spectrum, particularly due to increasing incidences of customer rage (Grove et al., 2004) and the associated negative short- and long-term consequences (Huefner & Hunt, 1995) for the individual concerned, the employees, and other customers who may be present.

The rise of this new and disturbing phenomenon known as "customer rage" has received much attention in the popular and business press. It was spawned by an article in *The Wall Street Journal* (Spencer, 2003), which chronicled some results from a study showing that 36% of customers admitted to raising their voice, yelling, and/or cursing at a service employee, and 45% of surveyed households reported at least one "serious problem" in the past year, with more than two-thirds experiencing "rage" over the way their incident was handled. Incidences of customer rage (some culminating in physical assault and even murder of employees) are becoming commonplace in service encounters. However, most organizations are ill-equipped to deal with these potentially dangerous situations because little is known about the causes, contexts, and consequences of customer rage, not to mention the most appropriate organizational responses (Grove et al., 2004).

Customer rage may be defined as an intense or extreme emotional reaction to dissatisfying elements of a service experience. Customer rage spectrum emotions may include feelings of exasperation, anger, fury, wrath, rage, outrage, hostility, ferocity, hate, spite, vengefulness, etc. but should *not* include lower level forms of anger or other negative emotions such as frustration, irritation, agitation, and annoyance. This conceptualization incorporates concepts drawn from a broad range of literature spanning from the clinical management of interpersonal rage in domestic relationships (e.g., Renshaw, 2002) to behavioral psychology research related to anger expression in driving (e.g., Deffenbacher et al., 2002; Lawton & Nutter, 2002) and road rage (Novaco, 1991).

Customer rage is a serious threat to companies and to society and clearly has both economic and social consequences. In July 2003, Jan Quintrall, president of the Better Business Bureau, wrote an article in *The Spokesman Review* entitled *"Consumer Rage Should Not Be Rewarded!"* outlining the consequences of these incidents for both service employees and businesses (Quintrall, 2003). Service employees are increasingly the victims of customer rage. For example, Barnett (2002) reports that each month bus drivers file hundreds of complaints with Seattle's Metro authorities about verbal harassments, property damage, and other threatening and dangerous behaviors by customers. Some examples included one passenger who yelled and kept banging his body against the coach, another who belligerently refused to pay a fare and blocked the front door of the bus after being told by the driver that he was not allowed to bring a large stackable lawn chair onto the bus, and another who slept past his stop and then when the driver would not return to the stop he harassed and loudly threatened the operator's job by calling the operator's supervisor on a mobile phone.

The increasing recognition of the importance of early detection of customer rage is demonstrated in new software being adopted by Fortune 500 companies that uses algorithms to detect rising levels of anger in callers that triggers a recording device and sends an alert to managers so that they can attempt to intervene and prevent escalation to customer rage (Chabrow, 2005). The program was developed by an Israeli company at a cost of over US$30 million.

ORGANIZATION-DIRECTED OUTCOMES

Previous work (Smith & Bolton, 2002; McColl-Kennedy & Sparks, 2003) has shown that customers who experience intense negative emotions may go to considerable lengths to "pay back" or "get even" with organizations who have wronged them (Bechwati & Morrin, 2003), even when the dollar amount of the original problem is very small (Bennett, Hartel, & McColl-Kennedy, 2005). These aggrieved customers may undertake a range of behaviors: (1) complain to an employee or manager of the organization in a calm manner; (2) scream abuse at the service provider (employee); (3) complain to a third party (e.g., consumer affairs); (4) spread negative word of mouth to family and friends; (5) seek revenge through non-violent means (e.g., exit, switch, boycott); (6) damage organizational property; (7) physically attack employees/other customers of the organization; (8) displace the anger; (9) internalize the anger (e.g., fume). Road rage research suggests violence was seen as necessary and justified because the perpetrator had been "wronged" and had suffered an injustice, and that this injustice had to be made "right." Since individuals experiencing rage emotions often feel that the offender needs to be "taught a lesson," retaliatory behavior toward organizations is often a consequence. Furthermore, it is clear from literature in psychology and sociology that anger results from a sense of injustice about what "should" and "should not" be done and that the provocateur is to blame and therefore should be punished (Indermaur, 1998). Indeed, the highest levels of anger were found when an event was viewed as intentional and personal (Lawton & Nutter, 2002). Consistent with these findings, work by McColl-Kennedy, Smith, and Patterson (2005) and McColl-Kennedy and Sparks (2003) found that cognitive assessments of a service failure triggered negative emotions such as anger, annoyance, and frustration and that customers appeared to engage in counterfactual thinking, i.e., thinking about what might have been. Results suggest that when customers felt that the service provider did not follow acceptable standards of what "should" have been done, the customer's negative emotions increased noticeably and if the customer perceived that they had been treated unfairly, their negative emotion escalated.

MEASUREMENT, MODELING, AND MANAGEMENT OF CUSTOMER EMOTIONS

Measurement of Customer Emotions in Service Failure and Recovery Encounters

Due to the lack of agreement and consistency in the definitions of emotion and the general tendency of consumer behavior and marketing researchers to rely on precedence (primarily based in psychology) when choosing measures for customer emotions, there is little consensus regarding how best to approach the measurement of customer emotions. For instance, many empirical studies of customer emotions have employed Izard's (1977) differential emotions scale (DES II), which consists of 30 items representing 10 fundamental emotions: interest, joy, anger, disgust, contempt, shame, guilt, sadness, fear, and surprise. Customers are usually asked to what extent they have experienced these emotions on a scale ranging from "almost never" to "very often." This scale typically results in a two-dimensional (positive and negative affect) representation of customer emotions.

Plutchik (1980) took a similar approach to emotion measurement by identifying eight "primary" emotions (consisting of fear, anger, joy, sadness, acceptance, disgust, expectancy, and surprise) and then developed an Emotions Profile Index (Plutchik & Kellerman, 1974) containing 62 forced-choice emotion descriptor pairs. Shorter versions of this scale were subsequently developed, adapted, and tested in a consumption context by Havlena and Holbrook (1986) and by Holbrook and Westwood (1989).

The emotions included in these scales also correspond to Ekman's (1994) characterization of a set of specific, discrete emotions that includes fear, anger, sadness, joy, love, and affection, and Shaver, Schwartz, Kirson, and O'Connor's (1987) list that includes love, joy, surprise, anger, sadness, and fear.

Another approach has been to measure emotional responses based on three (nearly) independent dimensions of pleasure, arousal, and dominance using the Pleasure, Arousal, Dominance (PAD) scale developed by Mehrabian and Russell (1974). Pleasure–displeasure distinguishes the positive–negative affective quality of emotional states, arousal–non-arousal refers to a combination of physical activity and mental alertness, and dominance–submissiveness is defined in terms of control versus lack of control. Specific emotions are inferred based on a customer's score as represented in a three-dimensional PAD emotion space. For example, "happy" is high on pleasure, moderate on arousal, while "angry" is high on displeasure, high on arousal, and moderate on dominance. Therefore, the 18-item semantic differential PAD scale does not measure emotions per se but rather the perceived pleasure, arousal, and dominance elicited by the stimuli. The PAD approach has been used to measure emotional responses to marketing stimuli such as atmospherics. Although some recent studies have used this three-dimensional approach to measure customer affect (Foxall & Greenley, 1999, 2000; Foxall & Yani-de-Soriano, 2005), it has generally been replaced by Russell's (1980) derivative: the circumplex model. This model assesses customer affect along just two of the original dimensions, namely pleasure and arousal, as dominance is believed to be an underlying dimension of cognition and perception (Donovan, Rossiter, Marccolyn, & Nesdale, 1994; Russell, 1980; Russell & Pratt, 1980).

Others have used the positive affect negative affect scale (PANAS) (Mano & Oliver, 1993; Watson, Clark, & Tellegen, 1988), which consists of 20 items representing specific positive and negative emotions scored on a 5-point scale that asks customers to indicate the degree to which they feel each emotion on a 5-point scale anchored by "very slightly, not at all" to "extremely" for a given time period (ranging from at the moment to past few days to past week to year to general). Therefore, this scale seems to be more suited for *trait* measures of affect than emotions related to a specific situation. It has been shown that *state* measures of affect vary over time and have a more dynamic influence on individual behavior (Schmukle, Egloff, & Burns, 2002).

Finally, Richins (1997) demonstrated that many commonly used direct measures of emotion (e.g., scales developed by Batra & Holbrook, 1990; Edell & Burke, 1987; Izard, 1977; Mehrabian & Russell, 1974; Plutchik, 1980) are unsuited for the purpose of measuring consumption-related emotions. She specifically pointed out the limitations of these measurement scales and also argued that some emotions used in the psychology and organizational behavior literature are irrelevant in marketing (consumer) contexts and that scales used to measure emotional responses to advertising are not designed to capture specific emotion states experienced during consumption. Therefore, Richins (1997) developed a consumption emotions set (the CES) representing the range of emotions consumers most frequently experience in consumption situations: anger (frustrated, angry, irritated); discontent (unfulfilled, discontented); worry (nervous, worried, tense); sadness (depressed, sad, miserable); fear (scared, afraid, panicky); shame (embarrassed, ashamed, humiliated); envy (envious, jealous); loneliness (lonely, homesick); romantic love (sexy, romantic, passionate); love (loving, sentimental, warm hearted); peacefulness (calm, peaceful); contentment (contented, fulfilled); optimism (optimistic, encouraged, hopeful); joy (happy, pleased, joyful), excitement (excited, thrilled, enthusiastic); surprise (surprised, amazed, astonished), and "other items" (guilty, proud, eager, relieved).

For the CES items, customers indicate how much a specified consumption situation made them feel each emotion on a 4-point response scale ("not at all," "a little," "moderately," "strongly"). Richins (1997) acknowledged that the CES represents a relatively broad but not exhaustive set of consumption emotion states and that some of the emotions included in the CES may be irrelevant to some phenomena studied in consumer research. The CES scale has subsequently been adapted and used in many empirical studies related to emotions in consumption situations (e.g., Ruth, Brunel, & Otnes, 2002). In studies of emotional contagion between customers in café/restaurant consumption settings, Tombs (2005) and Tombs and McColl-Kennedy (2005) measured customer emotions using Richins' CES scale. These studies found that Richins' consumption emotions outperformed PAD in terms of the variance explained by environmentally induced emotions influencing repurchase intentions.

As service encounters are a type of consumption-related situations, it seems that the CES scale may represent the most appropriate starting point for the measurement of customer emotions using a verbal scale. However, while consumer behavior and marketing researchers have traditionally relied on structured adjective-type scales to measure customer emotions, other techniques have also been employed. For example, measuring emotion via content analysis of verbal protocols (thought listings) is a technique that has been successfully used by other researchers (e.g., Fiebig & Kramer, 1998) and has been specifically applied in a study of the effects of customers' emotional responses to service failure and recovery encounters (Smith & Bolton, 2002). Because the use of words as descriptors to represent the underlying emotions felt by customers may be dependent upon their level of competence in articulating feelings or understanding the distinctions between similar emotional labels and descriptors, some researchers employ non-verbal cues in the measurement of emotions by using the coding of facial expressions (e.g., Derbaix, 1995; Ekman & Friesen, 1975; Kunin, 1955, 1998). Another approach to using non-verbal cues was applied in a study of service encounters by Mattila and Enz (2002) who captured displayed emotions via an index that measures the mechanics of expressed emotions and is composed of eye contact, smiling, and thanking behaviors (see Rafaeli & Sutton, 1989; Sutton & Rafaeli, 1988). The limitations of scales that use non-verbal cues are that they cannot adequately capture specific emotions and they may require respondents to have a high level of emotional intelligence.

The use of verbal, self-report measurement approaches has several advantages including ease of administration and analysis and the ability to distinguish between different types of emotions. However, they also have certain drawbacks such as customers' inability to identify their emotions, tendency to rationalize their emotions, and reluctance to share their emotions. In addition, these types of measures require both memory and cognitive effort. Consequently, some researchers employ non-verbal approaches that involve physiological, autonomic methods such as galvanic skin response, pupil dilation, and continuous process tracing methods. Although these methods have been helpful in measuring emotional responses to advertising, they would be very difficult to use and administer in a service encounter situation and they cannot be used to distinguish among specific emotions.

In studies of customer emotions involving service failure and recovery encounters, it is also important to clarify that the focus is primarily on stimulus-induced emotion (i.e., emotions that arise from a stimulus, which in this case would be the service failure) (Shiv & Fedorikhin, 1999) rather than task-induced emotion (i.e., emotions that arise directly from the structure or difficulty of the decision task itself), or ambient emotion (i.e., emotions that arise from background conditions such as fatigue or mood) (Isen, 1997; Yates, 1990). Another key aspect of service failure and recovery encounters, is that while customers' responses may be affected by their *general* emotional state (i.e., positive, neutral, or negative), it is also likely that their responses would be influenced by the type and intensity of *discrete* emotions (such as anger, disappointment, anxiety, etc.) that underlie their overall affective condition. A final consideration in the measurement of customer emotions in service failure and recovery encounters is that there is a temporal aspect to account for in that customers' emotions may change dramatically over the course of the encounter (i.e., after the failure versus after the recovery, depending on the effectiveness of the recovery, and depending on the duration of the encounter and the amount of time that lapses between the failure and the recovery or lack thereof). Therefore, in sum, all of these unique aspects of service recovery encounters suggest that multiple methods and a longitudinal, dynamic approach may be required to fully capture the nature and level of customer emotions.

Modeling of Customer Emotions in Service Failure and Recovery Encounters

In prior research models of customer satisfaction and other post-purchase processes, researchers have treated emotion as a mediator, a moderator, and as an independent variable. Because service failure and recovery encounters involve many different aspects and attributes, and occur over a period of time, there are various potential sources of positive and negative emotions. During a service encounter, emotions can also be related to past experiences with the type of service, past experience with the particular service provider, or to employee behaviors, the behavior of other customers, or to the customer's own behaviors. Emotion has been posited as a mediator between cognitive evaluations (such as expectations, performance, or disconfirmation) and customer satisfaction (Oliver, 1993b; Oliver & Westbrook, 1993). In a study of service failure and recovery encounters in the hospitality industry, Smith and Bolton (2002) found that emotion moderates the effects of recovery performance and other cognitive antecedents on service encounter satisfaction and that customers who respond with more emotion to service failures seem to process information more systematically and thoroughly. Andreassen (1999, 2000) found that initial negative emotion triggered by a service failure had a negative impact on customers' satisfaction with the organization's complaint resolution efforts and stimulated exit behavior. Other researchers have also demonstrated that emotion can contribute independently to satisfaction after accounting for the effects of cognitive antecedents (Oliver 1993b; Smith & Bolton, 2002). Therefore, in models of service failure and recovery encounters, emotions can directly and/or indirectly influence customers' perceptions, evaluations, satisfaction judgments, and behaviors.

Management of Customer Emotions in Service Failure and Recovery Encounters

Frontline service employees are critical to the management of customer emotions, not only because they are the ones who can observe and respond to customers during service encounters, but also because employee behaviors are often the trigger or cause of customer emotions stemming from service encounters, especially those involving service failure and recovery. Therefore, the services management literature tends to focus on human resource issues in terms of managing customer service and service quality (e.g., Bateson, 1995; Bowen, Schneider, & Kim, 2000). Prior research has also shown that displayed emotions serve as cues (Rafaeli & Sutton, 1990), which can enable employees to respond more appropriately and effectively to customers during service encounters.

Dubé and Menon (1998) argue that, if customers express negative emotions and the service provider successfully decodes them, then the service provider can change his/her performance and create higher levels of service encounter satisfaction. They cite evidence from several studies that suggests that service providers have been able to successfully employ these strategies in specific consumption situations such as hospitalization and delayed airline flights. This notion is consistent with prior research that has stressed how the social aspects of service encounters (personalization, friendliness, self-disclosure) are critical to customer satisfaction and loyalty (e.g., Goodwin & Gremler, 1996). Thus, knowledge of the impact of emotions experienced by customers during service failure and recovery encounters can help managers to engineer the service delivery process to maximize satisfaction.

They can do this by hiring employees with the ability to decode emotional cues and also by providing training to enhance this ability in current employees. In other words, employees should be able to recognize when customers are angry, disappointed, anxious, etc. Dubé and Menon (1998) argue that customers express negative emotions using distinct patterns of facial, postural, vocal, and verbal cues corresponding to discrete negative emotions. If such cues are not evident, service providers should encourage customers to verbalize their emotions so they can be recognized. Dubé and Menon (1998) and Tombs (2005) also suggest that empathic reactions such as "mimicking" customers' displays of negative emotions may give the service provider an opportunity to guide the customer toward a satisfactory service outcome. Finally, because customers exhibit varying types and levels of negative emotions during service failure and recovery encounters, providers should be trained to offer customized recovery efforts directed at improving the more emotional customer's situation on multiple dimensions by making an array of tools and resources available to frontline service employees (e.g., offers of compensation, goodwill gestures, apologies, timely response, empowerment, empathizing with the customer, taking the perspective of the customer, and thinking counterfactually) (McColl-Kennedy & Sparks, 2003).

RELATIONSHIP BETWEEN CUSTOMER EMOTIONS AND COGNITIONS

While there are varying theories and views about the distinction between and the nature of the relationship between cognition and affect, it is generally accepted that the two are somehow interdependent. Emotions have been shown to influence various aspects of cognitive processes including perceptions, evaluations, judgments, and behavioral intentions. Linkages have also been established between emotions and repurchase intentions (Oliver, 1997). Bagozzi et al. (1999) and Erevelles (1998) detail some of the effects that an individual's emotional state can have on memory, categorization, evaluations, attitudes, decision-making, and information processing as well as on post-purchase processes, volitions, and behaviors (see also Dubé, Ferland, & Moskowitz, 2003).

Therefore, while marketing and consumer researchers had typically taken the view that customers' evaluations are primarily based on cognitive-based assessments, subsequent research has established that independent positive and negative affective dimensions directly influence satisfaction and other post-purchase processes, and that these affective responses account for a significant amount of variance in customer responses, over and above traditional cognitive explanations (Westbrook, 1987). Emotions have also been shown to sometimes provide judgmental responses that are potentially faster, more predictive, and more consistent across individuals (Pham, Cohen, Pracejus, & Hughes, 2001). In addition, Bagozzi et al. (1999) argue that when processing of information is low (e.g., due to low motivation or involvement), affect has a direct and larger influence on attitude than cognition and even when information processing is high, affective state influences cognitive thoughts and, ultimately, evaluations. Finally, prior research also suggests that, for services high in experience or credence properties, customers may rely heavily on their affective reactions to derive satisfaction judgments (Alford & Sherrell, 1996). Therefore, in service failure and recovery encounters, we would expect emotions to have both direct and indirect influences on customer responses and behaviors.

Emotions and Customer Satisfaction

Customer satisfaction is considered to be a key outcome of service encounters whereby a comparison is made between expectations and actual performance (Oliver, 1980; Yi, 1990). In addition to expectations, performance, and attribute satisfaction, positive and negative affects have also been shown to be important determinants of customer satisfaction (Mano & Oliver, 1993; Oliver, 1993a; Westbrook, 1987; Westbrook & Oliver, 1991). Therefore, although early models of customer satisfaction focused mainly on cognitive processes to understand and explain customer satisfaction, it is now clear that emotions play a major role in customers' satisfaction judgments (Erevelles & Leavitt, 1992; Mano & Oliver, 1993; Yi, 1990), and particularly in customer satisfaction with service encounters (Liljander & Strandvik, 1997; Mattila & Enz, 2002; Smith & Bolton, 2002).

Research has shown that satisfaction judgments contain both cognitive and affective components and that affective responses can have a larger influence on customer satisfaction than cognitive evaluations (Dubé-Rioux, 1990; Mano & Oliver, 1993). For example, recent research has demonstrated that negative emotions displayed over service encounters involving customer penalties explain more variance in dissatisfaction judgments than disconfirmation does (Kim & Smith, 2005). Oliver (1993a) has not only shown that positive and negative affects are associated with satisfaction judgments, but also that attribute satisfaction influences affective responses such that these emotional responses act as a mediator in the relationship between attribute satisfaction and overall satisfaction. Therefore, we would expect that in service failure and recovery encounters, customers' responses will be largely driven directly and indirectly by emotions and that individual attributes of the service encounter may evoke different emotions that will ultimately affect satisfaction judgments and other post-purchase behaviors.

Emotions and Service Encounter Evaluations

Services researchers generally consider satisfaction and service quality from a cognitive perspective, viewing both concepts as post-consumption cognitive processes. Satisfaction and service quality levels traditionally have been assumed to be directly and positively related to the level of disconfirmation (Liljander & Strandvik, 1997; Zeithaml et al., 1993). Yet Strandvik (1994) found an asymmetrical relationship suggesting that customers have a zone of tolerance. Falling below this level has a greater impact on customers than when this level is exceeded. Price, Arnould, and Deibler (1995) found that negative emotions were generated when there was a failure by the service provider to provide the customer with a minimum standard considered by the customer to be appropriate for that service. While a strong positive emotion does not explain satisfaction, strong negative emotions can be associated with dissatisfaction (Liljander & Strandvik, 1997).

But it is important to recognize that a single encounter, particularly an extended service encounter, such as a shopping trip or a stay at a hotel or resort may elicit a number of different emotions and that negative emotions do not always result in dissatisfaction (Dubé & Menon, 2000; Liljander & Strandvik, 1997). For example, a consumer may experience excitement about going shopping only to find that the sales person is rude to the consumer, which makes them feel angry, and because the store is sold out of the size of shirt the customer needs, the customer feels sad and disappointed. Further, consider a customer who goes to see a film or the opera. The film/opera may make the customer feel sad and/or angry, but the customer may be simultaneously satisfied, possibly even very satisfied, with the film/opera itself (Liljander & Strandvik, 1997). Furthermore, Arnould and Price (1993) found that customers who experienced extreme negative emotions and customers who experienced extreme positive emotions both reported having high levels of satisfaction with a river rafting experience.

In a study of credence-based services (which are the most difficult for customers to evaluate), Alford and Sherrell (1996) propose that there may be two sources that may elicit customer emotions – the service itself and the focal service provider. Specifically, they found that both types of affect had an influence on customers' perceptions of performance, which, in turn, affected satisfaction judgments. In addition, Price et al. (1995) found that in a study of service encounters, extra attention by a service provider tends to induce positive emotions in customers while failing to meet minimum standards leads to negative emotions. Similarly, Mattila and Enz (2002) found that even in mundane, low-involvement service encounters, employee actions can affect customer emotions and that customers' displayed emotions are associated with both their service encounter evaluations and overall assessments of the firm.

Moreover, Muller, Tse, and Venkatasubramaniam (1991) propose that customer emotions are present in all aspects of a service encounter, including pre-purchase, interaction, and post-purchase phases. Liljander and Strandvik (1997) argue that this conceptualization can be extended to encompass a relationship perspective consisting of several encounters, where evaluations and emotions associated with each episode serve as inputs for the next encounter. Thus, based on prior research, it seems that customer emotions in service failure and recovery encounters should be studied in terms of: the different emotions that can be elicited by the service itself as well as the various employee actions over the course of the service encounter; the effects of customer emotions on different types of evaluations such as performance, service quality, and satisfaction judgments; and the influence of these emotions on both encounter-level and relationship-level assessments of the service provider.

Emotions and Attributions

Attribution theory accounts for how people make causal inferences, and previous studies show that inferred reasons for events influence customer responses and satisfaction judgments (Blodgett, Granbois, & Walters,

1993; Dubé & Menon, 2000; Folkes, 1984; Heider, 1958; Jones & Davis, 1965; Kelley & Michela, 1980). Researchers have suggested that attributions of locus (i.e., party or event responsible for causing the situation), control (i.e., degree of control over the situation), and stability (i.e., likelihood of the situation occurring again) will affect customer emotions and that attribution-driven emotions will vary depending on whether outcomes (e.g., as in service encounters) are positive or negative (Folkes, 1988; Oliver, 1989). Specifically, Oliver (1993b) posits that locus of control will affect customer emotions (and ultimately satisfaction). Also, recent research has demonstrated that attributions of controllability and stability have a significant direct influence on the cognitive and affective antecedents of dissatisfaction (Kim & Smith, 2005) in service encounters involving customer penalty incidents.

Therefore, attribution theory may be helpful in explaining customers' responses to service failure and recovery encounters, since research shows that negative events (e.g., service failures) elicit more attributional search and longer survey of causal information than positive or neutral events (Peeters & Czapinski, 1990; Wong & Weiner, 1981). As attributions are important in service failure and recovery encounters (see Sparks & Callan, 1996), it is important to include the influence of attributions and explore the specific role of these effects in models involving customer emotions and satisfaction with such incidents.

EMOTIONAL CONTAGION

Emotional contagion may be defined as the tendency to converge emotionally with others due to exposure to their displayed emotions, that is, if one can observe the emotions of others it is possible that these displayed emotions will influence that individual's affective state and subsequent behaviors (Hatfield, Cacioppo, & Rapson, 1994; Levy & Nail, 1993). Organizational behavior studies have demonstrated that emotional contagion occurs in work environments between employers and employees, between employees and employees (Ashforth & Humphrey, 1995; Barsade, 2002; McColl-Kennedy & Anderson, 2005), and in service environments between employees and customers (Hochschild, 1983; Howard & Gengler, 2001; Pugh, 2001; Tsai, 2001). Hochschild (1983) suggests that for positive customer emotions to be produced, employees must create and display positive emotions themselves (Tombs & McColl-Kennedy, 2003). Such a positive affective climate created by employees "infecting" customers with positive emotions will help to achieve important organizational objectives (Hochschild, 1983; Sutton, 1991; Sutton & Rafaeli, 1988). For example, Pugh (2001) showed that in a study of the interaction between bank tellers and their customers, positive emotions displayed by employees correlated with both the customers' positive affective states and their subsequent positive evaluation of the interaction. Furthermore, other studies have demonstrated that emotional contagion between employees and customers influences the customer's attitude toward products (Howard & Gengler, 2001), customer satisfaction (Brown & Sulzer-Azaroff, 1994; Homburg & Stock, 2004), and repurchase intentions (Tsai, 2001). Furthermore, a recent study by Tsai and Huang (2002) showed that employee affective delivery (EAD), which refers to an employee's "act of expressing socially desired emotions during service transactions" (Ashforth & Humphrey, 1993, pp. 88–89), had an influence on customer in-store emotional responses and behavioral intentions in retail environments.

Customers should not be regarded as "receptive objects" but rather as individuals who experience and display a range of emotions that can impact on others in the environment (Hatfield et al., 1994; Tombs & McColl-Kennedy, 2003). Holt (1995) showed that, in socially oriented settings, the displayed emotions of the individuals (baseball spectators) tend to become communal emotions and play a major part in the consumption experience. Furthermore, emotional contagion between customers is thought to be a significant factor in influencing both specific customer behaviors and the overall atmosphere of an environment (Tombs & McColl-Kennedy, 2003). This is demonstrated in a recent qualitative study by Tombs (2005), in which customers described how they were influenced by the emotions of others around them. As one customer explained, "… what I can say about the moods is that we generally consider the whole experience of going to a restaurant is a function of the food we eat plus the sort of atmosphere that is created. So we are conscious of other people's mood and the service quality and how that influences people's moods and how moods relate to the general atmosphere. In that sense the mood acts as a …. something that makes the experience more enjoyable or not." Another customer stated that, "I witnessed an argument with a customer and a waitress in a Chinese restaurant. I don't know what the cause was, but it was disruptive, it was unpleasant. You could sense that the mood in the restaurant dampened and it lingered even after the person left. I felt uncomfortable. And then I think we left earlier otherwise we may have lingered and ordered dessert. It took us actually quite a while before we went back." In this case the customer was recounting a service failure where she had no direct involvement but was infected by the emotions of others present. Further, Tombs (2005) has demonstrated that emotional contagion occurs between customers within the same environment, resulting in significant outcomes for the firm. For example, if the displayed emotions of some of the other customers are negative (such as anger and/or frustration), these emotions are likely to infect nearby customers and result in negative outcomes for the organization including negative word of mouth and customers being less likely to return and less likely to recommend the organization to others.

Tombs and McColl-Kennedy (2005) showed that when customers were exposed to overtly positive emotions, they experienced congruent positive feelings (contagion) or incongruent negative feelings (counter-contagion). When the customer's purchase occasion was a social or group occasion (such as a group birthday in a restaurant setting), they were more likely to enjoy the displays of positive emotions as this was seen as adding to the social atmosphere. On the other hand, if the occasion for which the customer purchased the service was private (such as a business meeting in a restaurant), then these customers appeared to resent the intrusion of emotions displayed by others, even when they were positive, thus resulting in negative feelings toward the other customers present and the firm.

INDIVIDUAL DIFFERENCES IN CUSTOMER EMOTIONS

Gender

It is widely acknowledged that leaders/supervisors often express positive emotions such as enthusiasm and optimism to motivate their colleagues as well as negative emotions such as anger and frustration in interactions. McColl-Kennedy and Anderson (2005), in a study of interactions between sales managers and sales representatives, found that gender combinations (male supervisor with male sales representative, male supervisor with female sales representative, female supervisor with male sales representative; and female supervisor with female sales representative) with leadership style produced different levels of frustration and optimism. They found that female manager–female sales representative with transformational leadership style was the best combination for producing positive emotions, self-esteem, and commitment to the organization. Conversely, female manager–female subordinate gender with management-by-exception style had the least favorable set of probabilities for positive emotions, self-esteem and organizational commitment. Larsen and Diener (1987) found that some individuals experience greater intensity of emotions when exposed to emotionally provocative stimuli. In a study of gender differences in six emotions across 37 countries, Fischer, Mosquera, van Vianen, and Manstead (2004) found that western men reported more powerful negative emotions (e.g., anger), whereas women reported more powerless negative emotions (e.g., sadness and fear). Although men and women reported the same intensity of powerful negative emotions (e.g., anger and disgust) and this finding did not differ across countries, significant differences were found for the negative emotions of fear, sadness, shame, and guilt, with women reporting a greater intensity of these negative emotions than men.

Although we are not aware of any published studies on gender differences in customer emotions during failures and recovery encounters, McColl-Kennedy, Daus, and Sparks (2003) clearly demonstrated significant differences between men and women regarding how service recovery should be handled. Specifically, the results revealed that female customers wanted to voice their concerns during service failure and recovery attempts, and that this resulted in greater levels of satisfaction and intention to return for women, but not men.

Culture

There is contradictory evidence regarding whether there are cultural differences in the way anger is expressed and demonstrated in behaviors. Lawton and Nutter (2002) found no significant differences in reported levels in expression of anger in everyday and automobile driving situations in terms of nationality of respondents (nationalities included American, European, Canadian, Brazilian, Malaysian, Japanese, and Chinese). In contrast, in a study of interpersonal aggression in Japanese, American, and Spanish students, Fujihara, Kohyama, Andreu, and Ramirez (1999) found that, although the basic factor structure of the Japanese, Spanish, and USA samples was similar, Japanese students showed a lower justification of indirect verbal aggression but a higher justification of direct verbal aggression than the American and Spanish students. Further, physical aggression in defense situations was more common in Americans. These authors assert that oriental cultures with an interdependent construal of self, seem more permissive of direct verbal aggression compared to Western cultures, but they have less tolerance for indirect verbal aggression. However, among highly collectivist Southeast Asian countries (China, Thailand, Indonesia, Malaysia), public displays of emotion (especially anger) are a clear sign of weakness (Holmes & Tangtongtavy, 1995; Triandis, 1995). Hence there exists a cultural norm of suppressing one's emotions in all but the direst circumstances. In Thailand, for example, *Jai Yen* (cool heart) is a core value. People learn from a young age to suppress any open displays of emotions such as anger, disappointment, and even frustration. Further, *Kreng Jai* (be considerate of others in most circumstances), and the desire for harmony are also core values that reinforce the cultural norm of not openly displaying emotions, especially extreme negative ones (Patterson & Smith, 2001, 2003; Triandis, 1995). However, to our knowledge, no significant cross-cultural empirical research has been conducted on customer rage, or even in terms of negative customer emotions in service failure and recovery encounters.

FUTURE RESEARCH DIRECTIONS

While service failure and recovery encounters have received much more attention from researchers over the past several years, there are still many areas that need to be explored in terms of customer emotions associated with such episodes. Therefore, a few avenues for future research in this important area are included here.

First, given the apparent rise in the levels of customer anger, especially in service failure situations and the negative (and sometimes potentially dangerous) consequences that result from such incidents for customers, organizations, and society, it is important to learn more about the triggers of these extreme emotions as well as the handling of such episodes. While anger is one of the most commonly experienced negative emotions in service encounters, it is surprising that extreme negative emotions such as rage, fury, ferocity, hostility, wrath, vengefulness, outrage (Shaver et al., 1987) have been neglected by consumer behavior and services marketing researchers. Current conceptualizations of consumption-related emotions that limit anger descriptors to "frustrated," "angry," and "irritated" (Richins, 1997) are inadequate for capturing more intense feelings. Therefore, research is needed to identify, define, and measure customer rage spectrum emotions (as triggered by service failure encounters) to determine how customers express these emotions, to examine how these experiences and expressions ultimately map onto specific behaviors directed toward the organization, and to provide organizations with guidelines for effectively responding to customer rage episodes.

Second, in addition to the overall refinement of scales and use of new techniques that may be needed to more specifically and effectively capture and measure customer emotions, several issues arise in terms of the modeling of customer emotions in service failure and recovery encounters that require further investigation. For instance, the importance of including both satisfaction and emotions in models pertaining to service failure and recovery encounters seems clear. However, the issue of whether satisfaction/dissatisfaction is phenomenologically distinct from certain positive/negative emotions continues to persist. In light of this, Bagozzi et al. (1999) argue that more rigorous empirical investigation is needed that specifies how satisfaction exists uniquely from many other positive emotions and how dissatisfaction can be clearly distinguished from certain negative emotions. In fact, Bagozzi et al. (1999) also suggest that, under certain situations, it is likely that certain positive and negative emotions are more important outcomes of purchase than satisfaction/dissatisfaction, and that the implications of emotional reactions in consumption situations on complaint behaviors, word-of-mouth communications, repurchase, and other behaviors may differ for various positive and negative emotions and be more relevant than satisfaction judgments per se.

Therefore, an avenue for future research would involve examining the roles of specific emotions and satisfaction in assessing customers' responses during and after service failure and recovery encounters. In general, it may also be useful to separate the different specific emotions and study their individual effects on customer responses to service encounters (i.e., satisfaction, complaining behavior, repurchase intentions, word-of-mouth communications, and other behaviors) or to look at patterns of emotions in order to find more varied relationships. Previous studies show that customers can be divided into clusters with different emotional profiles (Westbrook & Oliver, 1991; Oliver & Westbrook, 1993). Liljander and Strandvik (1997) conclude that these different emotional patterns may be related to a satisfaction continuum. Therefore, it would also be useful to identify customer groups with different emotional patterns and determine how these profiles are related to customer responses such as satisfaction. Both of these avenues of research should provide insights that would help managers to strategically leverage specific customer emotions to influence certain responses and behaviors.

Third, because service failure and recovery encounters typically involve mixed emotions, multiple interactions, and have a temporal aspect in terms of the timing and duration of events that occur during the encounter, it is important to examine how emotions change for better or worse over the course of the service encounter, depending on the actions taken by the service employees and how different types of cognitive appraisals correspond to specific emotions experienced by customers. It would also be useful to study how emotions felt during past service failure and recovery encounters influence subsequent evaluations of service encounters as well as more global evaluations of the service relationship and overall assessments of the organization. In addition, more research is needed to understand the complex nature of customers' emotional experiences during service failure and recovery encounters and to assess the nature and extent of coping mechanisms that customers can use to deal with negative emotions stemming from such episodes.

Finally, further research is needed to provide insights into the effective identification and management of customer emotions. Some of the keys to advancing knowledge in this area may involve studies that examine the effects of displayed emotions on both customers and employees or the influence of displayed emotions on both customers and employees via emotional contagion. Given that co-production of the service experience involves both the employee and the customer (Vargo & Lusch, 2004), it would be useful to investigate how these emotions are co-produced, specifically the role of emotional contagion for both positive and negative emotions and how emotions change over the course of the interactions between the customer and employee. Further, given that service failures often result in negative customer emotions such as anger, and because anger is one of the most contagious emotions, it is critical to provide guidelines to organizations on how customer-contact employees can respond most effectively in such situations. It is expected that some customers will express emotions differently to others, with some displaying more emotions than others. Research into gender and cultural differences is warranted. Moreover, additional research is also needed to examine the role of emotional expressiveness and emotional intelligence in helping to understand and manage customer emotions in service failure and recovery encounters.

ACKNOWLEDGMENTS

We gratefully acknowledge the contribution of Dr Alastair Tombs in reviewing our paper and providing helpful input and Sue Hogan for her editorial assistance.

REFERENCES

Alford, B. L., & Sherrell, D. (1996). The role of affect in consumer satisfaction judgments of credence-based services. *Journal of Business Research, 37,* 71–84.
Andreassen, T. W. (1999). What drives customer loyalty with complaint resolution? *Journal of Service Research, 1*(4), 324–332.

262 JANET R. McCOLL-KENNEDY AND AMY K. SMITH

26726726726762262 JANET R. McCOLL-KENNEDY AND AMY K. SMITH

Andreassen, T. W. (2000). Antecedents to satisfaction with service recovery. *European Journal of Marketing, 34*(1/2), 156–175.

Andreassen, T. W. (2001). From disgust to delight: Do customers hold a grudge? *Journal of Service Research, 4*(1), 39–49.

Arnould, E. J., & Price, L. L. (1993). River magic: Extraordinary experience and the extended service encounter. *Journal of Consumer Research, 20*, 24–45.

Ashforth, B. E., & Humphrey, R. H. (1993). Emotional labor in service roles: The influence of identity. *Academy of Management Review, 18*, 88–115.

Ashforth, B. E., & Humphrey, R. H. (1995). Emotion in the workplace: A reappraisal. *Human Relations, 48*, 97–125.

Ashkanasy, N. M., Hartel, C. E. J., & Zerbe, W. J. (2000). Emotions in the workplace: Research, theory, and practice – introduction. In: N. M. Ashkanasy, W. J. Zerbe & C. E. J. Hartel (Eds), *Emotions in the workplace: Research, theory, and practice* (pp. 3–18). Westport, CT: Quorum Books.

Bagozzi, R. P., Gopinath, M., & Nyer, P. U. (1999). The role of emotions in marketing. *Journal of the Academy of Marketing Science, 27*(2), 184–206.

Barnett, E. C. (2002). *Bus battles, seattle weekly, January 2*. Retrieved from http://www.seattleweekly.com/news/0201/news-barnett.php

Barsade, S. G. (2002). The ripple effect: Emotional contagion in groups. *Administrative Science Quarterly, 47*(4), 644–676.

Bateson, J. E. G. (1995). *Managing services marketing: Text and readings*. Fort Worth, TX: The Dryden Press.

Batra, R., & Holbrook, M. (1990). Developing a typology of affective responses to advertising. *Psychology and Marketing, 7*, 11–25.

Bechwati, N. N., & Morrin, M. (2003). Outraged consumers: Getting even at the expense of getting a good deal. *Journal of Consumer Psychology, 13*(4), 440–453.

Bennett, R., Härtel, C. E. J., & McColl-Kennedy, J. R. (2005). Experience as a moderator of involvement and satisfaction on brand loyalty in a business-to-business setting. *Industrial Marketing Management, 34*(1), 97–108.

Berry, L. L., & Parasuraman, A. (1991). *Marketing services: Competing through quality*. New York: Free Press.

Blodgett, J. G., Granbois, D. H., & Walters, R. G. (1993). The effects of perceived justice on complaints' negative word-of-mouth behavior and repatronage intentions. *Journal of Retailing, 69*(4), 399–427.

Bowen, D., Schneider, B., & Kim, S. (2000). Shaping service cultures through strategic human resource management. In: T. Swartz & D. Iacobucci (Eds), *Handbook of services marketing and management* (pp. 439–454). Thousand Oaks, CA: Sage.

Brown, C. S., & Sulzer-Azaroff, B. (1994). An assessment of the relationship between customer satisfaction and service friendliness. *Journal of Organizational Behavior Management, 14*, 55–75.

Chabrow, E. (2005). New support-center tool detects emotion in voice of disgruntled customers. *Information Week*, March 25.

Deffenbacher, J. L., Lynch, R. S., Oetting, E. R., & Swaim, R. C. (2002). The driving anger expression inventory: A measure of how people express their anger on the road. *Behaviour Research and Therapy, 40*(6), 717–737.

Derbaix, C. (1995). The impact of affective reactions on attitudes toward the advertisement and the brand: A step toward ecological validity. *Journal of Marketing Research, 4*(11), 470–479.

DeWitt, T., & Brady, M. K. (2003). Rethinking service recovery strategies. *Journal of Service Research, 6*(2), 193–207.

Donovan, R. J., Rossiter, J. R., Marcoolyn, G., & Nesdale, A. (1994). Store atmosphere and purchasing behavior. *Journal of Retailing, 70*(3), 283–294.

Dubé, L., Ferland, G., & Moskowitz, D. S. (2003). *Emotional and interpersonal dimensions of health services: Enriching the art of care with the science of care*. Montreal, Quebec: McGill-Queen's University Press.

Dubé, L., & Menon, K. (1998). Why would certain types of in-process negative emotions increase post-purchase consumer satisfaction with services? *Advances in Services Marketing and Management, 7,* 131–158.

Dubé, L., & Menon, K. (2000). Multiple role of consumption in post-purchase satisfaction with extended service transactions. *International Journal of Service Industry Management, 11*(3), 287–304.

Dubé-Rioux, L. (1990). The power of affective reports in predicting satisfaction judgments. *Advances in Consumer Research, 17,* 571–576.

Edell, J. A., & Burke, M. C. (1987). The power of feelings in understanding advertising effects. *Journal of Consumer Research, 14,* 421–433.

Ekman, P. (1994). Moods, emotions, and traits. In: P. Ekman & R. J. Davidson (Eds), *The nature of emotion: Fundamental questions* (pp. 56–58). New York and Oxford: Oxford University Press.

Ekman, P., & Friesen, W. V. (1975). *Unmasking the face: A guide to recognizing emotions for facial clues*. Upper Saddle River, NJ: Prentice-Hall.

Erevelles, S. (1998). The role of affect in marketing. *Journal of Business Research, 42,* 199–215.

Erevelles, S., & Leavitt, C. (1992). A comparison of current models of consumer satisfaction/dissatisfaction. *Journal of Satisfaction, Dissatisfaction and Complaining Behavior, 5,*104–114.

Fiebig, G. V., & Kramer, M. W. (1998). A framework for the study of emotions in organizational contexts. *Management Communication Quarterly, 11,* 336–372.

Fischer, A. H., Mosquera, P. M. R., van Vianen, A. E. M., & Manstead, A. S. R. (2004). Gender and culture differences in emotion. *Emotion, 4*(1), 87–94.

Fitness, J. (2000). Anger in the workplace: An emotion script approach to anger episodes between workers and their superiors, co-workers and subordinates. *Journal of Organizational Behavior, 21*(2), 147–162.

Folkes, V. S. (1984). Consumer reactions to product failure: An attributional approach. *Journal of Consumer Research, 10,* 398–409.

Folkes, V. S. (1988). Recent attribution research in consumer behavior: A review and new directions. *Journal of Consumer Research, 14,* 548–565.

Folkes, V. S., Koletsky, S., & Graham, J. L. (1987). A field study of causal inferences and consumer reaction: The view from the airport. *Journal of Consumer Research, 13,* 534–539.

Foxall, G. R., & Greenley, G. E. (1999). 'Consumers' emotional responses to service environments. *Journal of Business Research, 46*(2), 149–158.

Foxall, G. R., & Greenley, G. E. (2000). Predicting and explaining responses to consumer environments: An empirical test and theoretical extension of the behavioral perspective model. *The Service Industries Journal, 20*(2), 39–63.

Foxall, G. R., & Yani-de-Soriano, M. M. (2005). Situational influences on consumers' attitudes and behavior. *Journal of Business Research, 58*(4), 518–525.

Fujihara, T., Kohyama, T., Andreu, J. M., & Ramirez, J. M. (1999). Justification of inter-personal aggression in Japanese, American, and Spanish students. *Aggressive Behavior,* *25*(3), 185–195.

Fullerton, R. A., & Punj, G. (1993). Choosing to misbehave: A structural model of aberrant consumer behavior. *Advances in Consumer Research, 20,* 570–574.

Gardner, P. (1985). Mood states and consumer behavior: A critical review. *Journal of Consumer Research, 12,* 281–300.

Goodwin, C., & Gremler, D. D. (1996). Friendship over the counter: How social aspects of service encounters influence customer service loyalty. In: T. A. Swartz, D. E. Bowen & S. W. Brown (Eds), *Advances in services marketing and management* (Vol. 5, pp. 247–282). JAI Press Inc.

Grove, S. J., Fisk, R. P., & Joby, J. (2004). Surviving in the age of rage. *Marketing Management, 13*(2), 41–46.

Harris, L. C., & Reynolds, K. L. (2003). The consequences of dysfunctional customer behavior. *Journal of Services Research, 6*(2), 144–161.

Hartel, C. E. J., Zerbe, W. J., & Ashkanasy, N. M. (2005). Organizational behavior: An emotions perspective. In: C. E. J. Hartel, W. J. Zerbe & N. M. Ashkanasy (Eds), *Emotions in organizational behavior* (pp. 1–10). Mahwah, NJ: Lawrence Erlbaum Associates.

Hatfield, E., Cacioppo, J. T., & Rapson, R. L. (1994). *Emotional contagion.* Paris: Cambridge University Press.

Havlena, W. J., & Holbrook, M. B. (1986). The varieties of consumption experience: Comparing two typologies of emotion in consumer behavior. *Journal of Consumer Research, 13*(3), 394–404.

Heider, F. (1958). *The psychology of interpersonal relations.* New York: Wiley.

Hochschild, A. R. (1983). *The managed heart.* Los Angeles: University of California Press.

Holbrook, M. B., & Westwood, R. A. (1989). The role of emotion in advertising revisited: Testing a typology of emotional responses. In: P. Cafferata & A. M. Tybout (Eds), *Cognitive and affective responses to advertising* (pp. 353–371). Lexington, MA: Lexington Books.

Holmes, H., & Tangtongtavy, S. (1995). *Working with the Thais.* Bangkok: White Lotus.

Holt, R. R. (1970). On the interpersonal and intrapersonal consequences of expressing or not expressing anger. *Journal of Consulting and Clinical Psychology, 35,* 8–12.

Holt, D. B. (1995). How consumers consume: A typology of consumption practices. *Journal of Consumer Research, 22*(1), 16–33.

Homburg, C., & Stock, R. M. (2004). The link between salespeople's job satisfaction and customer satisfaction in a business-to-business context: A dyadic analysis. *Academy of Marketing Science Journal, 32*(2), 144–158.

Howard, D. J., & Gengler, C. (2001). Emotional contagion effects on product attitudes. *Journal of Consumer Research, 28*(2), 189–201.

Huefner, J. C., & Hunt, H. K. (1995). Extending the Hirschman model: When voice and exit don't tell the whole story. *Journal of Consumer Satisfaction, Dissatisfaction and Complaining Behavior, 7,* 267–270.

Indermaur, D. (1998). Preventing driving related violence. Paper presented at 7th international seminar on environmental criminology and crime analysis, Barcelona, 21–24 June. (http://www.roadrage.law.uwa.edu.au/welcome/publications)

Isen, A. M. (1997). Positive affect and decision making. In: W. M. Goldstein & R. M. Hogarth (Eds), *Research on judgment and decision making: Currents, connections, controversies* (pp. 509–534). Cambridge: Cambridge University Press.

Izard, C. E. (1977). *Human emotions.* New York: Plenum.

Izard, C. E. (1991). *The psychology of emotions.* New York: Plenum.

Jones, E. E., Davis, K. (1965). From acts to dispositions: The attribution process in person perception. In: L. Berkowitz (Ed.), *Advances in experimental social psychology* (Vol. 2, pp. 219–266). New York: Academic Press.

Keaveney, S. M. (1995). Customer switching behavior in service industries: An exploratory study. *Journal of Marketing, 59*(2), 71–82.

Kelley, H. H., & Michela, J. L. (1980). Attribution theory and research. *Annual Review of Psychology, 31*, 457–501.

Kim, Y. K., & Smith, A. K. (2005). Crime and punishment: Examining customers' responses to service organizations' penalties. *Journal of Service Research, 8*(2), 162–180.

Kunin, T. (1955). The construction of a new type of attitude measure. *Personnel Psychology, 9*, 65–78.

Kunin, T. (1998). The construction of a new type of attitude measure: The most widely cited article of the 1950s. *Personnel Psychology, 514*, 823–824.

Larsen, R. J., & Diener, E. (1987). Affect intensity as an individual difference characteristic: A review. *Journal of Research in Personality, 21*, 1–39.

Lawton, R., & Nutter, A. (2002). A comparison of reported levels and expression of anger in everyday and driving situations. *British Journal of Psychology, 93*(3), 407–423.

Lazarus, R. S. (1991). *Emotion and adaptation.* New York: Oxford University Press.

Levy, D. A., & Nail, P. R. (1993). Contagion: A theoretical and empirical review and re-conceptualization. *Genetic, Social, and General Psychology Monographs, 119*(2), 233–284.

Liljander, V., & Strandvik, T. (1997). Emotions in service satisfaction. *International Journal of Service Industry Management, 8*(2), 148–169.

Mano, H., & Oliver, R. L. (1993). Assessing the dimensionality and structure of consumption experience: Evaluation, feeling, and satisfaction. *Journal of Consumer Research, 20*, 451–466.

Mattila, A. S., & Enz, C. A. (2002). The role of emotions in service encounters. *Journal of Service Research, 4*(4), 268–277.

McColl-Kennedy, J. R., & Anderson, R. D. (2005). Subordinate-manager gender combination and perceived leadership style influence on emotions, self-esteem and organizational commitment. *Journal of Business Research, 58*, 115–125.

McColl-Kennedy, J. R., Daus, C. S., & Sparks, B. A. (2003). The role of gender in reactions to service failure and recovery. *Journal of Service Research, 6*(1), 66–82.

McColl-Kennedy, J. R., Smith, A. K., & Patterson, P. (2005). Exploring customer rage spectrum emotions, expressions, and behaviors in service failure encounters: Customer and employee perspectives. Paper presented at Frontiers in Services Conference. Phoenix, AZ, October.

McColl-Kennedy, J. R., & Sparks, B. A. (2003). Application of fairness theory to service failures and service recovery. *Journal of Service Research, 5*(3), 251–266.

Mehrabian, A., & Russell, J. A. (1974). *An approach to environmental psychology.* Cambridge, MA: MIT Press.

Muller, T. E., Tse, D. K., & Venkatasubramaniam, R. (1991). Post-consumption emotions: Exploring their emergence and determinants. *Journal of Consumer Satisfaction, Dissatisfaction and Complaining Behavior, 4*, 13–20.

Nguyen, D. T., & McColl-Kennedy, J. R. (2003). Diffusing customer anger in service recovery: A conceptual framework. Special issue: Emerging issues in services marketing: Emotions, e-marketing and encounters. *Australasian Marketing Journal, 11*(2), 46–55.

Novaco, R. W. (1991). Aggression on roadways. In: R. Baenninger (Ed.), *Targets of violence and aggression*. North-Holland: Elsevier.

Oliver, R. L. (1980). A cognitive model of the antecedents and consequences of satisfaction decisions. *Journal of Marketing Research, 42*(4), 460–469.

Oliver, R. L. (1989). Processing of the satisfaction response in consumption: A suggested framework and research propositions. *Journal of Consumer Satisfaction, Dissatisfaction and Complaint Behavior, 2*, 1–16.

Oliver, R. L. (1993a). A conceptual model of service quality and service satisfaction: Compatible goals, different concepts. In: A. T. Swartz, D. E. Bowen & S. W. Brown (Eds), *Advances in services management* (Vol. 2, pp. 65–85). Greenwich, CT: JAI Press Inc.

Oliver, R. L. (1993b). Cognitive, affective and attribute bases of the satisfaction response. *Journal of Consumer Research, 20*, 418–430.

Oliver, R. L. (1997). Emotional expression in the satisfaction response. In: *Satisfaction: A behavioral perspective on the consumer* (pp. 291–325). Boston, MA: Irwin/McGraw-Hill.

Oliver, R. L., Rust, R. T., & Varki, S. (1997). Customer delight: Foundations, findings, and managerial insight. *Journal of Retailing, 73*, 311–336.

Oliver, R. L., & Westbrook, R. A. (1993). Profiles of consumer emotions and satisfaction in ownership and usage. *Journal of Consumer Satisfaction, Dissatisfaction and Complaining Behavior, 6*, 12–27.

Patterson, P. G., & Smith, T. (2001). Modeling relationship strength across service types in an eastern culture. *International Journal of Service Industry Management, 12*(2), 90–113.

Patterson, P. G., & Smith, T. (2003). A cross-cultural study of switching barriers and propensity to stay with service providers. *Journal of Retailing, 79*(2), 107–120.

Peeters, G., & Czapinski, J. (1990). Positive-negative asymmetry in evaluations: The distinction between affective and informational negativity effects. In: W. Stroebe & M. Hewstone (Eds), *European review of social psychology* (Vol. 1, pp.33–60). Wiley.

Pham, M. T., Cohen, J. B., Pracejus, J. W., & Hughes, G. D. (2001). Affect monitoring and the primacy of feelings in judgment. *Journal of Consumer Research, 28*(2), 167–188.

Plutchik, R. (1980). *Emotion: A psychoevolutionary synthesis*. New York: Harper & Row.

Plutchik, R., & Kellerman, H. (1974). *Emotions profile index manual*. Los Angeles: Western Psychological Services.

Price, L. L., Arnould, E. J., & Deibler, S. L. (1995). Consumers' emotional responses to service encounters. *International Journal of Service Industry Management, 6*(3), 34–63.

Pugh, S. D. (2001). Service with a smile: Emotional contagion in the service encounter. *Academy of Management Journal, 44*(5), 1018–1027.

Quintrall, J. (2003). Consumer rage should not be rewarded. *Better Business Bureau Newsletter*, July/August.

Rafaeli, A., & Sutton, R. (1989). The expression of emotion in organizational life. In: L. L. Cummings & B. Staw (Eds), *Research in organizational behavior* (Vol. 11, pp. 1–42). Greenwich, GT: JAI.

Rafaeli, A., & Sutton, R. (1990). Busy stores and demanding customers: How do they affect the display of positive emotions? *Academy of Management Journal, 33*(3), 623–637.

Reichheld, F. F. (2003). The one number you need to grow. *Harvard Business Review*, (December), 1–9.

Renshaw, D. C. (2002). Rage 2002. *The Family Journal, 10*(2), 240–243.

Richins, M. L. (1997). Measuring emotions in the consumption experience. *Journal of Consumer Research, 24*(2), 127–146.

Russell, J. A. (1980). A circumplex model of affect. *Journal of Personality and Social Psychology, 39*(6), 1161–1178.

Russell, J. A., & Pratt, G. A. (1980). Description of the affective quality attributed to environments. *Journal of Personality and Social Psychology, 38*(2), 311–322.

Ruth, J. A., Brunel, F. F., & Otnes, C. C. (2002). Linking thoughts to feelings: Investigating cognitive appraisals and consumptions emotions in a mixed-emotions context. *Journal of the Academy of Marketing Science, 30*(1), 44–58.

Scherer, K. R. (1993). Studying the emotion-antecedent appraisal process: An expert system approach. *Cognition and Emotion, 7*(3/4), 325–355.

Scherer, K. R. (2004). Ways to study the nature and frequency of our daily emotions: Reply to the commentaries on emotions in everyday life. *Social Science Information, 43*(4), 667–689.

Schmukle, S. C., Egloff, B., & Burns, L. R. (2002). The relationship between positive and negative affect in the positive and negative affect schedule. *Journal of Research in Personality, 36*, 463–475.

Schneider, B., & Bowen, D. (1995). *Winning the service game.* Boston: The Harvard Business School Press.

Shaver, P., Schwartz, J., Kirson, D., & O'Connor, C. (1987). Emotion knowledge: Further exploration of a prototype approach. *Journal of Personality and Social Psychology, 52*(6), 1061–1086.

Shiv, B., & Fedorikhin, A. (1999). Heart and mind in conflict: The interplay of affect and cognition in consumer decision making. *Journal of Consumer Research, 26*, 278–292.

Smith, A. K., & Bolton, R. N. (2002). The effect of customers' emotional responses to service failures on the their recovery effort evaluations and satisfaction judgments. *Journal of the Academy of Marketing Science, 30*(1), 5–23.

SOCAP. (2003). *Consumer emotions study.* The Society of Consumer Affairs Professionals in Business Australia Inc. Melbourne.

Sparks, B. A., & Callan, V. J. (1996). Service breakdowns and service evaluations: The role of customer attributions. *Journal of Hospitality and Leisure Marketing, 4*(2), 3–24.

Spencer, J. (2003). Cases of customer rage mount as bad service prompts venting. *The Wall Street Journal,* September 17, p. D 4.

Stephens, N., & Gwinner, K. P. (1998). Why don't some people complain? A cognitive-emotive process model of consumer complaint behavior. *Academy of Marketing Science Journal, 2*(3), 172.

Strandvik, T. (1994). *Tolerance zones in perceived quality.* Doctoral dissertation 58, Publications of the Swedish School of Economics and Business Administration, Helsinki, Finland.

Sutton, R. I. (1991). Maintaining norms about emotional expression: The case of bill collectors. *Administrative Science Quarterly, 36*(2), 245–268.

Sutton, R. I., & Rafaeli, A. (1988). Untangling the relationship between displayed emotions and organizational sales: The case of convenience stores. *Academy of Management Journal, 31*, 461–487.

Tombs, A. G. (2005). *The social-servicescape: Influence of other customers on customers present.* Unpublished doctoral dissertation, University of Queensland, Brisbane, Australia.

Tombs, A. G., & McColl-Kennedy, J. R. (2003). Social-servicescape conceptual model. *Marketing Theory, 3*(4), 447–475.

Tombs, A. G., & McColl-Kennedy, J. R. (2005). The impact of social density, purchase occasion and displayed emotions of others on customer affect and behavioural intensions. Paper presented at 34th EMAC Conference. Milan, Italy, May.

Triandis, H. C. (1995). *Individualism and collectivism.* Boulder: Westview Press.

Tsai, W. C. (2001). Determinants and consequences of employee displayed positive emotions. *Journal of Management, 27,* 497–512.

Tsai, W., & Huang, Y. (2002). Mechanisms linking employee affective delivery and customer behavioral intentions. *Journal of Applied Psychology, 87*(5), 1001–1008.

Vargo, S. L., & Lusch, R. F. (2004). Evolving to a new dominant logic for marketing. *Journal of Marketing, 68,* 1–17.

Viriyapanpongsa, S., & Varghese, V. (2005). Dissatisfied customer thrashes his Toyota pickup, *The Nation* newspaper, p. 21 February 5 (Bangkok).

Watson, D., Clark, L. A., & Tellegen, A. (1988). Development and validation of brief measures of positive and negative affect: The PANAS scales. *Journal of Personality and Social Psychology, 54*(6), 1063–1070.

Weiner, B. (1985). An attribution theory of achievement, motivation and emotion. *Psychological Review, 92,* 548–573.

Westbrook, R. A. (1987). Product/consumption based affective responses and postpurchase processes. *Journal of Marketing Research, 24*(August), 258–270.

Westbrook, R. A., & Oliver, R. L. (1991). The dimensionality of consumption emotion patterns and consumer satisfaction. *Journal of Consumer Research, 18*(June), 84–91.

Wong, P. T. P., & Weiner, B. (1981). When people ask "why" questions, and the heuristics of attributional search. *Journal of Personality and Social Psychology, 40*(4), 650–663.

Yates, J. F. (1990). *Judgment and decision making.* Englewood Cliffs, NJ: Prentice-Hall.

Yi, Y. (1990). A critical review of consumer satisfaction. In: V. A. Zeithaml (Ed.), *Review of marketing* (pp. 68–123). Chicago: American Marketing Association.

Zeithaml, V. A., Berry, L. L., & Parasuraman, A. (1993). The nature and determinants of customer expectations of service. *Journal of the Academy of Marketing Science, 21*(1), 1–12.

CHAPTER 11

ATTRIBUTION AND NEGATIVE EMOTION DISPLAYS BY SERVICE PROVIDERS IN PROBLEMATIC SERVICE INTERACTIONS

Kay Yoon and Lorna M. Doucet

ABSTRACT

Recent research on service interactions indicates that negative displays of emotion by service providers play an important role in customer perceptions of the quality of the service. In this study, we examined the relations between attributions of responsibility for problems and the displays of negative emotions by service providers in service interactions. We hypothesized that attributions of responsibility for problems moderate the relation between the negativity of service providers' prior and subsequent emotion displays and the relation between the negativity of emotion display by customers and service providers. To test our hypotheses, we collected data from telephone service interactions in a large retail bank in the northeastern United States and measured the negativity of emotion displays by using the Dictionary of Affect in Language. Our results showed that (1) the negativity of service providers' prior emotion displays predicts the negativity of their subsequent displays, and (2) this relation is moderated by the attribution of responsibility for problems.

Individual and Organizational Perspectives on Emotion Management and Display
Research on Emotion in Organizations, Volume 2, 269–289
Copyright © 2006 by Elsevier Ltd.
ISSN: 1746-9791/doi:10.1016/S1746-9791(06)02011-6

INTRODUCTION

Recent research on service interactions indicates that displays of negative emotions by service providers play an important role in a customer's perceptions of service quality (Doucet, 2005) and, hence, the organizational profitability (Zeithaml, Berry, & Parasuraman, 1996). However, very little research has been done on the antecedents of the displays of negative emotions by service providers.

Earlier research has examined various antecedents of general emotion displays by service providers such as individual differences (Pugh, 2001), the type of service interaction (Gutek, 1995; Schneider & Bowen, 1995), and the context of service interaction (Pugh, 2001; Sutton & Rafaeli, 1988). Other antecedents of emotion displays have been proposed, but have yet to be tested empirically (Rafaeli & Sutton, 1989).

Research on service quality has found that service provider behavior during problematic service interactions can be a particularly important determinant of service quality (Rust, Zahorik, & Keiningham, 1996; Tax & Brown, 2000). Therefore, it is important to understand the antecedents of emotion displays in problematic service interactions. Past research in the general domain of problematic interpersonal interactions has shown that cognitive appraisals affect emotion displays (e.g., Betancourt & Blair, 1992). Building on these research streams, we examined the relations between cognitive appraisals and negative emotion displays in problematic service interactions. Specifically, we adopted the attributional theory of emotion and examined how attribution of responsibilities in problematic situations affects the consistency and contagion of emotion displays.

ATTRIBUTIONAL THEORY OF EMOTION

Attribution theories applied in emotion research suggested that cognitive processes are antecedents to emotion displays (Weiner, 1986). In proposing an attributional theory of emotion, scholars argued that particular emotional experiences such as anger and guilt are determined by an appraisal of causes for negative events (Lazarus & Smith, 1988; Smith, Hayes, Lazarus, & Pope, 1993; Weiner, 1985, 1986). More specifically, they theorized that people experience different types of emotion in negative events depending on who is perceived to be responsible for the problem and whether or not the person had volitional controllability of the causes of the problem. For example, feelings of guilt occur when the cause of a problem is within oneself, whereas feelings of anger occur when the cause of a problem is within another person. Also, one feels sympathy toward a person who suffers from a problem but has no control over its cause.

Empirical tests of attributional theory of emotion have been conducted in the areas of perception, help-giving decision, and conflict (e.g., Allred, 2000; Betancourt & Blair, 1992; Karasawa, 2001; Yamauchi & Lee, 1999). Karasawa (2001) examined subjects' interpretations of expressions of anger and guilt in response to negative events. He found that when subjects observed targets expressing anger, they inferred that the targets were less responsible for negative events than targets who were observed expressing guilt. In a study of help-giving decisions, Yamauchi and Lee (1999) found that the attribution of causal controllability influenced the feelings of sympathy that an observer has for a victim. Reading hypothetical scenarios in which causal controllability was manipulated, the subjects in the study felt more sympathetic toward the victims when they perceived that victims were less responsible for negative events.

Research in conflict and negotiation also suggests that attribution processes affect emotion displays (Allred, 2000; Betancourt & Blair, 1992; Johnson, Ford, & Kaufman, 2000). Allred (2000) described the impact of the judgment of responsibility on emotion displays in conflict situations. He theorized that the perception of responsibility affects emotion displays, which in turn affect the escalation of conflict and negotiation outcomes. Betancourt and Blair (1992) also confirmed the role of attribution as a determinant of anger and empathic emotions in conflicts. They examined perceived controllability and intentionality in conflict situations and found that attribution processes led to either anger or empathy, which in turn determined the degree of violence in the conflict.

ATTRIBUTION AND NEGATIVE EMOTION DISPLAYS

The empirical research described above provides ample support for the theory that feelings of guilt occur when the cause of a problem is within oneself whereas feelings of anger occur when the cause of a problem is within another person. Since previous research has shown that anger is a more negative emotion than guilt (Weiner, 1986; Whissel, 1989), we can simplify this by arguing that more intensely negative emotions are experienced when the cause of a problem is within another person than when the cause of a problem is in oneself. Furthermore, past research indicates that felt emotions are a good predictor of displayed emotions (see Ambady, Laplante, & Johnson, 2001 and Nowicki & Duke, 2001 for reviews). Hence, within the service interaction setting, we propose the following:

Hypothesis 1. In problematic service interactions, service providers will display more intensely negative emotions when they attribute responsibility for the problem to the customers than when they attribute responsibility for the problem to the bank (or a service provider for the bank).

INTRAPERSONAL CONSISTENCY

Theoretical or empirical research on the effect of prior emotion displays on subsequent emotion displays is scarce. However, at a more general level, a body of interpersonal communication literature addresses how prior communication behavior relates to subsequent communication behavior (see Cappella, 1984 for a review). This line of research examined whether or not general communicative behavior (verbal, non-verbal, and vocal) of individuals are consistent over time and across different social settings. The studies suggest that individuals' subsequent communicative behavior is reasonably well predicted by their prior behavior when situational variations are not pronounced. General consistency has been found in speech behavior related to floor time, vocalization, pausing, eye contact, gaze patters, and physical distance (Cappella, 1981; Cappella & Planalp, 1981; Daniell & Lewis, 1972; Jaffe & Feldstein, 1970; Libby, 1970). Cappella (1979) also found consistency of talk and silence styles in the individuals interacting in a group. Based on the consistency of communicative styles that was found in these studies, we argue that one's emotion displays may be consistent in service interactions. Therefore, we hypothesize that:

Hypothesis 2. In problematic service interactions, the negativity of service providers' prior emotion displays will be positively associated with the negativity of their subsequent emotion displays.

ATTRIBUTION AND INTRAPERSONAL CONSISTENCY

Although Cappella's research clearly suggests that prior communicative behavior is a significant predictor of subsequent behavior, it does not examine potential moderators of these relations. We argue that the appraisal of responsibility determines the degree to which one's prior emotion displays affect subsequent emotion displays through the mechanism of power differences. First, we argue that the appraisal of responsibility leads to power differences. Then we propose how these differences affect the relations between prior and subsequent emotion displays.

As we discussed earlier, responsibility for problems has been associated with feelings of guilt (e.g., Karasawa, 2001). Feelings and displays of guilt have also been associated with low level of power (Tiedens, 2001). Therefore, we expect those who feel responsible for problems will also feel more powerless than those who do not feel responsible. When one causes problems for another person and feels guilty, one may be yielding or accommodating to the other person as a form of compensation. In doing so, one surrenders one's power to the other person – and hence, feels less powerful vis-à-vis the other. Furthermore, anger has been associated with power (Tiedens, 2001). We expect those who experience problems caused by others are likely to feel angry, and hence more powerful, vis-à-vis those who are responsible for the problems.

This argument has been confirmed in empirical research. Based on survey data, Doucet and Yoon (2002) found that, in service interactions, people in interactions who were seen as responsible for the problems were perceived as less powerful than those who were not deemed responsible for these problems. This finding supports our claim that responsibility for problems is related to low-power status. Therefore, we argue that individuals who are deemed responsible for problems in service interactions are perceived as being less powerful than people who are not deemed to be responsible.

Research on power relations and self-construals suggests that power differences in interactions may moderate the relations between prior emotion displays and subsequent displays. Lee and Tiedens (2001) examined power relations as a predictor of self-construals and consistency of behavior. They argued that high-powered people are more likely to have independent self-construals, whereas low-powered people are more likely to have interdependent self-construals. In other words, high-powered people tend to perceive themselves independent of external factors such as social context and relationships with others, while low-powered people tend to perceive themselves with relation to others. Lee and Tiedens (2001) extended the arguments and posited that because high-powered people are less dependent on others, it is highly likely that they are less inhibited by external factors and more consistent in their behavior, whereas low-powered people are more likely to be constrained by the desires or behavior of others and less consistent in their own behavior. Therefore, the relations between prior and

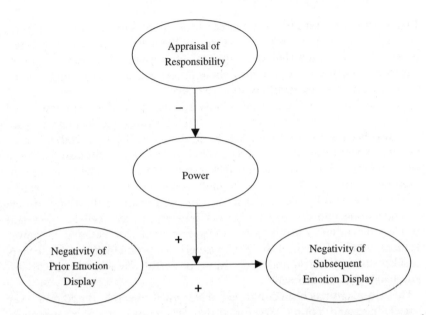

Fig. 1.   Relations between Appraisal of Responsibility, Power, and Intrapersonal
Consistency in Emotion Display.

subsequent behavior are likely to be moderated by power, so that these
relations are strongest for high-powered people and weakest for low-powered people.

To summarize, we theorize that the appraisal of responsibility in problematic interactions affects the extent to which an individual's subsequent
emotion display is affected by an individual's own prior display, via the
mechanism of power differences (see Fig. 1). We claim that attributional
processes are related to perceptions of power differences, which in turn
moderate the relations between prior and subsequent emotion displays.
Those who are not deemed responsible for problems are perceived as more
powerful in service interactions and, hence, are more likely to exhibit consistent emotional behavior. That is, the prior emotion displays are more
likely to predict subsequent emotion displays for the individuals who are not
seen as responsible for problems than for the individuals who are deemed
responsible for problems.

Hypothesis 3. In problematic service interactions, the attribution of responsibility moderates the relation between the negativity of prior and
subsequent emotion displays of service providers, so that this relation is

more positive when service providers attribute responsibility for the problem to the customers than when they attribute responsibility for the problem to the bank (or a service provider for the bank).

EMOTIONAL CONTAGION

Previous research has shown that emotions and other communicative behaviors are contagious (Cappella, 1980, 1981; Pugh, 2001). Research in emotions has shown that observers tend to experience (and display) emotions displayed by others in their social environment via emotional contagion (Barsade, 2001; Frodi et al., 1978; Hatfield, Cacioppo, & Rapson, 1994). For example, in a study of bank tellers, Pugh (2001) found that friendly behavior by service providers enhanced the positive mood of customers. Similarly, in a study of call center workers, Doucet (2005) found that hostile behavior by service providers influenced the hostility experienced by customers. Research in communication has examined this contagion mechanism for other types of communicative behavior. For example, Cappella (1981, 1984) found positive relations between prior communicative behavior of one partner in an interaction and subsequent communicative behavior of the other partner. He discovered these relations for communication behavior such as pauses, latencies, intensities, and length of utterance. Hence, based on the research evidence regarding the contagion process, we predict:

Hypothesis 4. In problematic service interactions, the negativity of customers' prior emotion displays will be positively associated with the negativity of subsequent emotion displays of service providers.

ATTRIBUTION AND EMOTIONAL CONTAGION

In addition to the main effect of emotional contagion, we also look at attribution processes as a moderating factor for the relations between prior emotion displays of one partner in an interaction and subsequent emotion displays of the other partner. Specifically, we argue that the appraisal of responsibility in problematic interactions determines the extent to which the degree of negativity of prior emotion displays of one partner influences the degree of negativity of subsequent displays of the other partner. As we have discussed in an earlier section, we argue that the appraisal of responsibility is related to differences in power between partners. Next, we argue that these power differences will affect the relations between the degree of negativity of prior emotion displays of one partner in an interaction and degree of negativity of subsequent displays of the other partner.

A body of research in organizational behavior and social psychology has dealt with the notion of power and the likelihood of one person's behavior affecting another's (Hsee, Hatfield, Carlson, & Chemtob, 1990; Pruitt & Carnevale, 1993). Essentially, much of this literature shows that the relations between prior behavior of one partner in an interaction and the subsequent behavior of the other partner are most positive when one partner is more powerful than the other.

As we mentioned earlier, people with less power in an interaction are more likely to have interdependent self-construal and to feel dependent upon their high-powered interaction partners. People with less power are more likely to attend to the behavior of high-powered people in interactions than vice versa. Assuming that attending to behavior increases the likelihood of behavioral contagion, we believe that the prior behavior of high-powered interaction partners are more likely to be predictive of subsequent behavior of the low-powered partners than vice versa. For example, Pruitt & Carnevale (1993) argued that in negotiations, the degree of cooperation exhibited by one interaction partner in the past can predict the degree of subsequent cooperation exhibited by the other partner only when the one partner is more powerful than the other.

Research on emotional contagion has produced similar findings. Hsee et al. (1990) argued that people in positions of less power are more likely to attend to the emotions of people in higher-power positions than vice versa. Empirical evidence in this area of research suggests that people in low-power positions are, indeed, more sensitive to the feelings of others than people in high-power positions (Hall, 1979; Snodgrass, 1985, 1992; Snodgrass, Ploutz-Snyder, & Hecht, 1999). If we assume that sensitivity to others' feelings is a precursor to behavioral contagion, we expect the following: the relations between the degree of negativity of prior emotion displays of one partner in an interaction and the degree of negativity of subsequent emotion displays of the other partner are moderated by power, so that these relations are strongest and most positive when one partner is more powerful than the other. Since attributions of responsibility are related to power differences, we can extend this argument to the following hypothesis:

Hypothesis 5. In problematic service interactions, the attribution of responsibility moderates the relation between the negativity of prior emotion displays of customers and the negativity of subsequent emotion displays of service providers, such that this relation is more positive when the service providers attribute responsibility for the problem to the bank (or service provider for the bank) than when the service providers attribute responsibility for the problem to the customers.

METHODS

Participants and Procedures

The data were collected from the telephone service center for a large retail bank located in the northeastern United States. The data include verbatim transcripts of service interactions between bank service providers and customers.

Over one thousand service interactions were audio taped for this study. The typical service interactions in this setting consist of bank customers contacting the service center for a variety of services. The most common types of service requests include inquiries concerning account balances, account transactions, general product information, checkbook ordering, and change of address requests. Service interactions typically last approximately 2 min and range from under 1 min to over 20 min in duration – depending on the complexity of the service request. Service providers in this environment handle approximately 20–25 service requests per hour.

Bank service providers were invited to participate in the study. Only those who agreed to participate were audio taped. A total of 215 service providers agreed. Interactions by each bank service provider were audio taped from a remote location. Service interactions at this telephone call center are routinely recorded for purposes of performance evaluation and feedback. Bank service providers are aware that 5–10 of their service interactions are recorded per month, but they are unaware of which particular interactions are being recorded. Hence, the research protocol did not significantly affect the service providers' sense of being monitored and evaluated. The recording facility used in this study was on a different floor from the bank service providers, which ensured that the service providers were not aware when their interactions were being recorded. Audio tapes of the interactions were transcribed.

Among the service interactions recorded, we selected the calls that involved mistakes or errors of either party in the interaction. We identified these interactions as being problematic and expected the parties in these

Table 1.   Total Number of Calls and Speaking Turns by Types of Calls.

	Customer Error	Bank Error	Total
Number of calls	15	34	49
Speaking turns	586	969	1,555

interactions to engage in attribution processes to assess responsibility for the problem. The total number of calls and speaking turns (defined as one party's continued speech without interruption from the other) is displayed in Table 1. The speaking turn is used as the unit of analysis.

Measures
Responsibility. In the verbatim transcripts of the service interactions, responsibility was identified based on which party made an error. When a call involved a situation in which the bank made an error either because of the system or an individual service provider, it was coded as bank/service provider error. On the other hand, when a call involved a customer's faulty behavior, it was coded as customer error. For example, when a customer lost his/her ATM card and called the service provider, the provider is likely to attribute the problem to the customer, and the customer is more likely to feel responsible for the problem. Likewise, when a customer calls regarding an error in his bank statement, the customer is likely to attribute the problem to the bank or a service provider, and the service provider is more likely to feel responsible for the problem on behalf of the bank.

Therefore, based on the assessment of errors, each call was coded as either bank/service provider error (1) or customer error (0). Accordingly, either 1 or 0 was assigned to each speaking turn in each call. The authors independently coded the error of all the calls. Cohen's κ was .91. Disagreements were discussed and resolved.

Negativity of Service Providers' and Customers' Emotion Displays. The negativity of the emotions displayed by each party in each speaking turn was measured by using Dictionary of Affect in Language (DAL) (Whissell, 1989). The DAL is a tool to measure emotions expressed in any type of text-based materials. DAL contains over 4000 words, and each word in the dictionary is accompanied by the scores along the affective dimensions of pleasantness, activation, and imagery. In this study, the pleasantness dimension was used in examining the negativity of emotions. The original scale for pleasantness in DAL ranges from 1 to 3, 1 being unpleasant and 3

Table 2. Illustration of Speaking Turns for Customer and Service Provider with DAL Mean Negativity Score.

Speaking Turn Label	Verbatim Talk	DAL Mean Negativity Score
R1	Hi! How may I help you today?	2.10
C1	I lost my ATM card somewhere and need to get another one	2.16
R2	May I have your account number and social security number?	2.10
C2	My account number is XXXX, and the social security number is XXX-XX-XXXX	2.10
R3	Oh, you've lost your card twice this month already	2.23
C3	That is right	1.95
R4	It is frustrating to be asked for a new card over and over again	2.20
C4	I'm sorry?	2.09
R5	I cannot believe you keep making the stupid mistakes over and over	2.40
C5	It's not like I lost it intentionally	2.17
R6	.....	
C6	.....	
...		
R (T-1)	You're all set.	2.18
C (T-1)	Thanks!	1.57
R (T)	Thank you. Have a nice day.	1.74

Note: "R" represents service provider and "C" represents customer.

being pleasant. However, to address the degree of negativity in this study, we reversed the scale so that 1 is least negative and 3 is most negative. Each word was assigned a negativity score using the DAL. Then, the scores for all the words in each speaking turn were averaged to create a degree of negativity for each speaking turn. Table 2 illustrates sample speaking turns for a customer and a service provider along with the degree of negativity for each of the speaking turns.

RESULTS

Table 3 provides correlations, means, and standard deviations for all variables used for analysis.[1] They include negativity of the service provider's prior emotion display, negativity of service provider's subsequent emotion

Table 3. Means, Standard Deviations, and Correlations[a].

Variable	Mean	SD	1	2	3	4	5
1.Negativity of service provider's prior emotion display	1.09	.24					
2. Negativity of service provider's subsequent emotion display	1.08	.26	.08**				
3.Negativity of customer's prior emotion display	1.02	.31	.03	.02			
4. Responsibility (bank error = 1, customer error = 0)	.62	.48	−.02	−.01	.03		
5. Negativity of service provider's emotion display for entire call	1.08	.05	.20**	.20**	.03	−.07**	
6. Negativity of customer's emotion display for entire call	1.02	.08	.02	.02	.22**	.16**	.17**

[a]$n = 1555$.
**$p < .01$ (two-tailed).

display, degree of negativity of customer's prior emotion display, negativity of service provider's emotion display for the entire call, and negativity of customer's emotion display for the entire call. We included the negativity of the entire call for the service provider and customer as control variables.

To test the hypotheses, we conducted a multiple regression analysis with five variables and two interaction terms in the model: negativity of service provider's prior emotion display, negativity of customer's prior emotion display, responsibility, negativity of service provider's emotion display for entire call, and negativity of customer's emotion display for entire call; negativity of service provider's prior emotion display × responsibility and negativity of customer's prior emotion display × responsibility (see Table 4). The dependent variable was negativity of the service provider's subsequent emotion display.

Attribution and Negativity of Emotion Display

Hypothesis 1 predicted that in problematic service interactions service providers would display more negative emotions when the customers were

Table 4. Summary of Multiple Regression Analysis for Predicting Negativity of Service Provider's Subsequent Emotion Displays ($N = 1,555$).

Variables	B	SE	β
Step 1			
Negativity of service provider's prior emotion displays (A)	0.08	0.03	0.08**
Negativity of customer's prior emotion displays (B)	0.02	0.02	0.03
Step 2			
Negativity of service provider's prior emotion displays (A)	0.04	0.03	0.04
Negativity of customer's prior emotion displays (B)	0.02	0.02	0.03
Responsibility (C)	0.00	0.01	0.01
(bank error = 1, customer error = 0)			
Negativity of service provider's emotion display for entire call	0.92	0.13	0.20**
Negativity of customer's emotion display for entire call	−0.11	0.09	−0.03
Step 3			
Negativity of service provider's prior emotion displays (A)	0.04	0.03	0.05
Negativity of customer's prior emotion displays (B)	0.02	0.02	0.03
Responsibility (C)	0.00	0.01	0.00
(bank error = 1, customer error = 0)			
Negativity of service provider's emotion display for entire call	0.94	0.13	0.20**
Negativity of customer's emotion display for entire call	−0.09	0.09	−0.03
A × C	0.21	0.05	0.11**
B × C	0.03	0.04	0.02

Notes: $R^2 = .08$ for Step 1 ($p < .001$); $\Delta R^2 = .04$ for Step 2 ($p < .001$); and $\Delta R^2 = .01$ ($p < .001$) for Step 3.
**$p < .001$.

responsible for the problem than when the service provider or bank was responsible for the problem. As can be seen from Table 4, this hypothesis was not supported. Variations in responsibility for the problem did not affect the degree of negativity of the service providers' emotion displays.

Intrapersonal Consistency

In Hypothesis 2, we predicted a positive association between the negativity of the service providers' prior emotion displays and the negativity of subsequent emotion displays. The regression results in Table 4 support this hypothesis. Service providers were found to be consistent in the negativity of their emotion displays.

Attribution and Intrapersonal Consistency

In Hypothesis 3, we predicted that responsibility would moderate the relations between the negativity of the service providers' prior and subsequent emotion displays. In Table 4 it can be seen that, consistent with our hypothesis, the negativity of service providers' prior emotion displays was a strong predictor of the negativity of their subsequent displays, with a significant interaction effect with responsibility. In other words, the negativity of bank service providers' prior emotion displays was more predictive of the negativity of their subsequent emotion displays when customers were responsible for the problems than when banks or service providers were responsible.

To interpret the nature of the interaction, we used procedures suggested by Aiken and West (1991). We centered degree of negativity of service providers' prior emotion displays, degree of negativity of service providers' subsequent emotion displays, and responsibility on the means. Next, we used unstandardized β coefficients from the regression equation to plot the relations between the degree of negativity of the providers' prior and subsequent emotion displays for two conditions: (1) bank error and (2) customer error. As shown in Fig. 2, the relations between the negativity of prior and subsequent emotion displays is more positive when customers were responsible for the problem than when the bank or service providers were responsible for the problem. These results support Hypothesis 3.

Emotional Contagion

With relation to emotional contagion, in Hypothesis 4 we predicted a positive association between the negativity of customers' prior emotion displays and service providers' subsequent emotion displays. The hypothesis was not supported (see Table 4). Contrary to our prediction, the negativity of service providers' subsequent emotion displays were not affected by the negativity of customers' prior emotion displays.

Attribution and Emotional Contagion

In Hypothesis 5 we predicted that responsibility would moderate the relations between the negativity of customers' emotion displays and service providers' emotion displays. In other words, we argued that the negativity of

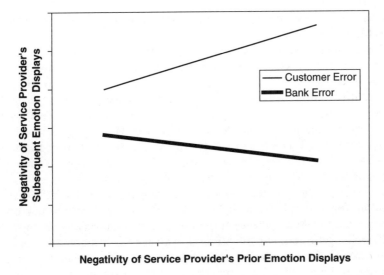

Fig. 2. Interaction Effect between Service Provider's Intrapersonal Consistency and Responsibility.

customers' prior emotion displays would predict the negativity of providers' subsequent emotion displays when the bank was responsible for the problem. Hypothesis 5 was not supported (see Table 4). The negativity of customers' prior emotion displays was not a significant predictor of the negativity of providers' emotion display regardless of who was responsible for the problem.

DISCUSSION

This study investigated the relations between attribution and emotion displays in problematic service interactions. Specifically, we examined whether responsibility for problems affects the negativity of service providers' emotion displays, the relations between service providers' prior and subsequent emotion displays, and the relations between customers' and service providers' emotion displays.

Contrary to our prediction, attributions of responsibility did not affect the negativity of service providers' emotion displays. Service providers did not display more negative emotions when customers were responsible for problems than when the bank or the service providers themselves were responsible for problems.

However, this study found a strong pattern of intrapersonal consistency in emotion display as well as a moderating effect of attribution. The negativity of service providers' subsequent emotion displays was predicted by the negativity of their prior displays. The consistency of service providers' emotional displays was more pronounced when customers were seen as being responsible for the problem. In other words, the negativity of prior emotion displays was more predictive of the negativity of subsequent emotion displays when customers were responsible for the problem than when banks or service providers were responsible for the problem.

In terms of the relations between the negativity of service providers' emotion displays and customers' emotion displays, contrary to our prediction, we did not find evidence for emotional contagion between customers and service providers nor did we find evidence for a moderating effect of responsibility on this relation. We offer two possible explanations for the lack of emotional contagion. First, the emotions displayed by customers and service providers may have been primarily a function of individual differences in trait affect as opposed to being a function of the situation. As Arvey, Renz, and Watson (1998) argue, individuals have predispositions to experience and display specific emotions. These predispositions can override situational factors, particularly in weak situations (Mischel, 1968). However, given that attributions for responsibility did affect the consistency of service providers' emotion displays, this argument is not consistent with all of our findings.

Another possible explanation for the lack of emotional contagion in our data may be the communication media used in these service interactions and its brief, transactional nature of the interaction (Gutek, 1995). The telephone is a relatively lean communication media compared with face-to-face communication (Carlson & Davis, 1998; Trevino, Daft, & Lengel, 1987). Fewer visual and physical cues are engaged, making interpersonal sensitivity and influence more difficult to achieve. The sample of service interactions used in this study would classify as transactions or pseudorelationships (Gutek, 1995), in which strangers engage in brief, standardized interactions, largely devoid of personal texture. These types of interactions tend to be more emotionally neutral and less personal, which would encourage little interpersonal dynamics of any type. Future research should explore different types of interactions as well as different communication media to identify when interpersonal influence is affected by responsibility for problems and when it is not.

This study contributes to the research on emotion displays in service interactions in two ways. First, it addresses interpersonal relations. Earlier empirical research has examined the emotion displays by service provider without paying much attention to interpersonal relations in such displays (see Doucet, 2005; Pugh, 2001 for exception). Our study investigated not only the intrapersonal consistency but also interpersonal influence in emotion displays. Although we did not find support for direct interpersonal influence via emotional contagion, we did find support for interpersonal consistency via attributions for responsibility. That is, perceived responsibility of a customer for a problem affects the consistency of service provider emotion displays.

Second, this study informs us of the likely complexity of the relations between responsibility and emotional contagion between service providers and customers in problematic interactions. Our conceptualization of responsibility for problems and its relation to power differentials was based on agency appraisal concerning responsibility for problems. However, the results of the study indicate that emotional contagion may not be affected by such a mechanism. There could be many other factors affecting emotional contagion between bank service providers and customers including communication media, the providers' relationship with the bank as a larger system, customers' possession of the appropriate documentation as the evidence of the problems, and customers' dependence on bank service providers' actions regardless of who is responsible for the problem. Clearly, further research is required to understand emotional contagion in service interactions.

The practical implication of this study is quite significant. We found that service providers are more consistent in their emotion displays when they consider customers responsible for problems than when they consider themselves (or the bank) to be responsible. This finding indicates that service providers are less sensitive and adaptive to customers when they attribute the cause of problems to customers. This lack of adaptability to customers may have a negative effect on the customers' perception of service quality. This effect may be especially important if service providers display negative emotions.

Although we found a main effect for consistency and a moderating effect for responsibility in the service providers' emotion display, the effect is relatively small. This result may stem from a lack of variance in the negativity of the service providers' emotion displays as well as theoretical or methodological limitations of this study. One theoretical limitation is in the conceptualization of responsibility and its relation to power. We assumed that service providers identify with the bank and, hence, feel personally responsible when the bank has made an error. However, this might not be the case. For example, service providers may not be held personally responsible for errors committed by the bank. In these cases, service providers may be perceived as customer advocates who represent the customers' interests in interactions with the bank bureaucracy. If so, service providers would not think of themselves as blame-worthy and responsible, but potentially as helpful, even powerful advocates against the system. Future research should measure perceptions of responsibility and power differentials more directly (e.g., immediately prior to the interaction) and should explore more contingencies surrounding "error" situations to better understand the determinants of perceived responsibility.

One methodological limitation comes from the use of DAL as a measure of the negativity of emotion displays. We used the verbatim transcripts of telephone conversations between customers and bank service providers to measure the negativity of emotion displays. It is true that the words used by conversation partners are important indicators when judging their emotions. However, the text-based data is not a comprehensive source for detecting emotions in verbal interactions. For example, negativity of emotion is also displayed through para-language such as vocal emphasis, voice inflection, and different tones. These channels for emotion displays are not captured by our method.

Service providers' emotion displays are important for the management of service quality. This study examined the negativity of emotion displays with relation to attributions of responsibility in problematic service interactions. The investigation of the relations between the attributional processes and the negativity of emotion displays contributes to the research on cognition and emotion and to the practical improvement of service interactions.

NOTES

1. In the analyses, the negativity of each service provider's speaking turn was used as both an independent variable (turn T-1) and a dependent variable (turn T). Due to concerns about this approach, we also conducted a separate analysis where the negativity of any service provider's speaking turn was only used as an independent variable (turn T-1) or a dependent variable (turn T), but never both. Results obtained using the second approach were not significantly different from results obtained using the first approach. Results reported in the manuscript are based on the first approach.

ACKNOWLEDGMENTS

We would like to thank the Wharton Financial Institutions Center and an anonymous retail bank for their generous support of this research. We would also like to thank Greg Oldham, Larissa Tiedens, and Peter Carnevale for their helpful comments and Karen Jaburek for her help with data collection.

REFERENCES

Aiken, L. S., & West, S. G. (1991). *Multiple regression: Testing and interpreting interactions.* Newbury Park, CA: Sage.

Allred, K. G. (2000). Anger and retaliation in conflict: The role of attribution. In: M. Deutsch & P. T. Coleman (Eds), *The handbook of conflict resolution: Theory and practice* (pp. 236–255). San Francisco, CA: Jossey-Bass Inc.

Ambady, N., Laplante, D., & Johnson, E. (2001). Thin slice judgments as measures of interpersonal sensitivity. In: J. A. Hall & F. J. Bernieri (Eds), *Interpersonal sensitivity: Theory and measurement* (pp. 89–101). Mahwah, NJ: Lawrence Earlbaum.

Arvey, R. D., Renz, G. L., & Watson, T. W. (1998). Emotionality and job performance: Implications for personnel selection. In: G. R. Ferris (Ed.), *Research in personnel and human resources management* (Vol. 16, pp. 103–147). Greenwich, CT: JAI Press.

Barsade, S. G. (2001). The ripple effect: Emotional contagion its influence on group behavior. *Administrative Science Quarterly, 47,* 644–675.

Betancourt, H., & Blair, I. (1992). A cognition-emotion model of violence in conflict situations. *Personality and Social Psychology Bulletin, 18,* 343–350.

Cappella, J. N. (1979). Talk and silence sequences in informal social conversations I. *Human Communication Research, 6,* 3–17.

Cappella, J. N. (1980). Talk and silence sequences in informal social conversations II. *Human Communication Research, 6,* 130–145.

Cappella, J. N. (1981). Mutual influence in expressive behavior: Adult-adult and infant-adult dyadic interaction. *Psychological Bulletin, 89,* 101–132.

Cappella, J. N. (1984). The relevance of the microstructure of interaction to relationship change. *Journal of Social and Personal Relationships, 1,* 239–264.

Cappella, J. N., & Planalp, S. (1981). Talk and silence sequences in informal conversations III: Interspeaker influence. *Human Communication Research, 7,* 117–132.

Carlson, P. J., & Davis, G. B. (1998). An investigation of media selection among directors and managers: From "self" to "other" orientation. *MIS Quarterly, 13,* 335–362.

Daniell, R. J., & Lewis, P. (1972). Stability of eye contact and physical distance across a series of structured interviews. *Journal of Consulting and Clinical Psychology, 39,* 172.

Doucet, L. (2005). Service provider hostility and service quality. *Academy of Management Journal, 47,* 761–771.

Doucet, L., & Yoon, K. (2002). Unpublished data. University of Illinois at Urbana-Champaign.

Frodi, A. M., Lamb, M. E., Leavitt, L. A., Donovan, W. L., Neff, C., & Sherry, D. (1978). Fathers' and mothers' responses to the faces and cries of normal and premature infants. *Developmental Psychology, 14,* 490–498.

Gutek, B. A. (1995). *The dynamics of service: Reflections on the changing nature of customer/provider interactions.* San Francisco, CA: Jossey-Bass Publishers.

Hall, J. A. (1979). Gender, gender roles, and nonverbal communication skills. In: R. Rosenthal (Ed.), *Skill in nonverbal communication: Individual differences* (pp. 32–67). Cambridge, MA: Oelgeschlager, Gunn & Hain.

Hatfield, E., Cacioppo, J. T., & Rapson, R. L. (1994). *Emotional contagion*. New York, NY: Cambridge University Press.

Hsee, C. K., Hatfield, E., Carlson, J. G., & Chemtob, C. (1990). The effect of power on susceptibility to emotional contagion. *Cognition and Emotion, 4*, 327–340.

Jaffe, J., & Feldstein, S. (1970). *Rhythms of dialogue*. New York: Academic Press.

Johnson, C., Ford, R., & Kaufman, J. (2000). Emotional reactions to conflict: Do dependence and legitimacy matter? *Social Forces, 79*, 107–137.

Karasawa, K. (2001). Anger vs. guilt: Inference of responsibility attribution and interpersonal reactions. *Psychological Reports, 89*, 731–739.

Lazarus, R. S., & Smith, C. A. (1988). Knowledge and appraisal in the cognition–emotion relationship. *Cognition and Emotion, 2*, 281–300.

Lee, F., & Tiedens, L. (2001). Is it lonely at the top?: The independence and interdependence of power holders. In: B. M. Staw & R. I. Dutton (Eds), *Research in organizational behavior* (Vol. 23, pp. 43–91). Greenwich, CT: JAI Press.

Libby, W. L. (1970). Eye contact and direction of looking as stable individual differences. *Journal of Experimental Research in Personality, 4*, 303–312.

Mischel, W. (1968). *Personality and assessment*. New York, NY: Wiley.

Nowicki, S., & Duke, M. P. (2001). Nonverbal receptivity: The diagnostic analysis of nonverbal accuracy (DANVA). In: J. A. Hall & F. J. Bernieri (Eds), *Interpersonal sensitivity: Theory and measurement* (pp. 183–198). Mahwah, NJ: Lawrence Earlbaum.

Pruitt, D. G., & Carnevale, P. J. (1993). *Negotiation in social conflict*. Pacific Grove, CA: Brooks/Cole.

Pugh, S. D. (2001). Service with a smile: Emotional contagion in the service encounter. *Academy of Management Journal, 44*, 1018–1027.

Rafaeli, R., & Sutton, R. I. (1989). The expression of emotion in organizational life. In: L. L. Cummings & B. M. Staw (Eds), *Research in organizational behavior* (Vol. 11, pp. 1–42). Greenwich, CT: JAI Press.

Rust, R. T., Zahorik, A. J., & Keiningham, T. L. (1996). *Services marketing*. New York: Harper Collins.

Schneider, B., & Bowen, D. E. (1995). *Winning the service game*. Boston: Harvard University Press.

Smith, C. A., Hayes, K. N., Lazarus, R. S., & Pope, L. K. (1993). In search of the "hot" cognitions: Attributions, appraisals, and their relation to emotion. *Journal of Personality and Social Psychology, 65*, 916–929.

Snodgrass, S. E. (1985). Women's intuition: The effect of subordinate role on interpersonal sensitivity. *Journal of Personality and Social Psychology, 49*, 146–155.

Snodgrass, S. E. (1992). Further effects of role versus gender on interpersonal sensitivity. *Journal of Personality and Social Psychology, 62*, 154–158.

Snodgrass, S. E., Ploutz-Snyder, R., & Hecht, M. A. (1999). *The effect of leadership expectations on interpersonal sensitivity*. Unpublished manuscript.

Sutton, R. I., & Rafaeli, A. (1988). Untangling the relationship between displayed emotions and organizational sales: The case of convenience stores. *Academy of Management Journal, 31*, 461–487.

Tax, S. S., & Brown, S. W. (2000). Service recovery: Research insights and practices. In: T. A. Swartz & D. Iacobucci (Eds), *Handbook of services marketing and management* (pp. 271–285). San Francisco: Sage.

Tiedens, L. (2001). Anger and advancement versus sadness and subjugation: The effect of negative emotion expressions on social status conferral. *Journal of Personality and Social Psychology, 80,* 86–94.

Trevino, L. K., Daft, R. H., & Lengel, R. L. (1987). Media symbolism, media richness, and media choice in organizations. *Communication Research, 14,* 553–574.

Weiner, B. (1985). An attributional theory of achievement motivation and emotion. *Psychological Review, 92,* 548–573.

Weiner, B. (1986). *An attributional theory of motivation and emotion.* New York: Springer-Verlag Inc.

Whissel, C. M. (1989). The dictionary of affect in language. In: R. Plutchik & H. Kellerman (Eds), *Emotion: Theory, research and experience* (Vol. 4, pp. 113–131). New York: Academic Press.

Yamauchi, H., & Lee, K. (1999). An attribution-emotion model of helping behavior. *Psychological Reports, 84,* 1073–1074.

Zeithaml, V. A., Berry, L. L., & Parasuraman, A. (1996). The behavioral consequences of service quality. *Journal of Marketing, 60,* 31–46.

CHAPTER 12

HOW TO FEEL RATIONALLY: LINKING RATIONAL EMOTIVE BEHAVIOR THERAPY WITH COMPONENTS OF EMOTIONAL INTELLIGENCE ☆

Matthias Spörrle and Isabell M. Welpe

ABSTRACT

Adopting the theoretical framework of Rational Emotive Behavior Therapy (REBT; Ellis, 1962, 1994), we examine the cognitive antecedents of functional behavior and adaptive emotions as indicators of emotional intelligence (EI) and test central assumptions of REBT. In an extension of REBT, we posit that adaptive emotions resulting from rational cognitions reflect more EI than maladaptive emotions, which result from irrational cognitions, because the former lead to functional behavior. The results of the first study using organizational scenarios in an experimental design confirm central assumptions of REBT and support our hypotheses. In a second correlational study we replicate the connection between rational

☆ Some parts of this chapter (especially regarding the first study) have already been published in a special issue of *Psicothema* on EI. The permission of the editors of *Psicothema* to include this material here is gratefully acknowledged.

Individual and Organizational Perspectives on Emotion Management and Display
Research on Emotion in Organizations, Volume 2, 291–322
Copyright © 2006 by Elsevier Ltd.
All rights of reproduction in any form reserved
ISSN: 1746-9791/doi:10.1016/S1746-9791(06)02012-8

cognitions and EI by measuring real person data using psychometric scales. Both studies indicate that irrational attitudes result in reduced job satisfaction.

INTRODUCTION

Emotional intelligence (EI) has emerged as an important and viable concept in organizational research (Ashkanasy & Daus, 2002; Cooper & Sawaf, 1997; Fisher & Ashkanasy, 2000; Goleman, 1995, 1998). Despite the conceptual differences in various approaches to EI, certain components of EI are present in most theoretical frameworks. These include the ability to perceive one's own emotions, regulate one's own emotions and to perceive the emotions of others (see Davies, Stankov, & Roberts, 1998). Some authors also include the capacity to regulate others' emotional states as an additional aspect (Goleman, 1998, Mayer & Salovey, 1997).

In addition to these four components, we suggest that a conceptual understanding of EI may benefit from the identification of which emotions are specifically detrimental to or supportive of EI. We argue that some emotions result in emotionally unintelligent behavior whereas other emotions facilitate emotionally intelligent behavior. Further, we suggest that someone experiencing emotions, which prevent them from behaving in an emotionally intelligent manner, will continue to behave in this manner (i.e., with low EI) unless they manage to control and change their emotional state. Hence, a conceptual distinction between adaptive ("emotionally intelligent") and maladaptive ("emotionally unintelligent") emotions might provide an important additional conceptual basis for EI.

In order to differentiate between adaptive and maladaptive emotions we argue that it is initially necessary to examine the cognitive antecedents of these emotions. We suggest that these emotions can be differentiated on basis of the thoughts, beliefs and evaluations that have caused these emotions. Hence, our work is based on the assumptions of cognitive emotion theories, and more precisely appraisal theories, which assume that emotions differ according to a person's (subjective) cognitions and evaluations (Scherer, 1999). Many empirical studies have demonstrated that the quality and quantity of emotional reactions toward an object depend on the individual's subjective appraisal of that object (e.g., Ellsworth, 1991; Roseman, 1984; Stein & Levine, 1987; Weiner, 1986, 1995). For instance, as noted by Weiner (1995), emotional reactions toward the negatively evaluated actions of another person (i.e., anger) depend on whether or not this person is considered to be responsible for the action. In addition to the discrimination between maladaptive and adaptive emotions there is another advantage of linking cognitive processes with the concept of EI: namely, since differential cognitive processes controlling emotional adaptation have been postulated to operate in persons with high vs. low EI (Matthews & Zeidner, 2000), knowledge of the cognitive antecedents of the emotions associated with emotionally intelligent and unintelligent behavior will also increase our understanding of individual variability in emotional adaptation.

The present research is based on the theoretical basis of Rational Emotive Behavior Therapy (REBT; Ellis, 1962, 1994), which can be classified as an appraisal theory of emotion. Although REBT itself has not been applied in organizational research so far, the value of using other appraisal theories of emotion as theoretical frameworks in organizational research has already been recognized, e.g., for predicting the consequences of work exhaustion (Moore, 2000) or co-workers' reactions to low performers (Lepine & van Dyne, 2001).

Albert Ellis (1962) introduced his appraisal theory of emotion while developing his pioneering and comprehensive system of cognitive therapy. Although REBT has become a widespread therapeutic method (Smith, 1982) with proven efficacy (Engles, Garnefsky, & Diekstra, 1993; Gonzalez et al., 2004; Grawe, Donati, & Bernauer, 1994; Lyons & Woods, 1991), to our knowledge its theoretical foundations have not yet been examined in an organizational setting. In the following section we briefly describe the theoretical assumptions of REBT regarding cognitions, emotions and behavior.

In introducing REBT, Ellis (1962) initially distinguishes between "irrational" and "rational" cognitions. Specifically, he argues that irrational cognitions are the primary source of emotional disturbances, because "practically all of them (i.e., emotional disturbances) arise from taking a sensible *preference* or *desire* and raising it to absolutist *must* or *demand*" (Ellis, 1995, p. 106). Ellis further points out that these irrational cognitions are characterized by absolutistic demands, such as "I must succeed" ... to attain a certain goal. Another specific aspect of these irrational cognitions concerns the linking of an individual's worth with the outcome of her or his actions: "If I do not succeed I will be worthless as a human being". By contrast, rational cognitions are characterized by wishes and preferences, such as "I would like", "I would prefer" or "it would be better" to succeed. Rational beliefs following a negative behavioral outcome are assumed to lead to self-acceptance (rather than negative self-evaluations) and not to be connected with self-worth.

We argue that an analysis of individual differences concerning these rational or irrational cognitions might result in an increased understanding of individual differences in EI and thus in an increased understanding of EI in general. As Matthews, Zeidner, and Roberts (2002) claim "a focus on individual differences may contribute to understanding EI in the more generalized sense" (p. 22).

With regard to emotional reactions, Ellis (1962) distinguishes maladaptive emotions such as anxiety, depression, rage and guilt from their adaptive counterparts, such as fear/concern, sadness, annoyance and regret. Additionally, Ellis (1962, 1973) hypothesizes a causal relationship between the appraisal dimensions (i.e., irrational vs. rational) and the emotional reactions (maladaptive vs. adaptive). Irrational cognitions (e.g., "I must succeed") are believed to lead to maladaptive emotions (e.g., anxiety while attempting to attain a goal and depression after failing to reach a goal) and emotional disturbances, whereas rational cognitions (e.g., "I would like to succeed") should maximize adaptive (e.g., fear/concern while attempting to attain a certain goal and sadness following failure) but not maladaptive emotions. However, Ellis and DiGiuseppe (1993) have also noted that according to REBT it is possible to experience both adaptive and maladaptive emotions simultaneously.

Overall, while Ellis (1962) provides a detailed description of the consequences of negatively evaluated emotional states (e.g., sadness or depression), positive emotions are not explicitly reconsidered in his classical works. In order to extend the theoretical framework of REBT to positive emotions, we introduce a fifth pair of emotions: joy and pride. Since Weiner (1986) maintains that pride is an emotion of increased self-worth, this emotional response to a positively evaluated event corresponds with irrational thinking: According to REBT, only irrational thinking can result in changes of self-worth, and consequently pride should be regarded as a maladaptive emotion. Joy, however, is not conceptualized as an emotion affecting self-worth and therefore should be regarded as an adaptive emotion. Since pride and joy share the positive evaluation of the emotion-provoking event, they can be regarded as a corresponding pair of emotion such as guilt and regret.

Additionally, since this general distinction between maladaptive and adaptive emotions is purely based on the theoretical assumptions, we also attempt to empirically assess perceived differences in functionality between adaptive and maladaptive emotions.

Regarding the behavioral consequences of these emotions, Ellis (1962, 1973) maintains that adaptive emotions result in functional behavior, whereas maladaptive emotions lead to dysfunctional behavior (i.e., behavior resulting in a decreased probability of successfully managing the emotion provoking event or situation).

This functionalistic understanding of the relationship between cognitions, emotions and behavior is in accordance with recent conceptualizations of EI as an index of the individual level of adaptive competence in emotion provoking contexts (Matthews & Zeidner, 2000).

Previous empirical tests (Försterling, 1985) of REBT theory have found that irrational cognitions were estimated to be more likely in the context of maladaptive emotions (rage, guilt and depression), whereas rational cognitions were seen as more likely to occur in the context of adaptive emotions (annoyance, regret and sadness). Moreover, recent research indicates that maladaptive emotions correlate significantly with irrational beliefs (David, Schnur, & Belloiu, 2002; David, Schnur, & Birk, 2004; David, Montgomery, Macavei, & Bovbjerg, 2005).

In our research we examine four potential connections between REBT with EI in the field of organizational research. First, we explore whether irrational beliefs actually lead to (emotionally unintelligent) maladaptive emotions and rational beliefs to (emotionally intelligent) adaptive emotions in an organizational context. Second, we test whether adaptive and maladaptive emotions lead to functional (emotionally intelligent) or dysfunctional (emotionally unintelligent) behavior, respectively, in an organizational setting. Third, we examine the assumption that if such beliefs (i.e., rational vs. irrational cognitions) and the resulting emotions (adaptive vs. maladaptive) are indicative of EI, the presence of rational beliefs and adaptive emotions should be judged as more emotionally intelligent than irrational cognitions and the resulting maladaptive affects. Hence there should be a negative correlation between individual levels of irrationality and EI. For instance, Ellis (1962, 1973) has argued that denying one's own ability to control emotions, which is a central aspect of EI, is part of the tendency to think irrationally. Hence, agreeing with such irrational beliefs will result in "emotionally unintelligent" behavior, i.e., failure to regulate one's own emotions. Fourth, on the level of individual differences, endorsements of irrational cognitions should be associated with indicators of emotionally intelligent behavioral consequences such as job- and/or life satisfaction.

By investigating these potential relationships between rationality and EI, we also provide an empirical test of Ellis' REBT theory in an organizational context. Hence, we hope to provide insights into the determinants and consequences of emotions, which might be relevant for EI, and cognitive appraisal theories of emotions.

To examine the relationships between rationality vs. irrationality, adaptive vs. maladaptive emotions, and EI, we conducted two studies. The first study, which utilized an experimental design, required participants to make judgments about hypothetical scenarios, a method that has been shown to be effective in emotion research (e.g., Reisenzein, 1986; Smith & Lazarus, 1993; Weiner, Russell, & Lerman, 1979). Specifically, participants were provided with descriptions of stimulus persons who were depicted in emotion-provoking situations. The stimulus persons were described on the basis of their cognitions (irrational vs. rational) and participants were asked to estimate their emotions by putting themselves in their position. Additionally, participants completed simple measures of irrational cognitions and of life and work satisfaction.

In the second correlational study, we attempted to further generalize the findings of the first study, which were based primarily on stimulus person data, by analyzing real person data. We used psychometric scales to assess individual levels of EI and irrationality, and again included simple measures of life and work satisfaction.

In our first study we sought to test the following four hypotheses:

Hypothesis 1. Adaptive emotions (fear, annoyance, sadness, regret, joy) will be expected from a rationally thinking stimulus person, whereas stimulus persons with irrational beliefs will be expected to experience maladaptive emotions (anxiety, rage, depression, guilt, pride).

Hypothesis 2. Adaptive emotions (fear, annoyance, sadness, regret, joy) will be perceived as being of higher functional value than their maladaptive counterparts (anxiety, anger, depression, guilt, pride).

Hypothesis 3. A rationally thinking stimulus person will be perceived to be more successful in perceiving and modifying emotional states (i.e., behaving emotionally intelligent) than an irrationally thinking person.

Hypothesis 4. Participants who identify strongly with stimulus persons who think irrationally in organizational contexts will be less satisfied with their organizational lives and to a smaller extent less satisfied with their lives in general.

In our second study we sought to test the following two hypotheses:

Hypothesis 5. On the level of real person data high levels of general irrationality will be associated with reduced levels of EI.

Hypothesis 6. On the level of real person data high levels of general irrationality will be associated with reduced satisfaction with occupational life, private life and life in general.

STUDY 1: METHOD

Participants

We obtained data from 113 persons (80 women, 33 men, mean age = 31.2 years, age range = 15–64 years) who were recruited by research assistants (where were they recruited from?). Fifty-five participants were students (49%), the others were either employees (30%), self-employed (4%), pupils (3%), apprentices (2%) or other (12%). With respect to educational level, 47% of participants had a university degree, the others had either a university entrance diploma (44%), had passed secondary school (8%) or had no qualification (1%).

Measures

Four dependent variables were assessed in the current study: (1) The emotions assumed to be felt by the stimulus persons; (2) the assumed ability of the stimulus person to perceive emotional states; (3) the assumed ability of the stimulus person to modify emotional states and (4) the extent to which participants identified with the stimulus person. Each dependent variable is discussed in greater detail as follows.

Emotions Felt by the Stimulus Person
In all scenarios, participants' assumptions about the emotions felt by the stimulus person were assessed using a forced choice question format. The emotions were administered pair-wise (e.g., sadness and depression) and the respondents had to assign one emotion to one stimulus person and the second emotion to the other individual in the scenario. All five pairs of emotions were used in each scenario. Consequently, the degree to which the emotion assignments to cognitions were in accordance with the theory served as the dependent variable.

Perception of Emotional States
In each scenario, participants estimated how well each stimulus person managed to perceive different emotional states in the ongoing situation. In the first situation, the emotional state described was that of a colleague who had not been promoted. In the second situation, it was the emotional state of the stimulus person, after they had been unable to successfully finish the work on the prototype. In the third situation, the emotional states of the associated team members had to be perceived. Thus, the emotional states of

the two stimulus persons, of another colleague or of a team were the object of perception. In each situation, participants indicated how well the two stimulus persons were able to perceive the emotional states on two 11-point rating scales ranging from 0 (*not at all*) to 10 (*optimal*).

Modification of Emotional States
Similarly to the assessment of the perception of the emotional states, participants were asked how well each stimulus person appeared to be able to modify the emotional states of the persons involved in order to help them return to efficient work. In the first situation, it was the emotional state of the disappointed colleague; in the second situation, it was the emotional state of the unsuccessful stimulus person and in the third situation, it was the disturbed emotional climate within the team. Again, participants indicated their belief as to how well the two stimulus persons were able to modify the emotional states of the persons involved on 11-point rating scales ranging from 0 (*not at all*) to 10 (*optimal*).

Participants' Identification with the Stimulus Persons
After reading each scenario, participants indicated the extent to which they identified with each (i.e., the rational vs. the irrational) stimulus person on two 11-point rating scales ranging from 0 (*not at all*) to 10 (*very strongly*). This measure of identification served as a very simple indicator of respondent's irrationality.

Additional Variables
In the second section of the questionnaire, we assessed the functionality of the emotions used. After reading the scenarios, respondents indicated the extent to which each of the 10 emotions was suitable to "deal with the person or situation better and more productively" on 11-point rating scales ranging from 0 (*not at all*) to 10 (*very*) made available on a separate sheet.

In the third and last section of the questionnaire the participants were asked to indicate how personally satisfied they were with their private life and their work life on two 11-point rating scales ranging from 0 (*not at all*) to 10 (*very*). Finally, in accordance with the procedure described by Myers (2000), respondents indicated how satisfied they were with their life overall on 11-point rating scales ranging from 0 (*not at all*) to 10 (*very*). For validation purposes, satisfaction is a characteristic that is relevant in the examination of EI and irrationality. Indeed, the theoretical relationship between EI and life satisfaction has already been demonstrated (e.g., Ciarrochi, Chan, & Caputi, 2000; Martinez-Pons, 1997), and based on such theoretical assumptions, we can also conclude that irrationality is inversely associated with satisfaction (for first empirical evidence see Ciarrochi & West, 2004). Life satisfaction is therefore a suitable validation criterion for both irrationality and EI.

Design and Procedure

We used a 2 (cognition: rational vs. irrational) × 3 (subject experiencing emotion: stimulus person himself vs. colleague vs. team members) repeated measures design in the current study.

Paper and pencil questionnaires were administered individually to the respondents. Research assistants were present while participants filled out the questionnaire. Respondents were allowed to ask questions for clarification.

The total time allowed for completion of the questionnaire was approximately 30 min. During the completion process, participants were allowed to ask for the investigator's help if they had difficulty understanding the content or the questions. Eight versions of the questionnaire differing in respect of the order of the items were created in order to minimize answering tendencies and response order effects (Schwarz, 1999).

RESULTS

T-tests (alpha adjusted according to Bonferroni) comparing the different versions of the questionnaire revealed no systematic significant mean differences between the two versions. We therefore analyzed the aggregated data. Furthermore, the *t*-tests revealed no systematic gender differences in participants' responses. Also, there was less than 1% missing data, indicating that the vast majority questionnaire items were answered.

Hypothesis 1 was based on the assumption that rational cognitions lead to adaptive emotions, whereas irrational cognitions result in maladaptive emotions. To test this hypothesis, we computed binomial tests of the percentage of adaptive emotions assigned to rational cognitions for all four pairs of emotions in all three scenarios.

The findings presented in Table 1 provide strong support for the first hypothesis. In each of the scenarios, participants estimated fear, sadness, regret, annoyance and joy to be more likely for the rational person and anxiety, depression, guilt, rage and pride to be more typical for the irrational stimulus person. It should be noted that, due to the question format, a

Table 1. Relative Proportions of Assignments of Emotions to Cognitions in Accordance with Theoretical Assumptions.

	Situation 1: Project Work	Situation 2: Prototype Construction	Situation 3: Teamwork
Fear	0.68	0.66	0.68
	$p<.001, g = 0.18$	$p<.001, g = 0.16$	$p<.001, g = 0.18$
Sadness	0.97	0.92	0.96
	$p<.001, g = 0.47$	$p<.001, g = 0.42$	$p<.001, g = 0.46$
Regret	0.91	0.96	0.96
	$p<.001, g = 0.41$	$p<.001, g = 0.46$	$p<.001, g = 0.46$
Annoyance	0.94	0.93	0.88
	$p<.001, g = 0.44$	$p<.001, g = 0.43$	$p<.001, g = 0.38$
Joy	0.88	0.89	0.88
	$p<.001, g = 0.38$	$p<.001, g = 0.39$	$p<.001, g = 0.38$

Notes: Cohen (1988) denotes a $g = 0.05$ as small, $g = 0.15$ as mean and $g = 0.25$ as a strong effect. N per cell respectively between 111 and 113.

correct assignment (e.g., sadness to the rational person) also resulted in an assignment the corresponding emotion (e.g., depression) to the irrational person. Additionally, this indicates that the newly included emotions joy and pride can indeed be regarded as a pair of emotions. Across all situations, the smallest effect was obtained for fear, indicating that a relatively high percentage of respondents attributed anxiety as a maladaptive emotion to the rationally thinking person. Nonetheless, in this case, most of the answers given are in accordance with the hypothesis. In each scenario, participants made over 50% of correct assignments, a rate which was found to be significant ($p<0.001$). For all emotion pairs, g was computed as an effect size measure. According to Cohen (1988), a g of 0.05 indicates a small effect size, a g of 0.15 a medium effect size and a g of 0.25 a large effect size. Effect sizes range from 0.16 to 0.47, indicating at least medium effect sizes for all emotions.

Hypothesis 2 suggests that adaptive emotions would be perceived to be of higher functional value than maladaptive ones. Comparisons of the mean differences between both types of emotions are reported in Table 2.

As expected, adaptive emotions were generally rated higher in functionality for each of the five emotion pairs. With the exception of the fear–anxiety pair, which failed to reach statistical significance, there is always a significant difference in the expected direction between adaptive and maladaptive emotions. The significant difference between joy and pride

Table 2. Means of Functionality of Adaptive and Maladaptive
Emotions.

Adaptive Emotions		Maladaptive Emotions
Fear		Anxiety
3.12		2.65
	$t(109) = 1.50, p < .15, d = 0.14$	
Sadness		Depression
5.07		1.02
	$t(109) = 14.82, p < .001, d = 1.41$	
Regret		Guilt
5.84		2.36
	$t(110) = 7.65, p < .001, d = 0.73$	
Annoyance		Rage
5.13		2.55
	$t(109) = 9.40, p < .001, d = 0.90$	
Joy		Pride
8.22		5.95
	$t(109) = 9.04, p < .001, d = 0.86$	
Overall adaptive		Overall maladaptive
5.49		2.89
	$t(110) = 13.52, p < .001, d = 1.28$	

Notes: Cohen (1988) denotes a $d = 0.20$ as small, $d = 0.50$ as mean and $d = 0.80$ as a strong effect. N per test respectively between 110 and 111.

supports our conceptualization that these two emotions form a complementary pair. Cohen (1988) suggests d as a measure of effect size for comparison of means with a $d = 0.20$ indicating a small effect, $d = 0.50$ indicating a medium effect and $d = 0.80$ indicating a large effect. With the exception of fear and anxiety, all effects can be regarded as large. Overall, the theoretically postulated difference between adaptive and maladaptive emotions can be demonstrated empirically by using respondents' judgments.

Hypothesis 3 linked irrational and rational cognitions with four central concepts of EI, namely the perception and modification of one's own and others' emotional states. The descriptive data from all three scenarios are summarized in Table 3.

We computed a 2 (type of cognition: Irrational and rational) × 2 (type of EI aspect: perception and modification) × 3 (target person experiencing the relevant emotional states: other individual, own person and other persons) repeated measures ANOVA to analyze the data. We obtained no significant

Table 3.   Means of Ability of the Rational and of the Irrational Person
to Perceive and Modify Emotional States.

	Perception		Modification	
	Rational	Irrational	Rational	Irrational
Situation 1: Project work (other person's emotions)	5.85 (2.39)	4.87 (2.56)	7.08 (1.90)	3.75 (2.11)
Situation 2: Prototype construction (own emotions)	6.86 (1.88)	3.41 (2.22)	7.93 (1.35)	2.69 (1.82)
Situation 3: Teamwork (group emotions)	6.96 (1.83)	3.35 (2.22)	7.42 (1.89)	2.70 (2.00)

Notes: Standard deviation displayed in brackets. Values are based on cases included in ANOVA ($N = 107$).

main effect for the two aspects of EI, $F(1, 106) = 0.63$, indicating that perception and modification were not generally rated differently, but a significant main effect for the type of cognition, $F(1, 106) = 247.55$, $p < .001$, $\eta^2 = .70$, indicating that, in agreement with our hypothesis, the rational stimulus person ($M = 7.02$) was generally perceived to exhibit more EI than the irrational person ($M = 3.46$). Based Cohen's (1988) effect size conventions (small: $\eta^2 = .01$, medium: $\eta^2 = .06$, large: $\eta^2 = .14$), this effect can be regarded as large. Moreover, we found a medium-sized significant main effect for the target person, $F(2, 199) = 6.11$, $p < .005$, $\eta^2 = .06$. Post-hoc tests confirmed that significantly more EI was attributed to the stimulus persons ($M = 5.39$) in the first scenario (the target person is a colleague) than in the third scenario (the target persons are the team; $M = 5.11$), and both values did not differ significantly from the second scenario (the target person is the stimulus person himself; $M = 5.22$). This indicates that, logically, participants generally assumed that it was easier for both stimulus persons to perceive and change the emotions of one person than the emotions of a whole team.

With respect to the interaction effects, we found a significant and large cognition × aspect of EI interaction, $F(1, 106) = 62.80$, $p < .001$, $\eta^2 = .37$. In line with the cognition main effect described above, the irrational person was generally perceived to behave with less EI than the rational person. Additionally, this interaction indicates that this difference is significantly greater for the modification (Difference: 4.43) than for the perception (Difference: 2.68) of emotional states. Additionally, we found a significant and large cognition × target person interaction, $F(2, 212) = 24.81$, $p < .001$, $\eta^2 = .19$, indicating that the overall EI difference between the rational and the irrational person depended on the target persons. In fact, the discrepancy between the two stimulus persons is smaller in the first scenario (including another person as target person (Difference: 2.16) than in the other two scenarios (Differences: Own person: 4.35; team member's emotions: 4.17). Finally, we also detected a comparatively small but significant cognition × EI aspect × target person interaction, $F(2, 212) = 3.79$, $p < .05$, $\eta^2 = .04$, indicating that the cognition × EI aspect interaction differs between the three target persons: specifically, the interaction is smaller for the other person as target (situation 1) than for the other to the other target persons.

Overall, these results support the hypothesis that the rationally thinking stimulus person would be perceived to behave with more EI with respect to the perception and modification of emotional states; this discrepancy is larger for modification than for perception of emotional states and smaller when it comes to perceiving and modifying the emotional states of one other person (compared with one's own emotions or the emotions of several others). All these effects can be regarded as large.

Hypothesis 4 suggested that respondents who identified with an irrationally thinking stimulus person would be less satisfied with their work life and to a smaller extent with their life in general. Since identification with either the rational or the irrational person correlated highly across the three situations (r's always $> .54$), we computed two mean values of identification, one with the rationally thinking stimulus person and one with the irrationally thinking person, across all three situations. The two indicators of identification (rational vs. irrational) correlated negatively ($r = -.63$, $p < .001$). As assumed, both variables correlated significantly ($p < .005$) with work life satisfaction: specifically, identification with the irrational person correlated negatively ($r = -.28$), whereas identification with the rational person correlated positively ($r = .29$). Since the two identification indices were computed from aggregated data obtained in scenarios and the other variable is an individual estimate at the end of the questionnaire, context effects can be disregarded as a possible explanation of these results.

To test the second part of our hypothesis, we correlated both identification indices with the measure of overall life satisfaction. We obtained slightly smaller but still significant ($p < .05$) correlations of $r = -.24$ (irrational identification) and $r = .21$ (rational identification).

There was no significant correlation between these two identification indices and the perceived satisfaction with private life. This suggests that irrational or rational cognitions specific to organizational life are not indicative of individual satisfaction with private life and, hence, provides evidence for the domain specificity of irrational beliefs. It is necessary to note that participants completed the identification indices and the measures of life satisfaction with reference to their personal situation rather than that of a hypothetical person. In the second study described in this paper, we attempted to replicate the relationship between rational thinking and EI and extend our focus using psychometric scales and real person data. The results of both studies will be discussed jointly.

STUDY 2: METHOD

Participants

One hundred and thirty six people (94 women, 42 men, mean age = 28.1 years, standard deviation = 10.0, age range = 18–73 years) participated in this study. All were approached on the University campus. Ninety-seven people were students, 20 were white-collar workers, five were self-employed and 14 persons were of other professions.

Measures

Data were collected using a questionnaire containing psychometric scales designed to measure EI, irrationality and life satisfaction. The measures are described separately below.

Emotional Intelligence
We used two standardized questionnaires to measure EI, namely, Wong and Law's Emotional Intelligence Scale (WLEIS; Wong & Law, 2002) and the Emotional Competence Inventory (ECI 2.0; Boyatzis, Goleman, & Rhee, 2000).

Wong and Law's questionnaire is aligned with Salovey and Mayer's (1990) definition of EI (Mayer & Salovey, 1993) and measures four components of EI by means of four items each: Self-Emotions Appraisal (SEA), Others-Emotions Appraisal (OEA), Use of Emotion (UOE) and Regulation of Emotion (ROE). The authors employed this instrument in three studies and reported reliabilities (what kind of reliabilities?) for each of the four dimensions, which ranged from satisfactory to good (SEA: 0.87, 0.89, 0.86; OEA: 0.90, 0.85, 0.82; UOE: 0.84, 0.88, 0.85; ROE: 0.83, 76, 0.79).

The questionnaire is not yet available in German and therefore six persons independently translated all 16 items. Subsequently, three more persons familiar with the concept of EI selected the translation they thought was most suitable for each item by means of a majority decision (see the appendix).

Version 2.0 of the ECI (see Boyatzis et al., 2000; Sala, 2002) consists of 72 items and relates to Goleman's concept of EI. It is actually a 360-degree measure in which a person is required to complete a self-assessment and is also assessed by his peers and superiors. These versions of assessment only differ on an item level in that either the first or the third person is used. In this investigation, only self-assessment was undertaken. The questionnaire is divided into four subscales: Self-Awareness (SeA), Self-Management (SM), Social Awareness (SoA) and Relationship Management (RM). In turn, these four dimensions are divided into 18 subgroups, although these were not examined in the current study. The reliability (Cronbach's alpha) reported by Sala (2002) with respect to the 18 sub-dimensions lies between 0.53 and 0.78. As there is no German translation of this instrument, a German version was developed as described above. As we wish to ensure that the questionnaire is not passed on to third parties, it is not included in the appendix. The HayGroup is responsible for distribution of the instrument.

Irrational Beliefs
Irrational beliefs were measured using the six irrational beliefs (IRBS) suggested by Försterling and Bühner (2003). We refrained from additionally measuring irrational attitudes by means of another instrument, because the ECI already made the questionnaire quite long.

Satisfaction Measures
Satisfaction with private life, work life and overall happiness with life were measured by means of the three items described in the first study.

Two different versions of the questionnaire were prepared in order to reduce sequential effects.

Procedure

Data were collected via a questionnaire comprised of three different sections. In the first section, participants were asked to imagine stimulus persons in three different scenarios before making judgments on forced choice measures and rating scales. Scenarios were examples of emotionally charged situations in an organizational context. In the second section, participants were asked to estimate the functionality of the 10 emotions of Ellis' REBT theory. Finally, in the third section, participants provided some personal information about themselves, and responded to items measuring work life satisfaction, private life satisfaction and general life satisfaction. Each section of the questionnaire is discussed in greater detail below.

The three scenarios used in the first section of the questionnaire involved two stimulus persons engaged in a workplace setting. In the first scenario, the stimulus persons work hard on a project in order to be promoted and succeed. In the second scenario two engineers try to complete their work on an important prototype and fail. Finally, in the third scenario, the two stimulus persons are the supervisors of two teams who want to present a successful submission to a potential customer and fail. The rationality of the cognitions (irrational vs. rational) was varied as first independent variable. In all three scenarios, the two stimulus persons are described as being identical with the exception of their thoughts. Specifically, in each scenario, one person is described as thinking rationally (e.g., in the first scenario: "it would be wonderful if I were promoted, but my value as human being would not be affected"), and the other one as thinking irrationally (e.g., in the first scenario: "I must be promoted at all costs, otherwise I would be worthless as a human being").

The emotional states as the object of perception and modification were manipulated across all three situations and represent the second independent variable in this study. In the first situation, this emotional state was that of a colleague who, in contrast to the stimulus persons, had not been promoted. In the second situation it was the emotional state of the stimulus persons themselves in the context of not having been able to successfully finish the work on the prototype. In the third situation the emotional states of the associated team members were targeted for perception and modification. Thus the emotional states of either the stimulus person, another person or of a team were the object of perception and modification.

RESULTS

With respect to the following reported scale values, it should be noted that higher values of the WLEIS denote lower levels of EI due to the format of the rating scale. In the case of all other instruments, a higher value denotes a higher level of the particular characteristic. As no significant differences were detected between the two sequences on any of the variables, the two groups were combined in the following analyses.

Psychometric Properties of Participants' Ratings

The reliabilities of the applied measures are described as follows. While the internal consistency (α) of the WLEIS is 0.82, the ECI has a reliability (Cronbach's Alpha) of 0.93. The subscales of the WLEIS also have respectable reliabilities (SEA: 0.76, OEA: 88, UOE: 0.83 and ROE: 0.88), while the subscales of the ECI have slightly lower reliabilities (SeA: 0.65, SM: 0.80, SoA: 0.72 and RM: 0.81). The reliabilities of the 18 subgroups of the ECI lie between 0.39 and 0.79 (eight are less than 0.50). Even when viewed in the context of these reliabilities, some of which are quite low, the interpretation of the 18 subdimensions does not appear meaningful. Overall, both scales seem to have quite good reliability, which, in the case of the ECI, can be partially explained by its large number of items. Both the instruments' four subdimensions have predominantly satisfactory reliability. It is also noticeable that in both instruments the reliability of the dimension concerning emotional management (SM and ROE) is measured well by both instruments. The fact that these reliabilities are comparable with those reported by the original instruments provides strong evidence that the first German translation of the instruments was also successful. For IRBS there is no satisfactory evidence of its accuracy of measurement, given its reliability of 0.63 and hence the results obtained using this measure should only be interpreted as preliminary in nature.

In order to examine Hypothesis 5 we computed correlation coefficients between the measures of EI and irrationality. These results are summarized in Table 4

Table 4 reveals that the partial correlations do not differ substantially or systematically from the correlations. As expected, with $r = -0.41$, $p < .01$, both EI measures correlate significantly. Although different conceptualizations of EI were used to develop the two instruments, a relationship can nevertheless be shown, providing evidence for the validity of the two instruments' criteria.

The presumed relationship between irrationality and EI is further supported, as the irrationality scale correlates significantly ($p < .05$) and in the expected direction with both EI measures, $r = 0.19$ (WLEIS) and $r = -0.21$ (ECI). In accordance with REBT theory, an examination of each of the four subscales reveals that the correlation of 0.34 (ROE, $p < .01$) and $-.23$ (SM, $p < .05$) with respect to the relevant emotional control dimension is significant and relatively high in comparison to the other dimensions. In examining the ECI subdimension of emotional self-control, a similar picture emerges such that, as expected, the scale correlates significantly with the

Table 4. Correlations between Measures of EI and Irrationality.

	WLEIS	SEA	OEA	UOE	ROE	ECI	SeA	SM	SoA	RM	IRBS
WLEIS	(.82)	.61	.54	.68	.64	−.41	−.35	−.39	−.09	−.38	**.19**
SEA	.62	(.76)	.32	.25	.14	−.10	−.13	−.09	−.07	−.04	.17
OEA	.55	.30	(.88)	.18	.04	−.20	−.11	−.14	−.20	−.21	−.06
UOE	.70	.26	.20	(.83)	.20	−.34	−.26	−.34	.02	−.36	−.02
ROE	.65	.16	.06	.22	(.88)	−.34	−.33	−.34	−.04	−.27	**.34**
ECI	−.40	−.07	−.21	−.36	−.32	(.93)	.79	.92	.58	.88	**−.21**
SeA	−.35	−.11	−.12	−.28	−.31	.79	(.65)	.71	.35	.57	−.30
SM	−.39	−.07	−.17	−.37	−.30	.91	.69	(.80)	.42	.72	**−.23**
SoA	−.07	−.01	−.15	.02	−.04	.59	.37	.44	(.72)	.36	.06
RM	−.38	−.02	−.23	−.36	−.27	.88	.56	.72	.38	(.81)	−.14
IRBS	.20	.16	−.05	.01	.33	−.18	−.26	−.18	.07	−.13	(.63)

Notes: WLEIS = Wong and Law (2002) Emotional Intelligence Scale (total scale), SEA = Self-Emotions Appraisal, OEA = Others-Emotions Appraisal, UOE = Use of Emotion, ROE = Regulation of Emotion, ECI = Emotional Competence Inventory 2.0 (total scale), SeA = Self-Awareness, SM = Self-Management, SoA = Social Awareness, RM = Relationship Management and IRBS = Irrational beliefs according to Försterling and Bühner (2003). Above the main diagonal the scales' correlations are indicated, underneath the main diagonal the scales' partial correlations are indicated below each other (controlled for age and sex). The main diagonal contains the reliabilities (Cronbach's alpha). All correlations stronger than .16 are significant on the level of 0.05 (2-sided). All correlations stronger than .25 are significant on the level of 0.01 (2-sided). N per cell respectively between 135 and 136. Cohen (1988) denotes an $r = 0.10$ as small, $r = 0.30$ as mean and $r = 0.50$ as a strong effect.

irrationality scale, $r = -0.25$, $p < .01$. Hence we can conclude that the theoretically postulated connection between irrationality and EI on the basis of emotional control is empirically supported. Note that both instruments also indicate a significant relationship between irrationality and the awareness of own emotions (SEA: $r = 0.17$, $p < .05$; SeA: $r = -0.30$, $p < .01$).

In order to test Hypothesis 6, we initially calculated the correlation between irrationality and EI, and then calculated the correlation between irrationality and indicators of life satisfaction. The results are shown in Table 5.

As shown, in accordance with our hypothesis and the existing findings, EI as well as irrationality are significantly associated with the aspects of life satisfaction. Looking at the overall scores of the EI scales, significant correlations exist with all three satisfaction measures, and only two correlations of the ECI did not reach statistical significance. On examination of the subscales it is noticeable that, in the case of both instruments, neither of the scales that address awareness of other people's emotions (OEA and SoA) achieve significance.

Table 5. Correlations of the EI Instruments and their Subscales as well as the Scale for the Measurement of Irrationality with Life Satisfaction Items.

	Satisfaction with Occupational Life	Satisfaction with Private Life	General Life Satisfaction
WLEIS	−.23	−.19	−.30
SEA	−.17	−.23	−.30
OEA	.05	.10	.09
UOE	−.19	−.25	−.37
ROE	−.20	−.09	−.16
ECI	.16	.10	.24
SeA	.18	.11	.21
SM	.15	.13	.28
SoA	−.07	.00	−.07
RM	.17	.08	.24
IRBS	−.34	−.31	−.31

Notes: WLEIS = Wong and Law (2002) Emotional Intelligence Scale (total scale), SEA = Self-Emotions Appraisal, OEA = Others-Emotions Appraisal, UOE = Use of Emotion, ROE = Regulation of Emotion, ECI = Emotional Competence Inventory 2.0 (total scale), SeA = Self-Awareness, SM = Self-Management, SoA = Social Awareness, RM = Relationship Management, IRBS = Irrational beliefs according to Försterling and Bühner (2003). All correlations stronger than .16 are significant on the level of 0.05 (2-sided). All correlations stronger than .23 are significant on the level of 0.01 (2-sided). $N = 135$. Cohen (1988) denotes an $r = 0.10$ as small, $r = 0.30$ as mean and $r = 0.50$ as a strong effect.

It is irrationality, however, that has the strongest relationships with the satisfaction measures, as it is significantly and moderately related to satisfaction in all three cases.

Since our findings indicate that EI and irrationality seems to be associated with each other and that both EI and irrationality correlate with life satisfaction, we used regression analyses to predict satisfaction from EI and irrationality. Three single regressions were calculated in which both the EI measures and the irrationality scale were used as predictors for each of the three aspects of contentment. The results of these three regressions are presented in Table 6. In examining these results, it can initially be seen that, as all three regressions are significant overall (F always greater than 5, $p < .005$), satisfaction can be significantly predicted in all three cases, but that it is evident from the R^2 that the predictive value remains relatively small and does not exceed 15% of the explained variance.

Furthermore, examination of the two measures of EI shows that they are not equally well suited as predictors of satisfaction. Namely, while the

Table 6. Regressions to Predict Occupational, Private and General Life
Satisfaction from Measures of EI and Irrationality.

	B	SE B	*β*	*R²*adj
Regression 1:				
Satisfaction with occupational life				
WLEIS	−.48	.28	−.16	
ECI	.20	.62	.03	
IRBS	−.93	.26	−.30**	$R^2 = .12$
Regression 2:				
Satisfaction with private life				
WLEIS	−.40	.25	−.15	
ECI	−.13	.55	−.02	
IRBS	−.76	.23	−.28**	$R^2 = .09$
Regression 3:				
General life satisfaction				
WLEIS	−.46	.19	−.21*	
ECI	.45	.43	.09	
IRBS	−.53	.18	−.25**	$R^2 = .15$

Notes: WLEIS = Wong and Law (2002) Emotional Intelligence Scale (total scale), ECI = Emotional Competence Inventory 2.0 (total scale), IRBS = Irrational beliefs according to Försterling and Bühner (2003). In all three regressions neither age nor sex prove to be significant predictors. For each regression a significant *F*-value results ($p < .005$), there were no problematic collinearities. $N = 134$.
*The regression coefficient is significant on the level of 0.05 (2-tailed).
**The regression coefficient is significant on the level of 0.005 (2-tailed).

WLEIS has three standardized regression coefficients in the expected direction in all three cases, the ECI does not achieve significance and even changes direction. More specifically, while the standardized regression coefficients of the WLEIS have a value of at least 0.15 (even achieving significance for general life satisfaction), all coefficients of the ECI are less than 0.10. On examination of the standard errors it is remarkable that these are relatively high for the ECI when compared to the two other scales, which suggests the possibility of greater inaccuracy when determining the strength of prediction.

In all three regressions irrationality proves to be a significant predictor of satisfaction, which can be classified as moderately strong with values of at least 0.25. The standard error turns out to be the smallest in each of the regressions. Hence we can conclude that when combining EI and irrationality to predict satisfaction, it is irrationality that offers the greatest predictive value.

GENERAL DISCUSSION

We examined the theoretical and predictive value of central REBT assumptions for EI research by using experimental and correlational data. By doing so, we aimed to enrich the theoretical foundations of the emerging field of EI by introducing a theory that, to our knowledge, has never been applied to this topic before.

Based on Albert Ellis' appraisal theory, we postulated that irrational vs. rational cognitions are central determinants of maladaptive vs. adaptive emotions and of emotionally unintelligent vs. emotionally intelligent behavior. In our first study we have applied these concepts to organizational behavior by means of experimentally manipulated scenarios, which represent concrete and typical individual and interpersonal situations at the workplace. In the second study we again tried to demonstrate the inverse connection between irrationality and EI by using correlational data.

The first hypothesis that rational cognitions lead to adaptive emotions whereas irrational cognitions result in maladaptive emotions was strongly supported. In all scenarios adaptive emotions were predominantly assigned to the person thinking rationally, whereas maladaptive emotions were attributed to the person thinking irrationally. These results support the theoretically postulated relationship between cognitions and emotions.

Our results also confirmed the differential functionality of adaptive and maladaptive emotions suggested in the second hypothesis. All adaptive emotions were perceived to have significantly higher functional value than maladaptive ones, with the exception of fear and anxiety. In accordance with theoretical assumptions, anxiety as a maladaptive emotion was perceived to be less functional than fear. However, this effect was not found to be significant. This finding may indicate that the participants found it difficult to discriminate between the words 'fear' and 'anxiety'. Overall (for four out of five emotion pairs) these results do, however, confirm the theoretical distinction between adaptive and maladaptive emotions as far as their functionality is concerned. We can therefore assume that those emotions attributed to an irrationally thinking person are in fact perceived to be of less functional value.

Due to the fact that REBT focuses primarily on negative emotions we tried to extend the theoretical basis of Ellis' theory by including the positive emotions joy and pride. We argued that even in case of positive emotions, maladaptive (pride) and adaptive emotions (joy) can be differentiated, since the former results from cognitions linking self-worth with behavior, which according to REBT can be classified as irrational, whereas the latter only results from a positive evaluation of the stimulus. Results confirmed our assumptions, which had not yet been empirically tested: across all situations joy was predominantly attributed to the rational stimulus person whereas the irrational stimulus person was assumed to feel pride. Moreover, joy was perceived to be of substantially higher functional value than pride. Hence, our research indicates that the functionality of an emotion has to be distinguished from its valence, as positive emotions can be perceived to be maladaptive. Based on these promising results it seems reasonable to integrate positively evaluated emotions in future research concerning REBT.

Additionally, we provided the first empirical evidence for the third hypothesis, namely that rational cognitions as conceptualized by REBT are associated with emotionally intelligent behavior. In this case, participants assumed that the rational stimulus person exhibited a greater ability to perceive and to regulate emotional states. This result was again replicated across all situations. The discrepancy between the two stimulus persons was larger for regulating than for perceiving emotional states which is in accordance with the REBT assumption that the denial of emotion control (not perception) is an explicit component of irrational thinking. In agreement with REBT we assume that emotions caused by irrational beliefs offer a potential explanation for this relationship between cognitions and emotionally (un)intelligent behavior, such that the quality of maladaptive emotions, such as depression or guilt, reduces an individual's capability to engage in functional behavior, including emotionally intelligent behavior.

In considering participants' life satisfaction in Hypothesis 4, we extended our findings that had until then been based on hypothetical stimulus persons, and were able to demonstrate that the participants' occupational life satisfaction decreased with increasing identification with the irrational stimulus person. Alternatively, however, identification with the rational stimulus person correlated significantly with increased occupational life satisfaction. These results provide evidence for the relationship between irrational cognitions and life satisfaction. Since there was no significant correlation between these identification measures and private life satisfaction, the results also provide the first evidence that domain-specific irrational thoughts might have a (domain-) specific impact.

Based on our results, there are three ways to explain this relationship between irrationality and reduced life satisfaction. First, from a REBT perspective, irrational beliefs might directly lead to reduced life satisfaction. A second possibility is that irrational beliefs result in maladaptive emotions, which might have a negative impact on life satisfaction. Finally, emotionally intelligent behavior as a result of rational beliefs might foster life satisfaction. Further investigation of these alternative explanations should be regarded as an important reason to simultaneously use real person measures of EI and irrationality in order to determine their predictive value for life satisfaction.

An important limitation of the first study is the measurement of emotions by means of a questionnaire. Emotions were not assessed directly; rather we measured cognitions about emotions. Moreover, the respondents were not personally involved, but were confronted with a story about somebody else in an emotion-provoking situation. Even though this method has successfully been used in many empirical studies it clearly places some limitations on our data. However, there are good reasons why our results should be seen as meaningful. First, real life examples of everyday situations were used. Furthermore, as Parrott and Hertel (1999) have pointed out, the limitations of this method of assessment can be reduced by ensuring that participants experience or imagine the emotional state vividly. In order to ensure this, the participants were asked to identify and empathize with the persons in the scenario. Nevertheless, the results of our first study should only be regarded as preliminary evidence for a potential causal relationship between rational cognitions and EI.

In order to reduce these methodological limitations we sought to replicate the relationship between rationality and EI by using real person data in the second study. Although this correlational design does not permit causal conclusions, it does provide evidence for the potential relationship between EI, irrationality and life satisfaction based on real person data.

As described earlier, two scales of EI, one irrationality scale and three items measuring life satisfaction, were utilized to test the fifth hypothesis. The scales of EI that were applied here are based on slightly different theoretical conceptualizations of EI and were translated into German for the first time. The reliabilities produced in the research are comparable to those of the originals and hence support the acceptability of the German versions of these two instruments.

In accordance with REBT and the results of our first study, an inverse correlation between EI and irrationality was obtained. Specifically, the more a person acceded to irrational attitudes, the lower the self-reported general EI was. As expected, an analysis of EI subdimensions revealed even stronger relationships between irrationality and the specific regulation and control of emotion dimension in both instruments, namely that increased irrationality is associated with reduced emotion control. In line with the assumption that irrational beliefs can be regarded as relatively stable and long-lasting structures that also go beyond aspects of emotional control, it seems reasonable to regard this as the causal factor of reduced emotionally intelligent behavior (especially reduced emotion control).

Both instruments also exhibited an unexpected relationship between irrationality and the awareness and evaluation of own emotions dimension. Subsequent investigations should examine the stability of this relationship.

With respect to Hypothesis 6, the second study also demonstrated that life satisfaction measures were positively associated with EI and negatively associated with irrationality. This replicates and extends the results of the first study in which we were able to show that identification with an irrationally thinking person was associated with reduced satisfaction. Multiple regression analyses further revealed that satisfaction could be significantly predicted, although irrationality and EI explained only about 15% of the variance. Compared to EI, irrationality was found to be the better predictor of satisfaction in all regressions. Since we only used measures of general irrationality in the second study, we were not able to replicate the results of the first study concerning the differential aspects of domain specific irrational attitudes. In future, organizational researchers should seek to develop reliable instruments of work-specific irrationality to further investigate the differential impact demonstrated in the first study. Furthermore, we only used relatively simple one-item indicators of satisfaction; hence the predictive value of irrationality (and to a smaller extent of EI) concerning life satisfaction should be replicated using more sophisticated measures of life satisfaction.

In summary, the second study provided empirical evidence for the theoretical link between irrationality and emotion control as a specific dimension of EI. This evidence was produced by means of two different instruments, which used slightly different conceptualizations of EI. It should be noted, however, that self-report questionnaires were used to measure EI. The relationships identified in this study should therefore be replicated using a task-oriented ability test for EI such as, for example, the MSCEIT V2.0 (Mayer, Salovey, Caruso, & Sitarenios, 2003) to increase the validity of the findings.

When the studies are compared from a methodological perspective, it is interesting to note that the relationship between irrationality and EI was demonstrated on the basis of stimulus and real person data; this convergence of results indicates that the use of scenario techniques can be regarded as a valid method in emotion research.

An important limitation of our second study is the low reliability of our irrationality scale; as such, our results concerning the relationship between irrationality and EI should be replicated using an instrument with higher accuracy, especially when trying to analyze the influence of specific irrational cognitions on emotional states and EI.

Moreover our data are primarily based on student samples and therefore results should be replicated by investigating employees of different educational status to extend the generalizability of our findings.

Another important methodical limitation of the second study concerns the use of self-report attitude scales to assess the constructs of EI and irrationality. Since both characteristics were measured using the same method, the relationship between EI and irrationality might be a result of common method bias, which is defined as follows: "If the measures of Construct A and the measures of Construct B [...] share common methods, those methods may exert a systematic effect on the observed correlation between the measures. Thus [...] common method biases pose a rival explanation for the correlation" (Podsakoff, MacKenzie, Lee, & Podsakoff, 2003, p. 879).

Since the relationship between EI and irrationality is the central proposition of our study, we reanalyzed the relationship between the EI subscales and irrationality by applying a procedure described by Podsakoff et al. (2003). Specifically, we used a structural equation model to analyze the relationship between the two constructs and included an unmeasured latent methods factor in the second step. The results of this procedure are summarized in Table 7.

In the first section the normal correlations between the two measures can be seen (including significance level), which are identical to the correlations described above. Subsequently, the correlations between the two latent variables EI and irrationality are displayed in the second section. These are no longer the correlations between the two mean values of the particular scales, but the correlations between the two latent variables used to predict the manifest values of the items of each of the concerning scale. As can be seen, the correlation between the two variables usually increases, which is not surprising since sub-optimal reliabilities no longer conceal the potential relationship. Additionally, it is evident that even large correlations do not reach statistical significance, since the estimate of the correlation includes more uncertainty.

In the third section the method factor is introduced into the same model. As a result, correlations predominantly decrease, confirming that there is indeed some common variance, which had inflated the former correlation. Also, when comparing the fit indices (*CFI* and *RMSEA*) between the models, it is evident that the second structural equation model offers a better description of the raw data than the first one: specifically, *CFI* always increases whereas *RMSEA* is mainly reduced (in two cases unchanged),

Table 7. Comparison of the Correlations between EI and Irrationality Obtained by Classical Procedure and Structural Equation Modeling Including Common Method Bias.

Pair of scales	Correlation between Scales		Model 1: Correlation between Latent Variables						Model 2: Correlation between Latent Variables Including Common Method Bias					
	r	p	r	p	χ^2	df	CFI	RMSEA	r	p	χ^2	df	CFI	RMSEA
SEA – IRBS	.17	.05	.21	n.s.	38,4	36	.99	.02	.11	n.s.	21,3	26	1.00	.00
OEA – IRBS	−.06	n.s.	−.08	n.s.	36,2	36	.99	.03	−.09	n.s.	24,5	27	1.00	.00
UOE – IRBS	−.02	n.s.	−.01	n.s.	56,1	36	.99	.06	−.17	.05	41,9	28	1.00	.06
ROE – IRBS	.34	.01	.47	.001	53,8	36	.99	.06	.40	.01	29,6	27	1.00	.03
SeA – IRBS	−.30	.01	−.71	n.s.	243,2	136	.99	.08	.15	.05	152,3	119	1.00	.05
SM – IRBS	−.23	.05	−.39	.001	727,9	406	.97	.08	−.45	.005	588,7	377	.98	.06
SoA – IRBS	.06	n.s.	.20	n.s.	228,1	136	.99	.07	.17	n.s.	135,1	118	1.00	.03
RM – IRBS	−.14	n.s.	−.21	n.s.	631,6	406	.98	.06	−.03	n.s.	535,0	377	.99	.06

Notes: IRBS = Irrational Beliefs (Försterling & Bühner, 2003), WLEIS = Wong and Law (2002) Emotional Intelligence Scale (total scale), ECI = Emotional Competence Inventory 2.0 (total scale), SEA = Self-Emotion Appraisal (WLEIS subscale), OEA = Others' Emotion Appraisal (WLEIS subscale), UOE = Use of Emotion (WLEIS subscale), ROE = Regulation of Emotion (WLEIS subscale), SeA = Self-Awareness (ECI subscale), SM = Self-Management (ECI subscale), SoA = Social Awareness (ECI subscale), RM = Relationship Management (ECI subscale), ESC = Emotional Self-Control (SM subscale), CFI = Comparative Fit Index (Bentler, 1990), value should exceed 0.95 to indicate a good model, and RMSEA = Root Mean Square Error of Approximation, value should be at least below 0.10, values below 0.05 indicate a good model (Browne & Cudek, 1993). Cohen (1988) denotes an $r = 0.10$ as small, $r = 0.30$ as mean, $r = 0.50$ as a strong effect.

suggesting a better fit of the second model. This is in accordance with an analysis of the χ^2 values of the models. As shown, the models of the second section do not obtain significance in two cases, whereas the models of the third section are significant in four cases; since significance indicates a discrepancy between the model and the underlying raw data, this also confirms a better fit of those models, which include a common method factor. Hence our data demonstrate that the inclusion of the common method bias offers a better description of the data.

As can be seen in the last section only the correlations between irrationality and emotional control remain significant and are even stronger than the values obtained by the correlation of the mean values. Hence this procedure confirms that our data are indeed influenced by common method bias (and reduced reliability), but that the consideration of this method factor cannot explain the major relationship between irrationality and emotional control as a central aspect of EI.

We set out to contribute to the literature by examining whether rationality as a determinant of adaptive emotions also influences emotionally intelligent behavior in an organizational context. By using a theoretical model from clinical psychology, linking it with EI concepts and applying this to an organizational setting, we were able to show a relationship between specific cognitions, resulting emotions and emotionally intelligent behavior, especially emotional control. Furthermore we were able to demonstrate a relationship between irrationality and life and job satisfaction. In our search for an integrative perspective, we hope that our results encourage future research to simultaneously integrate cognitions, emotions and behavior in empirical research in order to develop a comprehensive understanding of EI.

ACKNOWLEDGMENTS

We thank Jacob Eisenberg and Friedrich Försterling for their helpful comments about our first study and Sabine Aschmutat, Jennifer Stich, Andranik Tumasjan and Ingelore Welpe for their help in collecting the data.

REFERENCES

Ashkanasy, N. M., & Daus, S. D. (2002). Emotion in the workplace: The new challenge for managers. *Academy of Management Executive, 16*(1), 76–86.

Bentler, P. M. (1990). Comparative fit indexes in structural models. *Psychological Bulletin, 107*, 238–246.

Boyatzis, R. E., Goleman, D., & Rhee, K. S. (2000). Clustering competence in emotional intelligence: Insights from the Emotional Competence Inventory. In: R. Bar-On & J. D. A. Parker (Eds), *The handbook of emotional intelligence: Theory, development, assessment, and application at home, school, and in the workplace* (pp. 343–362). San Francisco, CA: Jossey-Bass.

Browne, M. W., & Cudek, R. (1993). Alternative ways of assessing model fit. In: K. A. Bollen & J. S. Long (Eds), *Testing structural equation models* (pp. 136–162). Newbury Park, CA: Sage.

Ciarrochi, J., & West, M. (2004). Relationships between dysfunctional beliefs and positive and negative indices of well-being: A critical evaluation of the common beliefs survey-III. *Journal of Rational Emotive and Cognitive Behavior Therapy, 22*(3), 171–188.

Ciarrochi, J. V., Chan, A. Y. C., & Caputi, P. (2000). A critical evaluation of the emotional intelligence construct. *Personality and Individual Differences, 28*(3), 539–561.

Cohen, J. (1988). *Statistical power analysis for the behavioral sciences* (2nd ed.). Hillsdale: Lawrence Erlbaum.

Cooper, R. K., & Sawaf, A. (1997). *Executive EQ*. New York: Grosset/Putnam.

David, D., Montgomery, G. H., Macavei, B., & Bovbjerg, D. H. (2005). An empirical investigation of Albert Ellis's binary model of distress. *Journal of Clinical Psychology, 61*(4), 499–516.

David, D., Schnur, J., & Belloiu, A. (2002). Another search for the "hot" cognitions: Appraisal, irrational beliefs, attributions, and their relation to emotion. *Journal of Rational Emotive and Cognitive Behavior Therapy, 20*(2), 93–132.

David, D., Schnur, J., & Birk, J. (2004). Functional and dysfunctional feelings in Ellis' cognitive theory of emotion: An empirical analysis. *Cognition and Emotion, 18*, 869–880.

Davies, M., Stankov, L., & Roberts, R. D. (1998). Emotional intelligence: In search of an elusive construct. *Journal of Personality and Social Psychology, 75*, 989–1015.

Ellis, A. (1962). *Reason and emotion in psychotherapy*. New York: Lyle Stuart.

Ellis, A. (1973). *Humanistic psychotherapy: The rational-emotive approach*. New York: McGraw-Hill.

Ellis, A. (1994). *Reason and emotion in psychotherapy* (Rev ed.). New York: Carol Publishing Group.

Ellis, A. (1995). Thinking processes involved in irrational beliefs and their disturbed consequences. *Journal of Cognitive Psychotherapy: An International Quarterly, 9*(2), 105–116.

Ellis, A., & DiGiuseppe, R. (1993). Are inappropriate or dysfunctional feelings in rational-emotive therapy qualitative or quantitative? *Cognitive Therapy and Research, 17*(5), 471–477.

Ellsworth, P. (1991). Some implications of cognitive theories of emotion. In: K. I. Strongman (Ed.), *International review of studies on emotion* (pp. 143–161). New York: Wiley.

Engles, G. I., Garnefsky, N., & Diekstra, F. W. (1993). Efficacy of rational-emotive therapy: A quantitative analysis. *Journal of Consulting and Clinical Psychology, 6*, 1083–1090.

Fisher, C. D., & Ashkanasy, N. M. (2000). The emerging role of emotions in work life: An introduction. *Journal of Organizational Behavior, 21*, 123–129.

Försterling, F. (1985). Rational-emotive therapy and attribution theory: An investigation of the cognitive determinants of emotions. *British Journal of Cognitive Psychotherapy, 1*, 41–51.

Försterling, F., & Bühner, M. (2003). Attributional veridicality and evaluative beliefs: How do they contribute to depression? *Journal of Social and Clinical Psychology, 22*(4), 369–392.

Goleman, D. (1995). *Emotional intelligence: Why it can matter more than IQ*. New York: Bantam.

Goleman, D. (1998). *Working with emotional intelligence.* New York: Bantam.

Gonzalez, J. E., Nelson, J. R., Gutkin, T. B., Saunders, A., Galloway, A., & Shwery, C. S. (2004). Rational Emotive Therapy with children and adolescents: A meta-analysis. *Journal of Emotional and Behavioral Disorders, 12*(4), 222–235.

Grawe, K., Donati, R., & Bernauer, F. (1994). *Psychotherapie im Wandel. Von der Konfession zur Profession [Psychotherapy in transition. From confession to profession].* Göttingen: Hogrefe.

Lepine, J. A., & van Dyne, L. (2001). Peer responses to low performers: An attributional model of helping in the context of groups. *Academy of Management Review, 26*(1), 67–84.

Lyons, L. C., & Woods, P. J. (1991). The efficacy of rational emotive therapy: A quantitative review of the outcome research. *Clinical Psychology Review, 11*, 357–369.

Martinez-Pons, M. (1997). The relation of emotional intelligence with selected areas of personal functioning. *Imagination, Cognition and Personality, 17*(1), 3–13.

Matthews, G., & Zeidner, M. (2000). Emotional intelligence, adaptation to stressful encounters, and health outcomes. In: R. Bar-On & J. D. A. Parker (Eds), *The handbook of emotional intelligence: Theory, development, assessment, and application at home, school, and in the workplace* (pp. 459–489). San Francisco: Jossey-Bass.

Matthews, G., Zeidner, M., & Roberts, R. (2002). *Emotional intelligence: Science and myth.* Cambridge: MIT Press.

Mayer, J. D., & Salovey, P. (1993). The intelligence of emotional intelligence. *Intelligence, 17*(4), 433–442.

Mayer, J. D., & Salovey, P. (1997). What is emotional intelligence? In: P. Salovey & D. Sluyter (Eds), *Emotional development and emotional intelligence: Educational implications* (pp. 3–34). New York: Basic Books.

Mayer, J. D., Salovey, P., Caruso, D. R., & Sitarenios, G. (2003). Measuring emotional intelligence with the MSCEIT V2.0. *Emotion, 3*(1), 97–105.

Moore, J. E. (2000). Why is this happening? A causal attribution approach to work exhaustion consequences. *Academy of Management Review, 25*(2), 335–349.

Myers, D. G. (2000). The funds, friends, and faith of happy people. *American Psychologist, 55*(1), 56–67.

Parrott, W. G., & Hertel, P. (1999). Research methods in cognition and emotion. In: T. Dalgleish & M. Power (Eds), *Handbook of cognition and emotion* (pp. 61–81). Chichester: Wiley.

Podsakoff, P. M., MacKenzie, S. B., Lee, J. Y., & Podsakoff, N. P. (2003). Common method biases in behavioral research: A critical review of the literature and recommended remedies. *Journal of Applied Psychology, 88*, 879–903.

Reisenzein, R. (1986). A structural equation analysis of Weiner's attribution–affect model of helping behavior. *Journal of Personality and Social Psychology, 50*(6), 1123–1133.

Roseman, I. J. (1984). Cognitive determinants of emotions: A structural theory. In: P. Shaver (Ed.), *Review of Personality and Social Psychology* (Vol. 5, pp. 11–36). Beverly Hills, CA: Sage Publications.

Sala, F. (2002). *Emotional competence inventory (ECI). Technical manual.* Boston: Hay Group.

Salovey, P., & Mayer, J. D. (1990). Emotional intelligence. *Imagination, Cognition and Personality, 9*(3), 185–211.

Scherer, K. R. (1999). On the sequential nature of appraisal processes: Indirect evidence from a recognition task. *Cognition and Emotion, 13*(6), 763–793.

Schwarz, N. (1999). Self-reports. How the questions shape the answers. *American Psychologist, 54*(2), 93–105.

Smith, C. A., & Lazarus, R. S. (1993). Appraisal components, core relational themes, and the emotions. *Cognition and Emotion*, 7, 233–269.
Smith, D. (1982). Trends in counselling and psychotherapy. *American Psychologist*, 37, 802–809.
Stein, N. L., Levine, L. J. (1987). Thinking about feelings: The development and organization of emotional knowledge, In: R. E. Snow, & M. Farr (Eds), *Aptitude, learning, and instruction* (Vol. 3, pp. 165–197). Cognition, Conation and Affect. Hillsdale, NJ: Erlbaum.
Weiner, B. (1986). *An attributional theory of motivation and emotion*. New York: Springer.
Weiner, B. (1995). *Judgments of responsibility: A foundation for a theory of social conduct*. New York: The Guilford Press.
Weiner, B., Russell, D., & Lerman, D. (1979). The cognition–emotion process in achievement-related contexts. *Journal of Personality and Social Psychology*, 37, 1211–1220.
Wong, C.-S., & Law, K. S. (2002). The effects of leader and follower emotional intelligence on performance and attitude: An exploratory study. *The Leadership Quarterly*, 13, 243–274.

APPENDIX. ITEMS IN THE WONG AND LAW EI SCALE (2002) IN ENGLISH (ORIGINAL) AND GERMAN (TRANSLATION)

	English	German
Self-Emotions Appraisal (SEA)	I have a good sense of why I have certain feelings most of the time.	Meistens habe ich ein gutes Gespür dafür, warum ich bestimmte Gefühle habe.
	I have good understanding of my own emotions.	Ich habe ein gutes Verständnis meiner eigenen Emotionen.
	I really understand what I feel.	Ich kann wirklich gut verstehen, was ich fühle.
	I always know whether or not I am happy.	Ich weiß immer, ob ich gerade glücklich bin oder nicht.
Others-Emotions Appraisal (OAE)	I always know my friends' emotions from their behavior.	Ich erkenne stets die Emotionen meiner Freunde an deren Verhalten.
	I am a good observer of others' emotions.	Ich bin gut darin, die Emotionen anderer zu beobachten.
	I am sensitive to the feelings and emotions of others.	Ich habe ein feines Gespür für die Gefühle und Emotionen anderer Menschen.
	I have good understanding of the emotions of people around me.	Ich habe ein gutes Verständnis von den Emotionen der Menschen um mich herum.
Use of Emotion (UOE)	I always set goals for myself and then try my best to achieve them.	Ich setze mir selber immer Ziele und versuche sie so gut ich kann zu erreichen.
	I always tell myself I am a competent person.	Ich sage mir selbst immer, dass ich eine fähige Person bin.
	I am a self-motivating person.	Ich bin jemand, der sich selbst motiviert.

	I would always encourage myself to try my best.	Ich würde mich selbst immer anspornen mein bestes zu geben.
Regulation of Emotion (ROE)	I am able to control my temper so that I can handle difficulties rationally.	Ich bin in der Lage, meine Stimmungen zu kontrollieren und mit Schwierigkeiten rational umzugehen.
	I am quite capable of controlling my own emotions.	Ich bin ziemlich gut in der Lage meine eigenen Emotionen zu kontrollieren.
	I can always calm down quickly when I am very angry.	Ich kann mich immer schnell wieder beruhigen, wenn ich sehr verärgert bin.
	I have good control of my own emotions.	Ich habe meine eigenen Emotionen gut unter Kontrolle.

ABOUT THE AUTHORS

Céleste M. Brotheridge is a professor of organizational behaviour with the Départment d'organisation et ressources humaines in the École des sciences de la gestion at the Université du Québec à Montréal. She completed her PhD in organizational behavior and research methods at the University of Manitoba. Dr. Brotheridge publishes and conducts research primarily in the areas of burnout, emotions, and bullying in the workplace. She is the chair of the Organizational Behaviour Division of the Administrative Sciences Association of Canada and a member of the editorial boards of the *International Journal of Stress Management* and the *Journal of Managerial Psychology.*

Stéphane Côté is an assistant professor of organizational behavior at the Rotman School of Management at the University of Toronto. He received his PhD and MA degrees from the University of Michigan, Ann Arbor, and his BSc degree from McGill University. He studies the influence of emotion regulation and emotional intelligence on job strain and well-being, job performance, and leadership. He has published in the *Administrative Science Quarterly, the Academy of Management Review, the Journal of Applied Psychology, and the Journal of Personality and Social Psychology.* He teaches courses on Leadership and Organizational Behavior at the Rotman School of Management.

Lorna M. Doucet is an assistant professor of business administration at the University of Illinois at Urbana-Champaign. She earned her PhD in management from the Wharton School, University of Pennsylvania. Her research focuses on emotions, performance, and cross-cultural interactions in organizations. She is particularly interested in the interplay between emotional and technical aspects of work.

Vanessa Urch Druskat is associate professor of organizational behavior at the Whittemore School of Business and Economics at the University of New Hampshire. Her research focuses on group structures and processes that increase group effectiveness and on effective formal and informal group leadership. It has appeared in publications such as *The Academy of Management Journal*, *Human Relations*, *The Journal of Applied Psychology*, *Leadership Quarterly*, *Sloan Management Review*, *Small Group Research*, and *The Harvard Business Review*. She is the lead editor on the book *Linking Emotional Intelligence and Performance at Work: Current Research Evidence with Individuals and Groups* published by Lawrence Erlbaum in the summer of 2005. In the winter of 2006 she will become associate editor of the Journal *Small Group Research*. She has an undergraduate degree in psychology from Indiana University, a master's degree in organizational psychology from Teacher's College at Columbia University, and a PhD in social and organizational psychology from Boston University.

Dorthe Eide is an assistant professor of organizational studies and management at the Bodø Graduate School of Business, in Norway. She is currently studying the role of emotions and social interactions in/for knowing and learning in organizations, proposing a broad situated-relational approach instead of seeing, knowing, and learning in practice only as a cognitive process of individuals or taking place as social cognition. She has mainly been teaching and doing research within organizational studies at college level, and in addition working with industries. Particularly she has an interest in different service sectors, where relations and emotions are of large importance in the social 'dance'. Besides literature within organizational studies, she draws upon philosophy, sociology, anthropology, and psychology, when exploring and elaborating emotions in organizations.

Andrea Fischbach is a junior professor of work- and organizational psychology at Trier-University, Germany. She received her diploma in Psychology (Dipl. Psych.) in 1999 from Goethe-University, Frankfurt, Germany and her PhD in work- and organizational psychology (Dr. rer. nat.) in 2003 at Georg-August-University, Göttingen, Germany. Her research is focused on emotional labor/emotion work, and cross-cultural psychology. She is particularly interested in how cultural, organizational, and personal factors influence service-interactions, and in the consequences of emotional demands on service workers, customers, and service organizations.

Markus Groth is a senior lecturer in organizational behavior at the Australian Graduate School of Management in Sydney, Australia. He received his PhD in Management from the University of Arizona in 2001. His research interests include service management, customer–employee interactions, the role of emotions in service deliveries, and organizational citizenship behavior. His work has been published in journals such as *Journal of Applied Psychology*, *Personnel Psychology*, *Journal of Management*, *Academy of Management Executive*, and *Journal of Marketing*. He has consulted with both private and public organizations on human resource management issues.

Thorsten Hennig-Thurau is a professor of management and media research at the Bauhaus-University of Weimar, Germany, and a visiting professor of marketing at London City University. His research interests include services management, relationship marketing, and media research. Hennig-Thurau's work has been published in, among others, the *Journal of Marketing, Journal of Academy of Marketing Science, Journal of Service Research, International Journal of Electronic Commerce, Journal of Interactive Marketing, Psychology & Marketing, International Journal of Service Industry Management*, and *Advances in Consumer Research*. He has published two books and is the co-editor of the monograph "Relationship Marketing" which has been translated into the Chinese. He also serves on the editorial board of three journals, including the *Journal of Service Research*. His previous achievements include several best paper awards, the JSR Excellence in Service Research Award, and the Literati Club Award for Excellence.

Annabelle Mark is professor of healthcare organisation at Middlesex University Business School UK and spent the first 10 years of her career as a manager in the UK National Health Service (NHS), since 1985 she has worked as an academic. A fellow of the Institute of Health Services Management and The Royal Society of Medicine, and a research associate of Oxford Health Care Management Institute Templeton College Oxford, her research interest and publications include the changing professional roles in healthcare, in particular doctors in the management role, teamworking, leadership, demarketing and managing demand, emotion in healthcare, and the development of NHS Direct. She is the founding academic of the biennel conference Organizational Behavior in Healthcare, chair of the Learned Society for the Study of Organising for HealthCare (SHOC) and director of the Pilot NHS Human Resource Management National Training Scheme in the UK.

Janet R. McColl-Kennedy is a professor of marketing at the UQ Business School, University of Queensland, Australia. She holds a BA with first class honors and a PhD from the University of Queensland. A key research focus is service recovery. She has published in several journals including *Journal of Service Research, Journal of Business Research, The Leadership Quarterly, Industrial Marketing Management, Journal of Services Marketing,* and *International Journal of Human–Computer Studies.*

Katrin Meyer-Gomes received her diploma in psychology (i.e. Masters of Science) in 2002 from the Georg-August-University, Göttingen, Germany. Her Master's thesis consisted of the development and validation of an English version of the Frankfurt Emotion Work Scales based on a sample of US-American teachers and travel agents. She is currently working on her PhD at the University of California in San Diego.

Christopher T.H. Miners is a doctoral candidate in the Organizational Behavior and Human Resource Management program at the Rotman School of Management at the University of Toronto. He received his BSc degree from McGill University. He studies the relations between personality, behavior, and emotion, and the relations between emotional intelligence, cognitive intelligence, and job performance. He has published articles in the *Journal of Behavioral Medicine and the Administrative Science Quarterly.* He teaches courses on Organizational Behavior at the Rotman School of Management.

Nanette Monin is a senior lecturer in the Department of Management and International Business, at Massey University's Auckland Campus, New Zealand. She has published papers on metaphor theory, dramatism, and the deconstruction of management theory in the *Journal of Management Studies, Organization* and the *Journal of Organizational Change Management,* and has written chapters in books published by John Benjamins, Routledge, and Longmans. She is the author of *Management Theory: A Critical & Reflexive Reading* (Routledge, 2004) and is the co-editor of books published by Longmans and Thomson Learning. She is a member of the Editorial Board of the *Journal of Management Studies.*

Sue Moon is a PhD student in the Organizational Behavior and Human Resource Management program at the Rotman School of Management at the University of Toronto. She received a Bachelor of Commerce degree and a Master of Industrial Relations degree from Queen's University. She has worked in the human resource departments of the Toronto Dominion Bank and Canadian Imperial Bank of Commerce. Her primary research interests include stress, diversity, and emotional intelligence.

Anthony T. Pescosolido is an assistant professor of organizational behavior and management at the Whittemore School of Business and Economics at the University of New Hampshire. His research interests are in team and group dynamics, particularly the role that informal leadership, group emotion and collective beliefs play in shaping the lives, and performance of groups and teams. His research has appeared in journals such as *Leadership Quarterly*, *Human* Relations, and *Small Group Research*, as well as multiple book chapters. He earned an A.B. in psychology from Harvard College and a PhD in Organizational Behavior from Case Western Reserve University.

Fleur Piper is a senior lecturer in the Department of Communication Studies, at the Auckland University of Technology, New Zealand. She has delivered papers on the experience of organizational emotions, and enhancing learning and interpersonal dynamics within groups. Currently, she is working on a paper for the *Australian Dispute Resolution Journal* on nonconventional ways of managing conflict resolution, particularly in relation to bullying issues. She is a member of the New Zealand Communication Association.

Johannes Rank is a doctoral candidate in the PhD program in Industrial/ Organizational Psychology at the University of South Florida and a research associate in the Department of Work and Organizational Psychology at the University of Giessen, Germany. He earned his Master's degree from the University of South Florida in 2000 and his German graduate degree (Dipl. Psych.) from the University of Hamburg in 2001. His research focuses on the impact of leadership, motivation and affect on innovative and proactive behavior in organizations. He is particularly interested in the implications of globalization processes and cultural value differences for innovation and performance management.

Arja Ropo is a professor of business administration, especially management and organizations in the Department of Management Studies and the vice rector at the University of Tampere, Finland. For over 20 years she has been doing research, primarily in managerial leadership in dynamic change contexts, entailing the emphasis on human and social competence. Her empirical area of specialty is cultural organizations.

Erika Sauer has recently received her doctorate at the School of Economics and Business Administration, at the Department of Management Studies in

the University of Tampere, Finland. Her research concentrates on the interplay of emotions, leadership, and creativity, which she has been studying
in arts organizations. She is also interested in the development of qualitative
social constructionist methodology.

Amy K. Smith is associate professor of marketing in the School of Business
at The George Washington University. Her research focuses on service
failure and recovery, customer service, customer relationship management,
customer satisfaction and retention, and customer assessments of services in
both business-to-consumer and business-to-business markets. Her research
has been published in the *Journal of Marketing Research*, the *Journal of
Service Research*, the *Journal of the Academy of Marketing Science*, and the
International Journal of Research in Marketing.

Matthias Spörrle studied psychology at the University of Munich (Diploma
in 2001). He has worked in several empirical research projects of applied
psychology such as: clinical and organizational evaluation, customer profile
analysis and customer satisfaction, gender studies, and entrepreneurship. At
present he is working at the Department of Psychology at the University of
Munich (Institute of General Psychology and Institute of Methodology) and
as lecturer for the Technology Transfer Office of the University of Munich.
Topics of current academic research are questionnaire design and question
formats, cognitive emotion theories, and emotional intelligence.

Ian Taylor is the leadership skills training manager of an international airline.
He has over 18 years experience as a management development practitioner.
His work involves him in a number of projects including the design and delivery of training and development interventions, the development of selection
and assessment processes, and change management initiatives. His qualifica-
tions include a BA (Hons) and MA in sociology, BSc (Hons), and an MSc in
occupational psychology from Birkbeck College, London University. The data
in this study were gathered for his MSc thesis. He is currently working toward
full Chartered Psychologist status with the British Psychological Society.

Gianfranco Walsh is a senior lecturer in marketing at Strathclyde Business
School in Glasgow. Before joining Strathclyde in 2004, Gianfranco was an
assistant professor of marketing at the University of Hanover, Germany.
His research focuses on consumer behavior, e-commerce, corporate

reputation, and services marketing. His work has been published in, among others, *Academy of Marketing Science Review, International Journal of Electronic Commerce, Journal of Consumer Affairs, Journal of Consumer Marketing, Journal of Interactive Marketing, Journal of Marketing Communications,* and *Journal of Marketing Management.* In addition, Gianfranco consults organizations in the retailing, energy, and Internet sector.

Isabell M. Welpe holds a master's degree in business administration (Ludwig-Maximilians-University Munich), a master's degree in European studies (London School of Economics), and a PhD (University of Regensburg). She has been a visiting fellow at the Massachusetts Institute of Technology in Boston, USA and the Carlson School of Management in Minnesota, USA, and a visiting scholar at the Hass School of Business in Berkeley, USA. Her research interests include theoretical and empirical work on human capital and emotional intelligence, entrepreneurship, and technology management. Presently she is working at the Institute for Information, Organisation and Management (Ludwig-Maximilians-University Munich).

Kay Yoon is a faculty in the Department of Communication at DePaul University and a doctoral candidate in the Department of Speech Communication at the University of Illinois at Urbana-Champaign. Her research interests include information sharing, communication, and task performance in small groups. Her recent research projects investigate how multicultural work groups recognize their members' expertise and how the expertise recognition processes affect their task performance and socioemotional experiences. She teaches small group communication, group decision-making, and organizational communication.

Dieter Zapf is a professor of work- and organizational psychology at Johann Wolfgang Goethe-University, Frankfurt, Germany. He studied psychology and theology in Neuendettelsau, Erlangen, Marburg, and Berlin, Germany. He received his diploma (Dipl. Psych.) in 1980 from Free University Berlin, Germany, his theological exam in 1983 from Ansbach, Germany; and his PhD in 1988 from Free University Berlin, Germany. He received his habilitation in 1993 from Justus-Liebig-University, Giessen, Germany. His research interests focus on psychological stress at work, stress-oriented job analysis, mobbing (bullying), emotion work, errors at work, and action theory.

SET UP A CONTINUATION ORDER TODAY!

Did you know that you can set up a continuation order on all Elsevier-JAI series and have each new volume sent directly to you upon publication? For details on how to set up a **continuation order**, contact your nearest regional sales office listed below.

To view related series in Business & Management, please visit:

www.elsevier.com/businessandmanagement

30% Discount for Authors on All Books!

A 30% discount is available to Elsevier book and journal contributors on all books *(except multi-volume reference works)*.

To claim your discount, full payment is required with your order, which must be sent directly to the publisher at the nearest regional sales office above.

2007 10 22